T0181865

Lecture Notes in Computer Science 13615

Shaoshan Liu · Xiaohui Wei (Eds.)

Network and Parallel Computing

19th IFIP WG 10.3 International Conference, NPC 2022
Jinan, China, September 24–25, 2022
Proceedings

 Springer

Editors
Shaoshan Liu
PerceptIn, Inc.
Fremont, CA, USA

Xiaohui Wei
Jilin University
Changchun, China

ISSN 0302-9743 ISSN 1611-3349 (electronic)
Lecture Notes in Computer Science
ISBN 978-3-031-21394-6 ISBN 978-3-031-21395-3 (eBook)
https://doi.org/10.1007/978-3-031-21395-3

This Springer imprint is published by the registered company Springer Nature Switzerland AG
The registered company address is: Gewerbestrasse 11, 6330 Cham, Switzerland

Preface

Welcome to the proceedings of the nineteenth edition of the International Conference on Network and Parallel Computing (NPC 2022), held in Jinan, China. First, we would like to thank all the committee members, from the various chairs to the local organizers and the reviewers. Of course, we should not forget the highly constructive influence, over the years, of Kemal Ebcioglu. A word of gratitude to the staff at IFIP for their tireless work. They have immensely contributed to improving the scientific impact of NPC. We acknowledge all the people we have interacted with for enhancing the scientific reach of NPC. They will recognize themselves. Thank you very much. We greatly appreciated their help and assistance.

A total of 89 submissions were received in response to our call for papers. These papers originated from Asia, Africa, Europe, and North America (USA). Each submission was sent to at least three reviewers, with an average of four reviewers per submission and up to five reviewers. Each paper was judged according to its originality, innovation, readability, and relevance to the expected audience. During the double-blind review process, we had the authors and the Program Committee (PC) members indicate any conflicts of interest and assigned reviewers accordingly to avoid such conflicts. Based on the reviews received, 23 full papers and eight short papers were selected to be published as LNCS proceedings (an acceptance rate 35%). Among these, five papers were further selected to be extended and submitted to a Special Issue of the International Journal of Parallel Programming. Five main themes were identified during the conference: Computer Architecture, Cloud Computing, Deep Learning, Emerging Applications, and Storage and IO, and the papers in this volume are grouped accordingly.

We would also like to recognize our three guest speakers who gave exciting presentations: Ao Kong from the United Nations, who discussed how computing innovations and cross-sector partnerships help the most vulnerable reach the UN Sustainable Development Goals, Denis Trystram from MIAI Grenoble Alpes, who explained sustainable resource managers for parallel and distributed systems, and Yuhao Zhu from the University of Rochester, who delved into visual computing for emerging applications such as AR/VR and autonomous machine computing.

We sincerely hope that you enjoy the proceedings of NPC 2022.

November 2022

Shaoshan Liu
Xiaohui Wei

Organization

General Co-chairs

Christophe Cérin   Université Sorbonne Paris Nord, France
Weimin Zheng   Tsinghua University, China

Program Co-chairs

Shaoshan Liu   PerceptIn, Inc., USA
Xiaohui Wei   Jilin University, China

Publication Chair

Xiangjiu Che   Jilin University, China

Publicity Chair

Bo Yu   PerceptIn, Inc., USA

Web Chair

Hengshan Yue   Jilin University, China

Finance Chair

Congfeng Jiang   Hangzhou Dianzi University, China

Steering Committee

Hai Jin (Co-chair)   HUST, China
Jean-Luc Gaudiot (Co-chair)   University of California, Irvine, USA
Stéphane Zuckerman (Vice Chair)   Université de Cergy-Pontoise, France
Chen Ding   University of Rochester, USA
Kemal Ebcioglu   Global Supercomputing, USA
Jack Dongarra   University of Tennessee, USA
Tony Hey   Science and Technology Facilities Council, UK
Guojie Li   ICT, China
Yoichi Muraoka   Waseda University, Japan
Viktor Prasanna   USC, USA

Daniel Reed	University of Utah, USA
Weisong Shi	Wayne State University, USA
Ninghui Sun	ICT, China
Zhiwei Xu	ICT, China

Program Committee

Jidong Zhai	Tsinghua University, China
Gaochao Xu	Jilin University, China
Parimala Thulasiram	University of Manitoba, Canada
Weifeng Liu	China University of Petroleum, China
Hailong Yang	Beihang University, China
Huimin Cui	Institute of Computing Technology, CAS, China
Chao Li	Shanghai Jiao Tong University, China
Quan Chen	Shanghai Jiao Tong University, China
Dingwen Tao	Washington State University, USA
Dezun Dong	National University of Defense Technology, China
Arthur Stoutchinin	ST Microelectronics, France
Éric Renault	ESIEE Paris, France
Heithem Abbes	University of Tunis El Manar, Tunisia
Anna Kobusinska	Poznan University of Technology, Poland
Bo Yu	PerceptIn, Inc., USA
Zishen Wan	Georgia Tech, USA
Weichen Xie	Clarkson University, USA
Tongsheng Geng	University of California, Irvine, USA
Tianze Wu	Institute of Computing Technology, CAS, China
Zhibin Yu	Shenzhen Institute of Advanced Technology, China
Keiji Kimura	Waseda University, Japan
Zhiliu Yang	Yunnan University, China
Hongliang Li	Jilin University, China
En Shao	Institute of Computing Technology, CAS, China
Gangyong Jia	Hangzhou Dianzi University, China
Songwen Pei	University of Shanghai for Science and Technology, China
Congfeng Jiang	Hangzhou Dianzi University, China
Abdulhalim Dandoush	ESME, France
Jingweijia Tan	Jilin University, China
Jie Tang	South China University of Technology, China
Jiajia Li	Pacific Northwest National Laboratory, USA
Xiaowen Xu	IAPCM, China
Angeliki Kritikakou	University of Rennes, France

Shang Gao   Jilin University, China
Xingwang Wang   Jilin University, China
Hongwei Liu   Harbin Institute of Technology, China
Xingwei Wang   Northeastern University, China
Nianmin Yao   Dalian University of Technology, China
Bing Chen   Nanjing University of Aeronautics and
                             Astronautics, China

Contents

Deep Learning

Emerging Applications

Storage and I/O

Architecture

A Routing-Aware Mapping Method for Dataflow Architectures

Zhihua Fan[1,2], Wenming Li[1,2(✉)], Tianyu Liu[1,2], Xuejun An[1,2],
Xiaochun Ye[1], and Dongrui Fan[1,2]

[1] State Key Lab of Processors, Institute of Computing Technology (ICT),
Chinese Academy of Sciences (CAS), Beijing 100190, China
liwenming@ict.ac.cn
[2] University of Chinese Academy of Sciences (UCAS), Beijing 100049, China

Abstract. Dataflow architecture is a promising parallel computing platform with high performance, efficiency and flexibility. Dataflow mapping algorithm offloads programs onto dataflow hardware, which has a significant impact on the performance of the architecture. Dataflow mapping methods in previous studies are hardly efficient as they rarely consider the requirements of routing resources. In this paper, we propose a routing-aware mapping algorithm by combining hardware resources and dataflow graph characteristics to explore better mapping schemes. Our method first focuses on the influence of predecessor and successor nodes when mapping a node, and then comprehensively considers the competition of computing resources and the routing cost, to find the mapping solution with the lowest overhead. Experiments demonstrate that our method can achieve up to 2.06× performance improvement and 12.8% energy consumption reduction compared to state-of-the-art methods.

Keywords: Dataflow architecture · Mapping · Routing balancing

1 Introduction

Dataflow architecture is an alternative to the "von Neumann" architecture [1,2]. In the "von Neumann" computer, the most important view point is that programs are stored in the memory, and they are executed one by one by the control of the program counter. On the contrary, dataflow programs are driven by data rather than program counter. The dataflow architecture is more aware of the value of data, which is a momentous breakthrough in traditional computer architecture.

Dataflow architecture is a prevailing parallel computing architecture, due to its high energy efficiency and flexibility [3–9]. In dataflow architecture, a program is represented by a dataflow graph (**DFG**). DFG consists of a set of nodes and directed edges that connect the nodes. The nodes represent the computing, and the edges between nodes represent data dependences. DFG is mapped to hardware through a mapping algorithm. The DFG mapping algorithm determines the location of DFG nodes in the PE array, as well as the communication distance between DFG nodes. The performance of dataflow architecture is sensitive

© IFIP International Federation for Information Processing 2022
Published by Springer Nature Switzerland AG 2022
S. Liu and X. Wei (Eds.): NPC 2022, LNCS 13615, pp. 3–16, 2022.
https://doi.org/10.1007/978-3-031-21395-3_1

to the efficiency of data supplement. Therefore, the DFG mapping algorithms have a significant impact on the performance of dataflow architectures.

Recently, many dataflow graph mapping methods have been proposed, and we divide them into two categories. One is depth-based mapping algorithm. The depth-based mapping approach aims at mapping the DFG nodes as many as possible to the same or adjacent PEs to shorten the data transmission distance, such as [10,12,13]. The disadvantage of these methods is that DFG nodes tend to be mapped to a portion of PEs, resulting in an imbalanced load. The other type is breadth-based mapping algorithm. The breadth-based DFG mapping approach map the dataflow nodes onto different PEs as many as possible to obtain workload balance of computational resources and higher node parallelism, such as [11,15,16]. However, these methods increase the distance of data transmission, hence increasing the delay of transmission, raising competition for routing resources and blocking the execution.

In this paper, we propose a routing-aware mapping algorithm by combining hardware resources and dataflow graph characteristics to explore more efficient mapping schemes. This paper mainly has the following contributions:

- We design a novel DFG mapping algorithm which first focus on the influence of predecessor nodes and successor nodes when mapping a DFG node, and then comprehensively considers the competition of computing resources and the routing cost.
- We evaluate our method by a wide range of benchmarks, and experiments demonstrate that our method can achieve up to 2.06× geomean performance improvement and 12.8% energy consumption reduction, compared to state-of-the-art methods.

The rest of this paper is organized as follows. In Sect. 2, the background and related works are presented. Section 3 is the motivation. Section 4 displays the details of our approach. The evaluation methodology and experimental results are presented in Sect. 5. Section 6 concludes our work.

2   Background and Related Works

Dataflow architecture is a popular parallel computing architecture, due to its high energy efficiency and flexibility. In this section, we will introduce the dataflow architecture and discuss several related works.

2.1   Dataflow Architecture

Figure 1 illustrates the high-level diagram of a dataflow architecture, which is comprised of a set of identical processing elements (PE), a micro-controller, a data buffer and external memory. The PEs are organized in a 2D array and connected through a dedicated network. Each PE consists of a local configuration buffer, several function units and register files. The function units merely perform operations, whereas the configuration buffer is responsible for controlling the function units. The memory hierarchy is composed of an off-chip memory, on-chip data buffers and local buffer in each PE. These global on-chip buffer are shared across all the PEs. The micro-controller is responsible for controlling the execution of the PE array and communicating with the host. The micro-controller receives dataflow mapping information and other configurations generated by the compiler. When the PE array accomplish the execution, the micro-controller sends end signal to the host. The results are sent to the host and external memory. During this process, the on-chip network is responsible for transferring configuration information and data between PEs.

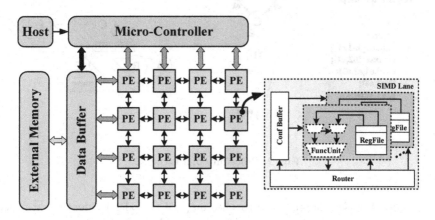

Fig. 1. A typical dataflow architecture.

Dataflow program execution model is a solution to exploit the data parallelism. It was proposed by Dennis [1]. The dataflow execution model is completely different from the control flow model. In the control flow model, the program is executed by the order of its instructions, while the programs in dataflow model are represented by a dataflow graph. A dataflow graph consists of a set of nodes and edges. The nodes represent calculations, and the directed edges represent data dependences between nodes. The basic principle of dataflow execution model is that any node can be fired as long as its operands are ready. In consequence, dataflow model exploits more instruction level parallelism without the limited instruction window and thus achieves a much higher performance.

The program offloaded to dataflow machine is called a **kernel**. The processing procedure of a kernel is displayed in Fig. 2. The dataflow compiler first converts the kernel into a DFG. Then the DFG is mapped to the hardware through a DFG mapping algorithm. The DFG mapping algorithm determines the location of the DFG nodes in a PE array, as well as the communication distance between DFG nodes and hardware utilization. Therefore, the DFG mapping algorithms have a significant impact on the performance of dataflow architectures.

2.2   Related Works

In recent years, many approaches have been proposed for mapping kernels onto dataflow architectures. In general, these methods can be divided into two main categories: depth-based methods and breadth-based methods.

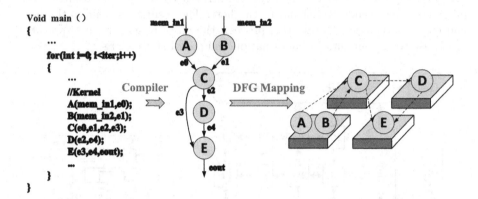

Fig. 2. Procedure of a kernel.

The depth-based mapping approaches map DFG nodes by depth-first order and aim to reduce the data transmission distance. Man et al. [10] propose a general pattern-based dynamic mapping method, which utilizes statically-generated patterns to straightforwardly determine runtime re-placement and routing so that runtime configuration creation algorithm has low complexity. Jiang et al. [12] design a mapping scheme based on a branch-and-bound algorithm map cores onto the NoC and allocate communications to different switching mechanisms simultaneously, such that the average communication latency and energy are optimized. Murali et al. [13] proposed a fast algorithm, called NMAP, to map applications onto mesh NoC architectures under bandwidth constraints. Hu et al. [14] focused on minimizing the communication energy and proposed a branch-and-bound algorithm to solve the mapping problem.

The breadth-based mapping algorithms map DFG nodes by breadth-first order. Fell et al. [11] introduce a mapping method that considers data dependence and path sharing. The technique of path sharing is proposed for improving the utilization of PEs. In [15], the express channel-based NoC is concentrated and a heuristic algorithm that runs in polynomial time is proposed for application mapping. Sahu et al. [16] presented a discrete particle swarm optimization-based strategy to map applications on both 2-D and 3-D mesh-connected NoC. Singh et al. [17] surveyed the mapping methodologies and highlighted the emerging trends for multi/manycore systems.

3   Motivation

In this section, we present our motivation by using an example and analyze the key factors affecting routing resource competition.

In dataflow architecture, the performance is sensitive to the efficiency of the data supplement. To fully exploit the performance of the dataflow architectures, data transfer with low latency between the DFG nodes is required. The data should be sent to the "consumer" node as soon as possible. However, the previous DFG mapping algorithms only consider the transmission distance between nodes or the computing resources. The routing resources are rarely considered, which will lead to competition for routing resources and thus block the execution.

As shown in Fig. 1, the computational resources in the dataflow architecture are uniform, while the routing resources on each processing unit are different. For example, a PE at the boundary can only exchange data to its neighbors, and a PE in the center can exchange data with PEs in multiple directions (east, south, west, north). That is, routing resources are actually heterogeneous in a homogeneous PE array.

A dataflow graph mapping approach that does not consider routing resources will lead to sub-optimal performance. If dataflow nodes with high out-degree are mapped to the processing elements with fewer routing resources, it will lead to the competition of routing ports. If dataflow nodes with small out-degree are mapped to the processing elements with enough routing resources, it will lead to the waste of routing resources.

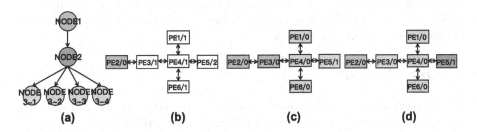

(a)   (b)   (c)   (d)

Fig. 3. An example of our motivation.

Figure 3 provides an example for our motivation. Figure 3 (a) is the DFG of a given kernel. Figure 3 (b) is the state of PE array during configuration period. We assume *node 1* has been mapped to PE 2. The variable in each PE is the number of DFG nodes that can be further mapped. In this situation, PE 5 can further accommodate 2 DFG nodes, and PE 1, 3, 4, 6 can only accommodate 1 DFG node. Then, we choose two state-of-the-art DFG mapping methods to discuss the challenges.

First, we use PBCT [10], a representative depth-based method to map the DFG to the hardware. To reduce the data transmission distance, the depth-based mapping approach aims to map the DFG nodes as many as possible to the same or similar PE. The mapping result is shown in Fig. 3 (c). In this method, node 2 is mapped to PE 3, and node 3-1, node 3-2, node 3-3, and node 3-4 are mapped to PE 1, PE 4, PE 5, and PE 6, respectively. As a result, the routing distance between node 2 and node 1 is short, and the calculation results in node 1 can be quickly transmitted to node 2. However, after the node 2 is completed, there is only a routing port in PE 3 that is linked to the eastern PE, and all the calculation results of node 2 need to be transmitted to the successor nodes through this port. The router can only send one network packet in one cycle, and it takes at least 4 cycles for the calculation results of node 2 that will be sent to successor nodes (we assume that the packet transmission can be pipelined).

Second, we use REGIMap [11], a typical breadth-based DFG mapping method. The breadth-based DFG mapping approach maps the dataflow nodes into different PEs as many as possible to obtain workload balance of computing resources and higher node parallelism. As shown in Fig. 3 (d), node 2 is mapped to PE 5, while node 3-1, node 3-2, node 3-3 and node 3-4 are mapped to PE 1, PE 3, PE 4 and PE 6, respectively. Similarly, this solution has the disadvantage that the successor nodes of node 2 need to wait for a long delay before obtain the data. It takes at least 4 cycles for the calculation results of node 2 to be sent to the successor node, and it enlarge the overhead of data transfer between node 1 and node 2.

When DFG nodes are mapped to an array of processing elements, it is impossible for all nodes to be mapped in the same PE because the PE is resource-constrained. If these nodes are mapped to the adjacent PEs, it will lead to strong resource competition and cannot fully exploit the parallelism among the nodes. If DFG nodes are mapped in different PEs, the inter-node parallelism can be utilized effectively, but it increases the distance of data transmission between nodes. The existing DFG mapping algorithms do not provide a better tradeoff between resources and parallelism.

4   Our Method

In this section, we first analyze the factors that need to be considered when mapping DFGs and provide a novel DFG mapping algorithm.

When designing a DFG mapping algorithm, both hardware resources and dataflow graph characteristics should be considered together to explore better dataflow graph mapping schemes. The hardware resources insight means it is necessary to consider the heterogeneity of hardware resources. The DFG characteristics insight refers to the need to consider not only the data transmission distance between the current node and its upstream node, but also the data dependency between the node and its downstream nodes.

Hardware Resources: Computing resource and routing resource should be both considered carefully in DFG mapping algorithm. Compute resources refer to the functional components inside the PE, such as arithmetic computing unit, logical operating unit. Routing resources are the number of PEs that can be directly connected, which is related to the PE topology and the hardware runtime.

DFG Characteristics: DFG mapping algorithms should consider the data dependences at the temporal level. As the kernel becomes more complex, the number of nodes in the DFG increases. It is necessary to consider not only the routing distance between the node and its upstream nodes, but also the mapping cost of the downstream nodes to avoid poor mapping solutions due to insufficient exploiting of DFG characteristics.

Based on above analysis, we propose a novel DFG mapping method which can improve routing load balancing (**RLBA**), as shown in a Algorithm 1. It is a search algorithm and incorporates efficient pruning, which reduces the execution time of the mapping algorithm.

The Algorithm 1 first sorts all the nodes in the dataflow graph in a breadth-first order. All nodes are sorted based on their position in the DFG, and data dependences between these nodes are preserved. The *BFSSort* function sorts the nodes and stores the order in *SD*. When evaluating the node cost, we treat the node and its predecessor and successor nodes as a group. We evaluate the cost of the entire group and choose the mapping scheme with the least cost. The *selectCandidateNode* function selects candidate nodes from the *SD*. Then, the Algorithm 1 finds all mappable schemes of the group by the *getmappingSlot* function. The *getMappingCost* function is used to calculate the cost of each scheme. Algorithm 1 selects the scheme with the lowest cost as the mapping result.

Algorithm 1. RLBA

Input: Dataflow Graph T, PE array P
Output: Mapping relationship $M: I \rightarrow P$
1: $bestGroupCost \leftarrow max$
2: $bestGroupMap \leftarrow node$
3: $SD = BFSSort(T)$
4: $L = selectCandidateNode(SD)$
5: **while** $L \neq NULL$ **do**
6:    $tmpGroupMap \leftarrow getMappingSlot(L, P)$
7:    **for** each vmap in tmpGroupMap **do**
8:       $tmpGroupCost \leftarrow GetMappingCost(vmap)$
9:       **if** $tmpGroupCost \leq bestGroupCost$ **then**
10:          $bestGroupCost \leftarrow tmpGroupCost$
11:          $bestGroupMap \leftarrow tmpGroupMap$
12:       **end if**
13:    **end for**
14:    $M \leftarrow M + mapSchedule(L, bestGroupCost)$
15:    $updateResourceMap(P)$
16:    $SD \leftarrow SD - L$
17:    $L = selectCandidateNode(SD)$
18: **end while**

The detail of *getMappingCost* is exhibited in Algorithm 2. The input of this algorithm is the node group and their mapping relationship to a set of PEs.

The algorithm first finds a valid set of processing elements by *findValidSlot*. In the set P, PEs with no available memory space will be eliminated. For each mappable PE, Algorithm 2 calculates the compute resource cost *pComputeCost* and the routing resource cost *pRoutingCost*. The *pComputeCost* is measured by: the number of mapped nodes/the number of computing components in the PE. For example, if a PE contains only one fixed-point pipeline, and N DFG nodes are mapped to it, the probability of each node being scheduled is $1/N$ on average. The *pRoutingCost* is measured by the delay of transfer data between nodes. It is simultaneously determined by the distance of the current node and its downstream nodes, network congestion *routingPortCost*, routing distance *transferCost*. For example, if a node has N downstream nodes, and it is mapped to a PE with M ports, then the data transfer costs at least N/M cycles. If data packets from other nodes need to pass through this data path at same time, the network will become blocked, and the routing cost will increase.

Algorithm 2. GetMappinpCost

Input: Map : Node-list $T \rightarrow$ PE-list P
Output: cost
1: $pGroupCost \leftarrow 0$
2: **for** each node in T **do**
3:     $validSlot \leftarrow findValidSlot(P)$
4:     **for** each slot in validSlot **do**
5:         $pComputeCost \leftarrow beScheduleCost(t, slot)$
6:         $pRoutingCost \leftarrow transferCost(t, slot) + routingPortCost(t, slot)$
7:         $pGroupCost \leftarrow pComputeCost + pRoutingCost$
8:     **end for**
9: **end for**

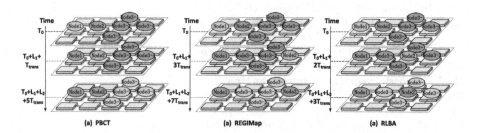

Fig. 4. Comparison between different mapping algorithms.

RLBA mapping algorithm divides DFG nodes into different candidate groups, and comprehensively considers the computing cost and routing cost to find the best mapping scheme. We take the example in motivation (Sect. 3) again. Figure 4 displays the comparison between different mapping algorithms. It is a time-extendtion diagram. In RLBA, node 2 is mapped to PE 4 (number in Fig. 3). In PBCT, the node 2 is mapped to the PE which is closest to node 1, while in REGIMap, the node 2 is mapped to the PE which has the most computing resources. Different from them, RLBA maps the node 2 to the PE which has the minimal computing cost and routing cost. As shown in Fig. 4, RLBA achieves the shortest execution latency.

5   Evaluation

5.1   Methodology

Simulator. We develop a cycle-accurate architecture simulator based SimICT [21], with parameters abstracted from real RTL design. Table 1 shows the hardware parameters. In this experiment, we use a RISC-V core as the host. And we implement a 4 × 4 PE array organized by a mesh NoC. Each PE supports a variety of data types to deal with multi-domain applications, including FP64/32, INT64/32, and logic units. We use Scratchpad memory as data buffer and we use 8 banks to increase the parallelism of memory access. In addition, we use Synopsys Design Compiler and a TSMC 12nm standard library to synthesize it and obtain power consumption.

Benchmarks. We select important workloads from Polybench [18], Mibench [19] and SPEC2000 [20] for experiments. SPEC2000 is an industry standardized CPU intensive benchmark suite. MiBench is a suite targeting a specific area of the embedded market, including automotive and industrial Control, security, and telecommunications. While PolyBench is a collection of benchmarks containing static control parts, extracted from operations in various application domains. Our benchmark contains digital signal processing, scientific computing and high performance computing kernels.

Table 1. Hardware parameters.

Module	Configuration
Micro-controller	RISC-V core, 1 GHz
PE	4X4, INT64/32, FP64/32, 1 GHz,
Network on Chip	2D-mesh, 1cycle/hop, X-Y routing
Data buffer	8Kb SPM, 8bank

Comparison. We choose two state-of-the-art DFG mapping methds to compare with our algorithm. PBCT [10] is a representative depth-based method to map the DFG to the hardware. It aims to map the DFG nodes to the closest PE and improve computing resources utilization. REGIMap [11] is a typical breadth-based DFG mapping method. It map the dataflow nodes to different PEs as much as possible to obtain load balancing of PEs and achieve higher parallelism.

5.2   Performance Improvement

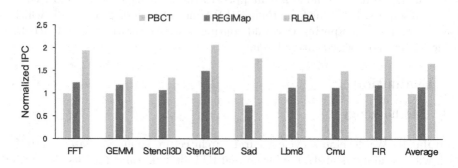

Fig. 5. IPC comparison.

We use the number of instructions executed per cycle (IPC, instruction per cycle) to evaluate the execution performance of the dataflow architecture. The higher the IPC, the better the performance of the kernel. Figure 5 demonstrates the IPC comparison normalized to PBCT. RLBA gains a 1.65 × geomean IPC improvement over PBCT and 1.45 × improvement over REGIMap. Compared with PBCT, RKBA achieves up to 2.06 × performance improvement. This is because in Stencil2D, the data dependencies between DFG nodes are complex, including a large number of DFG nodes with different out-degrees. The RLBA algorithm considers the out-degree of DFG nodes and the utilization of the routing resources. Thus RLBA algorithm can reduce the competition for routing ports and improve the data supply efficiency between DFG nodes. Meawhile, the performance improvement GEMM algorithm is not obvious, which is only 1.353 × over PBCT. This is determined by the algorithmic characteristics of the matrix multiplication. The relationship between the DFG nodes is simple and regular, and the competition of routing resources is not fierce.

5.3   Energy Saving

Figure 6 provides the energy consumption comparison between different mapping methods. We execute the benchmarks in the RTL environment and get the energy consumption of different kernels. Compared with PBCT, RLBA obtains a 12.8% energy reduction. And it achieves 6.4% energy reduction over REGIMap. This is because the RLBA algorithm takes into account computing resources and routing resources from the hardware side, so that the loads of computing resources and routing resources are balanced. The utilization rate of hardware resources is improved, and the energy consumption caused by control and blocking is reduced.

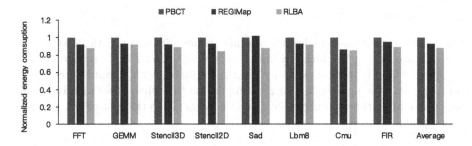

Fig. 6. Energy comsuption comparison.

5.4   Scalability

In our approach design, we do not make any assumption on PE array size and interconnection topology so that our approach can be applied to various dataflow architectures. To verify this, we first modified the architecture with typically network topologys (2-D mesh, 2-D torus). The PE array size is 4 × 4. The performance results are shown in Fig. 7. From this figure, we can find that our approach is flexible and efficient enough for different topologys.

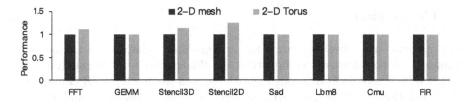

Fig. 7. Performance comparison normalized to 2-D mesh.

Second, we modify the size of PE array to 2 × 2, 4 × 4, and 8 × 8. The interconnection topology is the most typical 2-D mesh. We achieve the performance results shown in Fig. 8. It is worth noting that the improvement brought by our approach has tapered with the increase in the size in many cases. The reason is that the computing resources is the bottleneck when the size is small. In summary, our method has good scalability.

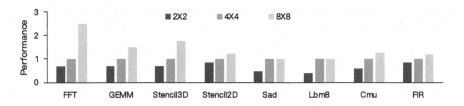

Fig. 8. Performance comparison normalized to 4 × 4.

5.5   Compilation Time

Since the compilation time decides whether the algorithm is practical, we report this indicator in Fig. 9, which is achieved on a Xeon 4116 CPU. To achieve a valid mapping with a better performance, RLBA evaluates both computing cost and routing cost, which may cause longer compilation time than other methods. The ratio of compile time to execution time is very small, so the cost of compilation is acceptable (Fig. 9).

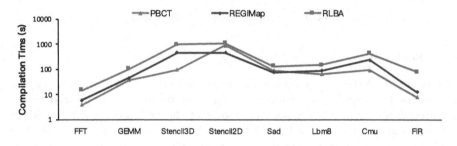

Fig. 9. Compilation times comparison.

6   Conclusion

The dataflow mapping algorithm has a significant relationship to the performance of the dataflow architecture. In this paper, we first analysis the design principle of DFG mapping algorithms. And we develop a DFG mapping algorithm that can take into account both computing resources and routing resources. When facing complex scenarios, the algorithm can obtain better solutions. Experiments demonstrate that our method can achieve an average of 2.06x performance improvement and 12.8% energy consumption reduction compared to state-of-the-art methods.

Acknowledgments. This work was partly supported by National Natural Science Foundation of China (Grant No. 61732018 and 61872335), Austrian-Chinese Cooperative R&D Project (FFG and CAS) (Grant No. 171111KYSB20200002), CAS Project for Young Scientists in Basic Research (Grant No. YSBR-029), CAS Project for Youth Innovation Promotion Association, Zhejiang Lab (Grant No. 2022PB0AB01), and the project of the state grid corporation of China in 2020 "Integration Technology Research and Prototype Development for High End Controller Chip" (Grant No. 5700-202041264A-0-0-00).

References

1. Dennis, J.B.: First version of a data flow procedure language. In: Programming Symposium, pp. 362–376 (1974)
2. Dennis, J., Gao, G.: An efficient pipelined dataflow processor architecture. In: Supercomputing, pp. 368–373 (1988)
3. Weng, J., Liu, S., Wang, Z., Dadu, V., Nowatzki, T.: A hybrid systolicdataflow architecture for inductive matrix algorithms. In: IEEE HPCA 2020, pp. 703–716 (2020)
4. Prabhakar, R., Zhang, Y., Koeplinger, D., et al.: Plasticine: a reconfigurable architecture for parallel paterns. In: ISCA 2017, pp. 389–402 (2017)
5. Guha, A., Vedula, N., Shriraman, A.: Deepframe: a profile-driven compiler for spatial hardware accelerators. In: PACT 2019, pp. 68–81 (2019)
6. Vilim, M., Rucker, A., Olukotun, K.: Aurochs: an architecture for dataflow threads. In: ISCA 2021, pp. 402–415 (2021)
7. Zuckerman, S., Suetterlein, J., Knauerhase, R., et al.: Position paper: using a codelet program execution model for exascale machines. In: EXADAPT Workshop: volume 10. Citeseer (2011)
8. Arteaga, J., Zuckerman, S., Gao, G.R.: Multigrain parallelism: bridging coarse-grain parallel programs and fine-grain event-driven multithreading. In: IPDPS2017, pp. 799–808 (2017)
9. Li, Z., Ye, Y., Neuendorffer, S., Sampson, A.: Compiler-driven simulation of reconfigurable hardware accelerators. In: 2022 IEEE HPCA, pp. 619–632 (2022)
10. Man, X., Liu, L., Zhu, J., et al.: A general pattern-based dynamic compilation framework for coarse-grained reconfigurable architectures. In: DAC 2019, pp. 1–6 (2019)
11. Hamzeh, M., Shrivastava, A., et al.: REGIMap: register-aware application mapping on coarse-grained reconfigurable architectures. In: DAC 2013, pp. 1–10 (2013)
12. Jiang, G., Li, Z., Wang, F., Wei, S.: Mapping of embedded applications on hybrid networks-on-chip with multiple switching mechanisms. IEEE Embed. Syst. Lett. $7(2)$, 59–62 (2015)
13. Murali, S., Micheli, G.D.: Bandwidth-constrained mapping of cores onto NoC architectures. In: Proceedings of the Design, Automation and Test in Europe Conference and Exhibition (DATE), pp. 896–901 (2004)
14. Hu, J., Marculescu, R.: Energy and performance-aware mapping for regular NoC architectures. IEEE TCAD $24(4)$, 551–562 (2005)
15. Zhu, D., Chen, L., Yue, S., Pedram, M.: Application mapping for express channel-based networks-on-chip. In: Proceedings of the Design, Automation and Test in Europe Conference and Exhibition, pp. 1–6 (2014)
16. Sahu, P.K., et al.: Application mapping onto mesh-based networkon-chip using discrete particle swarm optimization. IEEE Trans. VLSI. $22(2)$, 300–312 (2014)
17. Singh, A.K., et al.: Mapping on multi/many-core systems: survey of current and emerging trends. In: Design Automation Conference (DAC), pp. 1–10 (2013)
18. Pouchet, L.-N., et al.: Polybench: The polyhedral benchmark suite (2012). http://www.cs.ucla.edu/pouchet/software/polybench
19. Guthaus, M.R., Ringenberg, J.S., Ernst, D., Austin, T.M., Mudge, T., Brown, R.B.: MiBench: a free, commercially representative embedded benchmark suite. In: Proceedings of the Fourth Annual IEEE International Workshop on Workload Characterization. WWC-4 (Cat. No.01EX538), pp. 3–14 (2001). https://doi.org/10.1109/WWC.2001.990739

20. Standard Performance Evaluation Corporation. SPEC CPU2000 (2000). https://www.spec.org/cpu2000/. Accessed 27 Mar 2022
21. Ye, X., Fan, D., Sun, N., Tang, S., Zhang, M., Zhang, H.: SimICT: a fast and flexible framework for performance and power evaluation of large-scale architecture. In: International Symposium on Low Power Electronics and Design, pp. 273–278 (2013)

Optimizing Winograd Convolution on GPUs via Partial Kernel Fusion

Gan Tong[1], Run Yan[1], Ling Yang[1], Mengqiao Lan[1], Jing Zhang[1],
Yuanhu Cheng[1], Wentao Ma[1], Yashuai Lü[2], Sheng Ma[1], and Libo Huang[1(✉)]

[1] School of Computer, National University of Defense Technology,
Changsha 410073, China
libohuang@nudt.edu.cn
[2] Cambricon Technology Co., Beijing 100191, China

Abstract. Convolution operations are the essential components in modern CNNs (Convolutional Neural Networks), which are also the most time-consuming. Several fast convolution algorithms include FFT and Winograd, have been proposed to solve this problem. Winograd convolution is used to improve the inference performance of the convolution operators with small kernels, which are the mainstream in the current popular CNNs. However, the implementations of Winograd convolution in many highly optimized deep neural network libraries and deep learning compilers are not efficient. Due to the complex data dependencies of the four stages of Winograd convolution, it is very challenging to optimize it. In this paper, we improve the inference performance of the Winograd convolution operator on GPUs. We propose a sync-free implementation of the calculation stage of Winograd and furtherly propose methods of PKF (Partial Kernel Fusion) utilizing different memory levels of GPUs. We implemented PKF-Reconstructor based on TVM for PKF Winograd convolution. Evaluations on convolution operators from real-world CNNs show that our method achieves a speedup of 8.22×–13.69× compared to cuDNN and 4.89×–9.10× to the fastest vanilla TVM Winograd implementation.

Keywords: Winograd convolution · Convolution optimizing · Sync-free BGEMM · Partial kernel fusion

1 Introduction

Deep convolutional neural networks (CNNs) have achieved impressive results in many areas, such as computer vision [1], image classification [2], natural language processing [3]. Convolutions help improve machine learning with features of sparse interactions, parameter sharing and equivariant representations [4]. However, convolutions become the bottleneck of optimizing the running speed of

This work is supported in part by NSFC (No. 61872374, 62090023, 62172430), NSFHN (No. 2022JJ10064, 2021JJ10052) and NKRDP (No. 2021YFB0300300).

S. Liu and X. Wei (Eds.): NPC 2022, LNCS 13615, pp. 17–29, 2022.
https://doi.org/10.1007/978-3-031-21395-3_2

CNN models because of larger data sets and more complex models [5]. Therefore, there is still a growing demand for faster convolution implementation to reduce time consumption in the training and the inference of CNNs. While traditional convolution involves redundant multiplications, FFT (Fast Fourier Transform) and Winograd algorithms solve this problem by mapping the data to another space to replace part of the multiplications with additions and subtractions. Convolutions in modern CNNs usually have a small kernel (the most commonly used is 3×3), which performs well when using the Winograd convolution. Therefore, Winograd convolution has been implemented in various basic linear algebra libraries and DL (Deep Learning) frameworks to improve the performance of convolutions.

The NVIDIA CUDA Deep Neural Network library (cuDNN) library is the most popular backend implementation of existing DL frameworks. Both non-fused and fused Winograd convolution are implemented in cuDNN, but the fused one is not efficient enough and even inferior to the non-fused one in most cases. There also exists waiting overhead among warps in cuDNN implementation, which could be further optimized. Fused Winograd convolution via MegaKernel achieves considerable acceleration compared with fused Winograd convolution in cuDNN [6]. However, their algorithm relies on undocumented hardware features and violates the GPU programming model on data flow, possibly failing with new GPU architectures. Non-fused Winograd convolution implemented on TVM is inefficient but can obtain huge performance improvements after tuning. Nevertheless, we find that the search space of TVM can be further expanded in unexplored dimensions.

This paper proposes an algorithm to optimize Winograd convolution on GPU and implement it on deep learning compiler TVM. Our contributions include:

- We optimize the calculation stage of Winograd convolution and propose the **sync-free BGEMM** (Batched GEMM) algorithm.
- We propose two kernel fusion strategies using different memory levels and proposed a partial kernel fusion algorithm on Winograd convolution based on **sync-free BGEMM**, namely Partial Kernel Fusion (PKF).
- We implement PKF-Reconstructor to generate the proposed PKF Winograd on TVM over the limitations of TVM and evaluate the performance compared to existing implementations.

We select convolution operators in modern CNNs as workloads to evaluate PKF on NVIDIA RTX 2080Ti. The results show that PKF is up to $8.22\times$–$13.69\times$ faster than cuDNN Winograd convolution and $4.89\times$–$9.10\times$ faster than vanilla TVM Winograd convolution.

2 Background

2.1 Implementations of Convolution

Some implementations of convolution have been proposed, mainly divided into direct, GEMM-based, FFT-based and Winograd-based. The convolution is converted to GEMM through im2col-transformation in GEMM-based convolution.

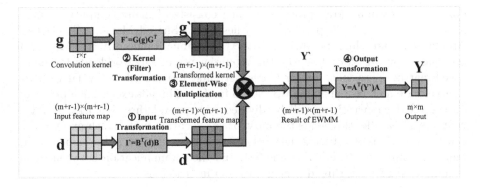

Fig. 1. Four stages of Winograd convolution.

GEMM is highly optimized in various BLAS (Basic Linear Algebra Subroutine) libraries, significantly improving performance. FFT-based convolution reduces unnecessary multiplication operations by mapping data to the complex number space. FFT-based convolution is more suitable when the input feature map and the kernel are close in size. Winograd-based convolution is similar to FFT-based convolution, but data is mapped to the rational number space. The Winograd convolution has better performance than the FFT-based convolution when the kernel size is small, shows considerable performance in most CNN applications.

2.2 Winograd Convolution

Winograd minimal filtering algorithm was first introduced in 2016 to calculate convolutions as an equivalent problem of FIR (Finite Impulse Response) filters problem [7]. The core idea of Winograd is to use additions and subtractions to reduce redundant multiplications by mapping data to another space, which can significantly improve performance on platforms where additions and subtractions are much faster than multiplications.

Two-dimensional Winograd convolution can be written in matrix form as:

$$O = A^T[[GgG^T] \odot [B^T dB]]A \qquad (1)$$

where $\odot$ denotes element-wise multiplication, g denotes input feature map, d denotes convolution kernel, O denotes output feature map, and G, B, A are respectively kernel transformation matrix, input transformation matrix and output transformation matrix. Winograd convolution can naturally be divided into four stages, namely **Input transformation (ITrans)**, **Kernel transformation (KTrans)**, **Element-wise matrix multiplication (EWMM)**, and **Output transformation (OTrans)**, as shown in Fig. 1.

2.3 NVIDIA GPU Architecture and Tensor Cores

The advantages of GPUs in matrix operations make it the preferred accelerator for deep neural network training and inference. An NVIDIA GPU consists of dozens of Streaming Multiprocessors, each consists of many computing units, a large number of high-speed register files and a Shared Memory (L1Cache). An L2Cache and a high-bandwidth DRAM (Dynamic Random-Access Memory) are shared by all SMs. To meet the requirements of DL workloads for high-speed matrix operations, Tensor Cores were first introduced to NVIDIA GPUs to accelerate matrix-matrix multiplication further. Threads executing a program on the GPU cooperatively will be divided into several thread blocks. A warp contains 32 parallel threads is the most basic execution unit, which execute the exact instructions on different data resources. All instructions in the same thread block can only be scheduled on one SM, and the communication between them is completed through thread synchronization instructions.

3   Related Work

Li et al. [8] introduce ReLU and pruning before the transformation of data and kernel respectively to make the two matrices of **EWMM** sparse, further reducing the number of multiplications. Meng et al. [9] optimize integer quantized convolutional neural networks by extending Winograd convolution to the complex number domain. Barabasz et al. [10] apply higher-order polynomials on Winograd convolution to reduce calculations on the bf16 data type and achieve better image recognition accuracy.

There are also some optimized studies for GPU. Yan et al. [11] redesign the division of workload and data layout to coalesce global memory access and eliminate bank conflicts in shared memory. They also hide memory access latency through software pipelines and enlarge block size to enhance the computational intensity. Finally, registers' utilization is optimized at the assembly level to avoid the recomputation of zero-padding masks. Their work combines high-level and low-level optimization, which is excellent but not conducive to expansion and transplantation. Huang et al. [12] and Wang et al. [13] implemented Winograd convolution on FPGA and three-dimensional Winograd convolution on GPU respectively.

Jia et al. [6] propose the fusion of Winograd convolution kernels based on MegaKernel. Compared with fused Winograd convolution in cuDNN, their algorithm achieves impressive performance improvements. However, their scheduling optimization depends on specific implementations of GPU platforms, such as the boot sequence of the GPU kernels. Since their scheduling algorithm violates the SIMT (Single Instruction Multiple Threads) programming models of GPUs, the difference in control flow will also bring substantial performance loss, as NVIDIA proved before [14].

4   Methodology

Before discussing, define the symbols in Table 1 to represent the parameters of a Winograd convolution operator (this paper only discusses unit-stride and non-dilation convolution).

Table 1. Parameters of a Winograd convolution operator.

Symbol	Description
N, C, H, W	The batch size, channel size, height and width of the input
K, KH, KW	The output channel size, height and width of the kernel
$ntiles$	The number of tiles into which the input is tiled
H_{tile}, W_{tile}	The height and width of input tiles
OH_{tile}, OW_{tile}	The height and width of output tiles

4.1 Optimizing EWMM Stage

BGEMM for Winograd Convolution. Computations in the Winograd convolution are concentrated in the EWMM stage with low arithmetic intensity. It is challenging to overlap memory access to execute such workloads on GPUs fully. The **ITrans** stage will tile the input tensor into overlapped tiles. Each tile will get a non-overlapping output tile at the end of the **OTrans** stage. According to the description of Winograd algorithm, we can get the following equations:

$$H_{tile} = OH_{tile} + KH - 1, W_{tile} = OW_{tile} + KW - 1 \qquad (2)$$

$$ntiles = ((H + pad \times 2 - H_{tile})/OH_{tile} + 1) \times ((W + pad \times 2 - W_{tile})/OW_{tile} + 1) \quad (3)$$

In the vanilla EWMM algorithm, after the input tensor is tiled, we get $ntiles$ transformed tiles of size $(N, C, H_{tile}, W_{tile})$. While the **KTrans** stage is done, a transformed kernel of size $(K, C, H_{tile}, W_{tile})$ is generated and then elementwise multiplication on the H_{tile} and W_{tile} dimensions and accumulate on the C dimension are performed. However, the arithmetic intensity of this method is very low, specifically $1/12$ for single-precision FP number, and needs to be further optimized.

Jia et al. [6] proposed to convert **EWMM** to **BGEMM** to improve the arithmetic intensity. The essence of their idea is that exchanging the dimensional order of the transformed input and the transformed kernel, that is, placing the reduction axis into the innermost layer. The arithmetic intensity AI_{BGEMM} of the **BGEMM** stage can be calculated as following:

$$AI_{BGEMM} = \frac{(ntiles * C * K + ntiles * C * K)FLOPS}{(ntiles * C + K * C + ntiles * K) * 4B} \qquad (4)$$

Let's bring in a typical convolution operator example, let $C = K = 64$, $KH = KW = 3$, $H = W = 224$, and m in Winograd convolution takes the commonly used 4. According to corresponding equations, the new arithmetic intensity AI_{BGEMM} is about 15.84, which is nearly 200 times that of AI_{EWMM}.

Sync-Free BGEMM. In order to use Tensor Cores to accelerate **BGEMM**, it is necessary to construct a computation in the **BGEMM** algorithm that can

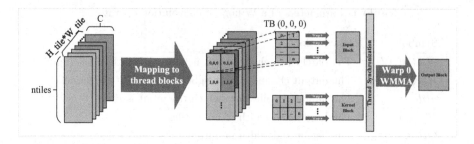

Fig. 2. Workload partition and data flow of the vanilla **BGEMM**. A synchronization instruction is required before warps perform WMMA instructions.

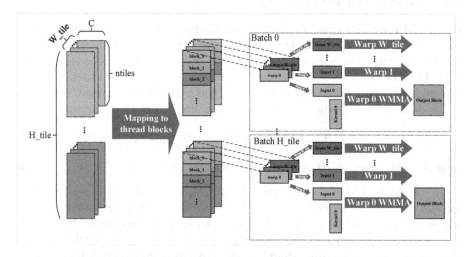

Fig. 3. Workload partition and data flow of the proposed **sync-free BGEMM**. Each warp can perform WMMA instruction immediately after reading the corresponding tile without synchronizing with other warps.

match the tensor intrinsic. In BGEMM, we constructed a matrix multiplication of $(ntiles, C) \times (C, K)$. By dividing the matrix into blocks, it is possible to call the tensor intrinsic to perform small-scale matrix multiplication directly. All Tensor Cores instructions are warp-level instructions, which means that all threads within a warp should execute the same instructions simultaneously. As shown in Fig. 2, batches of GEMM will be allocated to thread blocks, and each thread block will be responsible for calculating one of the output blocks. The warps within a thread block will cooperate to complete the data access corresponding to the output block. Then the threads within each warp cooperatively execute WMMA (Warp-level MMA) instructions to calculate one of the sub-matrices.

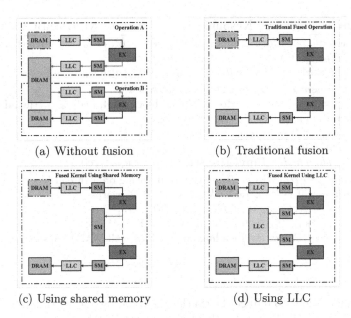

(a) Without fusion

(b) Traditional fusion

(c) Using shared memory

(d) Using LLC

Fig. 4. Data flow of different methods.

Here the question arises. After all warps within a thread block have already finished data access, a thread synchronization between warps is required to perform WMMA operations. This synchronization instruction inserted before the WMMA instruction will bring an inevitable synchronization overhead to the workload and affect the execution efficiency. In order to eliminate this overhead, we improved **BGEMM** to implement **sync-free BGEMM** (as shown in Fig. 3). $H_{tile} * W_{tile}$ batches of GEMM are no longer allocated to different thread blocks. We tile the workload along the *ntiles* dimension and allocate obtained blocks to thread blocks, while the data in the batch dimension is allocated to the same thread block. In other words, each thread block is now responsible for the GEMM of $H_{tile} * W_{tile}$ batches of sub-matrices. A thread block is composed of W_{tile} warps and iterates over H_{tile} batches to complete all calculations. At this time, the data accessed by each warp is consistent with the data used in the calculation. Therefore, each warp can perform WMMA instruction immediately after reading the corresponding tile, without waiting for other warps to reach the synchronization point of completing the data reading.

4.2 PKF (Partial Kernel Fusion)

New Fusion Methods. In DL compilation, operator fusion refers to combining operations into a fused operator. Unlike the loop fusion in traditional compilation, dependencies in operator fusion are implicitly given by the data flow graph and operator semantics [15]. Whether loop fusion or operator fusion, it tries to

Algorithm 1. Applying PKF-Shmem on ITrans and sync-free BGEMM

Input : packed input tiles $I(ntiles_{outer}, H_{tile}, W_{tile}, ntiles_{inner}, C)$, transformed kernel $F(H_{tile}, W_{tile}, K, C)$

Out : fused kernel output $O(ntiles_{outer}, H_{tile}, W_{tile}, ntiles_{inner}, K)$

1: **Shared** $shmem\_F[H_{tile}, W_{tile}, K, C] = \mathbf{LOAD}(F)$
2: **for** $n_{outer} = 0 \rightarrow ntiles_{outer}$ **do** // Thread block level, $ntiles_{outer}$ thread blocks
3:     **Shared** $shmem\_I[H_{tile}, W_{tile}, ntiles_{inner}, C]$;
4:     **for** $n_{inner} = 0 \rightarrow ntiles_{inner}$ **do**
5:         **for** $c = 0 \rightarrow C$ **do**
6:             $shmem\_I = \mathbf{InputTrans}(I[n_{outer}, :, :, n_{inner}, c])$
7:     **for** $h = 0 \rightarrow H_{tile}$ **do** // H_{tile} batches iterating on a thread block
8:         **for** $w = 0 \rightarrow W_{tile}$ **do** // Warp level, W_{tile} warps
9:             $K_{outer}, C_{outer} = \lceil K/K_{inner} \rceil, \lceil C/C_{inner} \rceil$
10:            **for** $k_{out}, c_{out} = 0 \rightarrow K_{outer}, C_{outer}$ **do**
11:                // Warp level loading and GEMM, call WMMA instructions here
12: **return** O

---

combine calculations to reduce the overhead of reading and writing intermediate results brought about by the bandwidth difference of the memory hierarchy.

According to the memory hierarchy of GPUs, we can theoretically have three fusion methods. The traditional fusion method is to directly use the result of the previous operator as the input of the next operator. The usual method is to merge the two operators into one operator through equivalent transformation or use local memory (registers) to temporarily store intermediate results as shown in Fig. 4(b). However, the four kernels cannot be fused into one kernel mathematically. Nevertheless, we can leverage shared memory (Fig. 4(c)) or LLC (Last-Level Cache) (Fig. 4(d)) to remap data to threads to fuse partial kernels of them with new fusion methods.

PKF for Winograd Kernels. Considering residing data using shared memory to fuse kernel **ITrans** and kernel **Sync-free BGEMM** (denoted as PKF-Shmem), we must tile data into tiles of appropriate size. Only a single warp can run on a single SM simultaneously. The WMMA API provides an interface that supports a few specific matrix sizes for matrix multiplication on a single warp. Defining the size of the matrix multiplication of $A_{M \times K}$ and $B_{K \times N}$ as $M \times N \times K$, there are three choices for them for half-precision floating-point matrix multiplication: $16 \times 16 \times 16$, $32 \times 8 \times 16$ and $8 \times 32 \times 16$, that puts forward requirements for the partition factor on $ntiles$, C and K dimension. The larger the $ntiles$ partition factor is, the more warps and threads are allocated in a thread block, making fuller use of computing resources. However, it also means that the transformed kernel needs to be repeatedly read more times, which will waste non-negligible memory bandwidth.

Unlike utilizing shared memory, using LLC for PKF can further keep the data residing in LLC (denoted as PKF-LLC). LLC is a bridge for data exchange between shared memory and off-chip DRAM. It is also an alternative fusion method to improve the hit rate of LLC through arranging the data layout used by the workload. The output data in the **ITrans** stage needs to be used immediately in the **BGEMM** stage. So the specific way is organizing the codes of two kernels together and synchronizing the threads to update LLC by inserting a thread synchronization instruction `__syncthreads();`. After the threads pass the synchronization point, they re-read the data required by the next kernel from LLC. As long as the data size can be controlled not exceed the capacity of LLC, the data access of a thread block will inevitably hit.

The PKF-Shmem algorithm is shown in Algorithm 1. The implementation of PKF-LLC is similar to PKF-Shmem. The difference is only in the explicit use of different levels of the memory hierarchy.

5   Implementation and Experiment

5.1   Implementation PKF on TVM

TVM. TVM [16] is a DL compiler that generates low-level optimized code for a diverse set of hardware back-ends. Unlike traditional compilers, the input of TVM is algorithms described by *compute* and *schedule* rather than high-level programming language codes. TVM uses *schedule* to indicate the mapping from tensor expressions to low-level code. *schedule* defines the implementation of *compute* by specifying how to do the computation. A well-performing *schedule* for a *compute* can be found by searching the scheduling space with various methods (such as learning-based methods [17]). Vanilla Winograd convolution implementation on TVM is composed of four separated kernels corresponding to the four stages of Winograd. Using the *compute* and *schedule* primitives on TVM, we can easily define and implement Winograd convolution using **sync-free BGEMM** to implement PKF further.

Challenges. There are still some challenges in implementing PKF Winograd on TVM. First, the vanilla TVM is unable to fuse the kernel **ITrans** and **BGEMM** due to their schedule with different warps. In addition, TVM will automatically insert thread synchronization instructions that are unnecessary in some cases while generating CUDA code. TVM checks the memory accesses during compilation to determine whether there are conflicts between threads, but only single-point accesses and read accesses after double buffer writes are analyzed to decide whether not to insert a synchronization instruction. In this way, it is possible to add unnecessary synchronizations to the workload. Tests show that synchronization instructions will still be inserted, although there is no memory dependency between warps in our **BGEMM** implementation.

PKF-Reconstructor. Modifying TVM's operator fusion logic and memory dependency analysis according to our needs will affect the fundamental basis of TVM. Therefore, we proposed a minimally costly implementation and implemented the PKF-Reconstructor. First, we use Compute and Schedule primitives to construct the prototype of PKF Winograd on TVM. Then we use TVM to generate intermediate CUDA code for the prototype. Finally, we use the PKF-Reconstructor to generate the final PKF Winograd CUDA code from the intermediate code and compile it into a GPU workload. The PKF-Reconstructor first finds the unfused **ITrans** and **BGEMM** kernel implementations and generates a fused parameter list based on the two kernels' parameter lists. Then, it extracts the code in the inner loop iteration bound to the thread block in the **BGEMM** kernel and inserts it into the corresponding loop of the **ITrans** kernel. After that, thread synchronization instructions after the warp loads are removed. Finally, PKF-Reconstructor modifies the partition of Grids and re-computes the iteration variables to get the correct PKF Winograd implementation. We also found that some other synchronization instructions can be removed without affecting the correctness of the program. Therefore, we try to remove all the synchronization instructions and confirm the removal if the correct output can be obtained.

5.2   Experiment

Experimental Setup. We evaluated the performance of PKF Winograd on a set of real-world convolution operators on the GPU. The main experimental setups are as follows.

- **Hardware platform**: We use NVIDIA RTX 2080Ti GPU with 11 GB memory, 5.5 MB LLC and 64 KB (per SM) shared memory.
- **Software platforms**: We use Apache TVM v0.7dev to implement basic Winograd convolution with **sync-free BGEMM** and generate intermediate CUDA C++ source code. The PKF-Reconstructor is written in Python and works with Python 3.8.4. Final GPU convolution workloads are compiled and linked with NVCC v11.0.
- **Workloads**: We have counted the parameters of the convolution operator in real-world CNNs base on Inception-V3, ResNet-V1, ResNet-V2, and DenseNet in MXNet Zoo. We choose the $C = K = 64$, $KH = KW = 3$ kernel with the highest frequency in the network as the workload. The size of the input feature map varies from 224 to 960.
- **Baseline**: We use the vendor-provided library cuDNN v8.5 to generate baseline Winograd convolution workloads. The performance measurement of each workload is repeated 100 times and averaged. For comparison, we also test vanilla Winograd implementation and a fine-tuned implementation generated by TVM.

Results and Analysis. Due to the limitation of using Tensor Core on the shape of the input matrix, there are only two choices for the partition factor of the available workload on the *ntiles* dimension, 16 and 32, respectively. We can obtain four implementations by combining them with the two PKF methods. We use a dash to attach the value of the division factor after the method name to distinguish between different approaches. We evaluate Winograd with and without fusion on cuDNN and take the faster one as the measurement result.

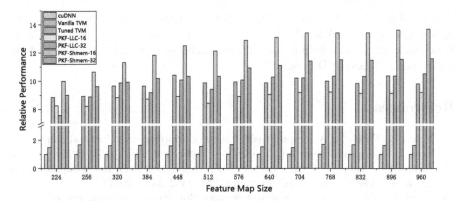

Fig. 5. The performance of applying different methods to the convolution operator. The relative performance of cuDNN is set to 1 as the baseline. The method PKF-Shmem-16 performed best, achieving an average speedup of 12.46.

The best performance among the four Winograd implementations on TVM is the result for vanilla TVM.

Experimental results (Fig. 5) show that, compared with cuDNN, the four PKF implementations have achieved considerable performance. Among them, PKF-Shmem-16 performed best, achieving an acceleration of 9.99 to 13.69 times. We can intuitively notice that the improvement increases with the growth of the feature map size with PKF-Shmem, while PKF-LLC does not. Compared with cuDNN, Vanilla TVM has an efficiency improvement of 47.54%–70.50%, but it is far from the four PKF implementations and the tuned TVM prototype.

Compared with the tuned prototype, PKF-LLC even has performance degradation because requiring additional thread synchronization. However, PKF-LLC-32 makes better use of computing resources, showing the advantages of fusion when the amount of calculation becomes larger. The performance of PKF-Shmem is impressive. It makes better use of the high-bandwidth shared memory without introducing synchronization overhead. PKF-Shmem-32 did not achieve the same profit as PKF-Shmem-16 does. By profiling the kernel of PKF-Shmem-32, we find that the hit rate of its LLC is much higher than the others. This usual increase in hit rate is caused by repeated access to the transformed kernel, which wastes the bandwidth of LLC. Further experiments on NVIDIA T4 GPUs also achieve similar results to NVIDIA 2080Ti, even though their architectures are Tesla and Turing respectively.

6   Conclusion

We propose **sync-free BGEMM** for Winograd convolution to utilize Tensor Cores. We further introduce PKF, which can effectively use memory hierarchy by partially fusing the kernels. Finally, we write PKF-Reconstructor based on TVM to implement PKF for Winograd convolution. Evaluations show that PKF

Winograd convolution achieves 8.22×–13.69× speedup over cuDNN and 4.89×–9.10× speedup over TVM. By leveraging lower-level cache in operator fusion, we hope our methods can help expand search space for auto-scheduling to look for better possibilities for DL compilers.

References

1. Patel, R., Patel, S.: A comprehensive study of applying convolutional neural network for computer vision. Int. J. Adv. Sci. Technol. **6**, 2161–2174 (2020)
2. Rawat, W., Wang, Z.: Deep convolutional neural networks for image classification: a comprehensive review. Neural Comput. **29**, 2352–2449 (2017)
3. Fathi, E., Shoja, B.M.: Deep neural networks for natural language processing. In: Handbook of Statistics, vol. 38, pp. 229–316 (2018)
4. Goodfellow, I., Bengio, Y., Courville, A.: Deep Learning. The MIT Press (2016)
5. Sze, V., Chen, Y.H., Yang, T.J., Emer, J.S.: Efficient processing of deep neural networks: a tutorial and survey. Proc. IEEE **105**(12), 2295–2329 (2017). https://doi.org/10.1109/JPROC.2017.2761740
6. Jia, L., Liang, Y., Li, X., Lu, L., Yan, S.: Enabling efficient fast convolution algorithms on GPUs via MegaKernels. IEEE Trans. Comput. **69**(7), 986–997 (2020). https://doi.org/10.1109/TC.2020.2973144
7. Lavin, A., Gray, S.: Fast algorithms for convolutional neural networks. Arxiv, September 2015
8. Li, S., Park, J., Tang, P.T.P.: Enabling sparse Winograd convolution by native pruning. arXiv e-prints arXiv:1702.08597, February 2017
9. Meng, L., Brothers, J.: Efficient Winograd convolution via integer arithmetic. arXiv e-prints arXiv:1901.01965, January 2019
10. Barabasz, B., Gregg, D.: Winograd convolution for DNNs: beyond linear polynomials. In: Alviano, M., Greco, G., Scarcello, F. (eds.) AI*IA 2019. LNCS (LNAI), vol. 11946, pp. 307–320. Springer, Cham (2019). https://doi.org/10.1007/978-3-030-35166-3_22
11. Yan, D., Wang, W., Chu, X.: Optimizing batched Winograd convolution on GPUs. In: Proceedings of the 25th ACM SIGPLAN Symposium on Principles and Practice of Parallel Programming, PPoPP 2020, pp. 32–44. Association for Computing Machinery, New York (2020). https://doi.org/10.1145/3332466.3374520
12. Huang, Y., Shen, J., Wang, Z., Wen, M., Zhang, C.: A high-efficiency FPGA-based accelerator for convolutional neural networks using Winograd algorithm. J. Phys. Conf. Ser. **1026**, 012019, May 2018
13. Wang, Z., Lan, Q., He, H., Zhang, C.: Winograd algorithm for 3D convolution neural networks. In: Lintas, A., Rovetta, S., Verschure, P.F.M.J., Villa, A.E.P. (eds.) ICANN 2017. LNCS, vol. 10614, pp. 609–616. Springer, Cham (2017). https://doi.org/10.1007/978-3-319-68612-7_69
14. Laine, S., Karras, T., Aila, T.: Megakernels considered harmful: wavefront path tracing on GPUs. In: Proceedings of the 5th High-Performance Graphics Conference, HPG 2013, pp. 137–143. Association for Computing Machinery, New York (2013). https://doi.org/10.1145/2492045.2492060
15. Kennedy, K., Allen, J.R.: Optimizing Compilers for Modern Architectures: A Dependence-Based Approach. Morgan Kaufmann Publishers Inc., San Francisco (2001)

16. Chen, T., Moreau, T., Jiang, Z., Zheng, L., Yan, E., et al.: TVM: an automated end-to-end optimizing compiler for deep learning. In: USENIX OSDI 2018, pp. 579-594. USENIX, USA (2018)
17. Chen, T., et al.: Learning to optimize tensor programs. In: Bengio, S., Wallach, H., Larochelle, H., Grauman, K., Cesa-Bianchi, N., Garnett, R. (eds.) NIPS 2018, vol. 31. Curran Associates, Inc. (2018)

Adaptive Low-Cost Loop Expansion for Modulo Scheduling

Hongli Zhong, Zhong Liu$^{(\boxtimes)}$, Sheng Liu, Sheng Ma, and Chen Li

College of Computer, National University of Defense Technology, Changsha, China
zhongliu@nudt.edu.cn

Abstract. This paper presents a novel modulo scheduling method, which is called Expanded Modulo Scheduling (EMS). Unlike existing methods which regard loop unrolling and scheduling respectively, EMS supports adaptive loop expansion, and provides a unified scheduling strategy with conflict elimination mechanism for all unrolled layers. EMS constructs the data dependence graph (DDG) only once for the initial loop, and the expansion step is performed on DDG rather than the loop itself. As a heuristic, EMS focuses on the criticality of operations and tries to schedule interdependent operations as close as possible, thus reducing the register pressure. The paper describes this technique and evaluates it on MT-3000, achieving an average of over $25x$ performance improvement for classical assemblies and better resource utilization against other methods.

Keywords: Instruction-level parallelism · VLIW · Software pipelining · Loop unrolling · Register requirement

1 Introduction

Loop optimization is the most critical aspect of modern compilers, since most of the program execution time is spent on loops. Besides, for programs running on VLIW architectures [1], the static instruction scheduling techniques determines their performance upper bounds in production environments.

Some of the approaches attempt to find the optimal resource-constrained schedule for loops, including integer linear programming [2] and constraint programming [3,4], which formulate the problem as an exact mathematical model and apply branch-and-bound or constraint solvers to compute the schedule. However, since scheduling with resource constraints is known to be NP-hard [4], the exponential complexity renders such techniques impractical for large loops. Similarly, techniques that apply evolutionary algorithms, such as simulated annealing and genetic algorithm [2,5,6], have been proposed but are only suitable for the scheduling of small loops.

Modulo scheduling [7], inheriting the idea of software pipelining, is an efficient instruction scheduling technique that exploits instruction-level parallelism (ILP) for loop optimization. The scheduling for each iteration is divided into several stages with iterative interval (II) cycles each, and the benefit derives from

© IFIP International Federation for Information Processing 2022
Published by Springer Nature Switzerland AG 2022
S. Liu and X. Wei (Eds.): NPC 2022, LNCS 13615, pp. 30–41, 2022.
https://doi.org/10.1007/978-3-031-21395-3_3

the repetitive execution of a regular pattern(called kernel) consisting of several stages from multiple iterations. Up to now, some proposals in the literature focus on achieving maximum instruction throughput [7–10] or minimizing register requirements [11–13], while others take power consumption into account [14,15].

Minimizing the iteration interval is the primary task of modulo scheduling, which means the most intensive instruction transmission frequency. The general procedure for modulo schedulers [7–15] is to first compute the minimum iteration interval (MII), and then attempt to schedule operations. If the operation cannot be scheduled due to resource constraints or the scheduling does not satisfy the loop carried dependency, then II is increased by 1 and the entire process is repeated. However, when hardware resources (e.g., functional units) far exceed the requirements of the target loop, the pursuit of only minimizing the iteration interval tends to low resource utilization.

In [16–18], researchers illustrate the benefit of loop unrolling before modulo scheduling. Loop unrolling can reduce or even eliminate the overhead of loop jumps and expand the size of the loop body for more scheduling opportunities. For loops with a sufficiently large number of iterations, this transformation potentially results in substantial performance benefits. However, excessive unrolling can rapidly increase register requirements and eventually lead to failed scheduling. The challenge is how to find an optimal unroll factor and how to schedule operations of replicas.

In [19], a register-sensitive loop unrolling algorithm (RSU for short) is proposed to estimate the upper bound of the unrolling factor before scheduling. The main drawback of RSU is that it ignores the effect of the scheduling process on the register requirements and is likely to get a larger upper bound than the actual one, thus missing out on better scheduling.

The high register overhead is a side effect of modulo scheduling, which means that the benefits from pipelining are likely to be reduced or even lost due to register spilling. In [12], researchers propose a lifetime-sensitive method called Swing Modulo Scheduling (SMS), which is state-of-the-art in relieving register pressure. SMS considers the criticality of operations and tries to arrange operations as close to their predecessors and successors as possible, thereby minimizing the lifetime of all variables. However, SMS does not distinguish unrolled loops in which register pressure can be further reduced.

In this paper, EMS is proposed to address the above issues, and its main features are as follows:

1. **Maximizing resource utilization** (e.g., functional units) under minimum iteration interval: EMS integrates adaptive loop unrolling and adopts an alternating heuristic scheduling strategy for all expansion layers.
2. **Relieving register pressure:** EMS considers the criticality of operations and schedules those interdependent operations as close as possible. Moreover, Instead of renaming variables blindly during loop unrolling, EMS renames variables after all operations are scheduled, and only performs on those with data conflicts.

3. **Reducing computational overhead:** In general, analyzing the data dependencies of a loop requires high computational overhead, especially for unrolled loops, whereas EMS requires only one dependency analysis towards the initial loop.

2 Expanded Modulo Scheduling

EMS is designed to provide a complete code generation framework capable of optimizing loops for realistic machine models, which inputs a standard loop with user hints and eventually outputs multiple optimized solutions.

The general structure of EMS consists of two layers of iterations, indexed by expansion count (EC) and II, respectively. The outer iteration is responsible for expanding the initial loop to the original $EC + 1$ times, i.e., creating EC copies. Loop layers consisting of original and copies are distinguished from each other and scheduled in an alternating manner.

In addition, to ensure the correctness and completeness of the solution, hints on the number of loop iterations are used to guide the code generation, which consists of two aspects. First, each solution must satisfy the requirement of the minimum number of iterations, that is,

$$SC \leq \left\lfloor \frac{LIT}{EC + 1} \right\rfloor$$

Second, since not all iterations will be pipelined, the remaining iterations needs to be processed. The division of loop iterations is as follows.

$$RT = \begin{cases} NT & , NT < SC \times (EC + 1) \\ NT\%(EC + 1) & , else \end{cases}$$
$$ST = NT - RT$$

where NT denotes the total number of iterations of the target loop at runtime. ST denotes the number of iterations used for pipelining while RT denotes the number of remaining iterations.

If NT is a compile-time constant, RT and ST are computed at compile-time, which means aggressive optimizations can be applied to the remaining iterations, such as dispatching the remainder to prologue/epilogue after de-looping. Otherwise, a copy of the loop will be constructed to perform the possible remaining iterations.

2.1 Data Dependence Graph

Since only the innermost loops that do not contain subroutine calls and conditional branches are handled, DDG-based scheduling is feasible. DDG consists of the following five elements ($\{V, E, \lambda, \omega, h\}$):

- V is the set of vertices (also called nodes or operations) in the graph, and any $u \in V$ represents a certain operation or a set of operations that can be executed in parallel.
- E is the set of directed edges, where each edge $e_{u,v} \in E$ represents a certain dependency from operation u to operation v. The dependency types only involve data dependencies (including register data dependencies and memory data dependencies), which can be unified into the flow-, anti-, and output-dependencies.
- $\lambda_{u,v}$ is the attribute of $e_{u,v}$ that represents the number of cycles required by operation u and operation v respectively. e.g., suppose there is a flow-dependency between Y and Z, denoted as $e_{Y,Z} \in E$, and Y takes 3 cycles, than $\lambda_{Y,Z} = <3,0>$, $\lambda_{Y,Z}(Y) = 3$, $\lambda_{Y,Z}(Z) = 0$.
- $\omega_{u,v}$ is the attribute of $e_{u,v}$ that represents the non-negative iterative distance from operation u to operation v. It means that operation v in the i-th iteration must wait until operation u in the $(i - \omega_{u,v})$-th iteration is completed.

Given an operation $u \in V$, $Pred(u)$ is a set of all the predecessors of u, and $Pred(u)^*$ contains only those operations in $Pred(u)$ that have been scheduled. Similarly, for all the successors of u, we have $Succ(u)$ and $Succ(u)^*$.

- h_u is the height of node u in the graph, which is defined as the maximum distance from node u to a node without successors. it is computed as below.

$$h_u = \begin{cases} 0 & , Su(u) = \emptyset \\ max(h_v + \lambda_{u,v}(u)), \forall v \in Su(u) & , otherwise \end{cases}$$

where $Su(u) = \{v | \forall v \in Succ(u), \omega_{u,v} = 0\}$.

2.2 Expansion Count and Iteration Interval

Unlike methods that treat scheduling and loop unrolling as independent of each other, the scheduling process in EMS is jointly directed by EC and II, striving to achieve maximum resource utilization while minimizing iteration interval. In other words, EMS preserves the expanded solution search space due to the non-integer iteration interval.

EC should be less than the minimum number of iterations (denoted as LIT) of the target loop obtained by compiler analysis or specified by user hints, i.e., $EC \in [0, LIT - 1] \in N$, and for each EC, $II \in [MII, +\infty) \in N$. Since increasing EC means higher register pressure, when EC exceeds a certain threshold, no more available schedules will be generated. Thus, an empirical upper bound for EC is used to avoid the negative effects of over-expansion.

MII is determined by two bounds, one bound is derived from the critical resource usage called resource MII (ResMII) while the other bound is derived from the critical recurrence circuit called recurrence MII (RecMII). MII equals the maximum value of ResMII and RecMII.

The ResMII of the target loop under any EC is computed as below.

$$ResMII = \lceil resp \times (EC + 1) \rceil$$

where $resp$ based on the initial loop is a float defined as below.

$$resp = \min_{s \in S} \left(\max_i \left(\frac{N_s^i}{U^i} \right) \right)$$

where S is a set containing all functional unit allocation schemes. N_s^i represents the number of units of class i required according to the scheme $s \in S$. U^i represents the number of identical units of class i available.

In EMS, a technique with low computational complexity is proposed for computing $resp$. The key step is to simulate the allocation of functional units under the assumption that there are no data-dependent constraints. The allocation strategy prioritizes the least used unit in the available options based on the real-time usage of each functional unit.

Cross dependencies between iterations of a loop can increase the latency between operations on the execution path, then the RecMII, based on the DDG, is defined as below.

$$RecMII = \max_{\forall c \in C} \left(\left\lceil \frac{\sum_{e_{u,v} \in C} \lambda_{u,v}(u)}{\sum_{e_{u,v} \in C} \omega_{u,v}} \right\rceil \right)$$

where C is a set containing all simple circuits of the graph.

2.3   Scheduling

All heuristic scheduling methods need to answer two fundamental questions based on a global perspective, one is in what order the operations should be selected, and the other is in which timeslot the operations should be placed. Due to data dependencies and resource constraints, the current operation is restricted by the scheduled operations and also affects the subsequent operations.

Selection. The critical path reflects the maximum time required for a single iteration of the target loop. An intuitive idea is to schedule non-critical operations into the remaining timeslots after the scheduling of critical operations to obtain compact schemes. Besides, considering the implicit dependencies between operations in the graph, the selection strategy here relies on the height of each operation (i.e., h).

EMS first divides all operations into groups based on their own height in the graph, and then selects the group with the largest height for scheduling. Three kinds of objects are arranged sequentially in each round, namely, the current critical operations, the legacy non-critical operations, and the current non-critical operations.

Since there is no explicit dependency between operations with the same height, critical operations with few successors are scheduled preferentially to relieve the register pressure.

Placement. In general, the timeslot in modulo reservation table (MRT) for any operation can be determined in two steps. First, all possible timeslots are computed based on the dependencies (i.e., anti, output, and flow) between the target operation and its scheduled predecessors/successors. Then, resource constraint tests are performed on each candidate in a certain order, and the first timeslot that passes the tests will be placed.

Given a DDG (denoted as G) and an operation to be scheduled (denoted as Y), $Y \in G$.

For any edge $e_{X,Y} \in G$, $X \in Prev(Y)^*$, the predecessor constraint interval (PCI) on Y is computed as below.

$$PCI_{X,Y} = \begin{cases} [r, r + II) & , X \xrightarrow{flow} Y \\ (r, +\infty) & , else \end{cases}$$

where $r = P_X + \lambda_{X,Y}(X) - \lambda_{X,Y}(Y) - \omega_{X,Y} \times II \in N$.

For any edge $e_{Y,Z} \in G$, $Z \in Succ(Y)^*$, the the successor constraint interval (SCI) on Y is computed as below.

$$SCI_{Y,Z} = \begin{cases} (s - II, s] & , Y \xrightarrow{flow} Z \\ (-\infty, s) & , else \end{cases}$$

where $s = P_Z - \lambda_{Y,Z}(Y) + \lambda_{Y,Z}(Z) + \omega_{Y,Z} \times II \in N$.

Then, the constrained interval involving all available slots for Y is defined as:

$$TS_Y = \bigcap_{X \in Prev(Y)^*} PCI_{X,Y} \bigcap_{Z \in Succ(Y)^*} SCI_{Y,Z}$$

To minimize the lifetime of all variables, each operation is placed as close as possible to its predecessors and successors. If operation Y has only predecessors (or only successors), then the front slots (or back slots) will be selected first.

2.4 Resolving Expansion Faults

In this section, the problem of data conflicts (variable conflicts and memory conflicts) among expansion layers will be resolved.

Figure 1a depicts part of the code of a loop after expanding twice. After the scheduling phase, the active intevals of variable x in the three expansion layers are shown in Fig. 1b, where the red area emphasizes the conflict between the first and second expansion layers. One way to effectively eliminate the above conflict is to choose either of these two extension layers to rename x. Notice that instead of renaming variables blindly, EMS renames variables after all operations have been scheduled, and only performs on those with data conflicts.

The reason for memory address conflicts is that multiple loop layers access the same memory address at the same time. In general, EMS modifies the address or the step size of the memory access according to the number of memory conflicts within the same timeslot to ensure the independence of different loop layers. Section 3.2 represents some modifications for MT-3000.

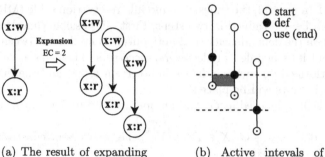

(a) The result of expanding
the part of a loop twice

(b) Active intevals of
variable x in different expansion layers

Fig. 1. An example to illustrate the problem of variable conflicts

2.5   Completing the MRT

Each schedule of EMS starts with an empty MRT, where each column represents
the stage with II cycles, and the column distance from the last non-empty column
(which contains at least one scheduled operation) to the first column equals
to stage count (SC). In this section, EMS performs the following two steps to
complete the MRT:

1. **Filling the MRT**: each original operation in the target MRT will be copied
   $SC - 1$ times in steps of II, thereby making up the code for the prologue,
   epilogue, and kernel.
2. **Insert loop count chain**: the loop count chain guides the execution of the
   kernel code and indicates that its total number of iterations is $ST - SC + 1$.
   The key step in scheduling counts and jumps is to ensure that the timing of
   the jumps is between adjacent iterations of the kernel code.

3   Performance Evaluation

3.1   Target Architecture

MT-3000 processor [20] is the target architecture used here. It is a heterogeneous multi-zone processor for HPC, which consists of four identical acceleration clusters. The experiments were executed on an acceleration cluster of a
preproduction MT-3000 chip.

In each acceleration cluster, one control core and 16 accelerator cores are
organized into an acceleration array. Each accelerator core organizes computation units in a VLIW manner, where three Multiply and Accumulate (MAC)
units, one Integer Execution Unit (IEU), and two Load/Store units are arranged
in parallel and up to six instructions are packed and issued concurrently to each
accelerator core in a single cycle.

Notice that in this architecture, write ports for the same functional unit may conflict. Suppose there is an instruction X with cycle i and an instruction Y with cycle j, which are successively dispatched by the same functional unit, and the dispatch interval is k cycles. If $i + k = j$, the write port of the target unit will conflict.

Jump instructions are delayed by 6 cycles, that is, the jump is issued at cycle i, but does not commit until cycle $i + 6$, and the jump event occurs before cycle $i + 7$. Thus, the first jump instruction will be dispatched to the position (i.e., the position of the last slot in the kernel $- 7$).

3.2   Adaptation of EMS

In terms of unit allocation, two constraints need to be considered when adapting the EMS to the MT-3000. One is the limited inventory, and the other is the need to avoid write port conflicts. Thus, two resource constraint tests will be applied in the scheduling phase.

The first test aims to ensure the exclusivity of the operation to the functional unit, and the specific steps are as follows:

1. Check whether there is a functional unit that can be assigned to the target operation (denoted as Y). If there is an available functional unit, denoted as U, proceed to the next step, otherwise, return failure.
2. Check whether the functional unit U is occupied in the slot whose index position in the MRT is equal to $P_Y + II \times n$, $n \in Z$. If the unit U in any checked slot is occupied, return failure.

The second test ensures that all assigned functional units have no write conflicts by maintaining a growing set (denoted as WS) containing write-back information of all scheduled operations. In WS, the write-back information of each operation is quantified as a unique integer identifier (called WP), and only those operations whose WP is unique in the WS can pass the test. The WP of operation Y is computed as below.

$$WP_Y = USZ \times (P_Y \% II) + UN$$

where UZS represents the total number of functional units, UN is an integer indicating the functional unit occupied by Y, $UN \in [0, USZ)$.

In terms of removing memory access conflicts among loop layers, the focus is on the update of address operands. If m loop layers have an address access conflict in a certain time slot, $2 \times m - 1$ updates are required (modifying the offset for the m operands + renaming the base address variable for the $m - 1$ operands). Since the updated offset is equal to the original offset multiplied by m, numerical overflow must be considered. To reduce register overhead, EMS prefers a constant offset if the number of significant bits is not greater than 18. EMS is terminated if the updated offset exceeds 36 significant bits.

Table 1. Experimental assemblies and configurations

Program	Description	Innermost loops	Input scale
gemm	$\alpha \times AB + \beta \times C$.	1	$A : 12 \times 384$ $B : 384 \times 64$
axpby	$\alpha \times x + \beta \times y$.	1	$n : 32768$
fir	FIR filtering algorithm	1	$nh : 8000$, $nr : 64$
dot	$x \cdot y$.	1	$n : 30720$
scal	$\alpha \times x$.	1	$n : 61440$
asum	$\sum_i |x_i|$.	1	$n : 61440$
fft_r2	DFT fast algorithm.	10	$n : 1024$

$^{*}A, B$ are matrices, α, β are scalars, and x, y are vectors of length n.

3.3 Experiment Setup

The experiment here is based on a small number of critical procedures in the field of signal processing. These programs written in assembly-layer language do not care about the arrangement of parallel instructions, the latency of instructions, and the allocation of registers and functional units. Table 1 describes these programs and their input scales. Besides, the following three methods are used to compare with EMS($EC \in [0, 7]$):

Base-Opt is an implementation of list scheduling that schedules operations sequentially according to their initial order. It is not only used as a baseline for evaluation but also to verify the correctness of scheduling schemes generated by other scheduling methods.

Top-Down is an implementation of modulo scheduling, which schedules operations sequentially according to their initial order. It doesn't care about the criticality of the operation, nor does it care about reducing register pressure.

U-TopDown first performs loop unrolling on the target loop, then uses Top-Down for scheduling. The number of loop unrolling is the same as the best schedule generated by EMS.

3.4 Experiment Results

Table 2 compares some performance metrics. The average resource utilization (avg-ResU) and register requirements (Reg) of each innermost loop after scheduling among the four methods are shown as well as the total number of beats (Beat). ResU is the ratio of the number of all allocated units to the total number of units in one iteration of a loop (only the functional units used for computation are considered). Overall, EMS achieves MII on all programs and improves the beat performance of all innermost loops by at least 18 times.

In terms of resource utilization, EMS outperforms other methods on 6 programs. The reason for the better resource utilization of Top-Down on scal is that ResU considers the loop count chain that occupies an IEU. Otherwise, the resource utilization of both methods is the same, i.e., 0.4. Although U-TopDown also performs loop unrolling, since loop copies are not distinguished

Table 2. Comparison of EMS with other scheduling methods

		$\sum II$	$\sum EC$	$\sum MII$	Reg	avg-ResU	Beat	BT*
axpby	Base-Opt	–	0	–	15	0.0190	43008	0
	Top-Down	7	0	2	15	0.1143	7188	4.9833
	U-TopDown	7	1	3	26	0.2143	3605	10.9300
	EMS	**3**	1	3	25	**0.5000**	1561	**26.5516**
fir	Base-Opt	–	0	–	13	0.0265	272000	0
	Top-Down	6	0	6	13	0.1500	48012	4.6653
	U-TopDown	9	7	9	97	0.7222	9016	22.9574
	EMS	**8**	7	8	**13**	**0.8125**	8017	**32.9279**
dot	Base-Opt	–	0	–	9	0.0217	22080	0
	Top-Down	6	0	6	9	0.0833	5770	2.8267
	U-TopDown	6	5	6	49 (spill)	0.4167	975	21.6462
	EMS	6	5	6	**9**	**0.4167**	975	**21.6462**
gemm	Base-Opt	–	0	–	9	0.0200	15360	0
	Top-Down	6	0	6	9	0.1000	2316	5.6321
	U-TopDown	6	5	6	49	0.5167	401	37.3042
	EMS	6	5	6	**9**	**0.5167**	401	**37.3042**
scal	Base-Opt	–	0	–	9	0.1852	51840	0
	Top-Down	1	0	1	9	**0.5000**	1939	25.7354
	U-TopDown	6	5	6	39	0.4167	1936	25.7769
	EMS	6	5	6	23	0.4167	1936	**25.7769**
asum	Base-Opt	–	0	–	9	0.0250	46080	0
	Top-Down	6	0	6	9	0.1000	11531	2.9962
	U-TopDown	6	4	6	37	0.4333	2319	18.8706
	EMS	6	4	6	21	**0.4333**	2319	**18.8706**
fft_r2	Base-Opt	–	0	–	210	0.0192	17760	0
	Top-Down	54	0	46	210	0.3317	1682	9.5589
	U-TopDown	56	6	52	282 (spill)	0.4100	1627	9.9158
	EMS	**44**	6	40	246	**0.4730**	1162	**14.284**

*Beat Times (BT) measures the performance of the target scheduling method compared to Base-Opt in terms of total beats.

during scheduling, independent operations in different unroll copies cannot be scheduled in advance, which may lead to scheduling failure (compared to EMS, U-TopDown generates larger iteration intervals for axpby and fir). EMS requires fewer registers than U-TopDown because EMS renames only variables with conflicts and tries to schedule the operation as close to its predecessors or successors as possible during the scheduling, thus shortening the lifetime of all variables.

On the 4 programs, EMS consumes more registers than Base-Opt and Top-Down, which is inevitable due to loop expansion. Benefit from the adaptive capability of loop expansion in EMS, the register pressure is still under control. Moreover, due to the register-sensitive scheduling strategy, on the other 3 programs, the register requirements after EMS processing are the same as the least case. In other words, EMS is efficient in register utilization, which means it can achieve higher performance for machines containing rich hardware resources, such as MT-3000.

4 Conclusion

We have proposed a novel modulo scheduling method that is called Expanded Modulo Scheduling (EMS). EMS integrates an adaptive loop expansion mechanism, and the overhead of analyzing data dependencies depends only on the initial loop, which means that it can trade lower overhead for a large search space compared to other methods that separate loop unrolling and scheduling. Moreover, as a heuristic technique, EMS focuses on the criticality of operations and makes those interdependent operations as close as possible, thereby shortening the lifetime of all variables and reducing the pressure on registers. EMS has been evaluated on MT-3000, achieving an average of over $25x$ performance improvement for classical assemblies and better resource utilization against other methods. In the future, we hope to adapt our method to more VLIW machines.

Acknowledgements. This work was supported by PDL Research Project (No. 2021-KJWPDL-11), NUDT Research Project (No. ZK20-04), National Key Research and Development Project (No. 2021YFB0300300), the NSFC (No. 62172430), and the NSF of Hunan (No. 2021JJ10052).

References

1. Fisher, J.A.: Very long instruction word architectures and the ELI-512. SIGARCH Comput. Archit. News **11**, 140–150 (1983)
2. Eriksson, M.V., Skoog, O., Kessler, C.W.: Optimal vs. heuristic integrated code generation for clustered VLIW architectures. In: Proceedings of the 11th International Workshop on Software & Compilers for Embedded Systems, SCOPES 2008, New York, NY, USA, pp. 11–20. Association for Computing Machinery (2008)
3. Govindarajan, R., Altman, E., Gao, G.: Minimizing register requirements under resource-constrained rate-optimal software pipelining. In: Proceedings of MICRO-27, the 27th Annual IEEE/ACM International Symposium on Microarchitecture, pp. 85–94 (1994)
4. Lozano, R.C., Carlsson, M., Drejhammar, F., Schulte, C.: Constraint-based register allocation and instruction scheduling. In: Milano, M. (ed.) CP 2012. LNCS, pp. 750–766. Springer, Heidelberg (2012). https://doi.org/10.1007/978-3-642-33558-7_54
5. Giesemann, F., Payá-Vayá, G., Gerlach, L., Blume, H., Pflug, F., von Voigt, G.: Using a genetic algorithm approach to reduce register file pressure during instruction scheduling. In: 2017 International Conference on Embedded Computer Systems: Architectures, Modeling, and Simulation (SAMOS), pp. 179–187 (2017)
6. Giesemann, F., Gerlach, L., Payá-Vayá, G.: Evolutionary algorithms for instruction scheduling, operation merging, and register allocation in VLIW compilers. J. Signal Process. Syst. **92**(07), 655–678 (2020)

7. Lam, M.S.: Software pipelining: an effective scheduling technique for VLIW machines. SIGPLAN Not. **39**, 244–256 (2004)
8. Ramakrishna Rau, B.: Iterative module scheduling: an algorithm for software pipelining loops. In: Proceedings of MICRO-27, the 27th Annual IEEE/ACM International Symposium on Microarchitecture, pp. 63–74 (1994)
9. Warter-Perez, N.J., Partamian, N.: Modulo scheduling with multiple initiation intervals. In: Proceedings of the 28th Annual International Symposium on Microarchitecture, MICRO 28, Washington, DC, USA, pp. 111–119. IEEE Computer Society Press (1995)
10. Rau, B.R., Glaeser, C.D.: Some scheduling techniques and an easily schedulable horizontal architecture for high performance scientific computing. SIGMICRO Newsl. **12**, 183–198 (1981)
11. Eichenberger, A., Davidson, E.: Stage scheduling: a technique to reduce the register requirements of a module schedule. In: Proceedings of the 28th Annual International Symposium on Microarchitecture, pp. 338–349 (1995)
12. Llosa, J., Ayguadé, E., Gonzalez, A., Valero, M., Eckhardt, J.: Lifetime-sensitive modulo scheduling in a production environment. IEEE Trans. Comput. **50**, 234–249 (2001)
13. Llosa, J., Valero, M., Ayguadé, E., González, A.: Hypernode reduction modulo scheduling. In: Proceedings of the 28th Annual International Symposium on Microarchitecture, MICRO 28, Washington, DC, USA, pp. 350–360. IEEE Computer Society Press (1995)
14. Yun, H.-S., Kim, J.: Power-aware modulo scheduling for high-performance VLIW processors. In:Proceedings of the 2001 International Symposium on Low Power Electronics and Design, ISLPED 2001, New York, NY, USA, pp. 40–45. Association for Computing Machinery (2001)
15. Bahuleyan, J., Nagpal, R., Srikant, Y.N.: Integrated energy-aware cyclic and acyclic scheduling for clustered VLIW processors. In: 2010 IEEE International Symposium on Parallel and Distributed Processing, Workshops and Phd Forum (IPDPSW), pp. 1–8 (2010)
16. Lavery, D.M., Hwu, W.-M.W.: Unrolling-based optimizations for modulo scheduling. In: Proceedings of the 28th Annual International Symposium on Microarchitecture, MICRO 28, Washington, DC, USA, pp. 327–337. IEEE Computer Society Press (1995)
17. Sánchez, J., González, A.: The effectiveness of loop unrolling for modulo scheduling in clustered VLIW architectures. In: Proceedings of the 2000 International Conference on Parallel Processing, ICPP 2000, USA, p. 555. IEEE Computer Society (2000)
18. Aiken, A., Banerjee, U., Kejariwal, A., Nicolau, A.: Instruction Level Parallelism. Springer, Boston (2016). https://doi.org/10.1007/978-1-4899-7797-7
19. Haibo, L.: Research on Software Pipelining Techniques for EPIC Architectures. Ph.D thesis, Tsinghua University (2003)
20. Lu, K., et al.: MT-3000: a heterogeneous multi-zone processor for HPC. CCF Trans. High Perform. Comput. (2022)

SADD: A Novel Systolic Array Accelerator with Dynamic Dataflow for Sparse GEMM in Deep Learning

Bo Wang, Sheng Ma$^{(\boxtimes)}$, Zhong Liu, Libo Huang, Yuan Yuan, and Yi Dai

National University of Defense Technology, Changsha, China
{bowang,masheng,zhongliu,libohuang,Yuanyuan,daiyi}@nudt.edu.cn

Abstract. Nowadays, deep learning is prevalent in many fields. The primary workload in deep learning is the General Matrix-matrix Multiplication (GEMM). The TPU is the state-of-the-art GEMM accelerator. However, it does not support sparsity. In this paper, we design and implement the SADD, a systolic array accelerator that supports sparsity and dynamic dataflow. First, we propose the Group-Structure-Maintained Compression (GSMC). Then, based on the GSMC, we propose the Sparsity-supported Weight Stationary Dataflow (SWS) and Sparsity-supported Input Stationary Dataflow (SIS) to exploit the sparsity for systolic arrays. Finally, by combining the SIS and SWS, we propose the Sparsity-supported Dynamic Dataflow (SDD), which can change dataflow according to the computing environment. The experimental results show that the SDD in the SADD perform efficiently in any computing environment. When running the AlexNet, the performance of the SADD is $2\times$ better than the TPU. In addition, the SADD brings only a small additional hardware overhead.

Keywords: Deep learning · Sparsity · Dynamic dataflow · Systolic array

1 Introduction

Deep learning has been widely used in many fields, such as data mining [1], machine translation [2], and personalized recommendation [3]. With the rapid development of deep learning, its computational complexity is quickly increasing [4]. In order to support such a large amount of computation in deep learning, the researchers have designed a variety of hardware accelerators. Since convolution operations are often translated into the General Matrix-matrix Multiplication (GEMM), the core operation in training and inference of most deep learning models becomes the GEMM [5]. Therefore, accelerating the GEMM has become the primary goal of hardware accelerator design. The state-of-the-art GEMM accelerator is the Google's TPU, which uses a systolic array as the hardware structure for computing the GEMM [6].

This work is supported in part by the National Key R&D Project No. 2021YFB0300300, the NSFC (62172430, 61872374), the NSF of Hunan Province (2021JJ10052, 2022JJ10064).
B. Wang and S. Ma—Contributed equally to this research.

The systolic array is a 2D array composed of several Processing Elements (PEs), which usually adopts three types of dataflows: the Output Stationary (OS), Weight Stationary (WS), and Input Stationary (IS) [7]. The systolic array is efficient for computing the dense GEMM, but it does not exploit the sparsity. Taking advantage of sparsity often leads to higher performance and lower power consumption and communication bandwidth requirements. However, previous accelerators using systolic arrays often cannot efficiently exploit the sparsity in the GEMM [6, 12–14]

In our work, first, we propose the Group-Structure-Maintained Compression (GSMC) method for the sparse matrix in the systolic array. Then, by applying GSMC to WS and IS dataflows, we develop the Sparsity-supported Weight Stationary Dataflow (SWS) and Sparsity-supported Input Stationary Dataflow (SIS). Based on experimental analysis, we find that the SIS and SWS have different performances in different environments. Then we propose the Sparsity-supported Dynamic Dataflow (SDD), a combination of the SIS and SWS design. The SDD can dynamically switch the dataflow to achieve high performance in all computing environments. Finally, we propose the SADD, a systolic array accelerator with dynamic dataflow.

In summary, this paper makes the following contributions.

1) We propose the GSMC method to compress the sparse matrix in the systolic array. Based on the GSMC method, we propose the SIS and SWS to make systolic arrays support sparsity.
2) We propose the SDD and a state-of-the-art systolic array accelerator SADD. The SDD used in the SADD combines SIS and SWS, which can dynamically switch the dataflow according to weight matrix size and input matrix size.
3) We analyze the performance of the systolic arrays using the WS, IS, OS, SIS, SWS, and SDD with different sizes of GEMMs, and shows that the SDD can achieve high performance in any computing environment.
4) We implement and evaluate the SADD. The performance of the SADD is $2\times$ better than the TPU when running the sparse AlexNet. And the SADD brings only a small amount of additional hardware overhead.

2 Background

2.1 Dataflows in the Systolic Array

The systolic arrays usually support three kinds of dataflow, namely the OS, WS, and IS. The main idea of the OS is to fix the calculation result into PEs of the systolic array. As shown in Fig. 1(b), the weight matrix elements are streamed column-wise into the top of the systolic array and continue to be passed down after being processed by the PE. The input matrix elements are streamed row-wise to the left of the systolic array and continue to the right after being processed. The partial sum is kept in the PE and not passed between PEs. The matrix multiplication operation is finish when all matrix elements have been processed.

Unlike the OS, the WS fixes the weight matrix into PEs of the systolic array. As shown in Fig. 1(c), the weight matrix elements are preloaded into PEs before the computation, and these elements do not change during the computation procedure. The input matrix elements are streamed row-wise to the left of the systolic array and continue to the right after being processed by PEs. After the PE processes the elements of the input matrix, the partial sum is generated. The partial sum is passed down after being processed by PEs. The final result is streamed out of the systolic array from the PEs of the last row.

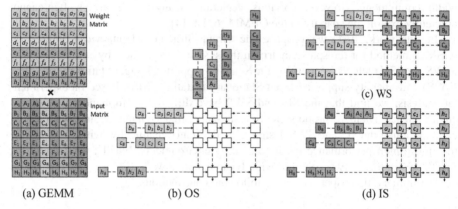

(a) GEMM   (b) OS   (c) WS   (d) IS

Fig. 1. Mapping of the GEMM in the OS, WS, and IS.

The IS fixes the input matrix into PEs of the systolic array. The IS is shown in Fig. 1(d). The input matrix elements are preloaded into PEs before the computation. The weight matrix elements are streamed column-wise into the systolic array during the calculation procedure. After being processed by PEs, the partial sum is passed down, and the input matrix elements are passed right. The final result is streamed out of the systolic array from the PEs of the last row.

2.2 Sparsity

The tensors in deep learning are always sparse. Many factors contribute to the sparsity of tensors in deep learning models. The ReLU activation function in CNN turns negative activation values into zeros [8]. The pruning technique of weights and activations makes the weights and activations sparse [9, 10]. GANs use transposed convolutions in degenerate networks, where the input data is amplified by inserting zeros between values. Then the activations in GANs become sparse [11].

Due to the sparsity in the tensors, there will be a lot of invalid data transmission and computation in the inference and training process. These invalid operations increase the computing, communication, and storage requirements of the accelerator. Proper utilization of sparsity can eliminate invalid computations. By processing computations with only non-zero values, the execution time and energy consumption can be reduced. Furthermore, by saving and transferring only non-zero values, the storage and communication requirements can be reduced. In order to take advantage of sparsity properly, accelerators often require specific designs.

3 SADD Architecture

In this section, first, we propose the Group-Structure-Maintained Compression (GSMC), a new compression method for matrices in systolic arrays. Second, based on the GSMC, we propose the Sparsity-supported Weight Stationary Dataflow (SWS) and Sparsity-supported Input Stationary Dataflow (SIS). Third, we analyze the performance of the SIS and SWS. Finally, we propose the Sparsity-supported Dynamic Dataflow (SDD) and the SADD accelerator.

3.1 Group-Structure-Maintained Compression

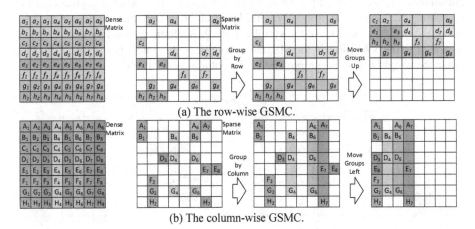

(a) The row-wise GSMC.

(b) The column-wise GSMC.

Fig. 2. The Group-Structure-Maintained Compression (GSMC) method.

Compressing sparse tensors can reduce the storage and communication requirements of the processor. To compress sparse matrices in the systolic array, we propose a new compression method: the Group-Structure-Maintained Compression (GSMC). Figure 2 illustrates the GSMC method. In the row-wise GSMC, some elements in a row are defined as a group. The left boundary of the group is the leftmost nonzero value in this row, and the right boundary is the rightmost nonzero value in this row. Each row has a group. If there is a space above, groups are moved up without changing the column. For example, in row 0 in Fig. 2(a), $a_2 \sim a_8$ is a group. This group contains three non-zero values (a_2, a_4, a_8) and five zeros. In row 2, c_1 is a group. In row 5, $f_5 \sim f_7$ is a group. Because there is space in row 0, the group c_1 can be moved to row 0. The rest space of row 0 is occupied by the group $a_2 \sim a_8$, so the group $f_5 \sim f_7$ cannot be moved to row 0. Moving groups up can reduce the number of rows in the matrix. In the column-wise GSMC, some elements in a column are defined as a group. The upper boundary of the group is the uppermost nonzero value in this column, and the lower boundary is the lowermost nonzero value in this column. Each column has a group. If there is a space to the left, groups are moved left without changing the row. Moving groups left can reduce the number of columns in the matrix.

3.2 The SIS and SWS

Like the WS in Sect. 2.1, the SWS fixes the weight matrix into PEs of the systolic array. As shown in Fig. 3(a), before the computation, the uncompressed weight matrix is fixed into PEs while the input matrix is compressed by the row-wise GSMC. The compressed input matrix is streamed row-wise to the left of the systolic array and continues to the right after being processed by PEs. After the PE processes the elements of the input matrix, the partial sum is generated. The partial sum is passed down after being processed by PEs. After processing a group of elements, the result leaves the systolic array via the forwarding link rather than passes down. The forwarding links of each PE link are independent and can feed the results from different groups to an accumulator outside the systolic array. For example, in Fig. 3(a), after 'h_1' reaches the PE containing 'A_1', the partial sum "h_1*A_1" will be passed to the PE containing 'B_1'. After 'h_3' enters the PE containing 'C_1', since the group "$h_1 \sim h_3$" has been processed, the partial sum "$h_1*A_1 + h_2*B_1 + e_3*C_1$" will leave the systolic array through the forwarding link. The SIS is similar to the SWS. But in the SIS, the uncompressed input matrix is fixed into PEs while the weight matrix is compressed by the column-wise GSMC.

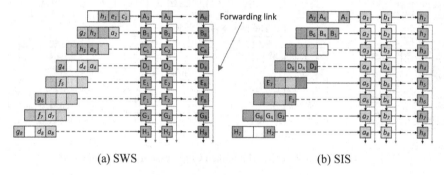

(a) SWS   (b) SIS

Fig. 3. Mapping of sparse GEMM in the SWS and SIS.

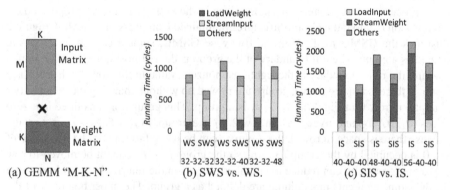

(a) GEMM "M-K-N".   (b) SWS vs. WS.   (c) SIS vs. IS.

Fig. 4. Performance analysis of the SWS, WS, SIS, and IS.

Figure 4(b) shows the performance of the SWS and the WS. Figure 4(c) shows the performance of SIS and IS. The sparsity of the input matrix and weight matrix in the experiment is 75% ("75% sparsity" is a reasonable assumption in [16]). The three numbers on the horizontal axis in Fig. 4(b) and (c) represent the size of the GEMM like Fig. 4(a). With the GSMC, the weight matrix in the SIS has fewer columns than the IS, and the input matrix in the SWS has fewer rows than the WS. So the time required to stream the weight matrix in the SIS is reduced, and the time required to stream the input matrix in the SWS is reduced. Therefore, the SWS's performance is higher than the WS's, and the SIS's performance is higher than the IS's.

3.3 The Performance of SIS and SWS with Different GEMM Sizes

Figure 5 shows the performance comparison of the SIS and SWS under different GEMM sizes. The sparsity in the experiment is 75%. The three numbers on the horizontal axis represent the size of the GEMM like Fig. 4(a). If the size of the input matrix is smaller than the size of the weight matrix, the performance of the SIS is higher. Otherwise, the performance of the SWS is higher. Both the SIS and the SWS contain fixed and streaming matrices. Replacing the fixed matrix in the systolic array requires additional time cost. So the fewer times the fixed matrix is replaced, the less running time is required. When the size of the weight matrix is smaller than the input matrix, if the SWS is used, the number to replace the weight matrix in the systolic will be less, and the performance will be higher. When the size of the input matrix is smaller than the weight matrix, if the SIS is used, the number to replace the input matrix in the systolic is less, so the performance of the SIS will be higher.

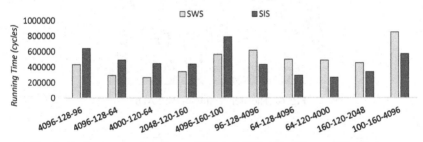

Fig. 5. Performance comparison of SIS and SWS with different GEMM sizes.

3.4 The SDD and SADD

Since the SIS and SWS perform differently with different matrix sizes, we developed the Sparsity-supported Dynamic Dataflow (SDD). The SDD is a combination of the SIS and SWS. The SDD switches between the SWS and SIS according to the matrix size during computation. When the weight matrix size is smaller than or equal to the input matrix size, the performance of the SWS is better than that of the SIS. The SDD switches to the SWS in this case. Otherwise, the SDD switches to the SIS. Therefore, the SDD can perform well with any matrix size.

We design the SADD, a systolic array accelerator that supports sparsity and dynamic dataflow. The dataflow used in the SADD is the SDD. As shown in Fig. 6, the SADD

includes ① Input Matrix FIFO, ② Weight Matrix FIFO, ③ Dataflow Selector, ④ Structured Compression Unit, ⑤ Systolic Array, ⑥ Accumulator. ① And ② store the input
matrix and weight matrix, respectively. ③ Controls the dataflow switching according to
the size of the matrix. When the size of the weight matrix is smaller than or equal to
the size of the input matrix, ③ fixes the weight matrix in ⑤ and sends the input matrix
to ④, and then the SWS can be realized. When the input matrix size is smaller than the
weight matrix size, ③ fixes the input matrix in ⑤ and sends the weight matrix to ④, and
then the SIS can be realized. ④ Performs the GSMC. ⑤ is a PE array that contains the
forwarding link (same as the forwarding link in Fig. 4). The new PE structure in ⑤ is
shown in Fig. 7. Compared with the previous PE structure, the hardware resources of
the new PE have changed little. The new PE only adds two 2-to-1 multiplexers, which
decide whether the partial sum is transmitted to the Forwarding Link or passed down. ④
And ⑤ are to support the SWS and the SIS in the SDD. ⑥ is used to accumulate multiple
matrices. Among them, ③, ④, and ⑤ are the main module used to support the SDD.

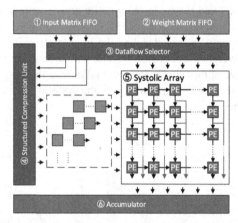

Fig. 6. The architecture of the SADD.

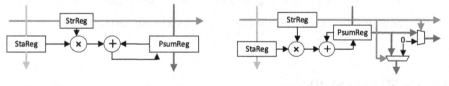

(a) The PE in previous systolic arrays.   (b) The PE in the SADD.

Fig. 7. PEs in previous systolic arrays and in the SADD.

4   Experimental Results

4.1   Experimental Setup

First, we compare the performance of the SDD with other dataflows in systolic arrays
with different GEMM sizes. We implement various systolic array accelerators using

the WS, IS, OS, SIS, SWS, and SDD. The systolic array accelerator using the SDD is our proposed SADD. We run GEMMs of different sizes with different sparsity on these systolic array accelerators and analyze the performance. Second, we take the WS systolic array to simulate state-of-the-art GEMM accelerator TPU. Then we compare the performance of SADD and TPU when running AlexNet's convolutional layers. Finally, we analyze the scalability and hardware overhead of the SADD.

We implement the above systolic array accelerators using RTL Verilog HDL. In our experiments, each systolic array contains 8 * 8 PEs with a data width of 8 bits. We use the Xilinx Vivado Design Suite for logic simulation and synthesis. The clock period during simulation is set to be 8 ns, and the main frequency during synthesis is set to be 125 MHz. Additionally, we implement the SADD and other systolic array accelerators with 16×16 PEs for scalability analysis.

4.2 Performance Comparison of Different Dataflows

Figures 8, 9 and 10 compares the performance of various dataflows with different GEMM sizes and different sparsity. The three numbers (M-K-N) on the horizontal axis represent the size of the GEMM. Additional time is required to load or replace the fixed data in the systolic array. The smaller the fixed data size, the fewer times the fixed data is loaded or replaced, and the less additional overhead is incurred. Therefore, the smaller the fixed data size, the higher the performance.

When the weight matrix size is larger than the input matrix size, in the IS, the fixed data size is small, and the streaming matrix size is large, so the performance is high. In the WS, the fixed data size is large, and the streaming matrix size is small, so the performance is poor. So the performance of the IS is better than WS. In the same way, the SIS has better performance than the SWS.

When the weight matrix size is smaller than the input matrix size, in the WS, the fixed data size is small, so the performance is high. In the IS, the fixed data size is large, so the performance is poor. Therefore, the performance of the WS is better than that of the IS. In the same way, the SWS performs better than the SIS. According to Sect. 3.2, the time to stream the data in the SIS or the SWS is reduced. So the SWS and SIS are smaller than WS, IS, and OS.

When the sparsity changes from 65% to 85% (Figs. 8, 9 and 10), the performance difference between the SWS and WS increases, and the performance difference between the SIS and IS increases. When the sparsity increases, the row amount of compressed streamed matrix reduces. So the time the streaming matrix enters the systolic array reduces, and the performance increases. Therefore, the higher the sparsity, the better the performance of the SIS and SWS.

When the weight matrix is larger than the input matrix size, the SDD switches to the SIS. Otherwise, the SDD switches to the SWS. So the performance of the SDD is higher than other dataflows. Overall, the performance of the SDD is $2\times$ better than the WS, IS, and OS on average. Moreover, the SDD can achieve good performance in GEMMs of any size.

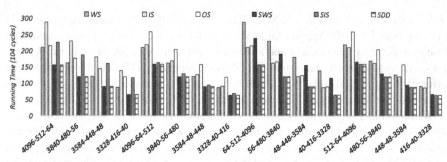

Fig. 8. The performance of different GEMM sizes with the 65% sparsity.

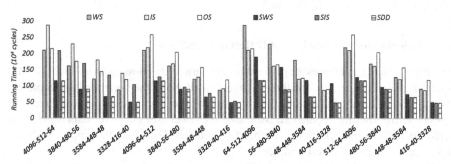

Fig. 9. The performance of different GEMM sizes with the 75% sparsity.

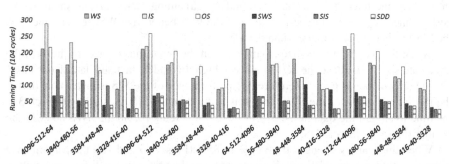

Fig. 10. The performance of different GEMM sizes with the 85% sparsity.

4.3   Comparison of the SADD and the TPU

Due to the small scale of the systolic array accelerator we implemented, we choose the small-scale neural network AlexNet. The convolution operation in the AlexNet is converted to GEMM, and we introduce 75% sparsity to these GEMMs in our experiments. Figure 11 shows the performance comparison of the SADD and the TPU. On average, due to the support of sparsity and dynamic dataflow, the performance of the SADD is 2× better than the TPU.

Layer Name	Kernel Size	Input Size	Output Size
Conv1	11×11	224×224×3	55×55×96
Conv2	5×5	27×27×96	27×27×256
Conv3	3×3	13×13×256	13×13×384
Conv4	3×3	13×13×384	13×13×384
Conv5	3×3	13×13×384	13×13×256

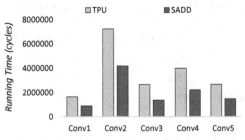

(a) Convolutional layers of the AlexNet.   (b) The performance of the TPU and the SADD.

Fig. 11. Performance comparison of the TPU and the SADD when running the sparse AlexNet.

4.4 Scalability Analysis

We implement the SADD and other systolic arrays with 256 PEs for scalability analysis. If a larger-scale SADD needs to be implemented, it is only necessary to add additional PEs and forwarding links. Figure 12 compares the performance of various dataflows in the systolic array with 256 PEs. The vertical axis is the running cycle, and the unit is ten thousand. The performance of SDD represents the performance of SADD. Compared to the 8×8 scale SADD, the larger-scale SADD has high performance similarly. Therefore, SADD has better scalability.

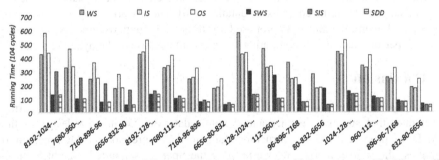

Fig. 12. The performance of different GEMM sizes with the 85% sparsity in 256-PE systolic array.

4.5 Hardware Cost Analysis

We compare the hardware overhead of the SADD with the WS, IS, and OS systolic arrays. Each of them contains 64 PEs. The experimental result is shown in Table 1. In the OS, because the result needs to be saved in PEs, there are additional registers. So the hardware overhead of the OS is higher than that of the WS and IS. The increase in the hardware resources of the SADD is mainly used for the Structured Compression Unit and the Dataflow Selector (shown in Fig. 6). Compared to the WS, IS, and OS systolic array accelerators, the SADD has a ~ 10% increase in hardware overhead. This overhead is acceptable relative to the $2\times$ performance increase.

Table 1. The hardware overhead of the SADD, WS, IS, and OS systolic array accelerators.

	WS systolic array	IS systolic array	OS systolic array	SADD
LUT	4060	4278	4819	4979
FF	3360	3419	3972	4071
BRAM	59	61	65.5	66

5 Related Work

The WinoCNN uses an optimized Winograd processing element [12]. It can support multiple convolution kernel sizes with the small computing resources in the systolic array. The AutoSA is a compilation framework for generating systolic arrays on FPGA [13]. It is based on the polyhedral framework and can incorporate a set of optimizations on different dimensions to boost performance. The CMSA is a flexible systolic array [14]. It keeps the original systolic array architecture and computing mode. Moreover, it can switch data mapping or dataflow by changing the data transmission direction. These works are based on the systolic array but do not consider the sparsity.

The Sparse-TPU contains an algorithm to pack sparse matrices by merging columns that allow collisions [15]. It can significantly reduce the number of zeros to the systolic array. To fully exploit the sparsity in CNNs, S2 Engine send the compressed feature and weight flows into the systolic array, and the processing element can dynamically select the aligned pairs from the compressed dataflow [16]. These works support the sparsity but not the dynamic dataflow. Our proposed SADD not only supports the sparsity, but also has high performance in any computing environment because of the dynamic dataflow.

6 Conclusion

In this paper, we design and implement the SADD, a state-of-the-art systolic array accelerator that supports sparsity and dynamic dataflow. During the design of the SADD, we propose the Group-Structure-Maintained Compression (GSMC) method to compress the sparse matrix, and we propose the Sparsity-supported Weight Stationary Dataflow (SWS), the Sparsity-supported Input Stationary Dataflow (SIS), and the Sparsity-supported Dynamic Dataflow (SDD) to support the sparsity in the systolic array. Experimental results show that for sparse GEMMs, the performance of the SDD used in the SADD is 2× better than the WS, IS, and OS on average, and the SDD can perform best in any computing environment. Moreover, the performance of the SADD is 2× better than the TPU when running sparse convolutional layers of the AlexNet. In addition, the SADD brings only a small amount of additional hardware overhead compared to previous systolic array accelerators.

References

1. Nguyen, G., et al.: Machine learning and deep learning frameworks and libraries for large-scale data mining: a survey. Artif. Intell. Rev. **52**(1), 77–124 (2019). https://doi.org/10.1007/s10462-018-09679-z

2. Yang, S., Wang, Y., Chu, X.: A survey of deep learning techniques for neural machine translation. arXiv preprint arXiv:2002.07526 (2020)
3. Acun, B., Murphy, M., Wang, X., Nie, J., Wu, C., Hazelwoodet, K.: Understanding training efficiency of deep learning recommendation models at scale. In: IEEE International Symposium on High Performance Computer Architecture (HPCA), pp. 802–814. IEEE (2021)
4. AI and Compute. https://openai.com/blog/ai-and-compute/ Accessed 01 May 2022
5. Qin, E., et al.: Sigma: a sparse and irregular gemm accelerator with flexible interconnects for dnn training. In: HPCA 2020, pp. 28–70. IEEE (2020)
6. Jouppi, N., Young, C., Patil, N., Patterson, D.: Motivation for and evaluation of the first tensor processing unit. IEEE Micro **38**(3), 10–19 (2018)
7. Samajdar, A., Zhu, Y., Whatmough, P., Mattina, M., Krishna, T.: A systematic methodology for characterizing scalability of DNN accelerators using SCALE-sim. In: Proceedings of the IEEE In-ternational Symposium on Performance Analysis of Systems and Software (ISPASS), pp. 58–68. IEEE (2020)
8. Krizhevsky, A., Sutskever, I., Hinton, G.E.: Imagenet classification with deep convolutional neural networks. Adv. Neural Inf. Process. Syst. **25**, 1097–1105 (2012)
9. Han, S., Pool, J., Tran, J., Dally, W.: Learning both weights and connections for efficient neural network. Adv. Neural Inf. Process. Syst. **28**, 1135–1143 (2015)
10. Albericio, J., Judd, P., Hetherington, T., Aamodt, T., Jerger, N.E., Moshovos, A.: Cnvlutin: ineffectual-neuron-free deep neural network computing. ACM SIGARCH Comput. Archit. News **44**(3), 1–13 (2016)
11. Yazdanbakhsh, A., Samadi, K., Kim, N.S., Esmaeilzadeh, H.: GANAX: a unified MIMD-SIMD acceleration for generative adversarial networks. In: 2018 ACM/IEEE 45th Annual International Symposium on Computer Architecture (ISCA), pp. 650–661. IEEE (2018)
12. Liu, X., Chen, Y., Hao, C., Dhar, A., Chen, D.: WinoCNN: kernel sharing Winograd systolic array for efficient convolutional neural network acceleration on FPGAs. In: 2021 IEEE 32nd International Conference on Application-specific Systems, Architectures and Processors (ASAP), pp. 258–265. IEEE (2021)
13. Wang, J., Guo, L., Cong, J.: AutoSA: a polyhedral compiler for high-performance systolic arrays on FPGA. In: The 2021 ACM/SIGDA International Symposium on Field-Programmable Gate Arrays, pp. 93–104. ACM (2021)
14. Xu, R., Ma, S., Wang, Y., Guo, Y.: CMSA: configurable multi-directional systolic array for convolutional neural networks. In: 2020 IEEE 38th International Conference on Computer Design (ICCD), pp. 494–497. IEEE (2020)
15. He, X., et al.: Sparse-TPU: adapting systolic arrays for sparse matrices. In: Proceedings of the 34th ACM International Conference on Supercomputing, pp. 1–12. ACM (2020)
16. Yang, J., Fu, W., Cheng, X., Ye, X., Dai, P., Zhao, W.: S2 engine: a novel systolic architecture for sparse convolutional neural networks. IEEE Trans. Comput. **71**(6), 1440–1452 (2021)

CSR&RV: An Efficient Value Compression Format for Sparse Matrix-Vector Multiplication

Junjun Yan[1,2], Xinhai Chen[1,2], and Jie Liu[1,2(✉)]

[1] Science and Technology on Parallel and Distributed Processing Laboratory,
National University of Defense Technology, Changsha 410073, China
{yanjunjun,chenxinhai16,liujie}@nudt.edu.cn
[2] Laboratory of Software Engineering for Complex System,
National University of Defense Technology, Changsha 410073, China

Abstract. Sparse Matrix-Vector Multiplication (SpMV) plays a critical role in many areas of science and engineering applications. The storage space of value array in general real sparse matrices accounts for costly. However, the existing compressed formats cannot balance the compressed rate and computational speed. To address this issue, we propose an efficient value compression format implemented by AVX512 instructions called Compressed Sparse Row and Repetition Value (CSR&RV). This format stores each different value once and uses the indexes array to store the position of values, which reduces the storage space by compressing the value array. We conduct a series of experiments on an Intel Xeon processor and compare it with five other formats in 30 real-world matrices. Experimental results show that CSR&RV can achieve a speedup up to 3.86× (1.66× on average) and a speedup up to 12.42× (3.12× on average) for single-core and multi-core throughput, respectively. Meanwhile, our format can reduce the memory space by 48.57% on average.

Keywords: Sparse matrix-vector multiplication · Value compression · Storage format · AVX512

1 Introduction

Sparse Matrix-Vector Multiplication (SpMV) is a kernel operation in many vital fields, such as parallel computing, scientific computation, and machine learning [1,2]. The expression of SpMV is $Y \leftarrow A*X$, where A is a sparse matrix and both X and Y are dense vectors. There are some classic sparse matrix storage formats have been proposed. For example, the Coordinates (COO) and the Compressed Sparse Row (CSR) [1]. The former uses the triple form $(row, col, value)$ to store all nonzero elements (nnz) while the latter compresses the row array to the row_ptr array, which only stores the start and end index of each row.

J. Yan and X. Chen—Contributed equally to this work.

S. Liu and X. Wei (Eds.): NPC 2022, LNCS 13615, pp. 54–60, 2022.
https://doi.org/10.1007/978-3-031-21395-3_5

Recent researches suggest that certain new features have arisen in the modern architecture of CPUs, for example, the increased number of cores and threads, the enhanced capacity of caches, and the improvement of Single Instruction Multi Data (SIMD) units [8]. There is a growing body of literature that redesigns and optimizes the classic formats by using those new features [2]. We generalize into two primary parts: first, taking full advantage of SIMD instructions for vectorization and using blocking algorithms to improve the data locality [2, 8, 10]; second, compressing the storage space to reduce the memory access [4, 5, 7], which depends on the feature of matrices [1].

In some applications, the sparse matrices have numerous repetitive values, which instructs us to compress the repeated elements in the value array to reduce memory access times and improve the SpMV efficiency [2]. Until recently, there are only litter studies about compression and optimization of the value array: Kourtis et al. [5] proposed the index and value compression approach to saving the memory of the value array but still not efficient in modern CPUs. Grigoras et al. [4] use the same idea in FPGA but also do not suit CPUs architecture. Therefore, it is necessary to design a new format to solve those problems.

This paper proposes an efficient value compression storage format named CSR&RV. The proposed format only stores the repetitive values once and compresses the original value array to a non-repetition value array and an index array. For each nnz, it uses the index array to store the position of the value array and loads the value indirectly. This operation compresses the storage space of the value array because the number of non-repetition values is much less than the number of nnz. What's more, we can further compress the storage space of the index array by using uint8 and uint16 to store the indexes (index compression).

We compare the CSR&RV format to five other formats with different evaluating criteria. The experimental results show that CSR&RV has the highest throughput and the lowest memory space overhead. Compared to the MKL-CSR [9], the proposed format can get an average of $1.66\times$ and $3.12\times$ speedup in single-core and multi-core throughput, respectively. Compared to other state-of-art formats [6, 8–10], it achieves an average of $1.36\times$ and $1.86\times$ speedup in single-core and multi-core throughput, respectively. With index compression, our format reduces an average of 48.57% (maximum of 58.13%) memory space on matrices saved in CSR format.

2   The Compressed Sparse Row and Repetition Value Format

2.1   CSR&RV Representation

The CSR-based storage format is not efficient enough in the matrices have extensive repetitive elements. Because SpMV will access the repetitive values in the value array many times, which leads to the precious memory bandwidth wasted. To overcome this disadvantage, the proposed format, as shown in Fig. 1, compresses the repetitive values in *csr_vals*. In CSR&RV, the *csrv_values* only stores each unequal value once. And for each nnz, we use an index array called *csrv_vals_idx* to point to the location of the value array. Therefore, the memory access for values indirectly uses *csrv_vals_idx* as indexes. Because the number of non-repetition values is much small than nnz, the *csr_vals* can be compressed to a same-length array *csrv_vals_idx* and a negligible array *csrv_values*. By changing the type of *csrv_vals_idx* (e.g. uint8), we can save the space further.

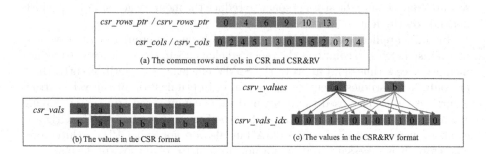

Fig. 1. The CSR&RV format.

2.2   SpMV Algorithm

Figure 2 shows the SpMV method implemented by AVX512 instructions. The proposed method vectorize the data by rows which means the elements in the same rows will be packed together into several vectors. There are five main steps to accomplish once floating multiply and add operation, which is a fundamental operation in SpMV (the type of *val_idx* array is uint8 as an instance):

(1) Loading eight indexes to the _val_idx_uint8 vector.
(2) Converting the indexes vector from uint8 to int32.
(3) Loading the columns from the *csrv_cols* array.
(4) Gathering the vector operand _x and _val.
(5) Executing once floating multiply and add operation in the FMA units.

Looping above five steps until the computation of one row is accomplished. After that, we can use the *reduce_add* instruction to sum the _y vector horizontally and write back the result to the y array corresponding to the row rank. The write position in y is prefetched before writing back. Repeating the procession until all the rows are computed and stored to y.

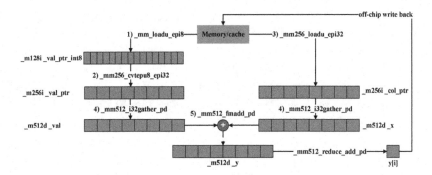

Fig. 2. The data flow in the SpMV algorithm.

3 Experimental Results

We compare our work with state-of-art open-source sparse matrix storage formats and SpMV algorithms. All the formats are implemented with the AVX512 instructions. The following 5 formats are compared: MKL-CSR [9], MKL-OPT (using the *mkl_sparse_optimize* function based on MKL-CSR), CSR5 [8], CVR [10], SPV8 [6]. We use 30 real-word sparse matrices downloaded from the SuiteSparse Matrix Collection [3]. Each matrix runs 1000 iterations and uses the single-iteration average time to evaluate. We run SpMV in double precision and record the run-time in different formats and threads (increased from 1 to 48). When evaluating the multi-core performance, we use the best run-time among all run-times. Normally, the maximal thread numbers (48) can get the best results.

3.1 Performance Comparison

Figure 3(a) presents the single-core performance of different formats. Compared to the MKL-CSR, CSR&RV can achieve an average of 1.66× and a maximum of 3.86× speedup. Figure 3(b) provides the multi-core performance. Compared to the best state-of-art formats, the proposed format can attain an average of 1.85× and a maximum of 7.92× speedup. These results suggest that the CSR&RV is better than other formats and the multi-core performance is better than the single-core. The possible reason for the phenomenon is that the optimization of arithmetic instructions can mainly influence the single-core performance because the bandwidth ability for one thread is enough. However, when considering multi-core, the increasing of thread numbers will gradually limit the bandwidth, which leads to the memory-access ability being the major influence and reflected by the storage space of formats.

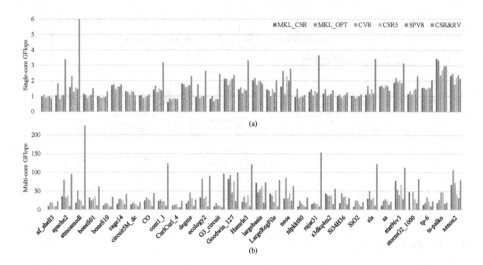

(a)

(b)

Fig. 3. The performance (GFlops) of different formats on the benchmark matrices.

3.2   Memory Overhead

Cause the memory space in the baseline formats is similar to the CSR format, we only compare our format with CSR. Figure 4 shows the memory overhead of different benchmark matrices. The memory space token by CSR&RV is smaller than CSR in all matrices. This article calculated the memory-reduction rate as the reduced size of CSR&RV divided by the original size of CSR. Compared with CSR, the memory space in the CSR&RV format is reduced by 48.57% on average and 58.13% on maximum. By reducing the memory overhead, we can reduce the memory-access bandwidth, which makes SpMV more efficient.

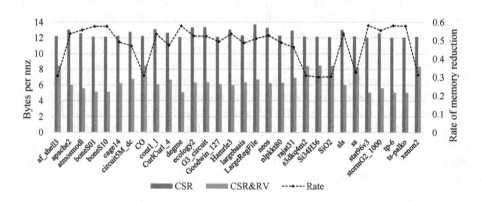

Fig. 4. Memory reduction in the CSR&RV format comparing to CSR.

3.3 Pre-processing

For the purpose of evaluating the practicability, this paper arranges all the tested matrices in the CSR format and measures the converting time from CSR to corresponding formats (except the MKL-CSR), which is called pre-processing in serval articles [6,7,10]. The pre-processing overhead is calculated as once single-core converting time divided by once single-core SpMV time. Table 1 shows that the pre-processing overhead in CSR&RV is the second lowest and only CVR is faster than it. This result indicates our format has the capability for actual use.

Table 1. The average processing overhead in different formats.

	CSR&RV	CSR5	MKL-OPT	SPV8	CVR
Processing overhead	3×	5×	10×	8×	2×

4 Conclusion

This paper proposes an efficient value compressed format named CSR&RV. The main idea of the proposed format is compressing the value array in CSR format to reduce the memory space and using AVX512 to improve the SpMV efficiency. We conduct a series of experiments on an Intel Xeon CPU and compare it with five state-of-art formats in 30 real-world sparse matrices. The experimental results show that CSR&RV can achieve the best throughput both in single-core and multi-core. Meanwhile, CSR&RV can reduce an average of about 50% (maximum of near 60%) of memory space compared to CSR. Moreover, this format has the advantage of being program-friendly and having low pre-processing overhead, which shows the potential to be employed in real-world applications. However, the CSR&RV format is mainly suited for sparse double-precision real matrices with many repetitive values. In future work, we will further extend our format to improve generality.

Acknowledgements. This research work was supported in part by the National Key Research and Development Program of China (2021YFB0300101).

References

1. Barrett, R.: Templates for the solution of linear systems: building blocks for iterative methods. In: Software, Environments, Tools, SIAM, Society for Industrial and Applied Mathematics (1994)
2. Chen, X., Xie, P., Chi, L., Liu, J., Gong, C.: An efficient SIMD compression format for sparse matrix-vector multiplication. Concurr. Comput. Pract. Exp. **30**(23), e4800 (2018)
3. Davis, T.A., Hu, Y.: The university of Florida sparse matrix collection. ACM Trans. Math. Softw. **38**(1), 1:1–1:25 (2011)

4. Grigoras, P., Burovskiy, P., Hung, E., Luk, W.: Accelerating SpMV on FPGAs by compressing nonzero values. In: 23rd IEEE Annual International Symposium on Field-Programmable Custom Computing Machines, FCCM 2015, Vancouver, BC, Canada, 2–6 May 2015, pp. 64–67. IEEE Computer Society (2015)
5. Kourtis, K., Goumas, G.I., Koziris, N.: Improving the performance of multi-threaded sparse matrix-vector multiplication using index and value compression. In: 2008 International Conference on Parallel Processing, ICPP 2008, Portland, Oregon, USA, 8–12 September 2008, pp. 511–519. IEEE Computer Society (2008)
6. Li, C., Xia, T., Zhao, W., Zheng, N., Ren, P.: SpV8: pursuing optimal vectorization and regular computation pattern in SpMV. In: 58th ACM/IEEE Design Automation Conference, DAC 2021, San Francisco, CA, USA, pp. 661–666, 5–9 December 2021. IEEE (2021)
7. Li, Y., et al.: VBSF: a new storage format for SIMD sparse matrix-vector multiplication on modern processors. J. Supercomput. **76**(3), 2063–2081 (2020)
8. Liu, W., Vinter, B.: CSR5: an efficient storage format for cross-platform sparse matrix-vector multiplication. In: Proceedings of the 29th ACM on International Conference on Supercomputing, ICS 2015, Irvine, CA, USA, 08–11 June 2015, pp. 339–350. ACM (2015)
9. Wang, E., et al.: Intel math kernel library. In: Wang, E., et al. (eds.) High-Performance Computing on the Intel® Xeon Phi™, pp. 167–188. Springer, Cham (2014). https://doi.org/10.1007/978-3-319-06486-4_7
10. Xie, B., et al.: CVR: efficient vectorization of SpMV on x86 processors. In: Proceedings of the 2018 International Symposium on Code Generation and Optimization, CGO 2018, Vösendorf, Vienna, Austria, 24–28, February 2018, pp. 149–162. ACM (2018)

Rgs-SpMM: Accelerate Sparse Matrix-Matrix Multiplication by Row Group Splitting Strategy on the GPU

Mingfeng Guo[1], Yaobin Wang[1(✉)], Jun Huang[1], Qingfeng Wang[1],
Yaqing Zhang[1], Mu Xu[2], and Fang Lu[2]

[1] School of Computer Science and Technology, Key Laboratory of Testing
Technology for Manufacturing Process in Ministry of Education, Southwest
University of Science and Technology, Mianyang 621010, China
gmfff12334@gmail.com, wangyaobin@foxmail.com
[2] Alibaba Group, Hangzhou, China

Abstract. The Sparse Matrix-Matrix Multiplication (SpMM) operation is widely used in different fields, especially the recently popular GNN framework. Researchers have designed many kernels on the GPU to accelerate the SpMM operation. Existing methods mostly adopt a row splitting strategy to obtain better parallelism and memory access efficiency. However, due to irregularities of sparse matrices such as short rows with few non-zero elements, current methods suffer from the under-utilization of thread resources in GPU. In this paper, We rearrange the distribution of non-zero elements in the sparse matrix and design the SpMM kernel based on the row group splitting strategy. In contrast to previous methods which assign a "row" task unit to a warp for processing, we combine short rows in a sparse matrix into "row groups" as a task unit, which allocate more appropriate non-zero elements tasks to the GPU resources. This method reduces the thread divergence in a warp and improves load balancing among warps. Our experimental data comes from the SNAP Matrix Collection. The results show that our kernel is faster than cuSPARSE and GE-SpMM, with an average speedup of 1.61 and 1.42 respectively.

Keywords: Sparse Matrix-Matrix Multiplication · GPU · Row group splitting

1 Introduction

Sparse Matrix Multiplication (SpMM) is a sparse matrix dense matrix multiplication as follows: C = AB where A is sparse and B, C are dense. It is one of the most widely used high-performance kernels in various applications, including data mining, and machine learning, especially the Graph Neural Networks (GNN) [1,2].

In the existing SpMM kernel, researchers found that the row splitting strategy works best for SpMM, that is, a row of the sparse matrix is assigned to a warp of

© IFIP International Federation for Information Processing 2022
Published by Springer Nature Switzerland AG 2022
S. Liu and X. Wei (Eds.): NPC 2022, LNCS 13615, pp. 61–66, 2022.
https://doi.org/10.1007/978-3-031-21395-3_6

GPU (one warp has 32 threads in Nvidia GPU). Unfortunately, in many sparse matrices, the number of elements in a row is much less than 32. Therefore, these short rows will cause thread divergence to affect parallel performance. At the same time, the huge difference in the number of non-zero elements from row to row will cause load imbalance among warps.

In order to solve the above challenges, we propose a novel method called Rgs-SpMM in this paper, which can more reasonably utilize the computing resources of modern GPUs. On the one hand, we will rearrange the sparse matrix according to the number of non-zero elements in each row, and use a new way to store the sparse matrix. On the other hand, we will adaptively combine the short rows in the sparse matrix into a row group, and hand over the row group to the appropriate GPU computing resources for processing. We use Rgs-SpMM on the SNAP Matrix Collection [8], and experiments show that our method can obtain an average 1.61 speedup over the cuSPARSE library and an average 1.42 speedup over the CSR-based state-of-the-art GE-SpMM on the modern GPU.

2   Related Work and Motivation

Since the birth of GPU, the acceleration of matrix multiplication on GPU has been studied such as SpMV (sparse matrix-vector multiplication) [3], and SpGEMM (sparse matrix-sparse matrix multiplication) [4]. In recent years, the wide application of SpMM and its huge computation cost has led to high demand to optimize SpMM for high performance. By learning the previous optimization method of matrix multiplication on the GPU, researchers have made a lot of efforts to optimize the SpMM kernel. In the cuSPARSE library [5], the SpMM kernel is also constantly updated to improve efficiency.

The only difference between SpMV and SpMM is that a single vector becomes a dense matrix with multiple columns, the method of SpMV optimization on GPU can be used to optimize SpMM. However, those well-known optimization methods are not fully applicable to SpMM kernels. On the one hand, compared to SpMV, SpMM emphasizes column-wise parallelism in the dense output matrix, which requires ensuring that memory accesses to each column of the dense matrix remain independent but coalesced. On the other hand, data reuse for sparse matrices in SpMM becomes more important relative to SpMV, because as the column dimension of the dense matrix becomes larger, memory transactions also increase. GraphBLAST [6] and GE-SpMM [7] use a row-splitting strategy to guarantee coalesced memory access and data reuse. Unlike the row-splitting strategy in SpMV, they achieved coalesced memory accesses 32 columns of a dense matrix instead of a single vector, which amortizes the cost of memory accesses. Although these existing row splitting kernels have good data locality and coalesced memory accesses, they do not take into account the irregular distribution of non-zero elements in sparse matrices. Especially for some rows with few elements, the algorithm allocates a few elements to a warp with 32 threads to process, which will cause thread divergence and affect parallel efficiency.

3   Rgs-SpMM Design

3.1   Data Organization in Rgs-SpMM

In the kernel of the existing row splitting strategy, "row" is used as the parallel granularity. All rows in a sparse matrix are stored in CSR format in row index order. The algorithm also allocates computing resources to each row in row index order, which results in different numbers of non-zero elements being allocated the same number of threads.

To avoid unreasonable allocation of computing resources, we propose a new method to store sparse matrices. We rearrange the sparse matrix according to the number of non-zero elements in each row. As shown in Fig. 1, assuming that the boundary is now 3, the number of non-zero elements less than 3 is moved to the front. In reality, we take 16 (warp_size/2) as the boundary to distinguish long and short rows. However, since the row index is scrambled, we need to use a new array row_Ind to record the previous index of the row. This method arranges short rows together, which makes it easy to group short rows into row groups. At the same time, it is ensured that the non-zero elements among the row groups are not much different, which will improve the loading balance.

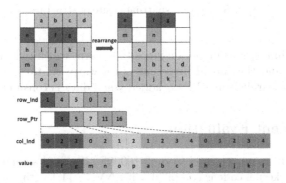

Fig. 1. The rearranged sparse matrix and storage format.

3.2   Row Group Splitting

To solve the problem of thread divergence caused by short rows, we design a row group splitting strategy for SpMM algorithm on GPU. As shown in Fig. 2, when the row is a short row, we will form a row group of several rows. And program hands all the elements in the row group to a warp for processing. These elements will first be loaded from global memory to shared memory. Each thread in the warp will be responsible for a column in the B matrix. In the register, calculating the partial result which is from each row element in the row group multiplied by the corresponding element of the column. Finally program gets the value of the partial area of the C matrix.

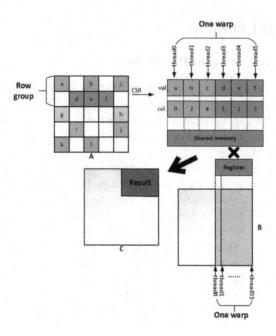

Fig. 2. Row group splitting strategy structure.

This algorithm assigns more non-zeros to a warp, which reduces the number of idle threads and the thread divergence in a warp. At the same time, more instruction-level parallelism (ILP) is added when data is consumed.

4   Experiment Evaluations

We run all the tests on the Intel Core i9-10900F CPU and a single Nvidia RTX 3070 GPU. Our kernel code is compiled using NVCC 11.1 with $-O3$ flag. For the experimental evaluation, we choose the SNAP dataset [8] which can be found in SuiteSparse Matrix Collection. This dataset contains 66 matrices, our report includes all matrix tests. We select two baselines to compare with our Rgs-SpMM method, one is the sparse matrix linear algebra library cuSPARSE from cuda 11.1, *cusparseSPMM* function, another one is called GE-SpMM, the state-of-the-art CSR-based SpMM kernel.

4.1   Overall Performance

Figure 3 shows the SpMM improvement with row group splitting strategy for dense matrix K = 256 on GPU. In our experimental results, our row group parameter is selected as 2, that is, two rows in the matrix are assigned to a warp in the GPU. The bar represents the throughput from 66 matrices in SNAP. Except that some matrices are too large to cause out-of-memory in our device,

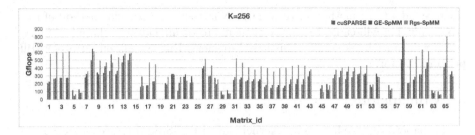

Fig. 3. The overall performance of Rgs-SpMM on RTX3070 is compared with cuS-PARSE and GE-SpMM, the abscissa is matrix_id, and the ordinate is throughput.

we can clearly see that our row group splitting method performs better than cuSPARSE and GE-SpMM in most matrices. On RTX 3070 device, our kernel has improved by 200 Gflops on average. Finally, our Rsg-SpMM achieved average speedups 1.61×, 1.42× on cuSPARSE and GE-SpMM, respectively. The highest speedup reached 3.11×, 2.91×. We have achieved good acceleration results in the dense matrix K = 128, K = 256, and K = 512. This also proves that our method is suitable for matrices of different sizes, that is, it can better adapt to different applications.

4.2   Analysis of Results

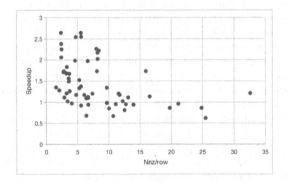

Fig. 4. The relationship between speedup brought by our strategy and Nnz/row.

To further analyze the reasons why our strategies perform differently on these matrices. We plot the relationship between speedup brought by our strategy and Nnz/row in Fig. 4. In matrices where Nnz/row is relatively small, our strategy almost always brings speedups, whereas, in matrices with Nnz/row greater than 10, our strategy does not perform very well. The SpMM operation of our method is even slower than GE-SpMM on these large Nnz/row matrices. We find that when we adopt our method in these large Nnz/row matrices, the method of row group splitting will cause too many elements to be allocated to shared memory, which will cause bank conflicts in shared memory. But overall, our strategy still performs better.

5   Conclusion

In this paper, we have proposed a kernel named Rgs-SpMM to accelerate SpMM operations on the GPU. We will rearrange the sparse matrix according to the number of non-zero elements in each row, and use a new way to store the sparse matrix. We designed the row group splitting strategy to solve the limitation of parallelism which is caused by the sparsity and irregularity of the sparse matrix on the GPU. Through these optimizations, our kernel reduced thread divergence. Our method was compared with Nvidia cuSPARSE and the state-of-the-art CSR-based GE-SpMM kernel on the SNAP Matrix Collection Benchmark, and finally achieved an average speedup of $1.61\times$ and $1.42\times$ respectively.

Acknowledgments. This work is supported financially by the National Natural Science Foundation of China (61672438), Natural Science Foundation of Sichuan, China (2022NSFSC0894, 2022NSFSC0940, 23NSFJQ0112), Special Project of China Association of Higher Education (21SZYB16).

References

1. Wang, M., Zheng, D., Ye, Z., et al.: Deep graph library: a graph-centric, highly performant package for graph neural networks. In: ICLR Workshop on Representation Learning on Graphs and Manifolds (2019)
2. Hu, Y., Ye, Z., et al.: FeatGraph: a flexible and efficient backend for graph neural network systems. In: Proceedings of the International Conference for High Performance Computing, Networking, Storage and Analysis, SC (2020)
3. Merrill, D., Garland, M.: Merge-based parallel sparse matrix-vector multiplication. In: Proceedings of the International Conference for High Performance Computing, Networking, Storage and Analysis, Salt Lake City, UT, USA (2016)
4. Winter, M., Mlakar, D., et al.: Adaptive sparse matrix-matrix multiplication on the GPU. In: Proceedings of the 24th Symposium on Principles and Practice of Parallel Programming - PPoPP 2019, pp. 68–81. ACM Press, New York (2019)
5. The API reference guide for cuSPARSE, the CUDA sparse matrix library (v11.4 ed.). http://docs.nvidia.com/cuda/cusparse/index.html
6. Yang, C., Buluç, A., Owens, J.D.: Design principles for sparse matrix multiplication on the GPU. In: Euro-Par 2018: Parallel Processing - 24th International Conference on Parallel and Distributed Computing, Turin, Italy, 27–31 August 2018, Proceedings, pp. 672–687 (2018)
7. Huang, G., Dai, G., Wang, Y., Yang, H.: GE-SpMM: general purpose sparse matrix-matrix multiplication on GPUs for graph neural networks. In: International Conference for High Performance Computing, Networking, Storage and Analysis (SC), pp. 1–12 (2020)
8. Davis, T.A., Hu, Y.: The university of Florida sparse matrix collection. ACM Trans. Math. Softw. **38**, 1–25 (2011)

Cloud Computing

Interference-aware Workload Scheduling in Co-located Data Centers

Ting Zhang[1], Dongyang Ou[1], Zhefeng Ge[1], Congfeng Jiang[1(✉)],
Christophe Cérin[2], and Longchuan Yan[3]

[1] School of Computer Science and Technology, Hangzhou Dianzi University,
Hangzhou 310000, China
{tingzhang,oudongyang,gezhefeng,cjiang}@hdu.edu.cn
[2] Université Sorbonne Paris Nord, LIPN UMR CNRS, 7030, 99 avenue Jean-Baptiste
Clément, 93430 Villetaneuse, France
christophe.cerin@univ-paris13.fr
[3] Information and Communication Corporation, State Grid Corporation of China,
Beijing 100053, China
lcyan@sgcc.com.cn

Abstract. Modern data centers typically contain thousands of servers, providing various computing and storage services for users. The strategy to provide reliable and high-performance online services is to over-allocate resources for online services, which results in a waste of cluster resources. Therefore, cloud vendors tend to co-locate online services and offline batch jobs into the same cluster to improve resource utilization. However, the co-location leads to contention on shared resources and causes mutual performance interference, which may degrade the QoS (Quality of Service) of online services. We present a performance interference model based on linear regression to predict the performance interference. Furthermore, the model can perceive the status of servers in real-time for more refined and accurate prediction. Then, we design an interference-aware workload scheduling strategy that can schedule batch jobs to the server while introducing minimal interference. The evaluation demonstrates that our scheduling strategy can at best increase the throughput of batch jobs by 48.95% and 27.09% compared with round-robin scheduling and random scheduling while guaranteeing the QoS of online services. The paper aims to provide some elements of answering the following general question: How do we design cloud systems and data centers scheduling strategies that can withstand the human pressure of global-scale use and still provide robust and secure services to end-users?

Keywords: Cloud computing · Workload co-location · Performance interference · Performance prediction · Workload scheduling · Data centers

1 Introduction

Cloud-based services have penetrated many aspects of people's lives, resulting in the scale of cloud data centers expanding rapidly. However, it is worth noting

© IFIP International Federation for Information Processing 2022
Published by Springer Nature Switzerland AG 2022
S. Liu and X. Wei (Eds.): NPC 2022, LNCS 13615, pp. 69–82, 2022.
https://doi.org/10.1007/978-3-031-21395-3_7

the resource utilization of the data center is usually less than 30%, which gives rise to a waste of resources. Therefore, improving resource usage and energy efficiency is the central issue within both the industry and academia.

The workloads deployed in a data center can generally be divided into two categories, namely online services that are latency-sensitive and offline batch jobs pursuing high throughput. To make full use of resources over-allocated for online services, cloud vendors usually co-locate online services with offline batch jobs in the same cluster [1]. This method is a way to master the problem with the uncertainy of the arrival of jobs that cause the under-utilization of the cloud data center. However, mutual interference induced by co-location remains a major challenge, which not only reduces the QoS or even violates the SLA (Service Level Agreement) of online services but also puts forward high requirements on resource management and workload scheduling.

Aimed for these problems, we concentrate on the performance interference on online services caused by batch jobs during co-location. The main contributions of this paper are summarized as follows:

(1) To quantify the performance interference on online services, the paper presents a metric called performance interference score for evaluation.
(2) This paper proposes a performance interference model based on linear regression, which predicts performance interference by extracting performance interference features of different batch jobs. The experimental results demonstrate that our model achieves great prediction accuracy.
(3) To optimize workload scheduling, this paper designs and implements an interference-aware workload scheduling strategy based on the performance, as mentioned earlier, interference model. And we also evaluate the performance of the strategy and compare it with round-robin scheduling and random scheduling. The evaluation confirms that our strategy can efficiently improve the throughput of batch jobs without violating the QoS of online services.

2   Related Work

The co-location of online services and offline batch jobs introduces mutual interference between workloads, which harms the QoS of online services. Considering plenty of factors such as the diversity of offline batch jobs, the heterogeneity of hardware facilities and so forth, it isn't easy to measure the performance interference on online services and to provide resource scheduling in the cluster [2]. As a result, an efficient performance interference model is necessary to optimize the management of workloads [3,4].

Workload scheduling strategies via prediction models are not new. Liu Q et al. [5] point out that in the Alibaba hybrid cluster, the estimated resource usage is set for each batch job through the cgroup mechanism, and use of idle resources by batch jobs can be dynamically adjusted at runtime to achieve flexible resource allocation. Lattuada M et al. [6] first allocate the minimum resource usage to batch jobs according to their execution deadline to minimize the interference to online services, and then predict the performance and completion time of batch job through methods such as machine learning and likelihood estimation. When it is predicted that batch jobs cannot be completed within the specified time or the resource allocation is seriously out of balance, the resources can be reallocated for optimization. Li Y et al. [7] dynamically adjust I/O concurrency level of online service and the disk I/O bandwidth of batch jobs by monitoring performance and throughput in real time, thereby optimizing response time of online service and throughput of batch jobs. However, our positioning is clearly towards utilizing a performance interference metric and not just a performance metric like the completion time. Having taken this precaution, we would also like to say that we have chosen to start with a linear regression model, which is a proven and solid technique. At the beginning of this project, we did not have strong arguments to use a more sophisticated approach. We hope that the study done in this article will serve as a starting point for other studies, considering the lessons learned from our work.

Several studies have been devoted to establishing a performance interference model by exploring the competition for shared resources. Zhao J et al. [8] point out that performance interference can be calculated via accumulating the contention on the shared resource of each CPU core. However, both these methods neglect the variability of different batch jobs and do not consider other resources competed by batch jobs such as caches. Zhang Y et al. [9] propose SMiTe for the scenario of co-location in different logical cores from the same physical core. However, SMiTe is only applicable to the condition of co-locating a single online service with a single offline batch job. Xu R et al. [10] present Pythia to predict the performance interference under the situation of co-locating memory-intensive online services with recurring batch jobs, regardless of some potential utilization features.

In summary, for prior researches concerning with co-location [9,11,12], they only explore the situation of co-locating online services with a single batch job. Or they apply Interference Additive Model (IAM) to accumulate the performance interference of different batch jobs as overall interference on the online service, which is a very rough approximation. Or they keep silent about how they characterize the contention and take no account of potential utilization characteristics. Hence in this paper, we consider a scenario of co-locating one online service with several batch jobs and define a clear metric to quantify the degradation of online services. Then we take into account competed resources to better build performance interference model. Finally, we further design an interference-aware workload scheduling strategy by using the proposed interference model.

3   Interference-aware Solution

3.1   Performance Interference Metric

The QoS generally describes the performance of online services, encompassing service availability, reliability, and response time. Given response time is highly corresponded with user experience for user-oriented online services, the increase in response time of the online service after co-location can be chosen to reflect the performance interference caused by co-located batch jobs. However, online services are so different from each other that using the response time increment has limitations. To address this problem, we define the performance interference score I_{score} as a metric instead in Eq. (1) to qualify the degradation of online service.

$$I_{score} = \frac{T_{co-location} - T_{solo}}{T_{solo}} \tag{1}$$

In the formula, $T_{co-location}$ and T_{solo} are the response time of online service with and without co-location respectively. I_{score} can be used to indicate the interference sensitivity of online services co-located with batch jobs. The higher the score is, the more sensitive the online service is to performance interference.

What's more, we measure the number of batch jobs currently co-located in a server via co-location level. For example, when there is only one batch job co-located with the online service, the co-location level of the server is 1, and when there are two batch jobs co-located with the online service, the co-location level is 2, and so forth.

3.2   Performance Interference Model Based on Linear Regression

In this section, we construct a performance interference model based on linear regression to predict the performance interference when co-locating one online service with multiple batch jobs.

Workload Selection. We use online services described in Table 1, and choose ten different batch jobs from CloudSuite and Phoronix-test-suite shown in Table 2.

Table 1. Online services overview.

Online service	Description
Data processing service	The server searches for required data and returns processed results according to the http requests of the client
Data query service	Query and processing of data based on Redis
Image processing service	Watermark-removing and rotation of the uploaded pictures

Table 2. Offline batch jobs overview.

Batch job	Test suite	Type
in-memory-analytics	cloudsuite	Model training in machine learning
amg	phoronix-test-suite	CPU-Intensive workload
aobench	phoronix-test-suite	CPU-Intensive workload
compress-7zip	phoronix-test-suite	CPU-Intensive workload
stream	phoronix-test-suite	Memory-Intensive workload
tinymembench	phoronix-test-suite	Memory-Intensive workload
ramspeed	phoronix-test-suite	Memory-Intensive workload
iozone	phoronix-test-suite	IO-Intensive workload
sqlite	phoronix-test-suite	IO-Intensive workload
git	phoronix-test-suite	Comprehensive workload

Feature Extraction. When co-locating ten batch jobs in Table 2 with each online service in Table 1, we monitor and record the changes of hardware metrics of the container where the online service is located, including the number of instructions per clock cycle (IPC), cache miss rate, branch prediction miss rate and so forth. Among these metrics, we observed that IPC is inversely correlated with the response time of online services. Figures 1, 2, 3 represent the correlation between response time and IPC of data processing service, image processing service, data query service, respectively. And their spearman correlation coefficients are -0.7996, -0.9001 and -0.7664. Consequently, we choose the IPC change of the online service due to interference when co-located with a batch job as performance interference feature. The interference feature F_{w_i} of each batch job w_i can be calculated in Eq. (2), where IPC_{w_i} and IPC_{solo} are IPC metrics with and without co-location with batch job w_i.

$$F_{w_i} = \frac{IPC_{solo} - IPC_{w_i}}{IPC_{solo}} \qquad (2)$$

Model Analysis. We use linear regression to derive the performance interference weights of different batch jobs on online services. The mathematical formula of the Batch-based Linear Regression Model (BLR) is defined in Eq. (3).

$$I_W = \sum_{w_i \in W} c_{w_i} \times \xi_{w_i} \times F_{w_i} + c_0 \qquad (3)$$

W is a set of batch jobs that are recurring in the cluster. The coefficient c_{w_i} represents the performance interference weight of batch job w_i on the online service. ξ_{w_i} indicates whether the batch job w_i is co-located, it is set to 1 when co-located and set to 0 otherwise. F_{w_i} is the interference feature of batch job w_i defined in Eq. (2). I_W is the performance interference score of the online service defined in Eq. (1), which will be used for scheduling later.

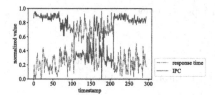

Fig. 1. The correlation between response time and IPC of data processing service.

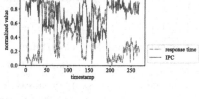

Fig. 2. The correlation between response time and IPC of image processing service.

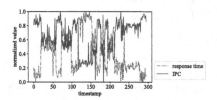

Fig. 3. The correlation between response time and IPC of data query service.

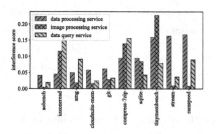

Fig. 4. Performance interference scores of different online services.

Moreover, in the real-world operation environment, there is a high possibility that external factors such as multiple users operating the server at the same time may change the status of servers, thereby causing inevitable performance interference on online services. For the sake of more accurate and refined prediction, we combine the current running status of the server (CPU utilization, memory utilization, etc.) with the interference features of batch jobs to propose a Server Status Aware and Batch-based Linear Regression Model (SABLR). Its mathematical expression in matrix form is shown in Eq. (4), in which K represents the number of sample and M represents the number of batch jobs:

$$
\begin{bmatrix}
\xi_{1,1}F_{w_1} & \xi_{1,2}F_{w_2} & \cdots & \xi_{1,M}F_{w_M} \\
\xi_{2,1}F_{w_1} & \xi_{2,2}F_{w_2} & \cdots & \xi_{2,M}F_{w_M} \\
\cdots & \cdots & \cdots & \cdots \\
\xi_{K,1}F_{w_1} & \xi_{K,2}F_{w_2} & \cdots & \xi_{K,M}F_{w_M}
\end{bmatrix}
\begin{bmatrix}
c_{w_1} \\
c_{w_2} \\
\cdots \\
c_{w_M}
\end{bmatrix}
+
\begin{bmatrix}
cpu_1 & mem_1 & \cdots & disk_1 \\
cpu_2 & mem_2 & \cdots & disk_2 \\
\cdots & \cdots & \cdots & \cdots \\
cpu_K & mem_K & \cdots & disk_K
\end{bmatrix}
\begin{bmatrix}
c_{cpu} \\
c_{mem} \\
\cdots \\
c_{disk}
\end{bmatrix}
=
\begin{bmatrix}
I_1 \\
I_2 \\
\cdots \\
I_K
\end{bmatrix}
\tag{4}
$$

To construct the model described above, a large number of data samples need to be collected. We suppose the co-location level of the server is limited to D, which means the maximum number of co-located batch jobs in a server is D, then the number of workloads combinations denoted as b_{case} can be calculated in Eq. (5) where d is the co-location level, M is the number of batch jobs we can choose from (in this paper M is ten), C_M^d is the combination formula.

$$b_{case} = \sum_{d=0}^{D} C_M^d \tag{5}$$

Due to the hardware restriction of our experimental environment, the maximum co-location level D is set to 3. According to Eq. (5), there are 176 different combinations for each online service. Since different online service has different interference sensitivity to the same batch job (as shown in Fig. 4), it is necessary to build an independent performance interference model for each online service, so a total of 528 different combinations needs to be considered.

In this experiment, we take all the 528 combinations into consideration and collect a total of 33897 data samples (13288 samples for data processing service, 10680 samples for image processing service, and 9929 samples for data query service) of which 87.5% is used for the training set, and 12.5% is used for the validating set. Each data sample includes the batch job combination, the running status of the server, and the corresponding performance interference score. We use the least square function in Eq. (6) as a regression equation to train the model, and use gradient descent algorithm to train and optimize the interference weight coefficient c. In addition, we can easily scale our method by obtaining data samples from the logs in the real-world operation environment when the online service can be mixed with much more batch jobs.

$$min \sum_{i}^{K} (y_{pred} - y_{true})^2 \tag{6}$$

3.3   Interference-aware Workload Scheduling

Different batch jobs will cause different performance interference to the online service, and different online services have different interference sensitivity to the same batch job. Therefore, this section uses this characteristic to propose an interference-aware scheduling strategy. The strategy predicts the interference the batch job to be executed will cause to each online service, and then schedules the batch job to the server with the least interference to the online service. Figure 5 illustrates the overall workflow. Algorithm 1 is a pseudo-code description of our scheduling strategy, and the main steps are shown as follows:

(1) The master control node obtains one batch job from the offline batch job queue composed of batch jobs to be scheduled;
(2) The master control node obtains the current batch job set and the current running status of each server deploying online services, and uses the corresponding interference model to predict performance interference score;
(3) Determine whether the interference score predicted in (2) exceeds the performance interference threshold $I_{threshold}$, select the server that can co-locate the batch job to be scheduled and add the server into $Server_{available}$;

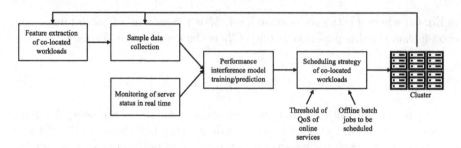

Fig. 5. Overall workflow of scheduling strategy.

Algorithm 1. Scheduling Strategy Based on SABLR.

Input: $batch_{queue}$; $threshold$

1: **for** $batch$ in $batch_{queue}$ **do**
2:    $available\_servers=\{\}$ //servers that can co-locate the batch job
3:    **for all** $server$ in $all\_servers$ **do**
4:       $W=get\_current\_colocated\_batches(server)$ //obtain current batch job set in the server
5:       $status=get\_server\_status(server)$ //obtain current running status of the server
6:       $model=get\_model(server)$ //obtain performance interference model
7:       $W.add(batch)$
8:       $score=model.predict(W,status)$ //obtain performance interference score
9:       **if** $score <= threshold[server]$ **then**
10:          $available\_servers[server]=score$
11:       **end if**
12:    **end for**
13:    //choose the server that introduces minimal interference
14:    $target\_server=select\_server\_by\_min\_score(available\_servers)$
15:    $schedule(batch, target\_server)$ //schedule batch job to the target server
16:    $update(target\_server, batch)$ //update batch job set in the target server
17: **end for**

---

(4) If the number of servers in $Server_{available}$ is more significant than 0, select the server with the least performance interference on online service from $Server_{available}$ as the target server and schedule the batch job to this server for execution;
(5) If the number of servers in $Server_{available}$ is equal to 0, it means that no server can deal with the batch job currently, so add the batch job back into the end of offline batch job queue;
(6) Repeat the steps above.

4   Experiment and Evaluation

In this section, we compare the prediction accuracy of different performance interference models and evaluate the throughput of different scheduling strategies.

4.1   Prediction Accuracy of Performance Interference Models

Based on Eqs. (3) and (4), we construct BLR that only uses the interference features as inputs and SABLR that takes both the server status and interference features into consideration, and choose IAM as the baseline model for comparison. Figure 6, 7 and 8 are scatter plots of the actual and predicted performance interference scores of IAM, BLR, and SABLR for data processing service, image processing service, and data query service.

These figures illustrate that the prediction error of IAM is significant, and both BLR and SABLR perform better than IAM. The interference score predicted by IAM in Fig. 7 is lower than the actual score, while that in Fig. 6 is relatively balanced, which further proves that different online services have different interference sensitivity to the same batch jobs combination, indicating that IAM cannot be applied to all different online services. While using linear regression to learn the different interference weight of batch jobs and introducing resource usage characteristics, SABLR can make a more accurate and fine-grained prediction of the performance interference of online services. For further evaluation, we calculate the following metrics: Coefficient of Determination (R^2), Mean Squared Error (MSE), Mean Absolute Error (MAE):

$$R^2 = 1 - \frac{\sum_i^n (y_{true}^i - y_{pred}^i)^2}{\sum_i^n (y_{true}^i - y_{avg})^2} \tag{7}$$

$$MSE = \frac{1}{n}\sum_i^n (y_{true}^i - y_{pred}^i)^2 \tag{8}$$

$$MAE = \frac{1}{n}\sum_i^n |y_{true}^i - y_{pred}^i| \tag{9}$$

Among them, MSE and MAE are standard metrics for prediction errors, while R^2 can reflect prediction performance. The closer the R^2 is to 1, the higher the prediction accuracy of the model is. Figure 9 is the comparison of R^2, MSE, MAE metrics using different models for different online services, where dps refers to data processing service, ips relates to image processing service, and dqs refers to data query service. The figure illustrates all three metrics of BLR and SABLR are significantly better than those of IAM, and the prediction effect of SABLR is slightly better than that of BLR. In conclusion, the SABLR method proposed in this paper can predict accurately.

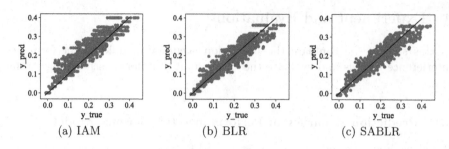

(a) IAM   (b) BLR   (c) SABLR

Fig. 6. Data processing service.

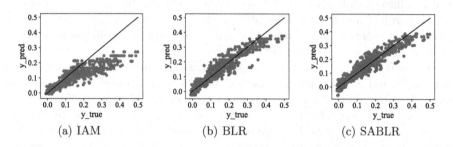

(a) IAM   (b) BLR   (c) SABLR

Fig. 7. Image processing service.

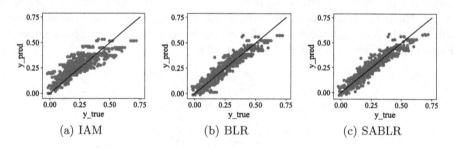

(a) IAM   (b) BLR   (c) SABLR

Fig. 8. Data query service.

4.2 Evaluation of Scheduling Strategies on Throughput

We built an experimental cluster composed of three servers. The kernel version of operating systems is Linux 3.10, and the release version is CentOS 7.6. The hardware configuration of each server is shown in Table 3. Three online services in Table 1 are respectively deployed in these three servers, and the client programs continuously send requests to the corresponding online service at a fixed rate.

During the experiment, ten batch jobs in Table 2 are placed in the offline batch job queue and are submitted to the cluster in turn. We set different performance interference thresholds (0.15, 0.2, and 0.25 separately) and calculate the time required to execute all batch jobs. Also, we compare our scheduling strategy based on SABLR with round-robin scheduling and random schedul-

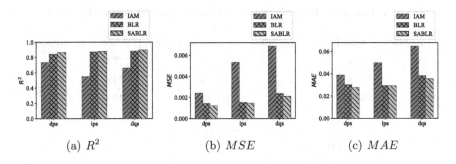

(a) R^2 (b) MSE (c) MAE

Fig. 9. Prediction accuracy.

ing. Round-robin (or Spread) and random scheduling are often used in Cloud computing, as baseline strategies, for instance in the Kubernetes[1] throughout a combination of a filtering and a scoring steps, and Docker ecosystems, making sound our comparison.

The three scheduling strategies above-mentioned determine whether co-locating the batch job to be scheduled violates the online service performance interference threshold according to the performance interference model before actual scheduling. If no server can handle the batch job, the batch job will be added back into the waiting queue, guaranteeing the QoS of the online service. Due to the uncertainty and randomness of random scheduling, we run the random scheduling strategy ten times and take the average. Table 4 records the execution time of all batch jobs under different scheduling strategies and different thresholds. Figure 10 shows a visualization of data in Table 4. It can be proved that our strategy can improve the throughput of batch jobs efficiently while guaranteeing the QoS of online services under different constraints of performance interference threshold.

Table 3. Experiment settings.

	Server 1	Server 2	Server 3
CPU	i5-8400 (2.80 GHz)	i7-7700 (3.60 GHz)	i7-9700 (3.00 GHz)
Physical Cores	6	4	8
Threads	6	8	8
L1 Cache	64 KB	64 KB	64 KB
L2 Cache	256 KB	256 KB	256 KB
L3 Cache	9 MB	8 MB	12 MB
Memory	16 GB	16 GB	16 GB

---

[1] See https://kubernetes.io/docs/concepts/scheduling-eviction/kube-scheduler/.

Table 4. Execution time of different strategies under different thresholds.

Threshold	Round-Robin Scheduling	Random scheduling	Scheduling proposed
0.15	1317 s	1204.4 s	1173 s
0.20	1347 s	1216.5 s	974 s
0.25	1663 s	1164.4 s	849 s

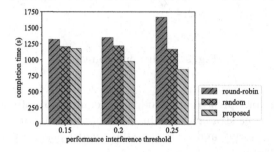

Fig. 10. Execution time of different strategies under different thresholds.

5   Conclusion

Co-location of online services and offline batch jobs may cause contention for shared resources, thus generating performance interference on online services. To solve these problems, the paper first proposes to use the performance interference score to evaluate the degree of interference with the online service quantitatively. Next, this paper considers several characteristics of server's running status and constructs a performance interference model based on linear regression, accurately predicting the performance interference caused by co-located batch jobs. Finally, this paper designs and implements an interference-aware workload scheduling strategy based on the model mentioned above, improving the throughput of batch jobs under the constraint of the performance interference threshold.

As future works, we propose investigating a more "dynamic" context where data arrives continuously and keeping the ideas of regression and scoring. Thus, the first general problem is to make the regression algorithm online, and the second one is controlling the scoring.

At last, we also propose to design meta-learning algorithms where automatic learning algorithms are applied to metadata about machine learning experiments. For instance, a Long Short-Term Memory based (LSTM-based) meta-learner is a technique to understand the exact optimization algorithm to be used to train another learner neural network classifier. The parametrization allows it to learn appropriate parameter updates specifically for the scenario where a set amount of updates will be made while also learning a general initialization of the learner (classifier) network that allows for quick convergence of training. The general question is what are the most appropriate meta-learning techniques for the performance interference problem introduced in our paper?

Acknowledgments. This work is supported by the National Natural Science Foundation of China (No.61972118), the Science and Technology Project of State Grid Corporation of China (Research and Application on Multi-Datacenters Cooperation & Intelligent Operation and Maintenance, No.5700-202018194A-0-0-00), and the Science and Technology Project of State Grid Corporation of China (No.SGSDXT00DKJS1900040). This work is also conducted during the Délégation with Centre National de la Recherche Scientifique (CNRS) of M Cérin. Thanks to the institutional supports of the CNRS, university of Grenoble Alpes and university Sorbonne Paris Nord.

References

1. Jiang, C., Han, G., Lin, J., Jia, G., Shi, W., Wan, J.: Characteristics of co-allocated online services and batch jobs in internet data centers: a case study from Alibaba cloud. IEEE Access **7**, 22495–22508 (2019)
2. Xavier, M.G., Matteussi, K.J., Lorenzo, F., De Rose, C.A.F.: Understanding performance interference in multi-tenant cloud databases and web applications. In: 2016 IEEE International Conference on Big Data (Big Data), pp. 2847–2852 (2016)
3. Rattihalli, G.: Exploring potential for resource request right-sizing via estimation and container migration in apache Mesos. In: 2018 IEEE/ACM International Conference on Utility and Cloud Computing Companion (UCC Companion), pp. 59–64. IEEE (2018)
4. DelValle, R., Rattihalli, G., Beltre, A., Govindaraju, M., Lewis, M.J.: Exploring the design space for optimizations with apache aurora and Mesos. In: 2016 IEEE 9th International Conference on Cloud Computing (CLOUD), pp. 537–544. IEEE (2016)
5. Liu, Q., Yu, Z.: The elasticity and plasticity in semi-containerized co-locating cloud workload: a view from Alibaba trace. In: Proceedings of the ACM Symposium on Cloud Computing, pp. 347–360 (2018)
6. Lattuada, M., Barbierato, E., Gianniti, E., Ardagna, D.: Optimal resource allocation of cloud-based spark applications. IEEE Trans. Cloud Comput. **10**, 1301–1316 (2020)
7. Li, Y., Zhang, J., Jiang, C., Wan, J., Ren, Z.: Pine: optimizing performance isolation in container environments. IEEE Access **7**, 30410–30422 (2019)
8. Zhao, J., Cui, H., Xue, J., Feng, X.: Predicting cross-core performance interference on multicore processors with regression analysis. IEEE Trans. Parallel Distrib. Syst. **27**(5), 1443–1456 (2015)
9. Zhang, Y., Laurenzano, M.A., Mars, J., Tang, L.: Smite: precise QOS prediction on real-system SMT processors to improve utilization in warehouse scale computers. In: 2014 47th Annual IEEE/ACM International Symposium on Microarchitecture, pp. 406–418. IEEE (2014)
10. Xu, R., Mitra, S., Rahman, J., Bai, P., Zhou, B., Bronevetsky, G., Bagchi, S.: Pythia: improving datacenter utilization via precise contention prediction for multiple co-located workloads. In: Proceedings of the 19th International Middleware Conference, pp. 146–160 (2018)

11. Mars, J., Tang, L., Hundt, R., Skadron, K., Soffa, M.L.: Bubble-up: Increasing utilization in modern warehouse scale computers via sensible co-locations. In: Proceedings of the 44th annual IEEE/ACM International Symposium on Microarchitecture, pp. 248–259 (2011)
12. Yang, X., Blackburn, S.M., McKinley, K.S.: Elfen scheduling: fine-grain principled borrowing from latency-critical workloads using simultaneous multithreading. In: 2016 USENIX Annual Technical Conference (USENIX ATC 2016), pp. 309–322 (2016)

FaaSPipe: Fast Serverless Workflows on Distributed Shared Memory

Ruizhe Tong[(⊠)]

Shanghai Jiao Tong University, Shanghai, China
tongruizhe@sjtu.edu.cn

Abstract. Serverless workflows consist of multiple chained functions that pass intermediate data through function invocations. Existing platforms implement data passing via remote storage services that incur significant performance and maintenance overhead. Some recent works optimize data passing with local shared memory but require specialized function scheduling support and are available only in constrained settings. In this paper, we observed that a simplified, peer-to-peer form of distributed shared memory (DSM) is sufficient and efficient to pass data in serverless workflows. With the observation, we propose *FaaSPipe*, a serverless workflow runtime built on the simplified DSM. FaaSPipe provides *PipeFunc*, a user-friendly shared memory-based serverless workflow programming model. To support PipeFunc and take full advantage of the simplified DSM, FaaSPipe designs the intra-workflow memory sharing scheme for address space coordination and builds full-duplex memory transfer channels to enable fast, non-blocking peer-to-peer data passing. Evaluation results on real-world workflow applications show that FaaSPipe reduces workflow latency by up to 61% and consumes up to $2.07\times$ less network traffic compared to state-of-art serverless platforms.

Keywords: Serverless computing · FaaS · Distributed shared memory

1 Introduction

Serverless computing has been a popular computing diagram for its easy maintenance, fine-grained billing and unlimited scalability. Serverless programmers write applications as *serverless workflows* and upload the workflows to the serverless platform, which is responsible for the workflow deployment and execution. Most well-known cloud providers have released their serverless workflow products, such as Huawei Cloud FunctionGraph [3], Google Cloud Composer [2], and AWS Step Functions [1].

A serverless workflow consists of multiple event-driven, chained functions and can be presented as a directed acyclic graph (DAG). Nodes in the graph represent functions, and edges present the invocation relation between functions. Specifically, an edge from A to B indicates that function A will invoke function B, where A is *parent* function and B is the *child* function. Edges also represent

© IFIP International Federation for Information Processing 2022
Published by Springer Nature Switzerland AG 2022
S. Liu and X. Wei (Eds.): NPC 2022, LNCS 13615, pp. 83–95, 2022.
https://doi.org/10.1007/978-3-031-21395-3_8

the data flow where parent functions pass intermediate data to child functions. A straightforward method to pass data is packing it in parameters and passing it along with the function invocation. However, this method cannot support many real-world applications that have large amount of states since platforms usually impose strict limits on the data format and size that can be passed between functions. For example, AWS Step Functions requires intermediate messages to be JSON texts with a length limit of 32 KB.

Serverless platforms solve the data passing problem by introducing shared remote storage services. To pass large amount of data between functions, the data producer uploads the data to remote storage, from which the consumer can download the data. The remote-storage-based data passing enables the large data passing between serverless functions but still has noticeable problems: (1) Performance: transferring data through remote storage significantly increases workflow execution latency since additional network overhead is introduced to access remote storage, especially when the remote storage service has high latency. (2) Maintainability: developers have to manually configure and manage the remote storage and write code to handle serialization, delivery, and deserialization of intermediate data, introducing additional labor and operational costs. (3) Impotence: since the access to the remote storage may be a non-idempotent operation, this method potentially destroys the stateless nature of serverless functions, thereby preventing the cloud computing platform from performing operations such as error retry on functions.

Efforts from industry and academia have been taken to optimize data passing in serverless platforms in two directions. Cloudburst [14], Pocket [11], and Jiffy [10] optimizes remote storage services for serverless to improve the performance of data passing. However, they still leave room for performance improvement and keep the other two problems unsolved. SAND [5], Faasm [13], and Nightcore [9] solve the data passing by local shared memory. When the parent and the child functions run on the same physical node, these systems establish shared memory between the functions to reduce data copy and avoid network communication. However, the performance gain of these systems can only be achieved when functions in a workflow are scheduled on the same node. Another solution would be using distributed shared memory (DSM) upon all nodes. But general DSM suffers from expensive consistency maintenance and leads to unacceptable performance downgrade.

Although general DSM is inappropriate for serverless computing, we find data passing between serverless functions only needs a simple form of DSM, which can be more efficient. The key observation is that data passing in serverless computing occurs only at the endpoint of a function's lifetime, from parents to children when a function is invoked, and from children to parents when a function returns. The DSM is simplified in three aspects. First, only two functions have access to the DSM: the parent and the child. Second, the DSM can be established when a function wants to pass data and destroyed when the data has been acquired by the other function. Third, data is prepared before the DSM is established and requires a single copy, which avoids the expensive consistency maintenance. As a result, instead of a general DSM, we can build a lightweight, peer-to-peer DSM to accelerate data passing between two functions. Based on the insight, we propose **FaaSPipe**, a serverless workflow runtime that allows data passing via simplified DSM. FaaSPipe provides **PipeFunc**, a serverless workflow programming model leveraging the simplified DSM to facilitate developing workflow. FaaSPipe designs the intra-workflow memory sharing scheme, enabling functions to share the address space distributedly. FaaSPipe builds a full-duplex communication channel to transfer memory between functions, allowing peer-to-peer data passing and hiding cold start latency. We evaluate FaaSPipe via two real-world serverless workflows, distributed word count and LightGBM, and analyze the results in detail. Experiments results show that FaaSPipe reduces workflow latency by up to 61% and network traffic by up to 2.07×.

The remainder of the paper is organized as follows. Section 2 discusses related work. Section 3 describes the design and implementation of FaaSPipe. In Sect. 3.1 we propose the PipeFunc programming model and discuss its benefits. From Sect. 3.2 to Sect. 3.4 we present the FaaSPipe workflow runtime in detail. Section 4 conducts rich experiments. Then we conclude in Sect. 5.

2   Related Work

Data Passing for Serverless Workflows. There are many systems that optimize intermediate data passing. Cloudburst [14] improves the distributed consistency of shared data in serverless computing based on the key-value storage service. Pocket [11] and Jiffy [10] build dedicated storage clusters with high elasticity and scalability. However, the above systems still rely on remote storage to pass intermediate data, incurring problems stated in Sect. 1. Other research works use shared memory to speed up intermediate data transfer in serverless workflows. Faasm [13] takes advantage of the software fault isolation capability provided by WebAssembly and uses shared memory for state sharing. Nightcore [9] splits interactive microservices into multiple functions and uses Linux FIFOs for data transfer between functions. However, these systems force functions scheduled on the same machine to use shared memory. We generalize the shared memory-based method to distributed scenarios and design FaaSPipe based on the characteristics of Serverless without introducing overhead in existing DSM systems.

Optimizing Cold Startup. Serverless functions suffer from high initialization latency, known as the cold boot problem. In a cold boot, serverless platforms create sandboxes, and functions do application-specific initialization. Researchers have proposed snapshot-based methods [8,15] to speed up the cold boot. The essential idea is to take a snapshot of the function after the initialization phase in advance and restore the function from the snapshot on startup. Some researcher [7,8,12] cache the pre-warmed function instance in memory and route function invocations to these pre-warmed function instances, bypassing part of the initialization phase. Unlike the snapshot-based and cache-based methods, FaaSPipe hides the cold boot latency rather than reduces it. The cold start stage overlaps with the memory transfer stage in FaaSPipe, leading to reduced end-to-end function execution latency.

3 Design and Implementation

3.1 The PipeFunc Programming Model

```
1    // PipeFunc API
2    Id              PipeFuncInvoke(entryFunc, inputDataPtr);
3    outputDataPtr PipeFuncJoin(Id);
4    void            PipeFuncCleanUp(Id);
5    // Sample word count workflow in PipeFunc
6    struct Task { vector<string>* lines; };
7    struct TaskResult { int cnt; };
8
9    TaskResult* ChildPipeFunc(Task *t) {
10       int wordCnt = countWordInLines(t->lines);
11       return new TaskResult{ .cnt = wordCnt };
12   }
13   TaskResult *ParentPipeFunc(int *n_worker) {
14       vector<Task *> tasks = fetchAndSplitWorkload(*n_worker);
15       vector<Id> childIds; int result = 0;
16       for (Task* t: tasks)
17           childIds.push_back(PipeFuncInvoke(ChildPipeFunc, t));
18       for (Id id: childIds) {
19           TaskResult* tr = PipeFuncJoin(id);
20           result += tr->cnt;
21           PipeFuncCleanUp(id);
22       }
23       return new TaskResult{ .cnt = result };
24   }
```

Listing 1. The PipeFunc API and sample word count workflow application

We propose PipeFunc, a distributed shared memory-based programming model for serverless workflows. Workflows in PipeFunc consist of several **pipe functions**. Different pipe functions may be scheduled on different FaaSPipe nodes for distributed and concurrent execution. Listing 1 shows the three key interfaces of the pipeFunc programming model. `PipeFuncInvoke` creates a *pipe function* with `entryFunc` as the entry point and `inputDataPtr` as the input. The calling pipe function becomes the parent function, and the new pipe function becomes the child function. `InputDataPtr` points to a memory address with the address space of the parent function. Typically, `inputDataPtr` points to the intermediate data. The child function visits its input data using the memory access instructions (`load/store`) directly through `inputDataPtr`. `PipeFuncInvoke` returns a unique identifier of the newly created pipe function. `PipeFuncJoin` blocks and waits for the termination of the pipe function specified by `Id`. Only parent functions can call `PipeFuncJoin` on their children. Upon termination of the child, `PipeFuncJoin` returns `outputDataPtr`, which is used to pass their output data to their parents. Finally, parent functions uses `PipeFuncCleanUp` to reclaim all the resources of their children.

The PipeFunc programming model enables developers to write distributed and parallel serverless workflows in a way similar to the single-machine multi-threaded programming method. Its advantages over remote storage-based workflows are as follows. First, the PipeFunc programming model follows the stateless requirement of serverless computing. With the assumption that functions are stateless, serverless platforms can easily perform fault-tolerant operations such as error retry. On the contrary, remote storage-based workflows are not impotent, leading to consistent issues. Second, PipeFunc frees developers from the burden of writing intermediate data transfer code and managing remote storage.

To better understand PipeFunc, we show a sample workflow application that counts the number of words in a large text distributedly. As shown in Listing 1, the starting pipe function begins at `ParentPipeFunc`. It fetches the workload, a large file containing many lines from a persistent storage, loads the file into memory and divides the lines into `n_worker` portions. Each portion corresponds to a `Task` object. Then the parent function invokes some child functions, each taking its `Task` object as the input and starting execution at `ChildPipeFunc`. Child functions access the assigned lines through the input pointer `t` and count the total number of words. They return a `TaskResult` describing the result. The parent function waits for the termination of children, obtains their output data pointers and calculates the sum. Finally, the parent function uses `PipeFuncCleanUp` to reclaim the resources of its children and returns the final result.

3.2   System Architechture of FaaSPipe

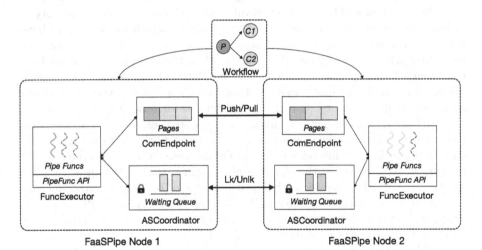

Fig. 1. FaaSPipe system architechture

FaaSPipe is a general-purpose serverless runtime, supporting PipeFunc and leveraging the simplified DSM. The prototype implementation of FaaSPipe is based on Faasm, which proposes Faaslet, a safe, lightweight serverless sandbox. Faaslet relies on the software fault isolation capability provided by WebAssembly and the resource management ability provided by the Linux kernel. Users can compile functions written in common programming into WebAssembly binaries to run in the Faaslet sandbox. FaasPipe uses Faaslet to provide isolation enviroments required by serverless computing for running functions.

Figure 1 shows the overall architecture of FaaSPipe. A single-process FaaSPipe runtime runs on each node in the FaasPipe cluster. Each FaaSPipe runtime comprises three core components: the function execution module (FuncExecutor), the communication endpoint module (ComEndpoint), and the address space coordinator module (ASCoordinator). FuncExecutor is responsible for initializing software environments for function and execution of functions. Inside it contains multiple pipe functions, each running in a dedicated Faaslet sandbox. Besides, FuncExecutor exposes the PipeFunc API (Sect. 3.1) that is linked to function instances. ComEndpoint (Sect. 3.4) establishes peer-to-peer communication channels to ComEndpoint on other nodes and transfers the intermediate data in the form of memory pages upon the channel in two directions, pushing and pulling. ASCoordinators (Sect. 3.3) on nodes of a workflow coordinate the address space allocation/deallocation operations and provide a consistent view of the address space through an distributed locking protocol.

3.3 Intra-workflow Memory Sharing

In FaaSPipe, all pipe function instances in a workflow instance share memory distributedly. Thus, input data pointers from parents via `PipeFuncInvoke` are valid in children, and output data pointers from children via `PipeFuncJoin` are valid in parents. The straightforward way to enable the shared memory is to build FaaSPipe atop conventional DSM systems, which are known to have poor performance and scalability. Instead, we observe that workflow functions have their private memory invisible to each other. Besides, memories shared via input/output data pointers are read-only for the receiver, eliminating network communications for memory updates. Based on these observations, we propose an infra-workflow memory sharing scheme suitable for serverless situations.

FuncExecutor hooks memory management system calls, so it has the complete ability to manage the memory of pipe functions. Each function dynamically creates and reclaims continuous ranges of virtual memory addresses (i.e., virtual memory areas, VMAs) in the shared address space. Each VMA in a workflow can be uniquely identified by a triple (*pipeFuncID*, *offset*, *length*), meaning that the function identified by *pipeFuncID* allocates the VMA of *length* in size at *offset*. At any time t, the union of all VMAs in the address space visible to the function f is called the *memory view* of f at t.

Child functions *inherit* the memory view of their parent function, thus guaranteeing that the input data pointers from parent functions are valid in child functions. As shown in Fig. 2, the parent has a VMA, and its two children also have this VMA in their memory view by memory view inheritance at `PipeFuncInvoke`. The input data pointer (inPtr) sits in the parent VMA and is passed to the children. After `PipeFuncInvoke`, the two children can use memory instructions (load/store) to access parent memory via inPtr and dynamically allocate their own non-overlapping VMAs that are invisible to each other.

Memory views of parents *merge* with child memory views when calling `PipeFuncJoin` on children in order to validate output data pointers returned by children in parents. As shown in Fig. 2, the parent function merges children's

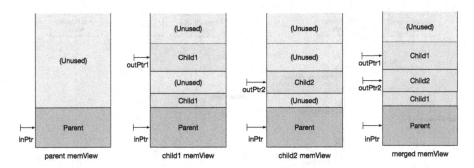

Fig. 2. An example of memory view inheritance and merging in FaaSPipe

memory views by putting their newly allocated VMAs into its address space. After merging, the two output data pointers from children, outPtr1 and out-Ptr2, sit in parent memory. Therefore, the parent function can use outPtr1 and outPtr2 to access the output data from children.

Although not required to provide consistency of memory contents, FaaSPipe still needs to coordinate address space operations for pipe functions. Pipe functions allocate and reclaim VMAs in the shared address space concurrently and dynamically. These VMAs cannot conflict, which means no two VMA address ranges can overlap. Otherwise, a single memory pointer will be ambiguous, pointing to memory allocated from different function instances. For example, if VMAs from child function conflict, the parent function can get the same value from multiple `PipeFuncJoin` calls and fail to distinguish the memory location pointed by the pointers.

FaaSPipe use distributed locks to coordinate the address space for pipe functions. Pipe functions allocate and reclaim VMAs in the shared address space concurrently. These VMAs must not conflict, which means no two VMA address ranges can overlap. Otherwise, a single memory pointer will be ambiguous. FaaSPipe has ASCoordinators on each node acting as agents to run a distributed locking protocol. Each workflow is assigned a lock, which must be acquired before performing address space operations (i.e., VMA allocation/reclamation) and released later. Internally, ASCoordinators maintain wait queues to decide the locking orders for pipe functions in the same workflow.

3.4 Full-Duplex Memory Transfer

We design peer-to-peer full-duplex memory transfer in FaaSPipe. Upon the memory view inheritance and merging, a full-duplex communication channel is established between the parent function node and the child function to transfer the memory. This section focuses on the memory transfer in the memory view inheritance.

When the parent function calls `PipeFuncInvoke` (i.e., memory view inheritance happens), it should pass its memory to the child. Figure 3 compares this process and data passing in the remote storage-based serverless platform. As shown in

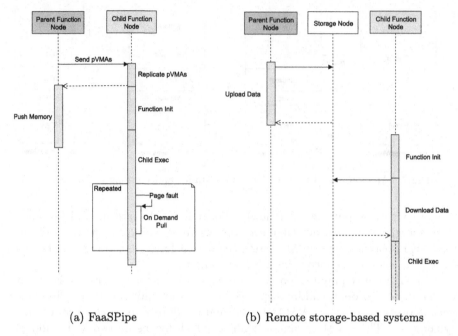

(a) FaaSPipe   (b) Remote storage-based systems

Fig. 3. The comparison of the intermediate data passing processes between FaaSPipe and remote storage-based serverless platforms

Fig. 3(a), the ComEndpoint on the parent node first sends all of the parent VMAs to the child ComEndpoint, which replicates VMAs to set up the address space for the child. At this time, access to child memory pages is prohibited by configuring the page table since the contents of these pages are still invalid. Then the parent ComEndpoint continuously pushes the memory pages to the child ComEndpoint. Upon the arrival of a page, the child ComEndpoint copies its content to the corresponding local page and restores its access permission. While the pushing phase is going on, the child FuncExecutor initializes the sandbox for the child pipe function and begins running the child function. Note that the child pipe function will trigger page faults because some pages have not been pushed, and these pages have not been granted permissions. In the page fault handler, the faulted page is pulled by the child ComEndpoint. The process of memory view merging is similar, so we briefly discuss it. After the parent function calls PipeFuncJoin, the parent function pulls the memory of the child function on demand, and the child function continuously pushes memory to the parent function. As a comparison, Fig. 3(b) shows intermediate data passing in the remote storage-based method. All stages in the method need to be executed sequentially. First, the parent function uploads the intermediate data to the remote storage node, then the child function starts and downloads the data, and finally starts execution.

Compared with data transfer based on remote storage, peer-to-peer memory transfer saves network round trips for FaaSPipe. Further, FaaSPipe overlaps the initialization of the function with the memory transfer, thereby hiding the startup latency, which can be used to alleviate the cold start problem. The on-demand pulling on the child side ensures that the execution of the child pipe function will not be blocked. Therefore, the child pipe function does not waste time waiting for the arrival of memory pages that will not be touched.

4   Evaluation

We implement FaaSPipe based on Faasm and conduct the experiments to compare FaaSPipe with Faasm, the state-of-art serverless platform that uses Redis as the remote storage service to enable distributed intermediate data passing. We use two real-world serverless workflow applications as benchmarks, compare the end-to-end latency of workflow execution and analyze the benefits of FaaSPipe in depth. We implement the workflow applications in FaaSPipe using the PipeFunc API and in Faasm using its *host interfaces*. We run FaaSPipe and Faasm runtime on two nodes, which is sufficient to demonstrate the feasibility and advantages of FaaSPipe. Each node is equipped with 28-core Intel(R) Xeon Gold 6238R CPUs with hyper-threading disabled. Each socket is equipped with 192 GB DDR4 memory. Additionally, Faasm needs a Redis server as the remote storage, equipped with 2-socket 40-core Intel(R) Xeon Gold and 377 GB DDR memory. All the nodes, including the Redis server, use Intel I350 1 Gb NIC.

4.1   Distributed Word Count

The distributed word count serverless workflow counts the number of words in a large file. The FaaSPipe version of this workflow is shown in Sect. 3.1. In the Faasm version, the main function stores the intermediate data (i.e., multiple groups of lines) to the Redis server, which is later downloaded by child functions. In the experiment, we assign a 200 MB file part to each child and adjust the number of the children functions that the main function spawns.

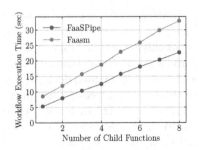

Fig. 4. End-to-end latency

Table 1. Latency breakdown

Stage (sec)	FaaSPipe	Faasm
Parent init - child invok	2.345	2.314
Data passing (P to C)	9.814	13.782
Avg. child init - return	3.650	2.350
Data passing (C to P)	0.167	0.165
End-to-end latency	12.558	18.61

Figure 4 shows the end-to-end latency of the workflow. In both FaaSPipe and Faasm, the latency increases linearly with the number of children since the size of the intermediate data to transfer is proportional to the child number. FaaSPipe shows better latency at all times. With four children functions, the workflow tasks 12.56 s in FaaSPipe and 18.61 s in Faasm. With one child, FaaSPipe has the best latency improvement, about 61%. We show the latency breakdown to analyze the execution speedup in detail in Table 1. Both FaaSPipe and Faasm spend 2.3 s on initializing software environments and execution til invoking child functions. Then the parent function creates child functions and passes data to them. In Faasm, the intermediate data is first uploaded to the Redis server and then downloaded by the child, taking 13.8 s. For FaaSPipe, we count the time of data passing as the latency to push the parent memory to the child node, which is 9.8 s. The peer-to-peer memory transfer reduces network roundtrips and overhead. Although the average interval between child initialization and returning in FaaSPipe is longer than Faasm, initialization and execution are overlapped with data passing in FaaSPipe. We can see that the end-to-end latency in Faasm equals the sum of latency for each step and is less than the sum in FaaSPipe.

4.2   LightGBM

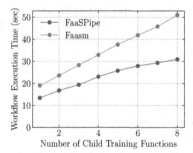

Fig. 5. End-to-end latency

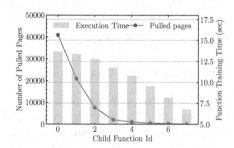

Fig. 6. Child latency and pulled pages

The LightGBM machine learning workflow trains ML models for inference using the LightGBM framework [4]. In this workflow, the main function loads the HIGGS [6] dataset and spawns a varied number of child functions, each training a decision tree by the LightGBM C++ library and sending trained models back. The main function then combines the models and evaluates the final decision tree on the test set. In FaaSPipe, the children return their decision trees as the output pointers, obtained by the main function using `PipFuncJoin`. In Faasm, child functions serialize the models and upload them to the Redis, later downloaded by the main function. We pick a 150 MB portion of the dataset and vary the number of child functions from 1 to 8. As shown in Fig. 5, both FaaSPipe and Faasm present linear end-to-end latencies against the number of child functions, similar to the results in the word count workflow. Additionally, with the increase in child functions, the latency growth trend slows slightly in FaaSPipe and keeps unchanged in Faasm. At eight child training functions, the latencies of FaaSPipe and Faasm are 30.8 s and 51.1 s. This is because the training dataset passed from the parent to the children has a fixed size of 150 MB. These child functions amortize the network overhead since they share the training dataset in memory. On the contrary, every child in Faasm has to download the training dataset and incur linear network overhead.

We notice that sibling child functions have different latencies related to the number of pulled memory pages in their execution in FaaSPipe. We pick the test where the parent spawns eight children and record the latency as well as pulled pages of each child. As shown in Fig. 6, the fewer pages pulled, the earlier child training functions finish, which is attributed to the implementation of the full-duplex memory transfer in FaaSPipe. A child must pull a page when a page fault occurs, indicating that the page has not been pushed from the parent. The parent pushes all the pages in the shared address space sequentially, so children receive pages in order and have different pages pushed at a timepoint. Child functions with fewer page pulling events run faster since a memory page pulling event pauses its execution.

4.3   Efficency of FaaSPipe vs. Faasm

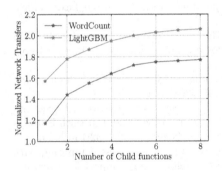

Fig. 7. Network traffic ratio

Table 2. Changed lines of code

Workflow	Total lines	Changed lines	
		FaaSPipe	Faasm
Word count	44	3	8
LightGBM	231	8	23

In this section, we discuss the efficiency of FaaSPipe over Faasm in two aspects, network overhead, and programming simplicity. Figure 7 shows the ratio of network traffic of Faasm to FaaSPipe. Faasm incurs at most 2.07× more network traffic in the word count workflow and 1.78× in the LightGBM workflow than FaaSPipe. This is because intermediate data goes through the remote storage in Faasm and is directly passed between nodes in FaaSPipe. The ratio increases with the number of child functions since some fixed network traffic (e.g., training dataset in LightGBM, stacks in both workflows) can be amortized. Table 2 shows the number of lines changed to rewrite multithreaded versions of the workflows in FaaSPipe and Faasm. Compared to the multithreaded version, workflows in Faasm need additional logic to cope with serialization/deserialization and interact with remote storage. However, FaaSPipe is based on shared memory, eliminating the tedious logic and making intermediate data ng passing easier. Most changed lines in the FaaSPipe version simply replace multithread calls with PipeFunc APIs.

5 Conclusion

We present FaaSPipe, a serverless runtime built upon simplified distributed shared memory. FaaSPipe designs the intra-workflow memory sharing scheme to enable distributed address space sharing and establishs a full-duplex memory transfer channel to make peer-to-peer data passing. Developers use the PipeFunc programming model to write workflows in FaaSPipe. Our evaluation demonstrates that FaaSPipe offers high-performance data passing for serverless workflows and efficiency in terms of network traffic and programming simplicity.

References

1. AWS Step Functions. https://aws.amazon.com/step-functions/?step-functions
2. Google Cloud Composer. https://cloud.google.com/composer
3. Huawei Cloud Function Graph. https://www.huaweicloud.com/intl/en-us/product/functiongraph.html
4. LightGBM's documentation. https://lightgbm.readthedocs.io/en/latest/index.html
5. Akkus, I.E., et al.: SAND: towards high-performance serverless computing. In: 2018 USENIX Annual Technical Conference, Boston, MA, USA, 11–13 July 2018, pp. 923–935
6. Baldi, P., Sadowski, P., Whiteson, D.: Searching for exotic particles in high-energy physics with deep learning. Nat. Commun. **5**, 4308 (2014)
7. Cadden, J., Unger, T., Awad, Y., Dong, H., Krieger, O., Appavoo, J.: SEUSS: skip redundant paths to make serverless fast. In: EuroSys 2020: Fifteenth EuroSys Conference 2020, Heraklion, Greece, 27–30 April 2020, pp. 32:1–32:15 (2020)
8. Du, D., et al.: Catalyzer: sub-millisecond startup for serverless computing with initialization-less booting. In: ASPLOS 2020: Architectural Support for Programming Languages and Operating Systems, Lausanne, Switzerland, 16–20 March 2020, pp. 467–481 (2020)
9. Jia, Z., Witchel, E.: Nightcore: efficient and scalable serverless computing for latency-sensitive, interactive microservices. In: ASPLOS 2021: 26th ACM International Conference on Architectural Support for Programming Languages and Operating Systems, Virtual Event, USA, 19–23 April 2021, pp. 152–166 (2021)
10. Khandelwal, A., Tang, Y., Agarwal, R., Akella, A., Stoica, I.: Jiffy: elastic far-memory for stateful serverless analytics. In: EuroSys 2022: Seventeenth European Conference on Computer Systems, Rennes, France, 5–8 April 2022, pp. 697–713 (2022)
11. Klimovic, A., Wang, Y., Stuedi, P., Trivedi, A., Pfefferle, J., Kozyrakis, C.: Pocket: elastic ephemeral storage for serverless analytics. In: 13th USENIX Symposium on Operating Systems Design and Implementation, OSDI 2018, Carlsbad, CA, USA, 8–10 October 2018, pp. 427–444 (2018)
12. Oakes, E., et al.: SOCK: rapid task provisioning with serverless-optimized containers. In: 2018 USENIX Annual Technical Conference, Boston, USA, 11–13 July 2018 (2018)

13. Shillaker, S., Pietzuch, P.R.: FaaSM: lightweight isolation for efficient stateful serverless computing. In: 2020 USENIX Annual Technical Conference, USENIX ATC 2020, 15–17 July 2020, pp. 419–433 (2020)
14. Sreekanti, V., et al.: Cloudburst: stateful functions-as-a-service. Proc. VLDB Endow. **13**(11), 2438–2452 (2020)
15. Ustiugov, D., Petrov, P., Kogias, M., Bugnion, E., Grot, B.: Benchmarking, analysis, and optimization of serverless function snapshots. In: ASPLOS 2021: 26th ACM International Conference on Architectural Support for Programming Languages and Operating Systems, Virtual Event, USA, 19–23 April 2021, pp. 559–572 (2021)

TopKmer: Parallel High Frequency K-mer Counting on Distributed Memory

Li Mocheng[1], Chen Zhiguang[2], Xiao Nong[1], Liu Yang[1], Luo Xi[3],
and Chen Tao[4(✉)]

[1] Institute for Quantum Information and State Key Laboratory of High Performance
Computing, College of Computer, National University of Defense Technology,
Changsha, China

[2] School of Computer, Sun Yat-sen University, Guangzhou, China

[3] Automotive Department, Shenzhen No. 2 Vocational and Technical School,
Shenzhen, China

[4] State Key Laboratory of Proteomics, Beijing Proteome Research Center, National
Center for Protein Sciences (Beijing), Beijing Institute of Lifeomics, Beijing, China
taochen1019@163.com

Abstract. High-throughput DNA sequencing is a crucial technology for
genomics research. As genetic data grows to hundreds of gigabytes or
even terabytes that traditional devices cannot support, high-performance
computing plays an important role. However, current high-performance
approaches to extracting k-mers cost a large memory footprint due to
the high error rate of short-read sequences. This paper proposes Top-
Kmer, a parallel k-mer counting workflow that indexes high-frequency
k-mers within a tiny counting structure. On the 2048 cores of Tianhe-2,
we construct k-mer index tables in 18 s for 174 GB fastq files and complete queries in 1 s for 1 billion k-mers, with a scaling efficiency of 95%.
Compared with the state of the art, the counting table's memory usage
is reduced by 50% with no performance degradation.

Keywords: k-mer counting · Distributed hash table · Space saving
algorithm · High scalability · Hybrid parallel

1 Introduction

Next-generation sequencing (NGS) technology has enabled the rapid development of genomics in recent years. The size of high-throughput sequencing
data has exploded, and conventional computers' memory and arithmetic power
are insufficient to support hundreds of GB or even larger data sizes. Besides,
short-read sequences of genomic dataset suffer from high error rates, short frag-
ments, and other problems requiring efficient and reliable splicing and correction
algorithms. Large data scale and data correction requirements mean genomic
sequence analysis is intensive in memory and computationally.

A mainstream practice of analyzing sequences is to slice short-read sequences
into k-mers by sliding windows into base sequences of length k for easy storage

© IFIP International Federation for Information Processing 2022
Published by Springer Nature Switzerland AG 2022
S. Liu and X. Wei (Eds.): NPC 2022, LNCS 13615, pp. 96–107, 2022.
https://doi.org/10.1007/978-3-031-21395-3_9

and statistics. Due to the high error rate of short-read sequences generated by NGS, the wrong k-mers occupy a large amount of space in the hash table.

Some algorithms introduce bloom filters but add extra computational overhead and exacerbate the load imbalance problem in the parallel case. Some sketch-based attempts limit the memory footprint but add a lot of computational overhead. There is currently no effective way to reduce memory usage without reducing performance.

In summary, k-mer counting in high-performance computing faces problems: reducing memory overhead while ensuring computational efficiency, optimising workflows, and solving potential load imbalance. In this paper, we carry out detailed work to address these points. The main contributions of our study are as follows:

- Inspired by the Top-k query, we designed a dedicated k-mer storage structure, a distributed multi-layer key-value hash table and its access method to work effectively at a tiny memory footprint. (Sect. 3)
- We designed a parallel framework for the structure, combining communication-computation overlap, hybrid MPI-OpenMP and communication load balance optimization based on hardware architecture. (Sect. 4)

In our study, on the 2048 cores of Tianhe-2, we completed all works of k-mer extraction, scale estimation, redistribution, and construction of hash tables in 28 s using 174 GB fastq files. The time overhead for communication and hash table construction is 18 s. The query for one million k-mers in a batch is 1 s, which accelerates 1.3× and 4.25× than state of the art with a similar structure. Compared to cutting-edge k-mer hash tables, we reduce memory footprint by 50% with no performance loss.

2   Background

2.1   Parallel K-mer Counting

Research on K-mer counting, or k-mer indexing, has a long history, and its parallel approach has been gaining attention in the last decade. Initially there were various thread-level parallel approaches such as Jellyfish [13], MSPKmerCounter [10,11], BFCounter [14], which can be efficiently applied in shared memory environments.

The process-level parallel k-mer counting algorithm has gained importance to accommodate the rapidly increasing data size because of its high scalability. The hash table structure for storing k-mers is divided into two factions: exact indexing based on key-value pairs and counting based on Filters. Some of the hash table k-mer counting examples are Kmerind [16] and Pan [17]. Kmerind designs a complete distributed k-mer indexing workflow, which got class-leading performance. Pan is designed based on a similar framework with a cache-friendly Robinhood algorithm, combined with MPI-OpenMP for hybrid parallelism and optimizations to obtain excellent performance. However, it does not filter low-frequency k-mers, resulting in a lot of memory space occupied by unnecessary data. One of the classic Bloom filter-based counters is BFCounter [14]. It adds each element in the filter with a counting structure. It stores k-mers with frequencies greater than a threshold in the hash table, thus reducing the hash table's inserting and querying pressure and memory overhead.

2.2 Heavy Hitters

Heavy Hitters is an important concept of the Top-k query [1,3,7], which originates from big data and streaming computing. Distinguished from k in k-mer, top-k aims to find the k items with the highest frequency. Heavy Hitter is defined as: there are m elements inside the data, find the k-1 elements occur more frequently than m/k. While facing limited memory and massive data, how to count Heavy hitter effectively becomes a key problem. Genomic analysis work is not sensitive to precision, and low-frequency k-mers are often discarded as untrusted data [2,9], making Top-k possible as a tool for k-mer counting.

There are four mainstream algorithms for finding Heavy Hitters. There are Lossy Counting [12], Misra-Gries [15], Space Saving and Count-min Sketch. In the field of gene sequence analysis, Hipmer [6] takes the lead in adopting a related method to screen extremely high-frequency k-mers to reduce the impact of load imbalance. Count-min Sketch [4] has been widely used in k-mer counting, i.e. SWAPCounter [5], TANKYALF [19]. However, it suffers from false positives and extra hash table access overhead, leading to low item access efficiency.

3 TopKmer Counter

3.1 Multi-layer Hash Table

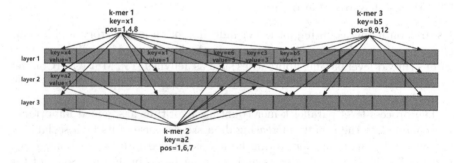

Fig. 1. Structure of TopKmer counter and its access method.

The core of TopKmer is a multi-layer hash table whose insertion and query algorithms are improved from the Space Saving algorithm. The structure and access method are shown in Fig. 1. Data access needs to traverse fixed storage space, so we designed a multi-layer hash table, which can obtain multiple candidate positions in one hash, reducing computational overhead.

We use the following notations. The counting table CT consists of L(default $L = 3$) levels, and the table size of each layer is S. Access to the element at position j of the ith layer of CT is denoted by $CT[i][j]$. For any i, j in $CT[i][j]$, it consists of a $tuple < key, value >$, where key is obtained by k- mer transformation, and $value$ is a parameter of improved Space Saving algorithm, which is also used as the fundamental basis for k-mer counting while querying.

3.2 Insert

The essence of the insertion algorithm is to use Space Saving algorithm to resolve conflicts. We hash L times to get L^2 slots from the L-level hash table. If there are empty slots, the k-mer is inserted; otherwise, the L^2 slots are regarded as filters to perform Space Saving algorithm to complete the insertion. The specific implementation is shown in Algorithm 1. Because Space Saving algorithm can reliably discard low-frequency data, the hash table can be compressed to a tiny size.

Algorithm 1. Insertion of TopKmer Counter

Input:
    $kmer$ to be inserted
1: $curKey \leftarrow getKey(kmer)$;
2: **for** $i \leftarrow 1$ to L **do**
3:   $pos[i] \leftarrow getPos(kmer, i)$;
4: **end for**
5: $minPos \leftarrow (1, pos[1])$;
6: $minEle \leftarrow HT[1][pos[1]]$
7: **for** $i \leftarrow 1$ to L **do**
8:   **for** p in pos **do**
9:     **if** $HT[i][p].value == 0$ **then**
10:      $HT[i][p] \leftarrow (curKey, 1)$;
11:      Return;
12:     **end if**
13:     **if** $HT[i][p].key == curKey$ **then**
14:      $HT[i][p].value \leftarrow abs(HT[i][p].value) + 1$;
15:      Return;
16:     **end if**
17:     **if** $abs(minEle.value) > abs(HT[i][p].value)$ **then**
18:      $minPos \leftarrow (i, p)$;
19:      $minEle \leftarrow HT[i][p]$;
20:     **end if**
21:   **end for**
22: **end for**
23: $HT[minPos].key \leftarrow curKey$;
24: $HT[minPos].value \leftarrow -abs(minEle.value) - 1$;

Note that in line 24, we make the values inserted after substitution negative. This operation uses the top bit of *value* to mark the replaced numbers. Any k-mer may be replaced and result in overcounting. Such k-mers require additional processing at query. However, if this number occurs a second time or more, it will be replaced again with a positive number(line 14), indicating that its *value* is included in the trusted category.

3.3   Query

When a k-mer is asked if it is in the hash table, the query algorithm traverses where it might appear and returns the result. Its detail is shown in Algorithm 2. The query and insert steps are very similar, and we only list the query logic of the algorithms. Replace lines 9–20 in Algorithm 1 with Algorithm 2 to count the complete query algorithm.

Algorithm 2. Query of TopKmer Counter

1: **if** $HT[i][p].key == curKey$ **then**
2:    **if** $HT[i][p].value < 0$ **then**
3:       return 1;
4:    **else**
5:       return $HT[i][p].value$;
6:    **end if**
7: **end if**
8: return 0;

We consider the ones marked as negative as low confidence k-mer and the rest as high confidence k-mer. The distribution of k-mers depends on sequencing quality. The high confidence k-mers are not easily replaced because of their high frequency, while low confidence k-mers multiple replacements may occur. So values for low confidence k-mers are not practical as a direct result and are treated as 1.

4   Parallel K-Mer Counting Framework

From fastq files to distributed k-mer counting tables, four basic steps are required: file read, k-mer disassembly from short-read sequences and redirection, exchange k-mers via communication, and insertion of hash tables. We introduce algorithm 3, which is the workflow of TopKmer, and is optimized in terms of communication load balancing on Tianhe II TH-express 2 [18].

The TopKmer working framework is a hybrid parallel algorithm on MPI-OpenMP. In line 1, we split the file into P blocks and distribute them to P processes for parallel reads, where P is the number of processes. In lines 2–7, we launch multiple threads, and each thread fetches a part of a file block to disassemble k-mers.

Algorithm 3. TopKmer workflow

Input:
    Number of nodes P
    Node id I for current node
Output:
    TopKmer Counter CT
1: Read a block of file into $rawData$
2: **for all** threads in parallel **do**
3:      **for all** $kmer$ in a piece of $rawData$ **do**
4:          Push $kmer$ into corresponding $sendBuffer$
5:          Update $hyperloglog$
6:      **end for**
7: **end for**
8: Global communicate and determine the $hyperloglog$ estimates
9: Set the hash table size according to the estimated value
10: **for** $p \leftarrow I$ to $I + P$ **do**
11:     Non-blocking send $sendBuffer[p\%P]$
12: **end for**
13: Non-blocking receive $recvBuf[(p+1)\%2]$ from node I itself
14: **for** $p \leftarrow I$ to $I + P$ **do**
15:     Wait non-blocking receive to complete
16:     Non-blocking receive $recvBuf[(p+1)\%2]$ from node $(p+1)\%P$
17:     **for all** threads in parallel **do**
18:         **for all** $kmer$ in $recvBuf[p\%2]$ **do**
19:             Insert $kmer$ into HT
20:         **end for**
21:     **end for**
22: **end for**

The size of the hash table for TopKmer is required to be predefined. Hyperloglog++ [8] provides the ability to accurately estimate the number of k-mers with a small estimating list. It maintains a list, thus allowing the estimation to be updated in real-time when traversing $rawData$, allowing multiple Hyperloglog lists to be merged. Line 5 represents its use to fit the multilevel parallel algorithm, and each thread has a separate Hyperloglog list. Line 8 contains three steps. First, all processes reduce the hyperloglog lists in multiple threads into process-level lists. Communication via *Allgather* reduces the process-level lists into a consistent list and finally computes a consistent estimate.

Lines 10–23 are the optimization strategies based on the Tianhe-2 communication architecture, which supplies high bi-directional bandwidth by fat-tree architecture. Using two receive buffers in rotation allows the next batch of data to be received while the current is processing. Each process receives data from itself because it has no communication delay and does not consume I/O bandwidth. Then the data sources received by each process, in turn, are staggered so that in an ideal state, only one receiving and one sending are performed simultaneously, thus achieving communication load balancing as shown in Fig. 2.

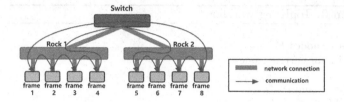

Fig. 2. Load balanced communication policy.

5 Results

5.1 Experiment Setup

We have done all our experiments on the Tianhe-2. One compute node in Tianhe-2 has 2 Intel Ivy Bridge CPUs, each with 12 cores and 32GB of memory, for 24 cores and 64GB of memory. For comparison experiments, some counters can only align the number of processes at 2^n, so we use 16 cores per node. We requested up to 128 nodes with 2048 cores for our experiments.

Table 1. Experimental datasets used for all evaluations.

Id	File count	Size (GB)	Source	Accession
R1	1	2.9	NCBI	SRP072055
R2	11	13.8	NCBI	SRP004241
R3	3	54.3	NCBI	SRP003680
R4	3	174.1	NCBI	SRP003680

The datasets we chose are shown in Table 1. For comparison experiments we chose Robinhood hashing from Pan [17] and SWAPCounter [5]. Robinhood hashing is a high-performance strategy that is cache-friendly and query efficient. It is a benchmark for state-of-the-art high performance distributed k-mer counter. Our goal is not to outperform it but to keep a minimal memory footprint with comparable performance. Swapcounter completes k-mer counting with low memory usage through the Count-min Sketch filter and then saves high-frequency k-mer into a hash table. We want our work to have better performance and scalability than SWAPCounter. Our figures use RH as short for Robinhood hashing, TK as short for our work TopKmer, and SC as short for SWAPCounter.

5.2 Quality of Counting

The quality of counters is closely related to their size. We use the memory footprint as a benchmark to compare the difference in counting quality to two other counters with similar memory footprints. TopKmer is a key-value pair counting without false positives. We choose to insert the k-mers of R1 into the counter and query one million of them to check the false negatives and counting accuracy.

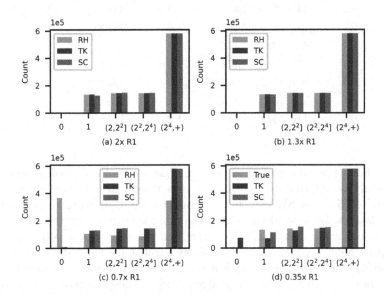

Fig. 3. Distribution of k-mers at varying memory footprint.

Our results are shown in Fig. 3, representing counter quality at different memory footprints, offering TopKmer's excellent performance in the extreme memory footprint. We list the counter query results from $2\times$, $1.3\times$, $0.7\times$, and $0.35\times$ R1 file sizes. To avoid the Robinhood hash table's insertion failure at too small memory, we discard the extra k-mer. All three hash tables perform well at (a) $2\times$ and (b) $1.3\times$. However, in (c) $0.7\times$, Robinhood hashing fails because many k-mers cannot be inserted and thus discarded. In (d) $0.35\times$, we compare the difference between TopKmer and SWAPCounter, where TopKmer dumps the untrustworthy k-mer, thus improving the credibility of the high-frequency k-mer. SWAPCounter cannot judge, leading to obvious false positives for high-frequency k-mers. In conclusion, if k-mers in $(4, +\infty)$ interval is required to be counted at the error rate less than 2‰, TopKmer's workable memory footprint is **54%** of Robinhood's and **70%** of SWAPCounter's.

5.3   Performance Comparison

Table 2. Performance

Dataset	Tool	Cores	Insert (S)	Query(S)	Mem usage (GB)
R2	RH	256	9.0	2.1	2.6
R2	SC	256	12.1	8.7	4.3
R2	TK	256	8.8	2.1	3.6
R3	RH	256	42.3	1.6	292.8
R3	SC	256	43.2	7.7	171.5
R3	TK	256	37.0	1.9	147.2
R4	RH	512	79.2	1.2	327.5
R4	SC	512	97.7	5.1	190.1
R4	TK	512	73.7	1.2	163.4

Table 2 shows that our performance is comparable to Robinhood hashing and significantly better than SWAPCounter in a variety of datasets. We speed up **1.7×** and **4.25×** over SWAPCounter in inserting and querying, respectively, on the R2 dataset. Because of the use of communication-computation overlapping, the communication delay has little impact on the algorithm's performance, so the improvement is significant for massively parallel and small datasets cases. In addition, to count high-frequency k-mers, SWAPCounter needs to insert a large amount of data into the hash table again, and all these operations significantly degrade the insertion performance. TopKmer circumvents these effects and significantly outperforms SWAPCounter in insertion and query performance.

The time overhead of TopKmer is linearly related to the size of the dataset, but the size of the counter is not significantly related to the file size. The counter size depends mainly on the number of unique k-mers. If there is a large dataset size with many duplicate k-mers, the dataset is high quality and does not require a too large counter to complete the statistics. The estimation function in the TopKmer workflow estimates the data size well and thus successfully predicts its counter size.

5.4   Scaling Capability

We used R4 as our experimental subject. Sixteen threads per node are used for Robinhood and TopKmer. We scale up to 128 nodes, i.e., a maximum of 2048 cores.

The experimental results are shown in Fig. 4. In terms of parallel efficiency, we still achieved good results. SWAPCounter is increasingly affected by communication delays as the number of processes increases, so its parallel efficiency gradually decreases. Compared to Robinhood, TopKmer still has some scalability

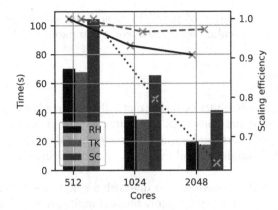

Fig. 4. Scaling experiments using 512 to 2048 cores on R4

improvements. Mainly, TopKmer is insensitive to collisions in the insertion algorithm. As parallelism increases and the hash table is refined, a slightly uneven distribution can significantly affect the performance of Robinhood.

5.5 Time Consumption Analysis

We use R4 and 512-2048 cores for the time overhead analysis. In this step, we add k-mer splitting and estimating into account to further analyze the factors affecting their parallel efficiency.

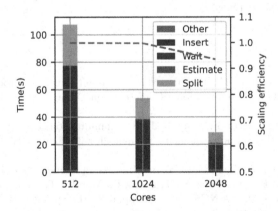

Fig. 5. Time consumption in each step on R4

According to the flow designed in Section III, the time overhead of all steps is shown in Fig. 5, except file I/O, which is not in our optimization scope. Except for a small number of non-parallelizable communication parts, the remaining steps maintain a high degree of parallelism, and the overall parallel efficiency stays above 95% when scaling up to 2048 cores compared to 512 cores.

6   Conclusion

In recent years, multiple k-mer counting methods are already available. However, we have noticed that previous data structures have difficulty solving the high error rate caused by short-read sequences, either by taking up a lot of memory space, adding extra computational overhead, or introducing the problem of false positives.

This paper provides TopKmer, a framework for high-frequency k-mer counting. We combine the Space Saving algorithm and multi-layer hash table to design a k-mer statistical method with high efficiency and low memory usage. In addition, we optimize for various aspects such as communication and load balance to achieve a high-performance counter. The memory footprint is reduced by 50% compared to hash table structured counters. The insertion is improved by 1.3 times, and the query is 4.25 times compared to similarly structured counters. For a 174GB dataset on 2048 cores, insertion is done in 18 s, the query of 1G k-mers in 1 s, and the parallel efficiency is kept above 95%. Our work has achieved excellent results in terms of algorithmic innovation and performance.

Acknoledgments. Thanks to Gao Qianwen, Guo Jiangyu and Wang Yifeng for their encouragement and support. Thanks to the reviewers for their dedication to this paper.

NSFC: U1811461 the Major Program of Guangdong Basic and Applied Research: 2019B030302002 Supported by the Program for Guangdong Introducing Innovative and Entrepreneurial Teams under Grant NO. 2016ZT06D211. Guangdong Natural Science Foundation (2018B030312002).

References

1. Babcock, B., Olston, C.: Distributed top-k monitoring. In: Proceedings of the 2003 ACM SIGMOD International Conference on Management of Data, pp. 28–39 (2003)
2. Boisvert, S., Laviolette, F., Corbeil, J.: Ray: simultaneous assembly of reads from a mix of high-throughput sequencing technologies. J. Comput. Biol. **17**(11), 1519–1533 (2010)
3. Charikar, M., Chen, K., Farach-Colton, M.: Finding frequent items in data streams. In: Widmayer, P., Eidenbenz, S., Triguero, F., Morales, R., Conejo, R., Hennessy, M. (eds.) ICALP 2002. LNCS, vol. 2380, pp. 693–703. Springer, Heidelberg (2002). https://doi.org/10.1007/3-540-45465-9_59
4. Cormode, G., Muthukrishnan, S.: An improved data stream summary: the count-min sketch and its applications. J. Algorithms **55**(1), 58–75 (2005)
5. Ge, J., Meng, J., Guo, N., Wei, Y., Balaji, P., Feng, S.: Counting k-mers for biological sequences at large scale. Interdiscip. Sci. Comput. Life Sci. **12**(1), 99–108 (2020)

6. Georganas, E., et al.: Hipmer: an extreme-scale de novo genome assembler. In: SC 2015: Proceedings of the International Conference for High Performance Computing, Networking, Storage and Analysis, pp. 1–11. IEEE (2015)
7. Gibbons, P.B., Matias, Y.: New sampling-based summary statistics for improving approximate query answers. In: Proceedings of the 1998 ACM SIGMOD International Conference on Management of Data, pp. 331–342 (1998)
8. Heule, S., Nunkesser, M., Hall, A.: Hyperloglog in practice: algorithmic engineering of a state of the art cardinality estimation algorithm. In: Proceedings of the 16th International Conference on Extending Database Technology, pp. 683–692 (2013)
9. Li, D., et al.: Megahit v1 0: a fast and scalable metagenome assembler driven by advanced methodologies and community practices. Methods **102**, 3–11 (2016)
10. Li, Y., Kamousi, P., Han, F., Yang, S., Yan, X., Suri, S.: Memory efficient minimum substring partitioning. Proc. VLDB Endow. **6**(3), 169–180 (2013)
11. Li, Y., et al.: MSPKmerCounter: a fast and memory efficient approach for k-mer counting. arXiv preprint arXiv:1505.06550 (2015)
12. Manku, G.S., Motwani, R.: Approximate frequency counts over data streams. In: VLDB 2002: Proceedings of the 28th International Conference on Very Large Databases, pp. 346–357. Elsevier (2002)
13. Marçais, G., Kingsford, C.: A fast, lock-free approach for efficient parallel counting of occurrences of k-mers. Bioinformatics **27**(6), 764–770 (2011)
14. Melsted, P., Pritchard, J.K.: Efficient counting of k-mers in DNA sequences using a bloom filter. BMC Bioinform. **12**(1), 1–7 (2011)
15. Misra, J., Gries, D.: Finding repeated elements. Sci. Comput. Program. **2**(2), 143–152 (1982)
16. Pan, T., Flick, P., Jain, C., Liu, Y., Aluru, S.: Kmerind: A flexible parallel library for k-mer indexing of biological sequences on distributed memory systems. IEEE/ACM Trans. Comput. Biol. Bioinf. **16**(4), 1117–1131 (2017)
17. Pan, T.C., Misra, S., Aluru, S.: Optimizing high performance distributed memory parallel hash tables for DNA k-mer counting. In: SC18: International Conference for High Performance Computing, Networking, Storage and Analysis, pp. 135–147. IEEE (2018)
18. Pang, Z., et al.: The TH express high performance interconnect networks. Front. Comp. Sci. **8**(3), 357–366 (2014)
19. Zhang, Q., Pell, J., Canino-Koning, R., Howe, A.C., Brown, C.T.: These are not the k-mers you are looking for: efficient online k-mer counting using a probabilistic data structure. PLoS ONE **9**(7), e101271 (2014)

Flexible Supervision System: A Fast Fault-Tolerance Strategy for Cloud Applications in Cloud-Edge Collaborative Environments

Weilin Cai[1], Heng Chen[1(✉)], Zhimin Zhuo[2], Ziheng Wang[1], and Ninggang An[1]

[1] Xi'an Jiaotong University, Xi'an 710049, China
hengchen@xjtu.edu.cn
[2] Beijing Institute of Electronic System Engineering, Beijing 100854, China

Abstract. With the development of cloud-edge collaborative computing technology, more and more cloud applications are transferred to edge devices. Some cloud applications in relatively unstable edge scenarios put forward higher requirements for fault tolerance. Therefore, we design and implement a flexible supervision system. The system provides a higher frequency of fault detection than existing cloud management platforms like Kubernetes. And It implements a more efficient checkpoint-restart fault handling scheme based on the distributed in-memory database. Meanwhile, we also consider minimizing the extra time costs caused by the fault-tolerance operations and saving cloud system resources including computing, storage, and network.

Keywords: Cloud computing · Fault-tolerance strategy · Flexible supervision system · Fault detection · Checkpoint restart

1 Introduction

In recent years, cloud computing technology has developed and matured rapidly, gradually forming increasingly large and complex cloud computing environment. Cloud computing tasks gradually spread out from traditional cloud computing centers to edge devices, forming the cloud-edge collaborative environment. Because of the unstable environment of edge devices, edge cloud nodes may face a higher failure probability than central cloud nodes.

Currently, there are many fault handling strategies in the cloud computing environment [1], including retry, checkpoint-restart, and replication. Each approach has advantages and disadvantages. In addition to fault handling strategy, fault detection is also an essential part of fault tolerance.

We design and implement a flexible supervisor system to achieve fault-tolerance of specific cloud applications in a large-scale cloud-edge collaborative environment. Its core is to solve two problems: 1. How to detect cloud application failures as quickly as possible? 2. How to continue the previous execution after the fault is detected?

© IFIP International Federation for Information Processing 2022
Published by Springer Nature Switzerland AG 2022
S. Liu and X. Wei (Eds.): NPC 2022, LNCS 13615, pp. 108–113, 2022.
https://doi.org/10.1007/978-3-031-21395-3_10

First, the system achieves faster fault discovery through high-frequency heartbeat detection among cloud nodes. Then, it saves application-level checkpoints in the distributed in-memory database to implement the checkpoint restart after discovering the fault.

Moreover, to minimize the extra time costs caused by the fault-tolerance operations, we propose an asynchronous double-buffer checkpoint scheme that automatically balances network transmission speed and checkpoint generation speed. In the real network test sample, the asynchronous double-buffer scheme reduces the extra time costs of fault tolerance by 95.8%. The application-level checkpoint we implemented is based on the original local checkpoint provided by Torch, so this scheme can be applied to other PyTorch model training as well.

2   Flexible Supervision System Architecture

As shown in Fig. 1, we establish a regional system in the cloud-edge environment to achieve fault tolerance for the specified cloud application. The flexible supervision system, which consists of a reliable distributed in-memory database, task manager, task executor, and task supervisor. And the deployment of the system has different scheduling algorithms and different configurations.

A reliable distributed in-memory database is the core of the flexible supervision system. Both the executor and supervisor need to establish a contact channel with it. In real cloud-edge scenarios, we would consider deploying it on secure servers, such as central cloud nodes or some reliable edge nodes.

The task manager acts as the interface to the cloud applications requests and schedules the deployment of executors and supervisors on cloud nodes.

The Task executor performs the actual computation. It can generate checkpoints and store them in the database during execution.

The task supervisor is responsible for monitoring whether the executor is alive. It holds the application container image and starts the container when discovers the executor's exception. It can download the checkpoint from the database and continues the previous execution. The supervisor needs to be deployed on a different cloud node than the executor, and a single supervisor can monitor multiple executors of different tasks at the same time.

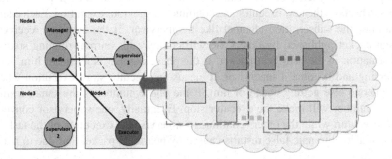

Fig. 1. The schematic diagram of building the flexible supervision system and the system architecture in a cloud-edge environment.

3 Fault Detection and Fault-Tolerance Strategy

Publish-Subscribe Heartbeat Detection. We design a publish-subscribe heartbeat detection mechanism based on Redis distributed in-memory database to achieve fault detection. The executor and supervisor of the same cloud application subscribe to the same channel. The executor will regularly publish heartbeat packets in the channel. And the supervisor will know whether the executor is abnormal by monitoring heartbeat packets in the channel.

The heartbeat packet contains three pieces of information: phase number, execution time, and sequence number. The phase number marks the recent phase that the executor has completed and saved successfully. It can also meet the requirements of some applications to store checkpoints for each phase, which can be retrieved from the database by the phase number index. The execution time indicates the execution duration. The sequence number will be informed to each executor and supervisor by the manager at the time of deployment.

This publish-subscribe heartbeat detection makes it convenient to implement an optional and variable number of supervisors to monitor an executor. When the executor fails, multiple supervisors can be synchronized through the same channel and transformed to an executor or supervise the new executor.

Asynchronous Double-Buffering Checkpoint. Due to the limitation of network bandwidth, uploading checkpoints to the distributed database may cost a lot of time in real cloud environments. We propose an asynchronous double-buffering checkpoint scheme, which can makes full use of network bandwidth to asynchronously upload checkpoints while ensuring the normal execution speed.

We use double checkpoint data buffers to prevent data conflict between the main process and the upload thread. When the upload thread discovers that there is updated checkpoint data in the buffer, it will package the data as a checkpoint and upload it. The main process avoids the uploading buffer and uses another buffer to store new checkpoint data.

Restart Process. Each supervisor maintains his own heartbeat countdown, which is refreshed each time a heartbeat packet is received. Once the countdown is over, the supervisor starts the cloud application container and downloads the checkpoint from the database. Then the supervisor becomes the new executor to continue the computation.

We propose a synchronization scheme to keep only one supervisor with the fastest progress to become the new executor and continue the previous execution. Each executor will monitor the subscription channel like a supervisor. If the executor receives the heartbeat packet published by others, he will compare his current running state with the information in the heartbeat packet. If the phase number is ahead of him, he will stop running and become a supervisor. It means an executor stops execution when he finds someone else getting ahead of him. If the phase number is the same, a smaller sequence number will make the executor stop. Eventually, one supervisor converts to the new executor, while the others continue to supervise the execution of the task. This design can also eliminate false restarts caused by heartbeat packet loss due to network fluctuations.

4 Experimental Evaluation

We implement object detection and model training cloud application based on Yolov5 to test our Flexible Supervision fault-tolerance system. We deploy cloud nodes within 30 km of Xi'an city, and the test is based on the real network environment.

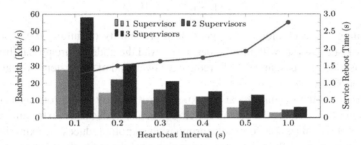

Fig. 2. The line indicates the service reboot time with different heartbeat detection intervals. And the bars indicate the network bandwidth occupied by heartbeat detection with a different number of supervisors.

Compared to the minimum interval of health check provided by Kubernetes, which can only be set to 1s, we have achieved a shorter interval of heartbeat detection. Figure 2 shows that the service reboot time is shortened by shortening the heartbeat interval. However, due to the fluctuation in the real network environment, high-frequency heartbeat detection is faced with the problem of misjudgment failure. And higher heartbeat frequency and more supervisors both increase the network overhead.

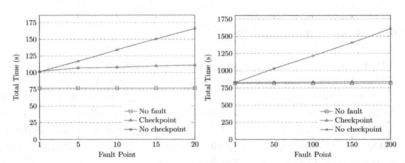

Fig. 3. In 20 and 200 iterations of model training, the total running time of normal operation without a fault and the total running time of handling a fault occurred at different phases with or without checkpoints.

We test the fault-tolerance effect of the checkpoint-restart mode on the Yolov5 model training cloud application. The training generates checkpoint data at the end of each iteration. And we use asynchronous checkpoints to automatically balance the speed of generation and transmission. As shown in Fig. 3, we test the total time costs of the case with no failure and the case that one failure occurs in different iterations.

The fault-tolerance reliability is related to the number of supervisors. The flexible supervision system ensures that a task can be completed as long as the executor or one of the supervisors is alive. If the failure probability of each cloud node is w and the number of supervisors corresponding to a task executor is s, the probability P that the task can be completed is:

$$P = (1 - w^{s+1}) \times 100\% \tag{1}$$

Assuming that each cloud node has a 30% probability of failure, it can achieve a 99.19% task success rate with three supervisors. And the node failure probability in real scenarios is much lower than 30%. To reduce the overhead of the system, we can choose fewer supervisors.

Compared to the original local checkpoint provided by Torch, our asynchronous checkpoint not only stores the data in the cloud but also reduces the extra time costs. In this real network test sample, our asynchronous checkpoint reduces the extra time costs of fault tolerance by 95.8% compared to our non-asynchronous checkpoint.

5   Related Work

As a widely used fault-tolerance method, the checkpoint is used to periodically back up the running state of the program. After the program fails, it can recover to the last running state by reading the checkpoint data. Due to the extra time and storage costs of checkpoints, there are many related types of research on checkpoint optimization for different scenarios and applications [2, 3]. With the development of cloud computing, fault-tolerance technologies in the past are gradually migrated to the cloud environment for integration and innovation [4, 5].

6   Conclusions and Future Work

We aim to provide a fault-tolerance strategy to solve the high availability problem of cloud applications in a cloud-edge collaborative environment. Therefore, we set up a regional flexible supervision system in the large-scale cloud environment to achieve the fault tolerance of specified cloud applications. In the future, we will further improve each detail of the system. And we are considering more convenient automated deployment and management. In addition, we will also consider improving this strategy as a plugin for cloud management platforms such as Kubernetes.

Acknowledgments. The work described in this paper was supported in part by the Key Basic Research Program of the China Basic Strengthening Program (2019-JCJQ-ZD-041).

References

1. Neto, J.P.A., Pianto, D.M., Ralha, C.G.: MULTS: a multi-cloud fault-tolerant architecture to manage transient servers in cloud computing. J. Syst. Archit. **101**, 101651 (2019)

2. Nakamura, J., Kim, Y., Katayama, Y., Masuzawa, M.: A cooperative partial snapshot algorithm for checkpoint-rollback recovery of large-scale and dynamic distributed systems and experimental evaluations. Concurr. Comput. Pract. Exp. **33**(12) (2021)
3. Tang, X., Zhai, J., Yu, B., Chen, W., Zheng, W., Li, K.: An efficient in-memory checkpoint method and its practice on fault-tolerant HPL. IEEE Trans. Parallel Distrib. Syst. **29**(4), 758–771 (2018)
4. Zhao, J., Xiang, Y., Lan, T., Huang, H.H., Subramaniam, S.: Elastic reliability optimization through peer-to-peer checkpointing in cloud computing. IEEE Trans. Parallel Distrib. Syst. **30**(4), 897–909 (2019)
5. Sinha, B., Singh, A.K., Saini, P.: A hybrid approach towards reduced checkpointing overhead in cloud-based applications. Peer-to-Peer Networking Appl. **15**(1), 473–483 (2021). https://doi.org/10.1007/s12083-021-01230-2

Adjust: An Online Resource Adjustment Framework for Microservice Programs

Lin Wang[1], Tianyuan Huang[1(✉)], Shichao Geng[2], Donghua Li[1], Xiaomin Zhu[3], and Huaxiang Zhang[1]

[1] School of Information Science and Engineering, Shandong Normal University, Jinan, China
tianyuanhuang@hotmail.com
[2] School of Journalism and Communication, Shandong Normal University, Jinan, China
[3] Shandong Institute of Big Data, Jinan, China
zhuxiaomin@sdibd.cn

Abstract. The categories of programs running in data centers are changing from the traditional monolithic program to loosely coupled microservice programs. Microservice programs are easy to update and can facilitate software heterogeneity. However, microservice programs have more stringent performance requirements. Estimating the resource requirements of each service becomes the key point to ensuring the QoS of the microservice programs. In this paper, we propose a QoS-aware framework Adjust for microservice programs. Adjust establishes a neural network-based microservice QoS prediction model. Moreover, Adjust identifies the causes of the abnormality of microservice programs, and determines performance assurance strategies on both system and microservice levels. By dynamically adjusting the resource allocation, Adjust can effectively guarantee the performance of microservice programs and improves system resource utilization at the same time.

Keywords: Microservices · QoS-aware framework · Resource allocation

1 Introduction

Nowadays, data centers are hosting various application programs [1, 2]. Most programs have to maintain expected availability while undergoing frequent update deployments. In order to deal with this issue, the design of data center applications has been evolving from the traditional monolithic application architectures to the single-purpose, loosely-coupled microservices architectures. Microservice programs are highly flexible and can offer a certain degree of availability and scalability. However, they also face new challenges. First, the performance requirements to microservice programs are more stringent. Second, each microservice has different resource requirements to fulfill its function, over-provisioning resource has no help to further improve performance but wasting resources. Therefore, ensuring the QoS of microservice programs while keeping high resource utilization is challenging [3].

S. Liu and X. Wei (Eds.): NPC 2022, LNCS 13615, pp. 114–119, 2022.
https://doi.org/10.1007/978-3-031-21395-3_11

The way to ensure the QoS of the microservice program is to accurately allocate the required resources to the microservices through characteristic metrics. In order to show a complex relationship between characteristic indicators and the performance of microservice programs, this paper proposes Adjust, a microservice QoS-aware framework capable of learning and utilizing this complex relationship. Adjust is composed of three components: Microservice Analyzer (MSA), Microservice Performance Prediction Model (MSPM) and Microservice Performance Guarantor (MSPG). Adjust uses MSA to obtain the runtime data of the program and passes the data to MSPM for predicting the program performance. MSPM further estimates the resource requirements of each microservice and judges the cause of possible QoS violation. Then MSPG dynamically allocates the required resources for each microservice. We compare Adjust with four other performance guarantee frameworks. Under the maximum load, Adjust can still effectively guarantee the QoS of microservice programs and improve system resource utilization.

2 A QoS Awareness Framework for Microservices

We adopt the neural network as an approach to build the performance prediction model for microservice programs. The model is able to learn the relationship between characteristic indicators and performance, identify the cause of QoS violations, and allocate appropriate resources to the microservice program. Using this approach, we propose a microservice QoS-aware framework Adjust shown in Fig. 1.

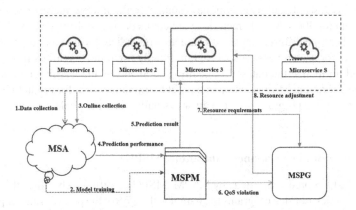

Fig. 1. A QoS awareness framework for microservice programs.

2.1 Microservice Analyzer (MSA)

The job of MSA is to collect the runtime data of each microservices for further analysis conducted by MSPM. MSA adopts the popular performance tools Perf and Docker stats to obtain the runtime data of the microservice programs on two levels [4]. The first level is the system level, the system level runtime event data such as Cache-misses, LLC-misses are collected. The second level is the microservice level, the microservice runtime event data such as CPU usage, Mem usage are collected.

2.2 Microservice Prediction Model (MSPM)

The performance prediction model for microservice programs is built by means of the basic neural network. The neural network model is powerful in capturing the relationship between microservice program performance and the input data. The output of the model is the predicted performance, that is, QoS of the program. In addition, we enrich the diversity of the dataset by different resource configurations. MSPM receives the input dataset and builds up the neural network-based model to reveal the complex relationship between the QoS of the microservice program and the input data.

Model Input and Output. To accurately predict the performance of microservice programs, we select a set of highly correlated characteristic indicators that can cover different levels of runtime characteristic. The input to the model chosen by our study includes both system-level and microservice-level information, which can fully cover and accurately describe the runtime characteristics of the microservice programs. The output of the model is the predicted performance, that is, QoS of the program.

Model Train. A rich dataset is the key point for training a successful prediction model. We enrich the diversity of the dataset by different resource configurations. Various combinations of core limit, main clock frequency and the request load are used to generate the training dataset. Under each unique resource configuration, the microservice program will run for 300 s. The characteristic indicators data are collected at fixed sampling intervals. Then, the different levels of characteristic indicators are combined to form an input dataset for each microservice program.Finally, we remove outliers from the input dataset and normalize the dataset. In addition, MSPM sets the learning parameters for training optimization. MSPM uses this dataset to train the model for predicting the QoS of the microservice program until the error is smaller than the predetermined value.

2.3 Microservice Performance Guarantor (MSPG)

Based on the QoS prediction made by MSPM, MSPG can effectively adjust the resource allocation to microservice programs to guarantee the QoS of the program and improve the system resources utilization. Next, we will introduce the microservices QoS assurance strategy in detail.

We define the basic concepts of a microservices QoS guarantee strategy. The QoS prediction value (i.e., the average latency) given by MSPM is defined as pre_QoS. The expected QoS of the microservice program is tar_QoS. The ratio of pre_QoS to tar_QoS is defined as the satisfaction rate st, as shown in Eq. 1.

$$st = pre\_QoS / tar\_QoS \tag{1}$$

A st value smaller than 1 means the predicted average latency is smaller than the expected average latency, the QoS is satisfied. Since the QoS of the microservice program is determined by the resource available, st really reflects the resource condition of the program. According to the value of st, MSPG divides the resource condition of the microservice program into three categories: abundant (sufficient resources), proper (moderate demand for resources), and urgent (urgent need for resources).

$$
resource\ condition = \begin{cases} abundant, & st \leq 0.8 \\ proper, & 0.8 < st \leq 1 \\ urgent, & st > 1 \end{cases} . \tag{2}
$$

The performance guarantee strategies are performed in three cases according to the program resource condition.

Case 1: When the resource condition is abundant, it indicates that the microservice program runs with a high resource configuration. So MSPG can use the resource recollect strategy to reclaim some resources and select a lower resource configuration that does not affect the QoS. The operation of the resource reclaim strategy is as follows: MSPG first reduces the main clock frequency step by step. When the clock frequency is at its lowest possible, MSPG reduces the number of cores allocated, started with one core, then more. After recollecting some resources, MSPG re-calculates the satisfaction rate st and evaluates the effect of resource re-collection.

Case 2: When the resource condition is proper, it indicates the microservice program is executing with an appropriate resource configuration. MSPG does not perform any actions.

Case 3: When the resource condition is urgent, it indicates the expected QoS of the microservice program is violated. MSPG has to examine the cause of the QoS violation. The first thing is to check whether the QoS violation is caused by the lack of resources or the microservice failure. MSPG retrieves the optimal resource configuration under the current request load from SRS, uses the optimal configuration to adjust the number of cores and main clock frequency, and then retrieves st again. If st now becomes smaller than 0.8, we can judge that the QoS violation is caused by lack of resources. If st is still larger than 0.8, it means that providing adequate resource cannot solve the QoS problem. We can get the conclusion that the QoS violation is caused by the failure of one or more microservices in this case. The MSPG takes the microservices with the greatest impact on QoS as bottlenecks and determines the root cause of the QoS violation.

3 Evaluation

Adjust is evaluated against four other performance guarantors to verify its effectiveness in resource allocation. The performance guarantors are Base, C_cpu, Heras, and Parts. Base does not perform resource adjustment so it is only a reference for base performance in comparison. C_cpu is a simple resource scaler that scales resources based on the CPU utilization of the key microservices. Heras and Parts borrow methods from Heracles and Parties respectively [5, 6]. They are task managers for latency-sensitive programs and batch programs. We made some adjustments to them based on the available documentation so as to adapt them to the microservice programs.

3.1 Performance Guarantee

Figure 2 shows the average latency of the microservice programs under different Performance Guarantors. When the request load reaches the maximum load level, the performance of the Base is the worst because its does not perform resource adjustment. Heras, Parts show good results, but they always supply microservices with the maximum resources. However, for C_cpu the QoS is not improved, for example, in the case when MediaService running with the maximum load. As shown in the figure, Adjust achieves the best average latency, which is 41% better than C_cpu, 18.6% better than Heras, and 25.45% better than Parts. Adjust can more accurately predict the execution performance, identify the bottleneck microservices, and tune the resource configuration for individual microservices.

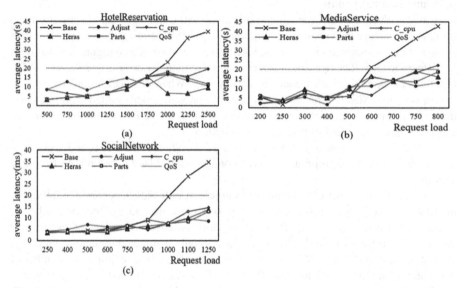

Fig. 2. The average latency of microservice programs under different performance guarantors.

3.2 Resource Re-collection

In this experiment, to express the usage of resources more accurately, the whole system resources are standardized up to 100%. Figure 3 shows the resource usage of the microservice programs under different Performance Guarantors. When the request load is low, Adjust reduces the resource usage of SocialNetwork from 60% to 30% while ensuring its QoS. Compared with other Performance Guarantors, Adjust can reclaim at least 17.28% of excessive idle resources, effectively reducing the waste of resources. When the request load is high, the resource usage of Adjust is about 25% higher than the Base because Base does not perform any resource adjustment and never increase resource provision for programs. However, Adjust reduces the resource usage by an average of 10.25% compared with other Performance Guarantors, which effectively improves the system resource utilization.

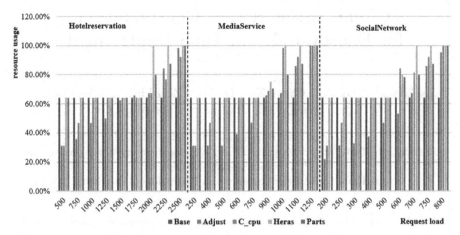

Fig. 3. The resource usage of the microservice program under different performance guarantees.

4 Conclusion

In this paper, we propose Adjust, a QoS-aware framework customized for microservice programs. A performance prediction model is established, and MSPG utilizes the performance prediction result to adjusts the resources for individual microservices and ensures the overall QoS of the microservice program. Experiment results show that Adjust can effectively enhance the QoS of microservice programs and effectively improve resource utilization.

References

1. Yadav, R., Zhang, W., Li, K., Liu, C., Laghari, A.A.: Managing overloaded hosts for energy-efficiency in cloud data centers. Clust. Comput. **24**(3), 2001–2015 (2021). https://doi.org/10.1007/s10586-020-03182-3
2. Kannan, R.S., Jain, A., Laurenzano, M.A., et al.: Proctor: detecting and investigating interference in shared datacenters. IEEE International Symposium on Performance Analysis of Systems and Software (ISPASS), pp. 76–86 (2018)
3. Guo, J., et al.: Who limits the resource efficiency of my datacenter: an analysis of Alibaba datacenter traces. In: Proceedings of the International Symposium on Quality of Service (IWQoS 2019). Association for Computing Machinery, pp. 1–10 (2019)
4. Mackenzie, J.M.: Managing tail latency in large scale information retrieval systems. SIGIR Forum **54**(1), 1–2 (2021). Article 18
5. Lo, D., Cheng, L., Govindaraju, R., Ranganathan, P., Kozyrakis, C.: Improving Resource Efficiency at Scale with Heracles. ACM Trans. Comput. Syst. **34**(2), 1–33 (2016). Article 6
6. Chen, S., Delimitrou, C., Martínez, J.F.: PARTIES: QoS-Aware resource partitioning for multiple interactive services. In: Proceedings of the Twenty-Fourth International Conference on Architectural Support for Programming Languages and Operating Systems. Association for Computing Machinery, pp. 107–120 (2019)

Cloud-Native Server Consolidation for Energy-Efficient FaaS Deployment

Lu Zhang[1], Yifei Pu[1], Cheng Xu[1], Du Liu[1], Zeyi Lin[1], Xiaofeng Hou[3],
Pu Yang[2], Shang Yue[2], Chao Li[1(✉)], and Minyi Guo[1]

[1] Shanghai Jiao Tong University, Shanghai, China
{luzhang,pkq2006,jerryxu}@sjtu.edu.cn, {lichao,guo-my}@cs.sjtu.edu.cn
[2] Tencent, Shenzhen, China
[3] The Hong Kong University of Science and Technology, Hong Kong, China

Abstract. The lack of function-oriented power management scheme has seriously hindered the serverless platform's cost efficiency. In this paper, we analyze the invocation pattern of serverless functions and investigate its implications on server energy efficiency. Rather than using a one-size-fits-all strategy, we propose DAC, a software-hardware co-design solution to offer differentiated cloud-native server consolidation. We build a proof-of-concept framework and show that DAC can improve the energy efficiency of tail function deployment by up to 23%.

Keywords: Serverless · Tail functions · Cloud-native consolidation

1 Introduction

In recent years, Function as a Service (FaaS) has attracted considerable attention due to its easy application deployment. To mitigate the overhead of cold start, most FaaS providers adopt a *keep-alive* policy [4,5]. However, Existing scheduling frameworks either deploy functions on servers with idle resources or activate a new server. This often leads to poor data center energy proportionality, due to the significant static power consumption. In addition, functions incur various invocation interval time(IIT) [3]. We refer to functions that can be kept in memory for frequent invocation as *native functions*. However, there are functions that seldom invoke which we call them as *tail functions*. The different IIT of functions bring challenges for optimizing energy efficiency of FaaS infrastructure.

A key insight driving our work is that energy-efficient consolidation scheme should distinguish tail functions from native functions. First, reserving computing resources for tail functions would waste energy. Second, mixing tail functions with native functions causes more servers alive for native functions, thus increasing static power. Thus, it is necessary to treat tail functions differently.

Enlightened by the above observations, in this paper we envision *cloud-native server consolidation* to explore differentiated function management. We maximally consolidate native functions on server cores with the keep-alive policy.

© IFIP International Federation for Information Processing 2022
Published by Springer Nature Switzerland AG 2022
S. Liu and X. Wei (Eds.): NPC 2022, LNCS 13615, pp. 120–126, 2022.
https://doi.org/10.1007/978-3-031-21395-3_12

Meanwhile, we opportunistically map tail functions on cores that run native functions. Although modern scale-out architecture has strict power limits for sustained workload, activating more computing resources for a very short time will not cause significant thermal/overloading issues [1,2]. Short-lived tail functions are well-suited to take advantage of this opportunity. To ensure high performance, we should also treat tail functions differently since some tail functions can still benefit from warm start while some tail functions cannot.

We devise *DAC* (*differentiate and consolidate*), a novel load management strategy for cloud-native server consolidation. First, *DAC* adopts a two-level classifier to classify functions. The first-level classifier aims to distinguish native functions from tail functions. The second-level classifier further identifies the power-performance sensitivity for native functions and the invocation pattern for tail functions. Second, *DAC* uses a consolidation controller to adaptively invoke tail functions. It works to optimize the energy efficiency of servers.

This paper makes the following contributions:

- We classify serverless functions as native or tail functions according to their IIT and discuss the key design considerations of functions' consolidation.
- We propose *DAC*, a novel cloud-native server consolidation strategy that can deploy functions in an energy-efficient way.
- We demonstrate that *DAC* can achieve the efficiency improvement of tail function deployment up to 23% by extensive experiments.

2   Key Design Considerations

Function Invocation Patterns. We investigate invocation patterns from the perspective of invocation rates and invocation intervals using the data set from Azure Functions [3]. Some functions are invoked frequently and we term these functions as *native functions* which can be kept on dedicated servers to ensure warm start. Differently, there are also troublesome functions whose IIT is larger than the given keep-alive value. We refer to them as *tail functions* and the system cost of maintaining warm start for tail functions could be prohibitively high.

We show examples of native functions in Fig. 1(a). The IIT is smaller than 10 min, which implies that they can be invoked with warm start under the keep-alive policy. Differently, tail functions can be classified into two categories: *explicit tail functions* and *implicit tail functions*. As shown in Fig. 1(b), the IIT of explicit tail functions is clearly longer than 10 min where all functions would suffer from cold start. However, the implicit tail functions have an uncertain invocation pattern as shown in Fig. 1(c). It is not easy to identify whether functions will suffer from cold start or warm start. The existence of implicit tail functions makes function power management a challenging problem.

Limitations of Current Solutions. The current FaaS load management solutions largely ignore the invocation rate of functions. They deploy functions according to the given policy and the current status. There are two key issues:

1) They mix tail functions with native functions. In this case, native functions have to be put on other servers which introduces cold start overhead. 2) It tends to activate more servers to process functions with load balancing. Since servers are far from energy-proportionality, doing so will increase energy consumption.

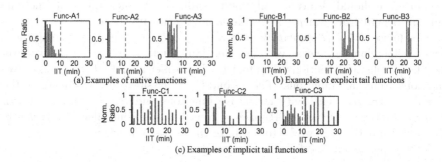

Fig. 1. The invocation interval time (IIT) of different Azure functions [3]

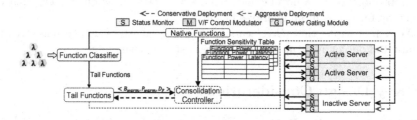

Fig. 2. Overview of the DAC design

We explore *cloud-native server consolidation* for tail functions, there are two deployment methods: *Aggressive Deployment* and *Conservative Deployment*.

Aggressive Deployment places tail functions with native functions. It faces two challenges. First, aggressive deployment would exceed the thermal/power constraint of servers. Servers must scale down the power level of cores, causing server-wide performance degradation. Second, due to the thermal limit, the chip can not support aggressive deployment for long time. Thus, incoming tail functions can not maintain the warm-start state.

Conservative Deployment has its merits. Native functions enjoy sufficient power budget for high performance. If tail functions are invoked successively, they can be deployed in the same server with warm start. The disadvantage of conservative deployment is that it increases the total energy consumption.

3   DAC Design

3.1   System Overview

Figure 2 gives an overview of the *DAC*. It consists of two main components to ensure efficient deployment of tail functions. The function classifier groups invoked functions into native or tail functions according to their IIT distribution. Meanwhile, a consolidation controller is used to coordinate the deployment of functions. The consolidation controller cooperates with a server-level power manager to robustly perform function consolidation. The controller monitors the status of servers and the collected information can be used to guide function deployment. The power manager can adjust server power consumption by activating/deactivating cores or manipulating the V/F levels of cores.

3.2   Function Classifier

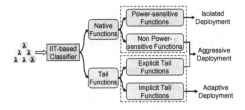

Fig. 3. *DAC* function classification

As shown in Fig. 3, the classifier further divides native functions into either *power-sensitive* and *non-power-sensitive* functions. We can opportunistically place tail functions to servers that run non-power-sensitive native functions. Power-sensitive native functions must be processed in an isolated way for high performance. We create a sensitivity table to store how power affects native functions' latency. Explicit tail functions can be deployed with native functions for energy saving purpose. Importantly, we need to carefully choose the deployment decision for implicit tail functions.

3.3   Consolidation Controller

The consolidation controller manage the status of native functions and opportunistically place tail functions with an adaptive algorithm. It requires two parameters to make the proper deployment decision for each function: 1) B_{warm}, the beneifts of functions' warm-start and 2) P_warm, the warm-start probability. B_{warm} is given by: $B_{warm} = \frac{D_{init}}{D_{total}}$, where D_{init} is functions' initialization time while D_{total} is the total duration. P_{warm} of each function is presented as $P_{warm} = \frac{Ivk_{warm}}{Ivk_{total}}$, where Ivk_{warm} is the frequency of invocations whose IIT is less than 10 min while Ivk_{total} is the total number of invocation.

The consolidation controller further utilizes an adaptive function deployment algorithm to deploy tail functions. The latency of functions is given by:

$$L_A = D_F, \qquad L_C = D_F * (P_{warm} * (1 - B_{warm}) + 1 - P_{warm})$$

where D_F is the duration of the function, L_A and L_C are the estimated latency of aggressive and conservative deployment. The system energy under the two methods is given by:

$$E_A = Power_{Dynamic} * L_A, \qquad E_C = Power_{total} * L_C$$

To identify the best trade-off between energy and performance, we use the metrics: $Eff = 1/(\alpha \frac{L_A}{L_C} + \beta \frac{E_A}{E_C})$. where α, β presents the importance of functions' latency and energy saving respectively $(\alpha + \beta = 1)$. If $Eff > 1$, it implies that the aggressive deployment is more energy-efficient and vice versa.

Table 1. The evaluated serverless functions

Function	Markdown	Img-resize	Sentiment	Ocr-img	Autocomplete	Matmul	Linpack	DD
Runtime	Python	Nodejs	Python	Nodejs	Nodejs	Python	Python	Python
B_{warm}	0.89	0.76	0.5	0.04	0.25	0.2	0.58	0.33

Table 2. Evaluated tail function pool

Tail function pool	Abbr.	Functions
Low Warm Ratio $(0 < B_{warm} < 0.3)$	LWR	ocr-img,matmul autocomplete
Medium Warm Ratio $(0.3 \leq B_{warm} < 0.65)$	MWR	dd, linpack sentiment
High Warm Ratio $(0.65 \leq B_{warm} < 1)$	HWR	img-resize markdown
Hybrid Function Pool $(0 < B_{warm} < 1)$	HFP	All functions combined

Table 3. Mixed function invocations

Case	Mixed functions
Case 1	LWR ($P=0$), MWR ($P=0.3$), HWR ($P=0.6$), HFP ($P=0.9$)
Case 2	LWR ($P=0.9$), MWR ($P=0$), HWR ($P=0.3$), HFP ($P=0.6$)
Case 3	LWR ($P=0.6$), MWR ($P=0.9$), HWR ($P=0$), HFP ($P=0.3$)
Case 4	LWR ($P=0.3$), MWR ($P=0.6$), HWR ($P=0.9$), HFP ($P=0$)

4 Evaluation

4.1 Methodologies

To validate and evaluate DAC under large-scale deployment, we implement a trace-driven evaluation framework. Our test bench takes realistic function execution trace as input. The information of tail functions is shown in Table 1. Tables 2 and 3 show various function pools (We use P as P_{warm} for brevity). We compare DAC with two deployment schemes: $PerFst$ and $EnerFst$. Like Open-Whisk, $PerFst$ deploys functions on individual servers for the best performance. Differently, $EnerFst$ applies aggressive deployment for tail functions to reduce the number of active servers which pursues energy saving [6].

4.2   Evaluation Results

Figure 4 shows the latency, energy and efficiency of different schemes. All results
are normalized to *PerFst* which yields the best performance. As seen in Fig. 4(a),
DAC achieves similar performance (up to 5% latency increase) under various
warm-start probability values.

As for energy (Fig. 4(b)), *DAC* consumes less energy than *PerFst*, but more
energy than *EnerFst* in some cases. When $P=0.9$ in MWR and $P=0.6/P=0.9$,
the latency of *EnerFst* could be very large. Although the dynamic power is
smaller than the total server power, significant latency degradation may neu-
tralize the benefits of power saving. Figure 4(c) shows the efficiency of different
schemes. *DAC* outperforms all other schemes.

In addition, we evaluate our design using hybrid function pools as shown in
Fig. 5. The efficiency of *DAC* outperforms *PerFst* by 18% when $P=0$ while the
improvement is 45% compared with *EnerFst* (when $P=0.9$).

We also investigate *DAC* under mixed functions shown Fig. 3. As shown in
Fig. 6, *DAC* achieves the best efficiency among all the evaluated schemes. On
average, *DAC* improve the efficiency by 6% and 23% compared to *PerFst* and
EnerFst, respectively. Although the latency of *DAC* is 2% larger than *PerFst*,
DAC can save 13% more energy. The high efficiency of *DAC* implies that it can
achieve a better design tradeoff between performance and energy.

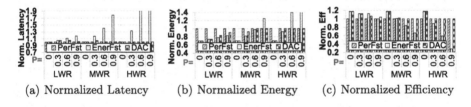

(a) Normalized Latency   (b) Normalized Energy   (c) Normalized Efficiency

Fig. 4. Comparison of different schemes under functions with different warm ratios

Fig. 5. Comparison of different
schemes under *HFP* (L:Latency,
E:Energy)

Fig. 6. Comparison of different
schemes under mixed function
invocation

5   Conclusion

To optimize the efficiency of FaaS infrastructure, we introduce cloud-native server consolidation and propose *DAC*. *DAC* differentiates functions according to invocation patterns and carefully consolidate tail functions. We hope that this paper can give insights to the design of energy-proportional FaaS platforms.

Acknowledgements. This work is supported in part by the National Natural Science Foundation of China (No. 61972247), and a Tencent Research Grant.

References

1. Esmaeilzadeh, H., Blem, E., Amant, R.S., Sankaralingam, K., Burger, D.: Dark silicon and the end of multicore scaling. In: ISCA, pp. 365–376 (2011)
2. Hou, X., Hao, L., Li, C., Chen, Q., Zheng, W., Guo, M.: Power grab in aggressively provisioned data centers: what is the risk and what can be done about it. In: ICCD, pp. 26–34 (2018)
3. Shahrad, M., et al.: Serverless in the wild: characterizing and optimizing the serverless workload at a large cloud provider. In: ATC, pp. 205–218 (2020)
4. Shilkov, M.: Cold starts in AWS lambda (2021)
5. Shilkov, M.: Cold starts in azure functions (2021)
6. Zhang, L., et al.: Tapping into NFV environment for opportunistic serverless edge function deployment. IEEE Trans. Comput. **71**(10), 2698–2704 (2021)

Deep Learning

NeuProMa: A Toolchain for Mapping Large-Scale Spiking Convolutional Neural Networks onto Neuromorphic Processor

Chao Xiao, Jihua Chen, and Lei Wang$^{(\boxtimes)}$

College of Computer Science and Technology, National University of Defense Technology, Changsha, Hunan, China
{xiaochao,jhchen,leiwang}@nudt.edu.cn

Abstract. Neuromorphic processors, the new generation of brain-inspired non-von Neumann computing systems, have the potential to perform complex computations with more energy efficiency than conventional architectures. Neuromorphic processors typically implement the spiking neural network (SNN)-based applications. However, a non-optimized mapping of SNNs onto the neuromorphic processor may increase the on-chip communication delay and data exchange between the off-chip and on-chip memory, especially when the size of the SNNs exceeds the capacity of the processor limited by the on-chip resources. This paper proposes a toolchain, called NeuProMa, to map large-scale spiking convolutional neural networks (SCNNs) onto resource-constrained neuromorphic processors. We exploit the implicit regular connections in the SCNNs and split the SCNNs into multiple sub-networks while reducing the data exchange between the off-chip and on-chip memory. Then, we partition the sub-networks into multiple clusters sequentially in a specific order, which significantly reduces the spike messages between neuromorphic cores. Finally, NeuProMa dispatches the clusters to the neuromorphic cores, minimizing the maximum workload of the routers. Our experiments using six SCNN-based applications show that NeuProMa can significantly reduce the data exchange between the off-chip and on-chip memory, and reduce the spike latency and energy consumption by up to 17% and 85%, respectively, compared with the state-of-the-art.

Keywords: Neuromorphic processor · Spiking convolutional neural networks · Splitting · Partitioning · Mapping

1 Introduction

Neuromorphic processors [8,10,15,20], the new generation of brain-inspired non-von Neumann computing systems, have the potential to perform complex computations with more energy efficiency than conventional architectures. The neuromorphic processors are generally multicore systems and adopt the Network-on-Chip (NoC) as the communication framework. They distribute the memory

© IFIP International Federation for Information Processing 2022
Published by Springer Nature Switzerland AG 2022
S. Liu and X. Wei (Eds.): NPC 2022, LNCS 13615, pp. 129–142, 2022.
https://doi.org/10.1007/978-3-031-21395-3_13

equally over cores and store parameters, such as synaptic weights and connections. Just as the GPUs serve for the conventional artificial neural network (ANN), those neuromorphic processors mainly support the execution of spiking neural networks (SNNs). SNN, the third generation of artificial neural networks, was proposed to mimic how information is encoded and processed in the human brain. Spiking convolutional neural network (SCNN), which has the CNN-like structure and adopts the spiking neuron as the fundamental computing element, has been applied to many machine learning tasks, such as image classification [16], object recognition [4], and the detection of Alzheimer's disease [19].

Although the neuromorphic processors provide parallel communication, a non-optimized mapping of SNNs to the neuromorphic processor may increase the spike communication traffic between neuromorphic cores, leading to NoC congestion and impairing execution performance. Besides, the limited computing resources and on-chip memory can only support the simultaneous execution of a limited number of neurons. For example, DYNAPs [10] comprises four cores and each core can accommodate 256 neurons. Table 1 lists the number of neurons and synapses in six SCNN-based applications. Obviously, when executing a large-scale SNN on DYNAPs, the four cores must be time-multiplexing.

Corelet [1] and PACMAN [7] are proprietary tools to map SNNs to the TrueNorth [15] and SpiNNaker [8], respectively. Other general-purpose mapping tools [2,3,14,17] have only addressed the case with unlimited hardware resources. They assume that the complete SNNs can be mapped onto the neuromorphic processor at once and aim at improving the NoC congestion and energy consumption. The case where the size of SNNs exceeds the capacity of neuromorphic processors is not taken into account in those mapping tools.

A second limitation of the general-purpose mapping methods is that they ignore the regular connections between neurons. They transform an SNN into a graph and employ some heuristic graph partitioning algorithms [11,12] to partition the SNN into several clusters, trying to reduce the number of spike messages on NoC. Unfortunately, those algorithms are easily trapped into the local optimum and unsuited for the SCNNs that have regular connections.

To address these challenges, we propose a systematic method, called NeuProMa (**Ma**pping large-scale SCNNs onto the **Neu**romorphic **Pro**cessor), which contains three parts: *splitting*, *partitioning*, and *mapping*. NeuProMa first splits a large-scale SCNN into several sub-networks to satisfy the on-chip resource constraints. Then, NeuProMa partitions the sub-networks into multiple clusters, reducing the spike messages on NoC. Finally, NeuProMa searches for the *cluster-to-core* mapping scheme. The contributions of this work are as follows:

(1) We exploit the implicit regular connections in the SCNNs and use the *linkSplit* selected from three splitting strategies to split large-scale SCNNs into multiple sub-networks. We show that the *linkSplit* can reduce the required memory and data exchange between the off-chip and on-chip memory.

(2) We partition the sub-networks sequentially according to the order of neurons' starting execution. The order is obtained by simulating the computing process of the entire SCNNs. This significantly reduces the spike messages on NoC, improving spike latency and energy consumption on NoC.

(3) In the mapping stage, we use an optimization algorithm to search for the best mapping scheme, minimizing the maximum workload of routers.

We evaluate NeuProMa with six SCNN-based applications. The experimental results show that the *linkSplit* can significantly reduce the memory requirement and data exchange between the off-chip and on-chip memory. Compared to SpiNeMap [2], NeuProMa achieves an average 2012× lower time consumed in the partitioning and mapping phases and reduces energy consumption on NoC by 85% and spike latency by 17%.

2 Background

2.1 Neuromorphic Processor

Neuromorphic processors, the new generation of brain-inspired non-von Neumann computing systems, implement near-memory computing. They distribute the memory close to multiple computing units called neuromorphic cores. The parameters, including synaptic weights, connections, routing tables, and neuron potentials, are stored in the on-chip memory in a distributed fashion.

NoC has been extensively used in neuromorphic processors to provide massively parallel communication due to its flexibility, scalability, and parallelism. If a spiking neuron generates a spike, the processor will query the routing table, get the addresses of destination cores where the postsynaptic neurons reside, and send packets with routing information to NoC. Neuromorphic processors generally adopt the *neuron-to-core* communication mechanism [5, 15]. The source core just sends one spike message to every destination core irrespective of the number of postsynaptic neurons in the destination core. Therefore, the total number of spike messages on NoC can be formulated as

$$T_{spike} = \sum_{i=1}^{|N|} S(i) \times C_{pos}(i) \tag{1}$$

where $S(i)$ is the number of spikes of the i_{th} neuron and $C_{pos}(i)$ is the number of destination cores where the postsynaptic neurons of the i_{th} neuron are distributed. Before all neuromorphic cores proceed to time step $t + 1$, the neuromorphic processor should ensure that all spikes generated at time step t have been received. Consequently, the high spike communication delay degrades the throughput performance.

2.2 Spiking Convolutional Neural Network

CNN is a supervised ANN specially used to process data with a similar grid structure. Although CNN has a good performance in many machine learning tasks, it is becoming increasingly complex and usually needs powerful computing platforms such as GPU for training or inference.

SNN, as the third generation of neural network, has attracted widespread interest due to its event-driven and low-power nature. Different from traditional ANNs, SNN transmits information via the precise timing of spike trains consisting of a series of spikes, rather than continuous values.

SCNN combines the advantages of those two models. SCNN has the CNN-like structure and adopts the spiking neuron as the fundamental computing unit. The research about how to train a deep spiking neural network directly is in infancy. An alternative approach is to convert the trained ANNs into SNNs [4,6,16]. The basic principle of converting ANNs into SNNs is that firing rates of spiking neurons should be equivalent to the activations of analog neurons. Rueckauer et al. [16] present the theoretical groundwork for this principle and the techniques to convert almost arbitrary continuous-valued CNNs into SCNNs. Their conversion of CNNs into SCNNs is nearly loss-less.

3   Related Work

Mapping is a process of placing neurons on specific cores and storing the parameters, such as synaptic weights and connections, in the on-chip memory. An optimized mapping can reduce the spike messages on NoC, improving the execution performance. In addition to the mapping tools for the specific neuromorphic processors, there are many general-purpose mapping methods. PSOPART [17] utilizes particle swarm optimization to partition SNNs. However, with the increasing size of SNNs, the search space soon becomes huge and unacceptable. SpiNeMap [2] and SNEAP [14] first transform an SNN into a graph by replacing the synaptic weights with the spike traffic between a pair of neurons. Then, SpiNeMap and SNEAP use Kernighan-Lin [12] and multi-level [11] graph partitioning algorithms, respectively, to partition an SNN into multiple clusters. Both partitioning algorithms traverse each neuron and put the neurons with frequent communication in the same cluster. Unfortunately, the intertwined connections within the network make the neurons' postsynaptic neurons be distributed in multiple clusters, which increases the number of spike messages on NoC and leads to NoC congestion and high energy consumption. Besides, those mapping approaches mainly confront the situation where the on-chip resources satisfy the needs of the entire SNN's execution, which makes them insufficient when mapping large-scale SNNs onto the resource-constraint neuromorphic processors.

4   NeuProMa

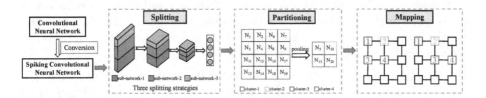

Fig. 1. The high-level overview of NeuProMa

Figure 1 shows the high-level overview of NeuProMa, which consists of three steps: splitting, partitioning, and mapping. *Splitting* is to divide the large-scale network into several sub-networks so that each sub-network can be accommodated on the processor. *Partitioning* is to partition the sub-networks into several clusters so that each cluster can be executed on a single core while reducing the spike messages on NoC. *Mapping* is a process to search for the *cluster-to-core* mapping scheme while improving the NoC congestion.

4.1   Splitting

The different splitting schemes lead to different spike communication traffic between sub-networks, which impacts the off-chip and on-chip data exchange and required memory to store the intermediate results. Here, we introduce three splitting methods and demonstrate the differences among them. Figure 2 shows that an SCNN is split into 9 sub-networks (marked in different colors) by the three strategies.

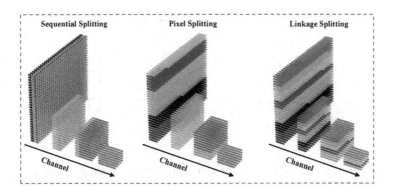

Fig. 2. An SCNN is split into 9 sub-networks. The structure of the network is Input $(32 \times 32 \times 3) \xrightarrow{Conv} (28 \times 28 \times 16) \xrightarrow{Pool} (14 \times 14 \times 16) \xrightarrow{Conv} (10 \times 10 \times 32) \xrightarrow{Pool} (5 \times 5 \times 32)$. The capacity of the neuromorphic processor is set to 2352.

Sequential Splitting (*seqSplit*): A simple method is to distribute the neurons into the sub-networks sequentially according to the spatial position. The left subfigure of Fig. 2 shows the splitting result by the *seqSplit*. The position of each neuron can be represented as (x, y, c, l) where x and y are the coordinates of the pixel in the feature map, c is the feature map index in the l_{th} layer, and l is the layer index in the whole network. The *seqSplit* just divides the network sequentially according to the coordinates.

Pixel Splitting (*pixSplit*): The *pixSplit* distributes the neurons located at the same pixel (x, y) into the same sub-network. The middle subfigure of Fig. 2 shows the splitting results by the *pixSplit*.

The connections in SCNNs are regular in a certain. Figure 3 shows the connections in the convolutional and pooling operations. For the convolutional operation, the same pixel's neurons of the latter feature maps receive spikes from the same presynaptic neurons in the preceding layer. For the pooling operation, although the neurons of the latter layer have different presynaptic neurons, those presynaptic neurons are located in the same pixels. Based on this observation, the *pixSplit* traverses every pixel of the feature maps sequentially and puts the same pixel's neurons into the same sub-network.

Compared with the *seqSplit* that may distribute the same pixel's neurons in multiple sub-networks, the *pixSplit* reduces the duplication of input spike trains from the off-chip to on-chip. Take the first layer of the SCNN in Fig. 2 for example. After the *seqSplit*, the same pixel's neurons are distributed in six sub-networks, which causes the input spikes should be transferred from the off-chip to the on-chip six times. After the *pixSplit*, most input spikes just need to be transferred once.

Linkage Splitting (*linkSplit*): Based on the *pixSplit*, the *linkSplit* places the connected neurons from different layers in the same sub-network. The right subfigure of Fig. 2 shows the splitting result by *linkSplit*.

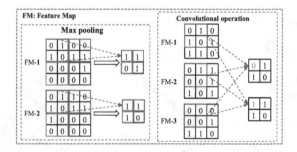

Fig. 3. The connections in the convolutional and pooling operations

The *seqSplit* and *pixSplit* divide the SCNNs layer by layer. After the execution of the preceding layer, the processor should record the neurons' firing information (intermediate results) of the preceding layer and store the intermediate results in the off-chip memory. When the following layer starts the computing, the processor should transform the intermediate results of the preceding layer into spike trains and load the spike trains from the off-chip to the on-chip.

Identical to the *pixSplit*, *linkSplit* distributes the same pixel's neurons in the same sub-network. The *linkSplit* traverses the pixels of the first layer sequentially. Once a new pixel of the first layer has been visited, the *linkSplit* checks whether the pixels of the other layers can be added to the current sub-network. The condition of adding a pixel is that the pixel's all presynaptic neurons have been already visited. As shown in the splitting result by *linkSplit*, the adjacent layers have a similar splitting structure. It is because the neurons from the adjacent layers have the local spatial correlation.

Each neuron from the fully connected layers can be treated as a single pixel. Therefore, the above three strategies can be applied to the fully connected layers.

4.2   Partitioning

After the initial large-scale SCNN is split into multiple sub-networks, each sub-network can be executed on the neuromorphic processor at once. The next step is to partition each sub-network into multiple clusters so that each cluster can be executed on a single core while reducing the spike messages between cores.

The desired result for optimal partitioning is to place the i_{th} neuron and its all postsynaptic neurons in the same core, which makes the $C_{pos}(i)$ equal to zero. However, the connections in a network are intertwined and such a result can be obtained for only a few neurons.

Inspired by the *linkSplit*, we simulate the entire computing process of the network, get the order in which all neurons start their computation, and partition the sub-networks into several clusters sequentially according to the computing order. Take the pooling operation, shown in Fig. 4, for example. N_5 has four presynaptic neurons (N_1, N_2, N_3, and N_4). Once the four presynaptic neurons have accomplished the computation, N_5 can start the computation. To get the computing order of the entire network, we first build a stack to store the neurons to be executed. Initially, all neurons in the first layer are pushed into the stack. Then, the first neuron is removed from the stack in turn, which means the neuron has accomplished the computation. Once all presynaptic neurons of a neuron that has not been pushed into the stack have accomplished the computations, we push the neuron into the stack. Repeat this process until the stack is empty. The order in which neurons are removed from the stack is the computing order. We partition each sub-network sequentially according to this computing order. It should be noted that the complete computing order is generated only once, which significantly reduces the end-to-end execution time (see Sect. 6.2).

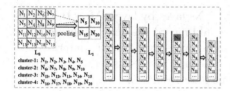

Fig. 4. The order of neurons' starting computation

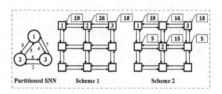

Fig. 5. Two candidate schemes for mapping a partitioned SNN

4.3 Mapping

After each sub-network is partitioned into multiple clusters, the next step is to map the clusters on the neuromorphic cores. Different mapping schemes lead to different workloads of routers, which impacts the spike latency. Figure 5 illustrates two alternate placements of a partitioned SNN to the neuromorphic processor with nine cores arranged in a 3×3 mesh topology. The routing algorithm is X-Y routing algorithm where a packet must be routed along the X-axis until it reaches the same column as that of the destination and then routed along the Y-axis. The number attached to the router is the total number of packets that pass through this router.

In the mapping stage, NeuProMa minimizes the maximum workload of routers. The neuromorphic processor is abstracted as a graph $\Phi(C, L)$ where C and L are the sets of cores and physical links, respectively. For every unmapped cluster, we explore all unallocated cores. We pre-map the current cluster on the selected core, simulate the spike communication according to the routing algorithm adopted by the target neuromorphic processor, and calculate the workloads of all routers. Then, by comparing with the historical optimal record, we choose the better mapping scheme where the maximum workload of routers is smaller.

5 Experiment Setup

5.1 Experiment Platform

Our experiment uses the hardware configuration of 6×6 2D-mesh NoC with X-Y routing algorithm. Noxim++ [2], a trace-driven and cycle-accurate NoC simulator, is employed to evaluate key performance statistics of NoC, such as energy consumption and spike latency. The capacity of a single neuromorphic core is set to 256. All experiments are performed on a system with the i7-10700 CPU, 16 GB RAM, and NVIDIA RTX2060 GPU.

5.2 Evaluated SCNNs

We use six SCNN-based applications to evaluate our proposed approach. Table 1 lists the six applications. Column 2, 3, and 4 report the number of neurons, the number of synapses, and the number of sub-networks after splitting the six applications, respectively. The six CNNs are first trained with the back-propagation algorithm using the training datasets. Then, the trained CNNs are converted into SCNNs using the SNN-TB tool [16].

Table 1. SCNN-based applications used for evaluation

SCNNs	Neurons	Synapses	No. of Sub-networks
LeNet-5-MNIST (LeNet-MN) [9]	5,814	286,120	1
CNN-FashionMNIST (CNN-FaMN) [21]	16,650	1,892,352	2
LeNet-5-Cifar10 (LeNet-Cifar10) [9]	19,894	2,343,464	3
CNN-Cifar10 [4]	35,018	5,675,904	4
AlexNet-ImageNet (AlexNet-ImaNet)* a [13]	185,285	101,099,584	21
VGG11-ImageNet (VGG-ImaNet)* b [18]	715,229	62,703,296	78

*On a subset of 6500 samples falling into 5 categories.
aInput (192 × 192 × 3) - [Conv, Pool] * 48 - [Conv, Pool] * 128 - [Conv, Conv] * 192 - [Conv, Pool] * 128 - FC(128) - FC(64) - FC(5)
bInput (192 × 192 × 3) - [Conv, Pool] * 8 - [Conv, Pool] * 16 - [Conv, Conv, Pool] * 32 - [Conv, Conv, Pool] * 64 - [Conv, Conv, Pool] * 64 - FC(128) - FC(64) - FC(5)

6   Experiment Results

6.1   Splitting Performance

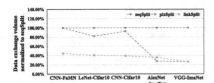
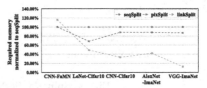

(a) The exchange volume of intermedi-   (b) Memory needs to store the interme-
ate results between the on-chip and on-   diate result
chip memory

Fig. 6. Splitting performance. (a) The exchange volume of intermediate results between the on-chip and on-chip memory normalized to the *seqSplit*. (b) The needed memory to store the intermediate results normalized to the *seqSplit*.

Figure 6(a) shows the exchange volume of intermediate results between the on-chip and on-chip memory normalized to the *seqSplit*. The neuromorphic hardware can accommodate the entire LeNet-MN network, so there are no intermediate results to be exchanged between sub-networks. Both *pixSplit* and *linkSplit* outperforms the *seqSplit* because they distribute the neurons located at the same pixel into the same sub-network, reducing the duplication of the same intermediate results. Figure 6(b) plots the memory required to store the intermediate results. The *linkSplit* outperform the *seqSplit* and *pixSplit* in most tasks. Moreover, with the expanding of network size, the *linkSplit* exhibits a superior advantage. This is because the *linkSplit* only needs to store less intermediate outputs by putting the connected neurons in the same sub-network.

6.2   Partitioning and Mapping Performance

To evaluate the partitioning and mapping algorithms, we conducted three experiments for the three splitting strategies. The results show that NeuProMa outperforms SpiNeMap and SNEAP regardless of the splitting strategy.

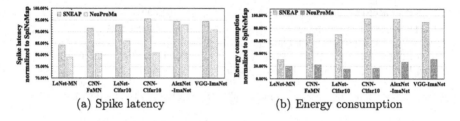

Fig. 7. Split the SCNNs using the *seqSplit*

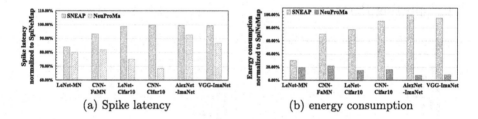

Fig. 8. Split the SCNNs using the *pixSplit*

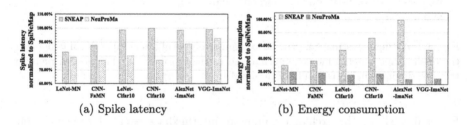

Fig. 9. Split the SCNNs using the *linkSplit*

Spike Latency on NoC. This is the average delay experienced by spikes on the NoC. Figure 7(a), 8(a), and 9(a) report the spike latency of our evaluated approaches normalized to SpiNeMap when using three splitting strategies. Compared with SpiNeMap and SNEAP, NeuProMa has the lowest spike latency (on average 17% lower than SpiNeMap, 11% lower than SNEAP).

Two reasons are responsible for this improvement. First, NeuProMa puts the neurons located at the same pixel into the same sub-network, which reduces the number of spike messages and alleviates NoC congestion. Second, in the mapping stage, NeuProMa minimizes the maximum workload of routers, which balances the workload indirectly.

Energy Consumption on NoC. This is the total energy consumption consumed by all spike messages on NoC. It can be formulated as

$$E_{total} = \sum_{i=1}^{N_s} [h_i \times E_S + (h_i - 1) \times E_L] \tag{2}$$

where N_s is the total number of spike messages, h_i is the number of hops the i_{th} spike message traverses between the source and destination, and E_S and E_L are the energy consumption on the physical links and hops, respectively.

Figure 7(b), 8(b), and 9(b) report the energy consumption of the evaluated approaches normalized to SpiNeMap. Compared with SpiNeMap and SNEAP, NeuProMa has the lowest energy consumption (on average 85% lower than SpiNeMap, 49% lower than SNEAP). Compared with SpiNeMap, NeuProMa reduces the energy consumption by more than 90% in both AlexNet-ImageNet and VGG11-ImageNet tasks. The main reason is that NeuProMa reduces the most of the spike massages on NoC among the three partitioning approaches.

Spike Count on NoC. This is the total number of spike messages on NoC (see Eq. (1)). Figure 10 reports the total number of spike messages on NoC of the evaluated methods normalized to SpiNeMap. Compared with SpiNeMap and SNEAP, NeuProMa achieves the minimum amount of spike messages (on average 82% and 52% lower than SpiNeMap and SNEAP, respectively). Both SNEAP and SpiNeMap partition the SCNNs using the heuristic algorithms, ignoring the implicit regular connections. Instead, NeuProMa exploits the regular connections and partitions the sub-networks according to the order of neurons' starting computation. After the partition by NeuProMa, the postsynaptic neurons of all neurons are centrally distributed in a few cores, which reduces the number of destination cores. The reduction in spike messages contributes to the reduction of energy consumption and spike latency.

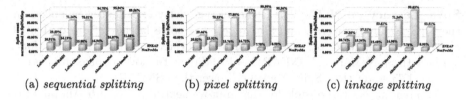

(a) *sequential splitting*   (b) *pixel splitting*   (c) *linkage splitting*

Fig. 10. The spike count normalized to SpiNeMap when using three splitting strategies

Execution Time. This is the time consumed for partitioning and mapping. Figure 11 reports the time under different methods. NeuProMa achieves 2012× and 149× lower execution time than SpiNeMap and SNEAP, respectively. There are two reasons accounting for this improvement. First, NeuProMa simulates the computing process and generates the computing order of all neurons once. Each sub-network is partitioned sequentially according to the order. Second, in the mapping stage, NeuProMa traverses the unallocated cores for the unmapped clusters, so the time complexity is $O(|V| \times |C|)$ where $|V|$ is the number of clusters and $|C|$ is the number of cores.

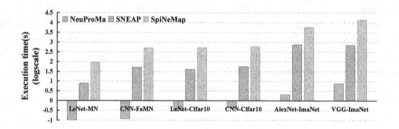

Fig. 11. Execution time

7 Conclusion

In this paper, we introduce NeuProMa, a toolchain to map large-scale SCNNs to the neuromorphic processor. Prior works have mainly addressed the case with unlimited hardware resources. Those approaches present significant limitations when mapping a large-scale SCNN onto a resource-constrained hardware. NeuProMa maps the SCNN-based applications in three steps: splitting, partitioning, and mapping. The *linkSplit* can reduce the intermediate results, which reduces the memory needs and exchange volume of intermediate results between the off-chip and on-chip memory. The partitioning algorithm of NeuProMa significantly reduces the spike messages on NoC, improving the spike latency and energy consumption on NoC. In the mapping stage, NeuProMa minimizes the maximum workload of routers. We have conducted experiments with six SCNN-based applications and demonstrate a significant increase in performance over current practices.

Acknowledgements. This work is founded by National Key R&D Program of China [grant numbers 2018YFB2202603].

References

1. Amir, A., et al.: Cognitive computing programming paradigm: a corelet language for composing networks of neurosynaptic cores. In: The 2013 International Joint Conference on Neural Networks (IJCNN), pp. 1–10 (2013)
2. Balaji, A., et al.: Mapping spiking neural networks to neuromorphic hardware. IEEE Trans. Very Large Scale Integr. (VLSI) Syst. **28**(1), 76–86 (2020)
3. Balaji, A., et al.: A framework to explore workload-specific performance and lifetime trade-offs in neuromorphic computing. IEEE Comput. Archit. Lett. **18**(2), 149–152 (2019)
4. Cao, Y., Chen, Y., Khosla, D.: Spiking deep convolutional neural networks for energy-efficient object recognition. Int. J. Comput. Vis. **113**(1), 54–66 (2015). https://doi.org/10.1007/s11263-014-0788-3
5. Davies, M., et al.: Loihi: a neuromorphic manycore processor with on-chip learning. IEEE Micro **38**(1), 82–99 (2018)
6. Diehl, P.U., Neil, D., Binas, J., Cook, M., Liu, S.C., Pfeiffer, M.: Fast-classifying, high-accuracy spiking deep networks through weight and threshold balancing. In: 2015 International Joint Conference on Neural Networks (IJCNN), pp. 1–8 (2015)
7. Furber, S., Galluppi, F., Davies, S., Rast, A., Sharp, T., Plana, L.A.: A hierachical configuration system for a massively parallel neural hardware platform. In: Proceedings of the 9th Conference on Computing Frontiers, pp. 183–192. Association for Computing Machinery (2012)
8. Furber, S.B., et al.: Overview of the spinnaker system architecture. IEEE Trans. Comput. **62**(12), 2454–2467 (2013)
9. LeCun, Y., Bottou, L., Bengio, Y., Haffner, P.: Gradient-based learning applied to document recognition. Proc. IEEE **86**(11), 2278–2324 (1998)
10. Moradi, S., Qiao, N., Stefanini, F., Indiveri, G.: A scalable multicore architecture with heterogeneous memory structures for dynamic neuromorphic asynchronous processors (DYNAPs). IEEE Trans. Biomed. Circ. Syst. **12**(1), 106–122 (2018)
11. Karypis, G., Kumar, V.: Multilevelk-way partitioning scheme for irregular graphs. J. Parallel Distrib. Comput. **48**(1), 96–129 (1998)
12. Kernighan, B.W., Lin, S.: An efficient heuristic procedure for partitioning graphs. Bell Syst. Tech. J. **49**(2), 291–307 (1970)
13. Krizhevsky, A., Sutskever, I., Hinton, G.E.: ImageNet classification with deep convolutional neural networks. Commun. ACM **60**(6), 84–90 (2017)
14. Li, S., et al.: SNEAP: a fast and efficient toolchain for mapping large-scale spiking neural network onto NoC-based neuromorphic platform. In: 30th Great Lakes Symposium on VLSI, GLSVLSI 2020, pp. 9–14 (2020)
15. Merolla, P.A., et al.: A million spiking-neuron integrated circuit with a scalable communication network and interface. Science **345**(6197), 668–673 (2014)
16. Rueckauer, B., Lungu, I.A., Hu, Y., Pfeiffer, M., Liu, S.C.: Conversion of continuous-valued deep networks to efficient event-driven networks for image classification. Front. Neurosci. **11**, 682 (2017)
17. Schaafsma, A.D.W.H.D.C.: Mapping of local and global synapses on spiking neuromorphic hardware. Quantitative Biology (2019)
18. Simonyan, K., Zisserman, A.: Very deep convolutional networks for large-scale image recognition. Comput. Sci. (2014)

19. Turkson, R.E., Qu, H., Mawuli, C.B., Eghan, M.J.: Classification of Alzheimer's disease using deep convolutional spiking neural network. Neural Process. Lett. **53**, 2649–2663 (2021). https://doi.org/10.1007/s11063-021-10514-w

20. Wang, L., et al.: LSMCore: a 69k-synapse/mm^2 single-core digital neuromorphic processor for liquid state machine. IEEE Trans. Circ. Syst. I Regul. Pap. **69**(5), 1976–1989 (2022)

21. Zambrano, D., Bohte, S.M.: Fast and efficient asynchronous neural computation with adapting spiking neural networks (2016)

Multi-clusters: An Efficient Design Paradigm of NN Accelerator Architecture Based on FPGA

Teng Wang⑩, Lei Gong⁽⊠⁾, Chao Wang, Yang Yang⑩, and Yingxue Gao⑩

School of Computer Science and Technology, University of Science and Technology of China, Hefei, China
{wangt635,greyyang,gyingxue}@mail.ustc.edu.cn,
{leigong0203,cswang}@ustc.edu.cn

Abstract. With the serial development of neural network models, choosing a superior platform for these complex computing applications is essential. Field-Programmable Gate Array (FPGA) is gradually becoming an accelerating platform that balances power and performance. The design of architecture in neural network accelerator based on FPGA is about two categories, stream and single-engine. Both design paradigms have advantages and disadvantages. The stream is easier to achieve high performance because of model customization but has low kernel compatibility. The single-engine is more flexible but has more scheduling overhead. Therefore, this work proposes a new design paradigm for the neural network accelerator based on FPGA, called the Multi-clusters (MC), which combines the characteristics of the above two design categories. We divide the original network model according to the calculated features. Then, different cores are designed to map these parts separately for efficient execution. The fine-grained pipeline is performed inside the cores. Multiple cores are executed by software scheduling and implement a coarse-grained schedule, thereby improving the overall computing performance. The experimental results show that the accelerator with the MC category achieved 39.7× times improvement of performance and 7.9× times improvement of energy efficiency compared with CPU and GPU, and finally obtained nearly 680.3 GOP/s computing performance in the peek.

Keywords: Accelerator · Architecture · FPGA · Neural network

1 Introduction

With the serial development of neural network models, choosing a superior platform for these complex computing applications is essential. Due to the low power consumption and reconfigurability, Field-Programmable Gate Array (FPGA) is gradually becoming an accelerating platform that balances power and performance [15]. Optimized for the computational process of the application and the data in the model, FPGA can achieve high parallelism and simplified logic. In

© IFIP International Federation for Information Processing 2022
Published by Springer Nature Switzerland AG 2022
S. Liu and X. Wei (Eds.): NPC 2022, LNCS 13615, pp. 143–154, 2022.
https://doi.org/10.1007/978-3-031-21395-3_14

the current implementation of neural network accelerators based on FPGA, its hardware architecture design is divided into two categories, stream and single-engine [2].

The overlap's thought is building a reusable processing engine to execute the common computing part of the algorithm, such as a systolic array, a multiply-adder tree, etc. [20]. The control of hardware units and operation scheduling is performed by host code [17]. Therefore, after a single compilation, the same bitstream can be used for many models without reconfiguration of the bitstream. It makes the accelerator more flexible and more compatible. However, the non-special approach makes the computing performance fluctuate on network models with different workload characteristics and has more scheduling overhead in the system [18].

Many accelerators based on stream mode have been proposed to alleviate the above problems [5,6]. The stream paradigm generates different hardware blocks for each computational operation of the target algorithm, where each block is individually optimized to exploit the parallelism of its layers, and all heterogeneous blocks are chained with the pipeline [3]. Therefore, this design pattern exploits the parallelism between layers through the pipeline and enables them to execute concurrently. The advantage of the stream paradigm is that it can be customized for the model, design different hardware parts to adapt to the computing characteristics and use different methods in each hardware unit to optimize the implementation and parallel solutions to improve the overall performance. Nevertheless, the compatibility of the hardware kernel is low, and the computing unit is usually reconfigured after the model is changed [21].

This work proposes a new design paradigm for the neural network accelerator based on FPGA, called the Multi-clusters (MC), combining the characteristics of the above two design paradigms, minimizing the external scheduling overhead and achieving high performance. First, we split the network model into slices containing a sequence of sequential operations. Then, different cores are designed to map these parts separately for efficient execution. The fine-grained pipeline is performed inside the cores. Multiple cores are executed by software scheduling and implementing a coarse-grained pipeline. Moreover, we developed an accelerator based on the MC paradigm in the experimental section. Our main contributions are summarized as follows:

- We identify shortcomings of previous single-machine and stream architectures, and propose a new design paradigm for neural network accelerator architecture, called the Multi-clusters (MC).
- We design a division strategy to split the network model and analyze the computational properties of different parts to process clustering.
- After the module clustering, the different parts are mapped to each processing engine. We perform the optimization for workload equilibrium to maximize computing efficiency and design exploration of architecture.
- In the experimental section, the results show that the accelerator with the MC category achieved 39.7× times improvement of performance and 7.9× times improvement of energy efficiency compared with CPU and GPU, and finally obtained nearly 680.3 GOP/s computing performance in the peek.

2   Background

2.1   Design Patterns of Accelerator

In implementing the computing accelerator based on FPGA, the current design of hardware architectures is divided into two types [2,12,14], the Overlap pattern and Stream pattern. As shown in Fig. 1, the thought of the Overlap method is mainly to design a reusable big processing engine to perform the calculation part of the algorithm [19]. At the same time, the hardware control and operation scheduling are executed by the host code in the upper layer [8,16]. Therefore, it can be expanded according to the input model and the available FPGA resources, as shown at the left of Fig. 1. The advantage of this design is that it is flexible, which we do not need to be reconfigured when the input model has changed, but the computing type has not changed [4]. However, due to a control mechanism similar to the general processor, it is not easy to achieve maximum efficiency in computing [9]. Because this one-size-fits-all approach may lead to the inconsistent final performance on network models with different workload characteristics [7,22]. Moreover, there are many kinds of non-linear functions between each computation part. So if running the model in the overlap pattern, achieving the optimal design size of the computing unit and the optimal processing schedule may be challenging.

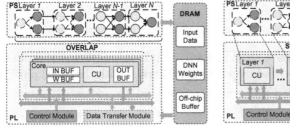 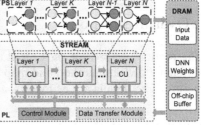

(a) The structure of overlap pattern   (b) The structure of stream pattern

Fig. 1. Common accelerator architecture on FPGA

Another design pattern, stream, is opposite to the overlap. It implements different hardware units for each computing part in the calculation flow of the target algorithm and optimizes them separately to take advantage of inter-block parallelism [3,5]. As shown in the right of Fig. 1, the computing units are connected in the order of the algorithm. After the data flow through each unit, the calculation can be completed and flowed into the next unit [6]. Therefore, the advantage of this design pattern is that according to the difference in the characteristics in different computing parts, we can use different ways to optimize the implementation and parallel scheme in each hardware kernel [11]. However, the disadvantage of stream pattern is that it is not flexible, and we should design the new hardware computing units for different network models.

2.2 Related Work

In the neural network accelerator design stage, zhang introduced the roofline model to analyze the computing characteristics of the network. He analyzed the optimal tilling strategy in different network layers [22]. However, due to the fixed hardware structure, the computational efficiency of this structure in different network layers will inevitably be different. MALOC introduces stream pattern to FPGA accelerator architecture design [5]. Under a given CNN model, each layer is mapped to a series of hardware blocks chained together as a coarse pipeline. Moreover, The performance-resource tradeoff of each block is individually tuned to meet the needs of each layer in the design space exploration phase to achieve high performance. Geng further deploys the stream architecture into the FPGA cluster to satisfy the enormous resource overhead requirements [3]. However, the customization of the stream also brings the disadvantage of insufficient flexibility. The OPU [21] is designed to make the computing unit suitable for various complex tasks. Under the overlap design, the domain-specific instruction set and compilation optimization are used to improve the overall computing efficiency. In OctCNN [12], Lou analyzes the internal difference between the two design structures. After analyzing the calculation characteristics of the model, the network is divided into two halves. One half is calculated in the stream mode, and the other half is run in the overlap mode [24] to perform the overall efficient calculation.

3 Overall Method

In this section, we present the overall method of MC, the multi-cluster strategy. We design a division method and map it to multi kernels with the inline pipeline structure. The details are as follows.

3.1 Division Method

We investigate the main differences between these two design paradigms in the past and find that the computation to communication ratio (CTC) [22] is a crucial factor. Because the value of CTC represents the maximum number of calculation results that can be produced by unit data in some calculation mode. Under the same computation mode, the larger value means the fewer data interaction, and the smaller value means the stronger correlation of data. Therefore, the difference between the network layers with the different CTC in the same computing mode leads to the difference in potential parallel performance. So the overlap structure is hard to achieve high computational efficiency. While in the stream pattern, the specific optimization for each layer will significantly improve the overall performance.

Based on the thought, we design a division method to split the neural network model by the value of CTC. First, we split the network model into several parts. And each contains a sequence of network layers. Then we calculate the

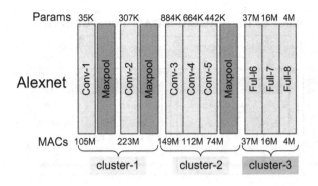

Fig. 2. The Alexnet Network is divided by the CTC with MC strategy, and the layers are clustered into three parts.

CTC value for each layer and perform subsequence division according to the CTC value. Finally, the layers with similar CTC in the same subsequence will be clustering to the same processing engine (PE). We take Alexnet [10] as an example for analysis. As shown on the left of Fig. 2, Alexnet has eight network layers, containing five convolution layers and three fully connected layers with different numbers of multiply accumulates (MACs) and parameters.

Furthermore, in the right of Fig. 2, we list the value of CTC between layer-1 to layer-8, respectively. After processing by our partitioning method, conv-1 to 2 will be mapped to the first PE, conv-3 to 5 will be mapped to the second PE, and FC-6 to 8 will be mapped to the third PE. In detail, the following section introduces the hardware mapping of each part with MC.

3.2 Architecture Design

The MC paradigm is different from the stream, which maps all the computing processes, or the overlap, which extracts the common computing feature. It is a design that balances two approaches to explore optimal computational performance. After we have split the process graph of the network model into several common subsequences according to the CTC value, we will now design architecture to support different subsequences executed on multiple PE, all of which can execute a part of the sequential operations in the network. As shown in Fig. 3(a), we give the overall architecture design with the previous example analysis. In Fig. 3(b), we give the inner architecture of the conv computing unit (CU). In the software layer, we can combine different PE with some order to complete the calculation of different network models. On the hardware level, these sequential operations run in a predetermined order inside the PE, with the pipeline technology dividing different stages and configuring different parameters to make the latency of each stage similar to obtain high computing efficiency. In this way, the computational performance of PE-i is shown in Eq. 1.

$$Performance_i = \frac{Frequency * GOPs}{MaxLatency(CUs)}. \tag{1}$$

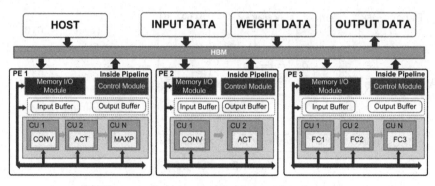

(a) The overall design architecture with sub-engines.

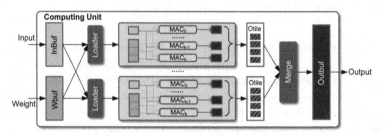

(b) The detail structure of conv computing unit.

Fig. 3. The overall accelerator architecture with MC strategy for example.

From Eq. 1 and Fig. 3, the overall performance of the MC is affected by the maximum latency of the computational units in the PE. Therefore, to optimize the computing performance and hardware utilization, we need to make the latency of each stage within the PE as close as possible in the design phase to ensure that the entire computing structure can run efficiently with simple software control.

3.3   Design Space Exploration

In previous sections, we focus on the division method, which makes it possible to complete the whole calculation by expressing several parts. Moreover, the overall performance of the MC is affected by the maximum latency of the computational units in the PE. So we introduce the design space exploration (DSE) method, which is inevitable for architecture design. This section discusses our DSE approach for the MC pattern to obtain the optimal computational performance with the given hardware platform. Therefore, we use equilibrium to measure the results after optimization to improve computing performance and hardware utilization, as shown in Eq. 2.

$$Equilibrium = k^{-1} * \sum_{i}^{k} (c_i * Timecost_i - \overline{Timecost})^2, \quad i \in \{k * PEs\}. \quad (2)$$

Therefore, to improve computing performance and hardware utilization, we need to reduce the value of equilibrium as much as possible. Therefore, we propose a workload equilibrium algorithm based on the greedy strategy to complete the DSE task.

As shown in Algorithm 1, after initializing parameters, we can obtain each computing unit component without parallelism optimization from the hardware template. First, we find the component with the max time cost in the current PE list. Then the component's internal configuration is modified with the increasing parallelism, and the computing unit component regenerates with the hardware template. Furthermore, because of the internal pipeline structure, the performance of PU can be accelerated by increasing the number of computing units and the pipeline balance. Moreover, resource checking determines whether the accelerated component is legally based on the current situation to improve the computing performance and reduce latency. Furthermore, if the state of resource check is a failure, we will decrease the parallelism of the whole design to search again. The algorithm updates the current and old values of the equilibrium. Finally, we will get the implementation of the computing unit with workload equilibrium according to the existing conditions.

Algorithm 1: The workload equilibrium algorithm for design space exploration of MC architecture.

Input: Calcultion Set, Data Size, FPGA Device, Cluster-PEs, Hardware Templates

Output: Implementation of the components

1 initialization;
2 CUs is the list of components' implement in Cluster-PEs;
3 c_i is the temporal times of pe_i;
4 init(PEs, c);   // Implementation initialization
5 equilibrium = CalEquilibrium(PEs, c);
6 old_equilibrium = equilibrium;
7 **while** $equilibrium <= old\_equilibrium$ **do**
8 $\quad$ pe_i = findMaxTimecost(PEs, c);   // Here is bottleneck
9 $\quad$ config = increaseParal(pe_i, c_i);
10 $\quad$ pe_i.CUs.update(genImplemente(config));   // Bottleneck speedup
11 $\quad$ flag = checkResource(PEs, fpga_device);   // Ensure resource usage
12 $\quad$ **if** $flag$ **then**
13 $\quad\quad$ **for** pe_k in PEs **do**
14 $\quad\quad\quad$ config = decreaseParal(pe_k, c_k);   // Reduce overall resources
15 $\quad\quad\quad$ pe_k.CUs.update(genImplemente(config));
16 $\quad\quad$ **end**
17 $\quad\quad$ old_equilibrium = CalEquilibrium(PEs, c);
18 $\quad$ **else**
19 $\quad\quad$ old_equilibrium = equilibrium;
20 $\quad$ **end**
21 $\quad$ equilibrium = CalEquilibrium(PEs, c);   // Refresh new value
22 **end**

3.4 Scheduling Strategy

In this section, we introduce the operation scheduling of our architecture. Our MC pattern makes overall scheduling easier after the design is complete. With the DSE handling, we have explored resource utilization and the number of different parts to ensure a more balanced latency. Because the calculation latency of each stage with the temporal times has been guaranteed to be similar in the design phase, the overall time consumption of each PE is also similar. Therefore, the scheduling part on the software side needs to consider how to logically connect the calculations of these PEs and the overall processing order.

As shown in Fig. 4, we give the schedule for the previous example architecture. Different colors represent different data sources; the solid box represents processing, while the dotted box represents temporal reuse with same PE. In short, the coarse-grained pipeline is performed between multiple PEs. Due to the similar latency of the internal stages in PE, PE-1, PE-2 and PE-3 can simultaneously complete computing tasks and write input results back to external memory. Initially, input-1 is first loaded from external memory to PE-1 to be computed with internal pipeline. Then, PE-2 processes the outputs of PE-1, and PE-3 processes the outputs of PE-2 in the next. Furthermore, the PEs write back these results to external memory, respectively. In particular, PE-1 is executing twice temporal times to process two network layers. PE-2 will be executing triple temporal times to process three network layers. In this way, computing resources can be fully utilized, and the external scheduling strategy is convenient.

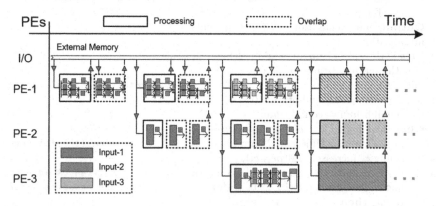

Fig. 4. The scheduling sequence diagram for the example.

4 Experiment

In this section, we implemented MC on Xilinx Alveo U50 FPGA, which has a total of 5,952 DSP slices, 1,344 BRAMs, 872K LUTs, and 1,743K FFs on this platform. We measure the overall performance on MC by running Alexnet and VGG-16. Then we perform a comprehensive comparison with the result of CPU, GPU, and other FPGA accelerators.

4.1 Experiment Setup

In this work, our MC is programmed on FPGA corresponding to the computation types using HLS-compatible C++, which forms the HLS core library with configurable parameters.

Experiment Platform. We deployed a neural network accelerator with an MC pattern on Xilinx Alveo U50. The clock frequency of our architecture is 200 MHz. The model we choose includes Alexnet and VGG-16. Each hardware is synthesized and generated with Xilinx Vitis HLS 2021.2, and we use Xilinx Vitis 2021.2 and Xilinx Vivado 2021.2 to synthesize and deploy the complete project. Moreover, the host CPU controls the accelerator and initial DDRs via the PCIe interface. The built-in power report in Vivado gives power consumption.

Table 1. Relative throughput of MC compared with CPU, GPU.

Device	Perf	Power	Efficiency
CPU	1×	88	0.125×
GPU	75.4×	245	0.308×
MC	39.7×	16.32	2.436×

Table 2. FPGA resource utilization in Alveo U50 platform.

	BRAM	DSP	LUT	FF
Used	1357	910	151k	228k
Available	2688	5952	871k	1743k
Utilization	50.48%	15.29%	17.33%	13.08%

4.2 Comparison with CPU and GPU

In this subsection, we compare performance and energy efficiency with CPU and GPU implementations. The detailed information is listed as follows:

1) *CPU Baseline*: Intel Core i7-4790K processor, including 16-GB DDR3 main memory, four physical cores, eight threads operating at 4 GHz, and the thermal design power (TDP) is 88 W.
2) *GPU Baseline*: NVIDIA Tesla K40C GPU card with 12 GB GDDR5 and 3584 hardware threads operating at 1481 MHz, working at 745–875 MHz, integrated with 15 SMs, 2880 hardware threads. We use the product of utilization and TDP power to estimate the actual CPU and GPU power consumption.

We first compare the speedup and energy benefit of the accelerator design with MC pattern against CPU and GPU implementation. The comparison results with running Alexnet on the Alveo U50 platform are shown in Table 1. Furthermore, the resource utilization of the accelerator with MC pattern is shown in Table 2. For performance, our accelerator achieves 39.7× compared with a CPU implementation. Compared to GPU implementation, we only achieve 0.526× speedup. However, we have achieved 19.488× and 7.909× energy benefits compared to CPU and GPU implementations.

4.3 Comparison with Previous FPGA Accelerators

As the implementation is shown in Table 3, we list some related work that design accelerator for Alexnet and VGG-16. To compare some Alexnet accelerator works [22] and [23] with ours, we achieve a 1.4–5.5× speedup in throughput and 1.5–6.3× improvement in the calculation efficiency. Further, their low efficiency is that the overlap type accelerator design brings a lot of control overhead and an unavoidable cost of data fragmentation in parallelism computation.

Moreover, because of the stream pattern, the works [1] and [5] achieve higher performance values, but we also maintain the same level of calculation efficiency when running VGG-16. This comparison also shows that our MC architecture can obtain similar computational efficiency to the stream type with configuration parameter optimization. Moreover, compared with other VGG-16 accelerator works, we achieve a 1.9–5.0× speedup in throughput and 1.7–2.6× improvement in calculation efficiency. It can prove that our paradigm is efficient for designing neural network accelerator architecture based on FPGA.

Table 3. Performance comparison with previous FPGA implementations

Work	[22]	[23]	[Ours]	[13]	[1]	[5]	[21]	[Ours]
Device	Virtex7 VX485T	Zynq 7Z045	Alveo U50	XC7Z 045	Virtex VU9P	Virtex-7 VX690T	XC7K 325T	Alveo U50
Network	Alexnet			VGG16				
DSP USage	2800	808	910	780	5349	2688	516	1929
Data format (bit)	32	16	16	16	16	16	8	16
Frequency (MHz)	100	200	200	150	214	150	200	200
Power (W)	18.61	7.2	16.32	9.63	49.25	31.2	16.5	18.2
Throughput (GOP/s)	61.62	247	340.36	137	1829	829.84	354	680.3
Efficiency (GOP/j)	3.31	14.2	20.86	14.22	37.14	26.6	21.45	37.38

5 Conclusion

This paper proposes a new design paradigm for neural network accelerators based on FPGA, called the sub-engines. We split the network model calculation process and generate different PEs to match them. Furthermore, we perform the pipeline processing inside the kernel, thereby improving the overall computing performance and minimizing the scheduling overhead of the upper layer. Through the experiment, the results show that the accelerator with the MC category achieved 39.7× times improvement of performance and 7.9× times improvement of energy efficiency compared with CPU and GPU, and finally obtained nearly 680.3 GOP/s computing performance in the peek.

Acknowledgments. This work was supported in part by the National Key R&D Program of China under Grants 2017YFA0700900 and 2017YFA0700903, in part by the National Natural Science Foundation of China under Grants 62102383, 61976200, and 62172380, in part by Jiangsu Provincial Natural Science Foundation under Grant BK20210123, in part by Youth Innovation Promotion Association CAS under Grant Y2021121, and in part by the USTC Research Funds of the Double First-Class Initiative under Grant YD2150002005.

References

1. Chen, Y., He, J., Zhang, X., Hao, C., Chen, D.: Cloud-DNN: an open framework for mapping DNN models to cloud FPGAs. In: Bazargan, K., Neuendorffer, S. (eds.) Proceedings of the 2019 ACM/SIGDA International Symposium on Field-Programmable Gate Arrays, FPGA 2019, Seaside, CA, USA, 24–26 February 2019, pp. 73–82. ACM (2019). https://doi.org/10.1145/3289602.3293915
2. Dhouibi, M., Ben Salem, A.K., Saidi, A., Ben Saoud, S.: Accelerating deep neural networks implementation: a survey. IET Comput. Digit. Tech. **15**(2), 79–96 (2021)
3. Geng, T., Wang, T., Sanaullah, A., Yang, C., Patel, R., Herbordt, M.: A framework for acceleration of CNN training on deeply-pipelined FPGA clusters with work and weight load balancing. In: 2018 28th International Conference on Field Programmable Logic and Applications (FPL), pp. 394–3944. IEEE (2018)
4. Gokhale, V., Zaidy, A., Chang, A.X.M., Culurciello, E.: Snowflake: an efficient hardware accelerator for convolutional neural networks. In: 2017 IEEE International Symposium on Circuits and Systems (ISCAS), pp. 1–4. IEEE (2017)
5. Gong, L., Wang, C., Li, X., Chen, H., Zhou, X.: MALOC: a fully pipelined FPGA accelerator for convolutional neural networks with all layers mapped on chip. IEEE Trans. Comput. Aided Des. Integr. Circ. Syst. **37**(11), 2601–2612 (2018). https://doi.org/10.1109/TCAD.2018.2857078
6. Gong, L., Wang, C., Li, X., Zhou, X.: Improving HW/SW adaptability for accelerating CNNs on FPGAs through a dynamic/static co-reconfiguration approach. IEEE Trans. Parallel Distrib. Syst. **32**(7), 1854–1865 (2021). https://doi.org/10.1109/TPDS.2020.3046762
7. Gong, Y., et al.: N3H-Core: neuron-designed neural network accelerator via FPGA-based heterogeneous computing cores. arXiv preprint arXiv:2112.08193 (2021)
8. Guan, Y., et al.: FP-DNN: an automated framework for mapping deep neural networks onto FPGAs with RTL-HLS hybrid templates. In: 2017 IEEE 25th Annual International Symposium on Field-Programmable Custom Computing Machines (FCCM), pp. 152–159. IEEE (2017)
9. Hameed, R., et al.: Understanding sources of inefficiency in general-purpose chips. In: Proceedings of the 37th Annual International Symposium on Computer Architecture, pp. 37–47 (2010)
10. Krizhevsky, A., Sutskever, I., Hinton, G.E.: ImageNet classification with deep convolutional neural networks. Commun. ACM **60**(6), 84–90 (2017). https://doi.org/10.1145/3065386
11. Liu, Z., Dou, Y., Jiang, J., Xu, J.: Automatic code generation of convolutional neural networks in FPGA implementation. In: 2016 International Conference on Field-Programmable Technology (FPT), pp. 61–68. IEEE (2016)
12. Lou, W., Gong, L., Wang, C., Du, Z., Xuehai, Z.: OctCNN: a high throughput FPGA accelerator for CNNs using octave convolution algorithm. IEEE Trans. Comput. **71**(8), 1847–1859 (2021)

13. Qiu, J., et al.: Going deeper with embedded FPGA platform for convolutional neural network. In: Chen, D., Greene, J.W. (eds.) Proceedings of the 2016 ACM/SIGDA International Symposium on Field-Programmable Gate Arrays, Monterey, CA, USA, 21–23 February 2016, pp. 26–35. ACM (2016). https://doi.org/10.1145/2847263.2847265

14. Venieris, S.I., Kouris, A., Bouganis, C.S.: Toolflows for mapping convolutional neural networks on FPGAs: a survey and future directions. arXiv preprint arXiv:1803.05900 (2018)

15. Wang, C., Gong, L., Li, X., Zhou, X.: A ubiquitous machine learning accelerator with automatic parallelization on FPGA. IEEE Trans. Parallel Distrib. Syst. 31(10), 2346–2359 (2020). https://doi.org/10.1109/TPDS.2020.2990924

16. Wang, C., Gong, L., Yu, Q., Li, X., Xie, Y., Zhou, X.: DLAU: a scalable deep learning accelerator unit on FPGA. IEEE Trans. Comput. Aided Des. Integr. Circ. Syst. 36(3), 513–517 (2017). https://doi.org/10.1109/TCAD.2016.2587683

17. Wang, C., Li, X., Chen, P., Zhang, J., Feng, X., Zhou, X.: Regarding processors and reconfigurable IP cores as services. In: Moser, L.E., Parashar, M., Hung, P.C.K. (eds.) 2012 IEEE Ninth International Conference on Services Computing, Honolulu, HI, USA, 24–29 June 2012, pp. 668–669. IEEE Computer Society (2012). https://doi.org/10.1109/SCC.2012.72

18. Wang, C., Li, X., Zhang, J., Zhou, X., Wang, A.: A star network approach in heterogeneous multiprocessors system on chip. J. Supercomput. 62(3), 1404–1424 (2012). https://doi.org/10.1007/s11227-012-0810-x

19. Wang, X., Wang, C., Cao, J., Gong, L., Zhou, X.: WinoNN: optimizing FPGA-based convolutional neural network accelerators using sparse Winograd algorithm. IEEE Trans. Comput. Aided Des. Integr. Circ. Syst. 39(11), 4290–4302 (2020). https://doi.org/10.1109/TCAD.2020.3012323

20. You, Y., et al.: New paradigm of FPGA-based computational intelligence from surveying the implementation of DNN accelerators. Des. Autom. Embed. Syst. 26, 1–27 (2022). https://doi.org/10.1007/s10617-021-09256-8

21. Yu, Y., Wu, C., Zhao, T., Wang, K., He, L.: OPU: an FPGA-based overlay processor for convolutional neural networks. IEEE Trans. Very Large Scale Integr. (VLSI) Syst. 28(1), 35–47 (2020). https://doi.org/10.1109/TVLSI.2019.2939726

22. Zhang, C., Li, P., Sun, G., Guan, Y., Xiao, B., Cong, J.: Optimizing FPGA-based accelerator design for deep convolutional neural networks. In: Proceedings of the 2015 ACM/SIGDA International Symposium on Field-Programmable Gate Arrays, pp. 161–170 (2015)

23. Zhang, X., et al.: DNNBuilder: an automated tool for building high-performance DNN hardware accelerators for FPGAs. In: Bahar, I. (ed.) Proceedings of the International Conference on Computer-Aided Design, ICCAD 2018, San Diego, CA, USA, 05–08 November 2018, p. 56. ACM (2018). https://doi.org/10.1145/3240765.3240801

24. Zhang, X., et al.: DNNExplorer: a framework for modeling and exploring a novel paradigm of FPGA-based DNN accelerator. In: 2020 IEEE/ACM International Conference On Computer Aided Design (ICCAD), pp. 1–9 (2020)

TrainFlow: A Lightweight, Programmable ML Training Framework via Serverless Paradigm

Wenting Tan[1,2], Xiao Shi[1(✉)], Zhengyu Lei[1,2], Dong Liang[1,2], Cunchi Lv[1,2], Xiaohong Wang[1], and Xiaofang Zhao[1]

[1] Institute of Computing Technology, Chinese Academy of Sciences, Beijing, China
{tanwenting,shixiao,leizhengyu,liangdong,lvcunchi,wxh,
zhaoxf}@ict.ac.cn
[2] University of Chinese Academy of Sciences, Beijing, China

Abstract. Distributed ML training is widely used to improve training performance. However, current distributed training frameworks bring undesirable burdens to application-oriented users due to its server-centric design. It is also difficult for users to customize training (e.g., with adaptive policies) to guarantee performance in dynamic environments. Thus, it is meaningful to make training framework lightweight and programmable. We argue that serverless paradigm can effectively help meet the demands. In this paper, we propose TrainFlow, adopting serverless paradigm to simplify and extend programmability of data-parallel training. First, the basic framework is built with a novel serverless process model, providing a high-level view and various state sharing. Then training can be divided into 2 processes with specific workflows. Second, TrainFlow provides an event-driven hook mechanism, allowing users to customize training workflow. We implement and evaluate TrainFlow with OpenFaaS. Experiments demonstrate its availability and programmability. For availability, TrainFlow can support various training patterns, and shows advantages of performance (e.g., $1.6\times$ higher speedup ratio than baseline) and resource consuming (e.g., at most 41.0% less memory consuming than baseline). For programmability, TrainFlow can work with adaptive policies as expected (e.g., at most $1.48\times$ higher throughput in a case).

1 Introduction

It is widely known that distributed computing can improve performance of machine learning (ML) training significantly, especially for data-intensive and compute-intensive tasks. The profit leads to many emerging patterns (e.g., data-parallel [1], model-parallel [2], pipeline-parallel [3]), optimizations (e.g., adaptive tuning [4]), and frameworks (e.g., TensorFlow [5], BytePS [6], Horovod [3]).

However, it is not as simple as it looks to practice distributed training, especially for application-oriented users. First, most frameworks require manual operations (e.g., scaling) due to their server-centric architecture, bringing undesirable burdens. Second, it is difficult to guarantee training performance due to dynamic environments in the cloud, such as anomalies of network congestion [7], and stragglers [8]. Recent studies show

S. Liu and X. Wei (Eds.): NPC 2022, LNCS 13615, pp. 155–167, 2022.
https://doi.org/10.1007/978-3-031-21395-3_15

that adaptive policies can effectively improve the performance and precision of training [4, 9]. But it needs quite well understanding and necessary programmable support. Thus, it is meaningful to construct a lightweight, programmable distributed ML training framework.

We argue that serverless paradigm is a proper choice. Compared with server-centric paradigm, it is famous for reducing programming complexity with loosely coupled functions and events, as well as providing great elasticity in high-level. Our goals are in line with the abstract of serverless. Nonetheless, there are still challenges to build serverless training. First, the stateful computing of training hinders serverless practice. Second, programmability needs a deliberate and systematic design.

In this paper, we present TrainFlow, a lightweight, programmable distributed ML training framework with data-parallel in serverless. TrainFlow is built on a novel serverless process model and divides training into two processes, task manager and worker. The process model provides a high-level view and necessary shared states for various training patterns, including Parameter Server (PS), ScatterReduce, and RingAllReduce. Then TrainFlow provides an event-driven hook mechanism that allows users to customize specific training workflow. For implementation, the training framework is systematically built, and the serverless runtime is based on OpenFaaS. Experiments demonstrate its availability and programmability. For availability, TrainFlow effectively supports essential training with various patterns, and shows performance (e.g., 1.6× higher speedup ratio than baseline) and resource cost (e.g., at most 41% less memory consuming than baseline) advantage compared with baselines. For programmability, TrainFlow can work well with extended adaptive policies as expected (e.g., at most 1.48× higher throughput in a case).

In summary, we make the following contributions:

1. We present a serverless process model. It can effectively support distributed ML training, including both programming and running requirements.
2. We design and implement TrainFlow in a complete serverless manner. It presents a method to realize various training patterns and brings the insight to handle performance fluctuations of training in cloud adaptively with programming support.
3. We evaluate TrainFlow's availability and programmability with a variety of training models. It is available to handle various training patterns as other server-centric approaches with performance and resource consuming advantages. It is also flexible to extend various adaptive policies for performance improvement in dynamic environments.

2 Background and Challenges

2.1 Distributed ML Training

Distributed ML training utilizes parallel computing to improve training performance. For example, a 90-epoch ResNet-50 training can be accelerated from days to minutes without losing accuracy [1, 10]. However, we observe that it is not as simple as it looks to practice distributed training, especially for application-oriented users (e.g., specialized ML scientists and engineers).

First, it is hard to manage facilities for distributed ML training. Since most training is designed with server-centric methods and they need to directly deploy within servers (e.g., VM, container), trainers or service providers have to concern operations (e.g., scalability) about the low-level, heterogeneous environments. Container clusters can help reduce the effort, while as long as training is server-centric, it requires extra work out of training itself.

Second, it is hard to guarantee distributed training performance in running due to the dynamics of cloud. For example, network congestion can slow down gradients aggregation among training workers, and heterogeneous environments may result in stragglers and performance decrement [8], as shown in Fig. 1. Studies suggest adaptive policies to improve performance [4, 9], though they are still at primary level. It inspires us that the basic framework can be extended for performance improvement, which requires programmability support. However, current frameworks can only provide limited programmability, which is not towards to this situation.

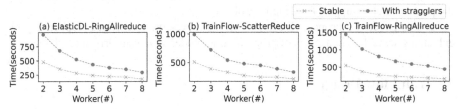

Fig. 1. Performance of training with same pattern varies in dynamic environments

2.1.1 Goals

Considering all the above, we argue that training can be benefit from:

1. **Making training framework lightweight**. The framework should be easy to use, maintain, and support further programmability extension.
2. **Providing wider programmability**. The framework should be flexible to extend user-defined functions, especially adaptive policies.

The goals are partially achieved in some works, while few of them provide both. Inspired by high-level abstract of serverless, we argue that it can be helpful for meeting the demands. First, serverless brings a Function-as-a-Service view, free from low-level operations, simplifies both programming and running. Second, the loosely coupled program structure with serverless functions is easy to achieve programmability. Serverless has been practiced in distributed ML training [11–14]. As we can see, it is helpful to improve training performance, but few works provide a direct and comprehensive view for our goals.

2.2 Challenges

Though serverless computing can be a good solution to achieve the goals, there are still some challenges related to basic frameworks and programmability extension.

First, the stateful computing of training hinders serverless practice, since serverless is currently more capable of stateless computing. Though some works have explored serverless training, trade-offs are made to bypass state management, like using VMs for stateful computing [12] and relying on cloud storage to reduce inter-function communication [13]. For various training patterns, they need differentiated support for state sharing. For example, PS requires specific parameter servers to aggregate gradients and update models instead of workers, RingAllReduce requires fine-grained communication between workers to synchronize gradients.

Second, the programmability can be multi-fold and needs a deliberate design. Hyperparameter tuning can be recognized as a basic pattern [4]. There are also other scenarios, like adaptive selections of training patterns (e.g., PS, RingAllReduce) or operators (e.g., SGD optimizer) in running. Few studies provide a systematic view. We focus on enabling the programmable support for adaptive policies.

In this paper, we propose TrainFlow which solves the challenges respectively by enhancing serverless in aspects of programming model and event-driven mechanism.

3 TrainFlow Design

3.1 Overview

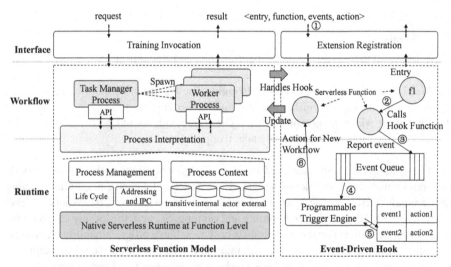

Fig. 2. TrainFlow architecture

TrainFlow provides users with a training service in complete serverless manner and can be customized easily with user-defined extensions.

It consists of interface, workflow, and runtime layers, as shown in Fig. 2. The interface layer allows users to invoke training and register extensions. To invoke training, users can use job-style or service-style interfaces to upload training model definitions and configurations. To register extension, users can submit an extension with a tuple. The workflow layer maintains the training program. When a training request arrives, it spawns processes of task manager and workers for training with serverless process models, supporting PS, RingAllReduce, and ScatterReduce. Meanwhile, extensions can be invoked and regulate specific workflows with event-driven hook mechanism in running. The runtime layer delivers low-level interpretation for process model and loads user-defined extensions to dynamically orchestrate the running workflows.

3.2 Serverless Process Model and Training Basics

3.2.1 Serverless Process Model

To simplify the design of TrainFlow, a novel serverless process model is adopted. It refers to concept of processes in operating systems. Similarly, the serverless process can create children processes and access the context of parent process. It can be spawned concurrently for parallel computing. A key point is that it provides a process context to deliver all shared states in the process. Thus, serverless functions can simply access the states with a context view. The model also identifies each function with process ID and function name. Then functions can communicate with each other.

In the model, shared states are categorized as transitive, internal, actor, and external, as shown in Table 1. A state is transitive when it may need to be accessed by all functions, so it is piggybacked by function invocations and each subsequent function saves it locally. This is suitable for small, basic sharing state. A state is internal when it needs to be accessed in message passing style, so the owner can send it actively. It is usually common for cooperation in parallel computing. An actor state uses a serverless actor function to manage state. Differently, an external state uses an external store, and needs no extra semantics. They all can be manipulated with high-level APIs.

To adopt the model, TrainFlow employs a runtime interpretation mechanism. Each process relies on the life cycle of all its functions and provides addressing with IPC. A unified context map for all active states is maintained in each process. The runtime adopts a design like Dapr [15] to forward high-level state APIs to real state backend. For transitive states, each function invocation will carry them and cache in receivers. For internal states, runtime interprets virtual addresses to IP addresses for message passing. For actor states, runtime extends actor function as a service. For external state, runtime uses Redis as a demo.

Table 1. Shared states in serverless process model and their usage

State type	Key APIs	Sharing method	Usage in TrainFlow
transitive	*get(key) → value* *put(key, value)*	Passed with each invoking	static worker state
internal	*send(dst, state)* *recv(src) → state*	By message passing	intermediate training state of RingAllReduce (optional)
actor	*get(dst, key) → value* *put(dst, key, value)*	Stored in an actor function	intermediate training state of PS (optional)
external		By accessing external stores	global state, intermediate training state of PS (optional), intermediate training state of ScatterReduce (optional)

3.2.2 Process and Workflow Definition

TrainFlow defines training with 2 processes, task manager and worker. Each process runs as an event-driven workflow, as shown in Fig. 3. The task manager acts as the main process, and workers are derived as children. Task manager mainly controls the epoch and step loops in training. In each step, it spawns worker processes according to degree of parallelism from hyper-parameters. Each worker fetches a task, loads model, calculates gradients via SGD, if necessary, synchronize and aggregate gradients, updates model, and exits when its workflow finishes. Workflow of a worker process can be implemented in different ways. For example, the worker with ScatterReduce can split a coarse-grained worker function into gradient calculation and aggregation without affecting the performance.

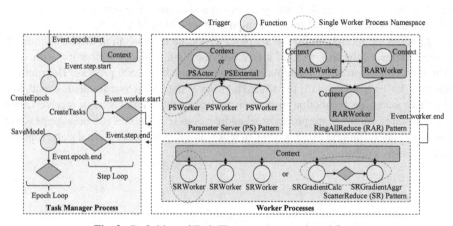

Fig. 3. Definition of TrainFlow processes and workflows

For training state requirements, TrainFlow groups states into global state, static worker state, and intermediate training state. The global state mainly contains model configurations, dataset path, epoch number, and tasks. It is mostly needed for initialization, and needs no further processing, so we define it as external type. The static worker state mainly contains a process map for communication, can be transitive for every function. The intermediate training state includes gradient and model variables. They are dynamic, highly shared, and vary in training patterns. TrainFlow comparatively studies the options (in Sect. 5.1): PS with actor or external, RingAllReduce with internal, and ScatterReduce with external. The details of state management are all transparent for training developers.

3.3 Programmability Extension with Event-Driven Hook

TrainFlow uses an event-driven hook mechanism to extend training programmability. In the mechanism, an extension can be defined with a tuple, <entry, function, events, action>. In each function defined in Sect. 3.2, a hook handler is set at the end of processing. Each handler corresponds to a hook entry. It can invoke a user-defined hook function. Currently, we transfer it as a serverless function. The function is free to be defined according to business requirements. Importantly, if it produces new events, the events can be recognized by triggers and affect following processing. The <events, action> pair can be registered to a programmable trigger which is available to handle composite events and actions. Thus, complicated conditions can be defined by combining user-defined (e.g., network.congestion) and built-in events (e.g., epoch.start). As shown in Fig. 2, a user can upload self-defined extensions (step 1); when a hook entry is reached, it invokes the registered hook function (step 2); the hook function may push a new event into event queue (step 3), then the event is consumed by programmable trigger (step 4); the trigger looks for an action table (step 5) and generates a new workflow orchestration. For adaptive policies, its adaptive algorithm (e.g., adaptive selection of existing methods) can be defined in a hook function with specific events, the action can be indications of a new workflow (e.g., representing the selected method). We illustrate it with 2 simple but heuristic cases.

Case 1: Adaptive selection of training patterns. It can help reduce the effects of stragglers by using computing patterns that need lower synchronization frequency. The functions (e.g., RARWorker, SRGradientAggr) with gradient synchronization is used as entry, the hook function follows a simple algorithm that when it detects a large fluctuation of synchronization time, it reports a new event (pattern.async) and orders to select a pattern with lower synchronization frequency in next epoch (with event epoch.start). Here, it switches from RingAllReduce (with BSP strategy [16]) to ScatterReduce (with SSP strategy [16]), to PS (with ASP strategy [16]).

Case 2: Adaptive selection of synchronization strategy. It can help reduce communication overhead with network congestion. Similarly, when the synchronization becomes slower, it uses events (sync.adapt and epoch.start) to change synchronization strategy from S-SGD to AD-PSGD [17].

4 Implementation

The implementation of TrainFlow contains 2 aspects, including the serverless runtime and training program.

For the serverless runtime, we enhance OpenFaaS to support the serverless process model and event-driven hook mechanism. Serverless process is added as a new kind of entity in OpenFaaS. First, a library, managing process and state, is built for programming, and running. Second, the OpenFaaS gateway is extended to recognize invocations of serverless processes and invoke the following workflows. Third, the OpenFaaS watchdog integrates the process library to convert high-level APIs to low-level OpenFaaS operations, such as address translation, store querying, and actor accessing. For each state type defined in the model, the watchdog can provide corresponding access support. Then the OpenFaaS triggers are updated to be programmable, similar to TriggerFlow [18], allowing entries to be added as <events, actions>.

For serverless training program, the processes are defined based on the runtime, and workflows are defined for different training patterns, including PS, RingAllReduce, ScatterReduce. For implementation of some low-level training operators, we rely on some common libraries, such as TensorFlow.

5 Evaluation

In this section, we demonstrate the availability and programmability of TrainFlow. The experiments are evaluated with 3 ML models, including ResNet50, DeepFM, and LeNet, as shown in Table 2. They are trained with Cifar10, Frappe, and MNIST respectively. All experiments are carried out in a CPU cluster, while the training patterns are also suitable for GPUs. For ResNet50, we provide 4CPUs and 16GB of RAM for each worker. For the other models, 2CPUs and 4GB of RAM are allocated for each worker. The training time is the computation time to complete 2 epochs.

Table 2. Experimental models and datasets

Model	Size (M)	Dataset	Setting
ResNet50	89	Cifar10(26 K)	Mini-BatchSize $= 256$, LearningRate $= 0.01$
DeepFM	1.4	Frappe(200 K)	Mini-BatchSize $= 256$, LearningRate $= 0.01$
LeNet	0.4	MNIST(60 K)	Mini-BatchSize $= 128$, LearningRate $= 0.01$

5.1   Availability

For availability, we consider 3 training patterns: PS, ScatterReduce, and RingAllReduce, with all 3 models. In PS pattern, 3 training frameworks are compared. The baseline is ElasticDL (ElasticDL-PS). And the other two are TrainFlow with actor (TrainFlow-PS-Actor), and external state (TrainFlow-PS-External) respectively. In ScatterReduce and RingAllReduce patterns (grouped as AllReduce pattern), 3 training frameworks are compared. The baseline is ElasticDL with RingAllReduce (ElasticDL-RingAllReduce). The others are TrainFlow with ScatterReduce (TrainFlow-ScatterReduce) in BSP from LambdaML, and with RingAllReduce (TrainFlow-RingAllReduce). The availability can be proved from 2 aspects.

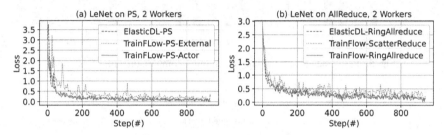

Fig. 4. Loss convergence comparison

First, all models get trained successfully with TrainFlow, as shown in Fig. 4. In each model, TrainFlow shows a similar trend of loss convergence to ElasticDL, and can achieve comparable model accuracy. Here, we use LeNet as an example. Most of the time, the loss convergence of TrainFlow is competitive with ElasticDL. TrainFlow-PS-Actor usually performs better than TrainFlow-PS-External in average due to the better performance of actor function. In addition, the TrainFlow practice shows that PS converges faster than RingAllReduce in loss convergence as expected.

Second, TrainFlow shows great scalability in all cases, as shown in Fig. 5 and Fig. 6. With increment of parallelism, the performance of TrainFlow is explicitly improved, and the memory consuming of workers in TrainFlow decreases sometimes. Since TrainFlow with all training patterns shows similar trends, we mainly explain TrainFlow-PS-Actor with 8 of degree of parallelism. In terms of training time, it is 39.3%, 44.3%, and 12.2% faster than ElasticDL-PS for ResNet50, DeepFM, and LeNet. In terms of speedup ratio, it is 1.6× higher than ElasticDL-PS. In terms of memory consuming, it is 41.0%, 21.2%, and 22.2% less than ElasticDL-PS for ResNet50, DeepFM, and LeNet. In addition, TrainFlow-RingAllReduce outperforms TrainFlow-ScatterReduce due to its advantage in reducing data transfer of synchronization as expected. In total, the profits are earned from lightweight and fine-grained design of training, taking less effort for running.

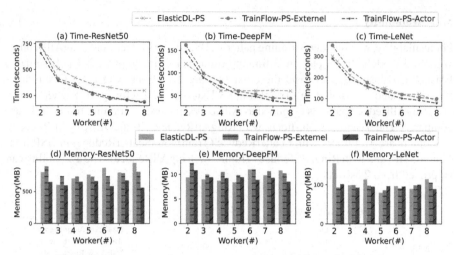

Fig. 5. Performance and memory consuming comparison with PS pattern

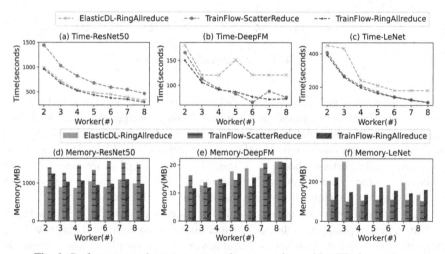

Fig. 6. Performance and memory consuming comparison with AllReduce pattern

5.2 Programmability

For programmability, we consider the 2 cases discussed in Sect. 3.3. It is measured with ResNet50. In the adaptive selection of training patterns (case 1), the baseline is TrainFlow-RingAllReduce. In the adaptive selection of synchronization strategy (case 2), the baseline is TrainFlow-RingAllReduce with S-SGD. In both cases, some background workloads are used to meet the conditions of adaptive selection. The programmability can also be viewed from 2 aspects.

First, TrainFlow can effectively support the programming and running of adaptive policies. TrainFlow handles both cases as expected. For case 1, when the number of stragglers increases step by step, selections happen twice in turn, reducing the influence

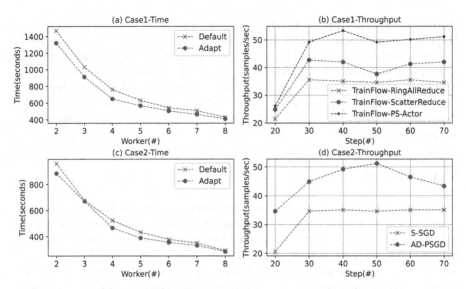

Fig. 7. Performance of adaptive selections of training patterns and synchronization strategy

of stragglers. For case 2, selection is made once, reducing the data transfer in running time successfully.

Second, the adaptive policies can improve the training performance in practice, and the programmability of training framework is worth further promotion, as shown in Fig. 7. In both cases, the performance is improved explicitly with adaptive policies. In case 1, each time a selection is made, the training throughput increases. For example, the increment is 1.2 and 1.3×, when the step is 40. In case 2, the training throughput also increases. For example, the throughput is 1.48× higher when step is 50. Based on this, the effectiveness of adaptive policies is preliminarily verified. We argue that finer grained adaptive policies can further improve performance in TrainFlow.

6 Related Work

6.1 Classic ML Training

Many high-level frameworks have been proposed for large-scale distributed ML training. TensorFlow [5] is an end-to-end ML platform, providing flexible synchronous and asynchronous training strategies. ElasticDL [19] is a Kubernetes based DL framework built on TensorFlow that supports fault tolerance and elastic scheduling. They focus on optimization of distributed ML training, regardless of underlying running environments, such as server management. TrainFlow adopts a complete serverless architecture, and provides a covenant-lite, low maintenance ML training workflow.

6.2 Serverless ML Training

Studies have been devoted to leveraging serverless to build ML systems for scalability, cost efficiency. Cirrus [12] implements a PS on the top of VMs and adopts serverless functions as workers, while all workers communicate with the centralized PS. Siren [11] presents an asynchronous ML framework based on AWS Lambda, workers update models through storage services. LambdaML [13] presents a FaaS-based training system to determine the cases where FaaS holds a sway over IaaS. Crucial [20] provides a fine-grained state management solution with better performance and could be considered as an implementation of state management within a training framework. Differently, TrainFlow focus on improving the serverless experience to make training lightweight and programmable.

7 Conclusion

In this paper, we present a lightweight and programmable distributed training framework design with serverless paradigm. It can effectively support various training. Compared with server-centric methods, it shows simple program structure, performs better scalability (e.g., 1.6× higher speedup ratio than baseline) and resource consuming (e.g., at most 41.0% less memory consuming than baseline), and supports wider programmability. The profit is gained from a novel serverless process model and event-driven hook mechanism. These methods help overcome the challenges of stateful computing and simplify programmability design. We argue that the methods in this paper can also be extended to support other workloads, and adaptive training is worth a further exploration.

References

1. You, Y., Zhang, Z., Hsieh, C., Demmel, J., Keutzer, K.: ImageNet training in minutes. In: The 47th International Conference on Parallel Processing (ICPP '18) (2018)
2. Yuan, J., Li, X., Cheng, C., Liu, J., Guo, R., Cai, S., et al.: Oneflow: redesign the distributed deep learning framework from scratch. arXiv preprint arXiv:2110.15032 (2021)
3. Harlap, A., Narayanan, D., Phanishayee, A., Seshadri, V., Devanur, N., Ganger, G., et al.: Pipedream: fast and efficient pipeline parallel DNN training. arXiv preprint arXiv:1806.03377 (2018)
4. Mai, L., Li, G., Wagenländer, M., Fertakis, K., Brabete, A.O., Piezuch, P.: KungFu: marking training in distributed machine learning adaptive. In: The 14th USENIX Symposium on Operating Systems Design and Implementation (OSDI '20) (2020)
5. Abadi, M., Barham, P., Chen, J., Chen, Z., Davis, A., Dean, J., et al.: TensorFlow: a system for large-scale machine learning. In: The 12th USENIX Symposium on Operating Systems Design and Implementation (OSDI '16) (2016)
6. Jiang, Y., Zhu, Y., Lan, C., Yi, B., Cui, Y., Guo, C.: A unified architecture for accelerating distributed DNN training in heterogeneous GPU/CPU clusters. In: The 14th USENIX Symposium on Operating Systems Design and Implementation (OSDI '20) (2020)
7. Wang, G., Venkataraman, S., Phanishayee, A., Devanur, N., Thelin, J., Stoica, I.: Blink: fast and generic collectives for distributed ML. CoRR, abs/1910.04940 (2019)
8. Cipar, J., Ho, Q., Kim, J.K., Lee, S., Ganger, G.R., Gibson, G., et al.: Solving the straggler problem with bounded staleness. In: The 2013 Workshop on Hot Topics in Operating Systems (HotOS '13) (2013)
9. Wagenländer, M., Mai, L., Li, G., Pietzuch, P.: Spotnik: designing distributed machine learning for transient cloud resources. In: The 12th USENIX Workshop on Hot Topics in Cloud Computing (HotCloud '20) (2020)

10. Jia, X., Song, S., He, W., Wang, Y., Rong, H., Zhou, F., et al.: Highly scalable deep learning training system with mixed-precision: training ImageNet in four minutes. arXiv preprint arXiv:1807.11205 (2018)

11. Wang, H., Niu, D., Li, B.: Distributed machine learning with a serverless architecture. In: The 2019 IEEE International Conference on Computer Communications (INFOCOM '19) (2019)

12. Carreira, J., Fonseca, P., Tumanov, A., Zhang, A., Katz, R.:. Cirrus: a serverless framework for end-to-end ML workflows. In: The 2019 ACM Symposium on Cloud Computing (SoCC '19) (2019)

13. Jiang, J., Gan, S., Liu, Y., Wang, F., Alonse, G., Klimovic, A., et al.: Towards demystifying serverless machine learning training. In: The 2021 ACM International Conference on Management of Data (SIGMOD '21) (2021)

14. Sánchez-Artigas, M., Sarroca, P.: Experience paper: towards enhancing cost efficiency in serverless machine learning training. In: The 22nd ACM International Middleware Conference (Middleware '21) (2021)

15. DAPR, Distributed Application Runtime. https://dapr.io/. Accessed 18 March 2020

16. Verbraeken, J., Wolting, M., Katzy, J., Kloppenburg, J., Verbelen, T., Rellermeyer, J.S.: A survey on distributed machine learning. ACM Computing Surveys (CSUR), **53**(2), 1–33 (2020)

17. Lian, X., Zhang, W., Zhang, C., Liu, J.: Asynchronous decentralized parallel stochastic gradient descent. In: The 35th International Conference on Machine Learning, PMLR 80 (2018)

18. López, P.G., Arjona, A., Sampé, J., Slominski, A., Villard, L.: Triggerflow: trigger-based orchestration of serverless workflows. Future Gener. Comput. Syst. **124**(1), 215–229 (2021)

19. ElasticDL: A Kubernetes-native deep learning framework. https://elasticdl.github.io/

20. Barcelona-Pons, D., Sutra, P., Sánchez-Artigas, M., París, G., García-López, P.: Stateful serverless computing with crucial[J]. ACM Trans. Softw. Eng. Methodol. **31**(3), 1–38 (2022)

21. Sergeev, A., Balso, M.: Horovod: fast and easy distributed deep learning in TensorFlow. arXiv preprint arXiv:1802.05799 (2018)

DRP:Discrete Rank Pruning for Neural Network

Songwen Pei[1,2,3]([✉]), Jie Luo[1], and Sheng Liang[1]

[1] University of Shanghai for Science and Technology, Shanghai 200093, China
swpei@usst.edu.cn
[2] State Key Laboratory of Computer Architecture, Institute of Computing
Technology, Chinese Academy of Sciences, Beijing 100190, China
[3] Engineering Research Center of Software/Hardware Co-designed Technology
and Application, Ministry of Education (East China Normal University),
Shanghai 200062, China

Abstract. Although deep neural networks (DNNs) have achieved excellent performance in computer vision applications in recent years, it is still challenging to deploy them on resource-limited devices such as mobile phones. To solve this problem, we propose a novel filter pruning method for neural network named Discrete Rank Pruning (DRP). Moreover, many methods apply sparse regularization on the filter weights of the convolution layers to reduce the degradation of performance after pruning. We analyze these methods and find that it is necessary to consider the influence of the bias term. Based on these, we propose a novel sparse method named Consideration Bias Sparsity (CBS). Extensive experiments on MNIST, CIFAR-10 and CIFAR-100 datasets with LeNet-5, VGGNet-16, ResNet-56, GoogLeNet and DenseNet-40 demonstrate the effectiveness of CBS and DRP. For LeNet-5, CBS achieves 1.87% increase in accuracy than sparse regularization on MNIST. For VGGNet-16, DRP achieves 66.6% reduction in FLOPs by removing 83.3% parameters with only 0.36% decrease in accuracy on CIFAR-10. For ResNet-56, DRP achieves 47.45% reduction in FLOPs by removing 42.35% parameters with only 0.82% decrease in accuracy on CIFAR-100.

1 Introduction

Deep Neural Networks (DNNs) have achieved great success in computer vision tasks, such as object detection [1], image classification [2] and video analysis [3]. However, there are challenges in deploying them in edge devices such as mobile phones, robotics and wearable devices due to their high computation costs and memory footprint. To solve this problem, many approaches of model compression have been proposed, including network pruning [4], quantization [5], knowledge distillation [1], and low-rank decomposition [6].

Among the above approaches, network pruning has been a promising technology due to the convenience for practical application. Network pruning can be divided into two categories empirically. i.e. unstructured pruning and structured

© IFIP International Federation for Information Processing 2022
Published by Springer Nature Switzerland AG 2022
S. Liu and X. Wei (Eds.): NPC 2022, LNCS 13615, pp. 168–179, 2022.
https://doi.org/10.1007/978-3-031-21395-3_16

pruning. Unstructured pruning prunes insignificant neurons and their connections by exploring the attribute of network. It causes the network suffering from the defect of irregular calculation and topological structure. Manufacturers require to designing specific software or hardware to support its practical deployment. In contrast, structured pruning does not have this limitation since redundant filters and corresponding channels are removed entirely. For structured pruning algorithms are more hardware-friendly, a wide range of researchers have tried to study further. The typical scheme of structured pruning algorithms consists of three stages: (1) pre-training a neural network model; (2) pruning the model by property importance; (3) fine-tuning the pruned model to recover the decrease in accuracy caused by pruning.

This paper is focused on structured pruning, aiming to remove inessential filters under maintaining high accuracy. We propose a novel filter pruning algorithm for neural network named Discrete Rank Pruning (DRP), as shown in Fig. 1. The inspiration for DRP comes from HRank [7]. HRank empirically demonstrates that the average rank of feature maps generated by a single filter is almost unchanged. Filters with low-rank feature maps are less informative and thus less important to preserve accuracy, which can be removed first. It is observed that the distribution of the average rank of feature maps is very concentrate. Many important filters will be pruned by mistake. As a result, it is necessary to discretize the distribution of average rank. According to former research [8], the small weights in the neural network are less contribution to the accuracy of DNNs. It is unwise to extract the average rank of feature maps directly. Because small weights will noise the final the average rank set. To address this problem, DRP adds a sparsity training stage to obtain the discrete rank set.

During the sparsity training stage, we analyze the existed sparse methods and find that the influence of bias term is not considered. These existed sparse methods usually set small weights to zero directly, regardless of bias term of the convolutional layer. It is an improper manner. For example, a weight in the feature map is small but with a big value of bias. It is arbitrary to set this weight to zero directly. Because activations of this weight are not zero and still contribute effect to the next layer. Based on this observation, we propose a novel sparse method named Consideration Bias Sparsity (CBS).

The main contributions of our work are listed below:

1. It is verified that the average rank of feature maps generated by a single filter will distribute more discretely after sparsity training. Based on this verification, we propose Discrete Rank Pruning (DRP) to effectively conduct filter pruning of DNNs. It is convenient to deploy large scale models on resource-limited devices.
2. We analyze existing sparse methods and find that it is necessary to consider the influence of bias term in the network. Based on this observation, we propose a novel sparse method named Consideration Bias Sparsity (CBS).
3. Extensive experiments on MNIST, CIFAR-10 and CIFAR-100 datasets with LeNet-5, VGGNet-16, ResNet-56, GoogLeNet and DenseNet-40 architectures demonstrate the efficacy of CBS and DRP. And the outstanding experiment

result on different architectures and datasets show the flexibility and extensibility of CBS and DRP.

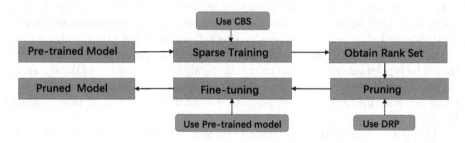

Fig. 1. The framework of DRP.

2 Related Work

In this section, the closely compression techniques will be reviewed. Because this paper is mainly focused on sparse method and structured pruning algorithm, the advantages and disadvantages of previous related researches will be summarized.

2.1 Compression Techniques

To enable DNNs running on resource constrained devices, various model compression techniques have been proposed. Liu et al. [5] proposed an instance-aware dynamic neural network quantization technique to reduce memory footprint by using fewer bits instead of 32-bit full precision to represent weight parameters. Phan et al. [6] proposed a stable low-rank tensor decomposition to compress DNNs. It approximates convolutional operations by representing the weight matrix as a low-rank product of two smaller matrices to reduce the computation cost. Kang et al. [1] proposed an instance-conditional knowledge distillation technique. It utilizes a student network to imitate the soft output of a larger teacher network to obtain fast-to-execute models for object detection.

2.2 Sparse Method

Sparsity is a method by assigning zero values to reduce the number of parameters in neural networks. To reduce more memory footprint and improve the prediction performance of neural network, many existing sparse algorithms apply sparse regularization on the filter weights. For example, Wen et al. [9] proposed a sparse algorithm called SSL to alleviate the damage of the pruning process. SSL adds sparsity learning on the structure to make the pruned model adapt to hardware platforms. Li et al. [10] propose a sparse method called group sparsity. Group sparsity makes a hinge between filter pruning and decomposition to compress network networks. However, these sparse methods all ignore the influence of bias term. CBS sets a threshold to estimate the importance of bias term.

2.3 Structured Pruning

At present, the mainstream structured pruning algorithms are channel pruning and filter pruning. Zhao et al. [11] proposed a channel pruning algorithm called variation pruning. Variation pruning removes redundant channels by the distribution of channel saliency via variation inference automatically. The great strength of variation pruning is to save the computation costs of fine-tuning. DRP uses the pre-trained model to restore the performance of the model on the fine-tuning stage. This operation also saves many computation costs. Li et al. [12] proposed a filter pruning algorithm called PFEC. PFEC measures the relative importance of filters by calculating the sum of its absolute weights. Filters with small absolute weights will be pruned, because they contribute less to the accuracy of the model. Lin et al. [7] proposed a filter pruning algorithm called HRank. HRank removes inessential filters by calculating the average rank of feature maps. The experimental comparison of these methods with DRP will be displayed in Section Experiment & Evaluation.

3 Consideration Bias Sparsity

Existing sparse methods [9,10] apply sparse regularization on the filter weights of convolutions to produce structured sparsity. The training objective function can be shown as follows:

$$W^{(l)} = \lambda \cdot \overrightarrow{L}\left(W^{(l-1)}\right) + \beta^{(l-1)} \tag{1}$$

$W^{(l)}$ represents the weights of the l_{th} convolutional layer. $W^{(l-1)}$ represents the weights of the $(l-1)_{th}$ convolutional layer. $\beta^{(l-1)}$ represents the bias of the $(l-1)_{th}$ convolutional layer. The $\overrightarrow{L}(\cdot)$ is the objective function of the normal training. λ is the factor of controlling the strength of sparsity. Existing sparse methods set $\beta^{(l-1)}$ to zero directly during sparsity training. However, a significant issue is ignored here:

λ and β are independent on the filter weights of convolutions. λ is a scaling factor to indicate the importance of weight. β is a shifting factor to affect activations of this convolutional layer. It is improper to set β to zero directly due to ignoring the influence of shifting factor. For example, some small weights will be set to zero by utilizing the scaling factor λ. However, the value of shifting factor β is very big. It is unwise to set these weights to zero, because activations of this layer are not zero and still affect the next layer.

To remedy this issue,Formula (1) is reformulated as follows:

$$W^{(l)} = \theta_1 \cdot \lambda \cdot \overrightarrow{L}\left(W^{(l-1)}\right) + \theta_2 \cdot \beta^{(l-1)} \tag{2}$$

θ_1 and θ_2 are two different thresholds. θ_1 is used to determine whether a weight is important. θ_2 is used to determine whether a bias is important. When the weight is unimportant and corresponding shifting term is unimportant, this weight can be set to zero. This is the principle of CBS. To describe in more details, the pseudocode of CBS as follows:

Algorithm 1. Consideration Bias Sparsity(CBS)

Input: Pre-trained Model: PTM; Threshold1: θ_1; Threshold2: θ_2; Max layer: L;
Output: Sparity Model: SM;
1: **for** l=1, ..., L **do**
2:     **if** weigth of $PTM < \theta_1$ and corresponding bias $< \theta_2$ **then**
3:         weight = 0 and bias = 0;
4:     **end if**
5: **end for**

---

4   Discrete Rank Pruning

The key of filter pruning is identifying and removing the unimportant filters. Most of prior study work is finding a criterion to measure the importance of filters, which can be summarized as an optimization problem:

$$\min \sum_{i=1}^{M} \sum_{j=1}^{N} \vartheta_j^i L \left(filter_j^i \right) \tag{3}$$

We assume a deep neural network has M convolutional layers and a convolutional layer has N feature maps. $filter_j^i$ represents the j_{th} filter of i_{th} convolutional layer. $L(\cdot)$ is a function used to measure the importance of a filter. The codomain of $L(\cdot)$ is N filters of each layer. If the filter is determined to be important, ϑ_j^i is set to 1, or else ϑ_j^i is set to 0. The function of minimizing Formula (3) is to remove insignificant filters.

Different prior study work, Lin et al. [7] proposed a method called HRank. HRank designed a function $L'(\cdot)$ on the feature maps. By calculating the average rank of feature maps, it can determine significant filters. This operation can be calculated by:

$$\min \sum_{i=1}^{M} \sum_{j=1}^{N} \vartheta_j^i L' \left(feature\ map_j^i \right) \tag{4}$$

where $L'(\cdot)$ is used to extract the average rank of feature maps. $feature\ map_j^i$ represents j_{th} feature map of i_{th} convolution layer. Explicitly, $L'(\cdot)$ can be formulated as follows:

$$L'(\cdot) = Rank \left\{ feature\ map_1^1,\ ...,\ feature\ map_j^i, ...,\ feature\ map_M^N \right\} \tag{5}$$

$Rank\{\cdot\}$ is a set of the average rank of feature maps. After obtaining the rank set of filters, HRank will prune filters with low-rank feature maps, because they contain less information. However, the rank distribution of HRank is relatively concentrated according to actual observation. It will prune many significant filters by mistake. This operation will result in a drop in the accuracy of model. Therefore, it is necessary to design a function to optimize the rank set:

$$\min \sum_{i=1}^{M} \sum_{j=1}^{N} \vartheta_j^i L'' \left(Rank\{\cdot\} \right) \tag{6}$$

Research [8] has proved that the weights with small values are unimportant. Corresponding neurons can be pruned. Based on this research, weights with small values in the feature maps will noise the extraction of average rank. Before obtaining the rank set, it is wise to set small weights in the feature maps to zero. As a result, the function $L''(\cdot)$ can be described as follows:

$$L''(\cdot) = Sparse\{W_1^1, ..., W_j^i..., W_M^N\} \tag{7}$$

W_j^i represents the weights of j_{th} feature map of i_{th} convolutional layer. $Sparse\{\cdot\}$ is a objective function used to set small weights to zero. After sparsity training, the distribution of rank will be more discrete. By using the discrete rank, more parameters compression can be obtained. This is the principle of DRP. To describe in more details, the pseudocode of DRP as follows:

Algorithm 2. Discrete Rank Pruning(DRP)

Input: Pre-trained Model: PTM; Pruning rate: p; Training epoch: E; Mini-batch B;
Output: Pruned Model: PM;
1: Use CBS to train PTM;
2: Obtain sparisty model SM;
3: **for** b=1, ..., B **do**
4:     Extract the average rank of SM;
5: **end for**
6: Obtain the discrete rank set;
7: **for** e=1, ..., E **do**
8:     Prune unimportant filters by using discrete rank set and p;
9:     Use PTM to fine-tune iteratively;
10: **end for**

---

5 Experiment and Evaluation

In this section, extensive experiments on several benchmark datasets with different network architectures demonstrate the effectiveness of CBS and DRP.

5.1 Datasets and Network Models

Datasets. MNIST is a handwritten digit dataset, which contains 60,000 training images and 10,000 testing images. Each image is a fixed size (28×28) with values from 0 to 1. CIFAR-10 and CIFAR-100 are color image datasets, which contains 50,000 training images and 10,000 testing images. And they are drawn from 10 and 100 classes respectively. Each image of them is cropped as 32×32 randomly.

Network Models. LeNet-5 [13] is a typical network model, which is composed of 3 convolutional layers and 2 fully connected layers. VGGNet-16 [14], ResNet-56 [15], GoogLeNet [16] and DensNet-40 [17] is a network with a plain structure, a residual block, an inception module and a dense block respectively.

5.2   Implementation

Training Strategy. For CBS, LeNet-5 is trained and tested on MNIST with a batch size of 64 and 30 epochs. VGGNet-16 is trained and tested on CIFAR-10 with the same setting. For DRP, VGGNet-16, ResNet-56, GoogLeNet and DenseNet-40 are trained and tested on CIFAR-10 and CIFAR-100. Among them, VGGNet-16 is trained with a batch size 256 and 150 epochs for total. Other networks are trained with a batch size 256 and 300 epochs due to the depth of network. The SGD optimizer is utilized to solve the optimization problem with momentum 0.9. 5 batch size images are used to estimate the average rank of feature maps.

Evaluation Metric. Numbers of parameters and Floating Point Operations (FLOPs) are used to measure the model size and computation cost respectively. To evaluate the task-specific capabilities, top-1 accuracy of sparsity training model on MNIST, CIFAR-10 and CIFAR-100 is used to demonstrate the superiority of CBS and DRP.

5.3   Results and Analysis on CBS

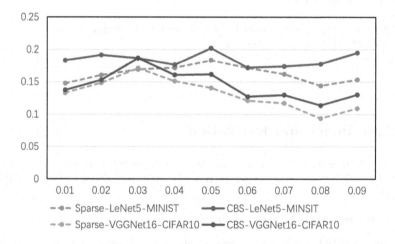

Fig. 2. The accuracy of sparse models with different threshold of weight.

Table 1 shows the accuracy of sparse models with different thresholds. Based on actual observation, most of bias terms are less than 0.1. Thus the range of bias can be narrowed to [0.01, 0.1]. In the process of selecting the threshold of bias, the threshold of weight is set to 0.01. From Table 1, the best accuracy of sparse model on LeNet-5 is 18.32%, where the threshold is 0.06. The best accuracy of sparse model on VGGNet-16 is 13.72%, where the threshold also is 0.06. Therefore, the appropriate threshold of bias can be determined as 0.06.

Table 1. The accuracy of sparse models with different threhold of bias

Threshold	0.01	0.02	0.03	0.04	0.05	0.06	0.07	0.08	0.09	0.10
LeNet	15.20%	15.60%	17.57%	16.24%	16.31%	18.32%	17.19%	16.62%	15.90%	16.87%
VGGNet	11.79%	12.50%	9.20%	10.94%	12.11%	13.72%	10.16%	11.33%	11.72%	11.19%

Figure 2 shows the accuracy of sparse models variation of different threshold of weight. The horizontal axis represents the threshold and the vertical axis represents the accuracy of sparse method. When the threshold of weight is greater than 0.08, weights of some convolutional layers all are 0. Meanwhile, the gradient of models will disappear and lead to the failure of backpropagation. Thus, the range of weight can be narrowed to [0.01, 0.08]. The bias terms of sparse regularization all are set to zero. The bias terms of CBS that are less than 0.06 will be set to zero. From Fig. 2, the accuracy of CBS is greater than the accuracy of sparse regularization regardless of different threshold. When the threshold is 0.05, the accuracy of LeNet-5 on MINIST is best. Meanwhile, the accuracy of sparse regularization is 18.34% and the accuracy of CBS is 20.21%. CBS achieves 1.87% increase than sparse regularization. When the threshold is 0.03, the accuracy of VGGNet-16 on CIFAR-10 is best. Meanwhile, the accuracy of sparse regularization is 17.11% and the accuracy of CBS is 18.67%. CBS achieves 1.56% increase than sparse regularization.

Based on extensive experiments, the thresholds of weight on VGGNet-16, ResNet56, GoogLeNet, and DenseNet-40 can be determined to 0.03, 0.04, 0.06, 0.04 respectively. The thresholds of bias on all network models can be determined to 0.06. Considering the length of paper, The complete data is not displayed.

5.4   Results and Analysis on DRP

Table 2 shows the performance of different network models on CIFAR-10 dataset. To demonstrate the superiority of DRP, the existing pruning algorithms such as PFEC, VCNNP and HRank are used to compare.

The accuracy of VGGNet-16 on CIFAR-10 is 93.46% after pre-training and the number of parameters is 14.98M. When VGGNet-16 performs the image classification task on CIFAR-10, the floating-point operations (FLOPs) is 313.73M. From Table 2, DRP can remove 83.3% parameters with relatively small loss of accuracy. Meanwhile, the FLOPs of VGGNet-16 can be removed 66.66% due to the decrease of parameters.

Compared to existing structured pruning algorithms, PFEC can prune 64% parameters with 0.56 loss of accuracy by calculating the absolute value of weight. VCNNP can prune 73.3% parameters with 0.78 loss of accuracy by the distribution of scaling factor on Batch Normalization (BN) layer. The parameter compression and model performance all are weaker than DRP. This is because the used pruning criterion is not imprecise enough. It is difficult to identify inconsequential channels and filters on the late pruning stage.

Figure 3 show the distribution of feature maps' average ranks before and after sparsity training. HRank prunes insignificant filters by using original rank.

Table 2. Results on CIFAR-10

Model	Accuracy	Parameters	PR	FLOPs	PR
VGGNet-16	93.96	14.98M	-	313.73M	-
PFEC [12]	93.40	5.4M	64%	206M	34.2%
VCNNP [11]	93.18	3.92M	73.3%	190M	39.1%
HRank [7]	93.43	2.51M	82.9%	145.61M	53.5%
DRP	93.60	2.50M	83.3%	104.78M	66.66%
ResNet-56	93.26	0.85M	-	125.49M	-
DRP	92.50	0.24M	70.0%	34.78M	72.3%
GoogLeNet	95.05	6.15M	-	1.52B	-
DRP	94.86	2.09M	65.8%	0.39B	73.9%
DenseNet-40	94.81	1.04M	-	282.00M	-
DRP	94.59	0.39M	61.9%	113.08M	59.9%

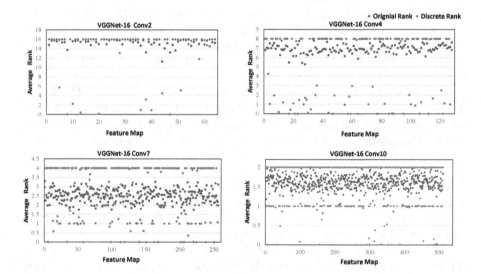

Fig. 3. The distribution of average rank.

It can prune 82.9% parameters with 0.53 loss of accuracy. After using CBS to train the pre-trained model, the average ranks of feature map distribute more discrete, as shown ret dots in Fig. 3. By using the discrete rank, DRP can prune more parameters with the 0.17 increase of accuracy than HRank.

With the increase of pruning ratio, the accuracy of the model will decrease inevitably. The VGGNet-16 on the CIFAR-10 is adopted to show the accuracy variation via different pruning ratio. The results are demonstrated in Fig. 4. When the pruning ratio of parameter is less than 80%, the accuracy of pruned model stabilizes around baseline. However, when the pruning ratio of the parameter is set around 85%, the accuracy of pruned model begins to drop dramatically. If the pruning ratio of parameter is more than 90%, the pruned model will lose the ability to perform image classification. Moreover, from the Fig. 4, the performance of DRP is over HRank and DRP-Sparse (DRP-Sparse is a method use sparse regularization to train VGGNet-16) regardless of the pruning ratio.

To further explore the advantages of DRP, ResNet-56, GoogLeNet and DensNet-40 are pruned on the CIFAR-10 dataset respectively to verity extendibility of DRP. As demonstrated in Table 2, 70% parameters of ResNet-56 are removed with the 0.76 decrease in accuracy. Under the same condition, 65.8% parameters of GoogLeNet and 61.9% parameters of DenseNet-40 are removed with 0.19 and 0.22 decrease in accuracy respectively. These decreases in accuracy are compromising because of the huge savings in memory footprint.

To demonstrate the flexibility of DRP,the pruning results with different network architecture on CIFAR-100 are shown in Table 3. By using DRP, 66.60% FLOPs of VGGNet-16 are removed by pruning 82.58% parameters with only 0.88 decrease in accuracy. In the same situation, 47.45% FLOPs of ResNet-56 are removed by pruning 42.35% parameters with 0.82 decrease in accuracy. The network structure of ResNet-56 is more complex than VGGNet-16, so it is more difficult for ResNet-56 to improve the pruning ratio than VGGNet-16. The same reason applies to GoogLeNet and DensNet-40. GoogLeNet can achieve 73.68% FLOPs reduction by pruning 64.39% parameters with 2.33 loss of accuracy. DenseNet-40 can achieve 41.54% FLOPs reduction by pruning 41.35% parameters with 2.5 loss of accuracy. The decrease in accuracy of GoogLeNet and DenseNet-40 is a bit large. One reason is that the classification results of the model on CIFAR-100 is not outstanding, and the other reason is that training network is random.

Table 3. Results on CIFAR-100

Model	Accuracy	Parameters	PR	FLOPs	PR
VGGNet-16	72.17	14.98M	-	313.73M	-
DRP	71.29	2.55M	82.58%	104.78M	66.60%
ResNet-56	70.73	0.85M	-	125.49M	-
DRP	69.91	0.49M	42.35%	65.95M	47.45%
GoogLeNet	79.39	6.15M	-	1.52B	-
DRP	77.06	2.19M	64.39%	0.40B	73.68%
DenseNet-40	72.48	1.04M	-	282.00M	-
DRP	69.98	0.61M	41.35%	164.94M	41.51%

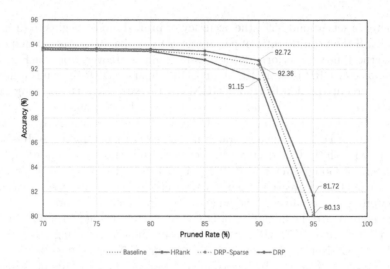

Fig. 4. The accuracy of sparse models with different threshold of weight.

6   Conclusion

In this paper, we propose Discrete Rank Pruning (DRP) for removing insignificant filters in DNNs. We verify that average rank of feature map will distribute more discretely after sparsity training. In the process of analyzing the existing sparse regularization, we find that it is necessary to consider the influence of bias term of convolutional layer and propose a novel sparse method named Consideration Bias Sparsity (CBS). The extensive experiments on different datasets and mainstream network models demonstrate the outstanding performance of CBS and DRP. In the future, we plan to explore a better way to select a threshold and conduct DRP on large-scale datasets to verify the effectiveness of DRP further.

Acknowledgments. The authors would like to thank the anonymous reviewers for their invaluable comments. This work was partially funded by the National Natural Science Foundation of China under Grant No. 61975124, Shanghai Natural Science Foundation (20ZR1438500), State Key Laboratory of Computer Architecture (ICT, CAS) under Grant No. CARCHA202111, and Engineering Research Center of Software/Hardware Co-design Technology and Application, Ministry of Education East China Normal University under Grant No. OP202202. Any opinions, findings and conclusions expressed in this paper are those of the authors and do not necessarily reflect the views of the sponsors.

References

1. Kang, Z., et al.: Instance-conditional knowledge distillation for object detection. In: Advances in Neural Information Processing Systems (NIPS), pp. 16468–16480 (2021)

2. Rao, Y., et al.: Global filter networks for image classification. In: Advances in Neural Information Processing Systems (NIPS), p. 34 (2021)
3. Tang, Y., et al.: Coin: a large-scale dataset for comprehensive instructional video analysis. In: Proceedings of the IEEE/CVF Conference on Computer Vision and Pattern Recognition (CVPR), pp. 1207–1216 (2019)
4. Pei S., et al.: Neural network compression and acceleration by federated pruning. In: International Conference on Algorithms and Architectures for Parallel Processing (ICA3PP), pp. 1–10 (2020)
5. Liu, Z., et al.: Instance-aware dynamic neural network quantization. In: Proceedings of the IEEE/CVF Conference on Computer Vision and Pattern Recognition (CVPR), pp. 12434–12443 (2022)
6. Phan, A.-H., Sobolev, K., Sozykin, K., Ermilov, D., Gusak, J., Tichavský, P., Glukhov, V., Oseledets, I., Cichocki, A.: Stable low-rank tensor decomposition for compression of convolutional neural network. In: Vedaldi, A., Bischof, H., Brox, T., Frahm, J.-M. (eds.) ECCV 2020. LNCS, vol. 12374, pp. 522–539. Springer, Cham (2020). https://doi.org/10.1007/978-3-030-58526-6_31
7. Lin, M., et al.: HRank: filter pruning using high-rank feature map. In: Proceedings of the IEEE/CVF Conference on Computer Vision and Pattern Recognition (CVPR), pp. 1529–1538 (2020)
8. Han, S., et al.: Learning both weights and connections for efficient neural network. In: Advances in Neural Information Processing Systems (NIPS), p. 28 (2015)
9. Wen, W., et al.: Learning structured sparsity in deep neural networks. In: Advances in Neural Information Processing Systems (NIPS), pp. 2074–2082 (2016)
10. Li, Y., et al.: Group sparsity: The hinge between filter pruning and decomposition for network compression. In: Proceedings of the IEEE/CVF Conference on Computer Vision and Pattern Recognition (CVPR), pp. 8018–8027 (2020)
11. Zhao, C., et al.: Variational convolutional neural network pruning. In: Proceedings of the IEEE/CVF Conference on Computer Vision and Pattern Recognition (CVPR), pp. 2780–2789 (2019)
12. Li, H., et al.: Pruning filters for efficient convnets. arXiv preprint arXiv:1608.08710 (2016)
13. Lecun, Y., et al.: Gradient-based learning applied to document recognition. Proc. IEEE **86**(11), 2278–2324 (1998)
14. Simonyan, K., et al.: Very deep convolutional networks for largescale image recognition. arXiv preprint arXiv:1409.1556 (2014)
15. He K, et al.: Deep residual learning for image recognition. In: Proceedings of the IEEE Conference on Computer Vision and Pattern Recognition (CVPR), pp. 770–778 (2016)
16. Szegedy C., et al.: Going deeper with convolutions. In: Proceedings of the IEEE Conference on Computer Vision and Pattern Recognition (CVPR), pp. 1–9 (2015)
17. Huang G., et al.: Densely connected convolutional networks. In: Proceedings of the IEEE Conference on Computer Vision and Pattern Recognition(CVPR), pp. 4700–4708 (2017)

TransMigrator: A Transformer-Based Predictive Page Migration Mechanism for Heterogeneous Memory

Songwen Pei[1,2(✉)], Jianan Li[1], Yihuan Qian[1], Jie Tang[3],
and Jean-Luc Gaudiot[4]

[1] University of Shanghai for Science and Technology, Shanghai 200093, China
swpei@usst.edu.cn
[2] State Key Laboratory of Computer Architecture, Institute of Computing
Technology, Chinese Academy of Sciences, Beijing 100190, China
[3] South China University of Technology, Guangzhou 510641, China
[4] University of California, Irvine, CA 92617, USA

Abstract. Page migration strategies are crucial to the performance of a
hybrid main memory system which consists of DRAM and Non-Volatile
RAM. Previous locality-based migration strategies have limitations on
deciding which pages should be placed in limited DRAM. In this paper,
we propose TransMigrator, a transformer-based predictive page migration mechanism. TransMigrator uses an end-to-end neural network to
directly predict the page that will be accessed most in the near future, by
learning patterns from long memory access history. The network achieved
0.7245 average accuracy of prediction with 0.804 MB model parameter
size. Besides, a threshold-based method is used at the same time to
make the system robust. TransMigrator reduces access time by 23.59%
on average compared with AC-CLOCK, THMigrator and VC-HMM.

1 Introduction

The development of the data-intensive application exposes limitations of DRAM,
such as unscalable capacity and huge static energy consumption. Recent research
[5] has revealed that DRAM consumes 30%–48% energy of the whole system.
Thus, Non-Volatile RAM (NVM) emerged in order to solve these problems,
which promises higher storage density and lower static energy consumption
[2,3,18]. However, compared to conventional DRAM, NVM also shows lower
performance, like slower data access especially in data writing, limited write
endurance and higher write energy consumption.

Considering these defects, NVM cannot replace DRAM entirely. Instead,
hybrid memory system which formed with DRAM and NVM has been proposed
to take both advantages and disadvantages of the two devices into consideration.
[4,9,15,22]. In this system, hot pages which are accessed more frequently could

© IFIP International Federation for Information Processing 2022
Published by Springer Nature Switzerland AG 2022
S. Liu and X. Wei (Eds.): NPC 2022, LNCS 13615, pp. 180–191, 2022.
https://doi.org/10.1007/978-3-031-21395-3_17

be placed in DRAM and cold pages which are accessed less frequently could be placed in NVM.

Hybrid memory system has two organizations, **vertical** and **horizontal**. In the vertical organization, DRAM is used as a cache for NVM. When a request missed in DRAM, a copy of the accessed page will be made for further requests. DRAM also could be by passed (i.e., access NVM directly) in this organization like THMigrator [16].

In the horizontal organization, DRAM and NVM are combined into one address space. In some designs, a page could only exist in one device, such as CLOCK-DWF [11] and AC-CLOCK [10]. We name these strategies **exclusive strategy**. In some other designs, a page cloud exist in two devices, such as APMigrate [19] and VC-HMM [17]. We name these strategies **redundant strategy**. The vertical organization naturally belongs to the redundant strategy, because a page could appear both in DRAM and NVM.

In order to take advantage of the hybrid memory system, pages should be placed in DRAM and NVM carefully through hotness evaluation. CLOCK-DWF only migrates dirty pages (i.e., pages being written) to DRAM, while AC-CLOCK migrates pages being both read and written. THMigrator migrates pages through a fixed threshold, which is hard to fit different kinds of applications. APMigrate and VC-HMM update threshold by the benefit of a previous migration. But the initial value of the threshold makes the system fragile. If the initial threshold is too small, a lot of low beneficial migrations will be performed. These migrations are not detected until they are evicted back. So, the threshold will become very large when these pages are migrated back and prevent the following migrations from NVM. This pitfall is shown in our experiments.

To catch the most frequently accessed page accurately, we use the **neural network** which has the ability to learn the regular pattern of memory access.

Some works have already used neural networks in page migration in hybrid memory system. Kleio [6] trains individual neural network for each important pages to predict the access count of each page in the next duration. Instead, we prefer a single network to simplify the system design. DeepSwapper [20] uses LSTMs to predict the next memory access sequence from previous sequence. It uses differences of adjacent addresses as input and output. However, in our experiments, it is very unstable to recover the addresses from differences due to the low precision. To address the problem, we designed an end-to-end network to predict the hot page directly. The main contributions are summarized as follows:

- A transformer-based end-to-end predictor is proposed for hot page prediction.
- A robust hybrid memory architecture, TransMigrator, is proposed. TransMigrator integrating the predictor with a fallback threshold-based method to achieve low access latency even when the predictor makes a mispreciton.
- Our design is evaluated on various benchmarks in SPEC 2006 and achieves remarkable results.

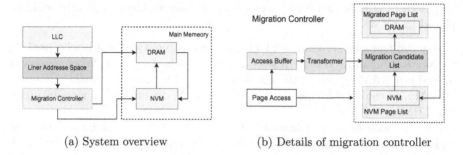

(a) System overview   (b) Details of migration controller

Fig. 1. Migration controller

2 TransMigrator

Figure 1a shows the overview of TransMigrator in system level. TransMigrator is designed for the horizontal organization with a redundant strategy for a hybrid memory system. All the LLC misses are intercepted by the migration controller (MigC). The MigC is responsible for address translation and page migration between DRAM and NVM. Details of MigC are shown in Fig. 1b.

TransMigrator contains a migration part and a prediction part.

The left part of Fig. 1b is the prediction part. Page numbers are stored in a buffer prepared as the network input. The predictor is a stander transformer [21].

The right part of Fig. 1b depicts the migration part. The NVM Page List (NPL) is used to track pages in NVM, and the Migrated Page List (MPL) is used to track pages in DRAM. Besides, the Migration Candidate List (MCL) is used to store the pages might be hot. Pages in MCL will be migrated to DRAM when being accessed again. But they will be removed from MCL if their lifetimes expire. In order to track the lifetime, we need a request counter. The expired time is set to the current counter value plus the lifetime. The MCL is the bridge between the migration part and the prediction part.

The predictor may perform not well on some benchmarks. Instead of relying on the predictor alone, we also use a fixed threshold method in parallel with the predictor, which will makes the system more robust.

2.1 Design of Neural Network

The end-to-end network uses a sequence of page numbers as the input to directly predict the page number that will appear most in the next sequence. Figure 2 shows the details of the network. We model the problem as a classification problem. Page numbers are treated as words, and every word is corresponding to an embedding vector. To reduce the dictionary size, page numbers are split into small tokens like approaches in natural language processing.

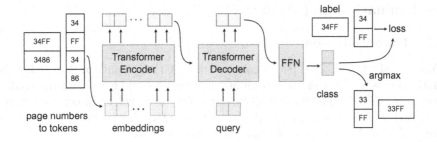

Fig. 2. Details of the neural network.

Input and Output. The input is a sequence of L_{seq} page numbers. Each page number is split into N small tokens in L_{token} bits, used as indices to select embeddings. The output is a sequence of N small tokens which can be assembled back to a page number.

Considering our traces are small, we set the address space 32 bits. We use 4 KB page size, so the page number is 20 bits. Zeros are padded to the high bits if 20 is not the multiple of L_{token}.

Network. Dimension of token embeddings and model dimension of the transformer are same, denoted as d_{model}. The dimension of feedforward networks in the transformer is $2 * d_{model}$. Tokens are converted to embeddings as the input of the transformer encoder. The input of the transformer decoder is N learnable embeddings. Features of the decoder output will be transformed from d_{model} to C by a linear layer. C is the dictionary size, i.e. $2^{L_{token}}$. The cross entropy between decoder output and real labels is minimized.

2.2 Page Migration

A memory access will trigger two data paths simultaneously. One is the predictor. The page number will be added to the access buffer, and all page numbers will be fed into the predictor if their numbers reach L. The predictor could add its output page number to MCL anytime with lifetime L_{seq}.

The other path is the migration routine. The accessed page is denoted as P. The MigC will first do one of the following: 1. P is in MPL. P will be moved to MPL head. And mark it dirty if the request is a write request. 2. P is in MCL. P will be migrated to DRAM from NVM. If DRAM is full, the page at the tail of MCL (P_{tail}) will be evicted to NVM. P_{tail} will be written back anyway if P_{tail} is not in NPL. Otherwise, only dirty P_{tail} need to be written back. After ensuring there is room in DRAM, P will be copied to DRAM leaving its original data in NVM. In this way, only dirty pages need to be written back. 3. P is in NPL. Increase P's access counter. If it reaches the migration threshold T, add P to MCL with lifetime $life$. 4. Not find P. Ensure DRAM has room like above, load P from store device to DRAM, and place P at MPL's head. Then, the MigC remove all pages that run out their lifetimes from MCL.

3   Evaluation and Analysis

3.1   Trace Collection

Traces of SPEC CPU2006 [8] are collected using GEM5 simulator [14]. 10 benchmarks are used and run for 100 million instructions. Table 1 shows the configuration of GEM5 simulation. We simulated the prevalent architecture of three level caches. An AtomicSimpleCPU is used for better simulation speed, because the timing of the traces is not required in our simulation.

Table 1. GEM5 simulation configuration.

CPU	AtomicSimpleCPU
L1 data cache	32 KB (8-way, 64-byte line)
L1 instruction cache	32 KB (8-way, 64-byte line)
L2 cache	512 KB (8-way, 64-byte line)
L3 cache	4 MB (16-way, 64-byte line)

3.2   Network Training

Dataset. The dataset used to train and validate the network is the mixture of all traces. The input sequence length of the network is noted as L_{seq}. The traces are first split into small sequences in the length $2 * L_{seq}$. The first half of a sequence is used as input while the latter half of a sequence is used for producing real labels. The label is the first page number that appears most in the latter half sequence. A stride of $0.5 * L_{seq}$ is applied in splitting in order to get more sequences. Then, all sequences are split randomly into training set and validation set in 7:3 ratio.

However, the data of training set is severe imbalanced in terms of benchmarks which would undermine the performance of the network. A weighted sampler is used to tackle this problem. The number of sequences of benchmark i is noted as n_i. $\frac{1}{n_i}$ is used as the weight for sequences of benchmark i. Thus, small traces have more opportunity to be sampled into a training batch.

Table 2. Network training configuration.

Encoder layers	2	Learning rate	0.001
Decoder layers	2	Batch size	2048
Number of heads	2	Dropout	0.0
Model dimension	64	Seed	43
Sequence length	30	Loss	Cross entropy
Token length	8	Optimizer	Adam

Network Configuration. Table 2 shows the configuration of the network. In order to get stable convergence, we use a cosine learning rate scheduler with a warm-up stage. It calculates the learning rate factor following Eq. 1. i represents iterations in batches, w represents warm-up steps and m represents the max iteration.

$$\text{lr factor} = \begin{cases} 0.5(1 + cos(\frac{i}{m}\pi)) & , i \geq w \\ i/w & , i < w \end{cases} \tag{1}$$

Results. Traces are split into sequences of length L, and check whether the predicted page is the page that appears most in the next sequence. The network achieved 0.7245 prediction accuracy with 0.804 MB estimated model parameter size.

3.3   Migration Simulation

A trace simulator is developed to evaluate kinds of page migration strategies. The neural network is simulated by preparing the predicted results in individual file for each benchmark in advance. A predicted page number will be read from corresponding file as needed.

Configurations. AC-CLOCK [10], THMigrator [16] and VC-HMM [17] are used as the comparisons. AC-CLOCK has no hyperparameters. THMigrator, VC-HMM and our design have two parameters, threshold and lifetime, which are set to 32 and 256 respectively. Besides, VC-HMM also uses a small DRAM as a direct mapping victim cache between DRAM and NVM.

In order to simulate the intensive memory usage, we set the NVM size for each benchmark to the approximate memory footprint. The DRAM size, NVM size and victim cache size are set as the ratio $1 : 8 : \frac{1}{16}$ to align with the real world usage and VC-HMM.

Table 3. Memory characteristics

Attributes	DRAM	NVM
Latency read (ns)	15	50
Latency write (ns)	15	150
Energy read (mJ/GB)	12.1857	15.62
Energy write (mJ/GB)	3.0469	150
Energy static (mW/GB)	100	1

Calculations. Total access time and total energy consumption are calculated according to Eqs. 2 and 3. These equations are adopted from APMigrate with some modification.

Variables in Eqs. 2 and 3 are explained in Table 4. t_{mig} is 380 times of t_{dr} according to APMigrate. Other variable values are adopted from [23] and listed in Table 3.

$$t_{total} = n_{dr} * t_{dr} + n_{dw} * t_{dw}$$
$$+ n_{nr} * t_{nr} + n_{nw} * t_{nw} \qquad (2)$$
$$+ n_{mig} * t_{mig}$$

$$e_{total} = data_{dr} * e_{dr} + data_{dw} * e_{dw}$$
$$+ data_{nr} * e_{nr} + data_{nw} * e_{nw} \qquad (3)$$
$$+ (p_d * size_d + p_n * size_n) * t_{total}$$

Table 4. Variables in computation

n_{dr}	DRAM read count	$data_{dr}$	Total data of DRAM read
n_{dw}	DRAM write count	$data_{dw}$	Total data of DRAM write
n_{nr}	NVM read count	$data_{nr}$	Total data of NVM read
n_{nw}	NVM write count	$data_{nw}$	Total data of NVM write
n_{mig}	Migration count	e_{dr}	DRAM read energy
t_{dr}	DRAM read latency	e_{dw}	DRAM write energy
t_{dw}	DRAM write latency	e_{nr}	NVM read energy
t_{nr}	NVM read latency	e_{nw}	NVM write energy
t_{nw}	NVM write latency	p_d	DRAM static power
t_{mig}	Migration latency	p_n	NVM static power
$size_d$	DRAM size	$size_n$	NVM size

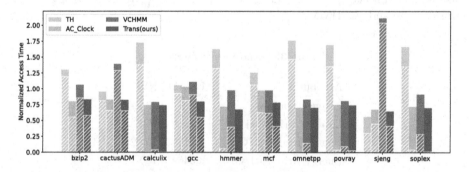

Fig. 3. Normalized access time. The whole bar is the total access time. The shadow part is the access time of NVM.

3.4   Access Time

Figure 3 shows the access time of different migration strategies. Data are normalized by dividing their mean for each benchmark for more consistent scales.

Our method reduces the average access time over THMigrator, VC-HMM and AC-CLOCK by 38.72%, 26.27% and 5.41% respectively.

THMigrator is conservative in our experiment setting. It makes fewer migrations than other approaches and results very low energy consumption. But it leaves too many pages in NVM and boosts the access time dramatically. On benchmark gcc and sjeng, THMigrator achieves better performance by more page migrations. Given that DRAM has limited capacity, it is necessary to migrate certain pages for better performance. Too few migrations will undermine the performance of the system. On benchmark sjeng, VC-HMM also reflects a defect of a class of strategies that update the threshold by benefits. There is usually a long duration between migration beginning and threshold adjustment. When low beneficial migrations are detected, the threshold will be pushed to an extreme value that prevents the following migrations and prevents the threshold back to normal range as well. Even if VC-HMM has the possibility to fall in the trap, it performs better than THMigrator in most cases. AC-CLOCK achieves relative low access time than THMigrator and VC-HMM, and robust in all the benchmarks. Our design achieves lower access time than AC-CLOCK except on benchmark bzip2. TransMigrator has more NVM writes than AC-CLOCK on benchmark bzip2. Pages have many write accesses may not be migrated in terms of access count, because read and write are not distinguished in our design. In most benchmarks, TransMigrator has robust and good performance. It achieves low access time in benchmark cactusADM, even if the prediction accuracy is only 40.10%. This proves the co-work of the predictor and the fallback method is effective and robust.

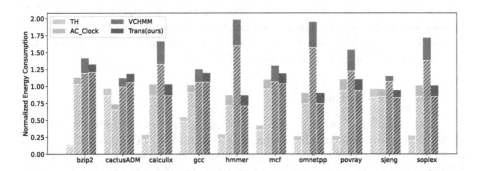

Fig. 4. Normalized energy consumption. The whole bar is the total energy consumption. The shadow part is the energy consumption of NVM.

3.5   Energy Consumption

Figure 4 shows the total energy consumption of different migration strategies. Data are normalized by dividing their mean for each benchmark. Our method

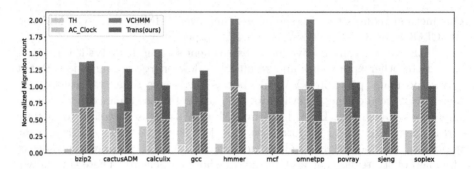

Fig. 5. Normalized migration count. The shadow part is the actual write back count of NVM. Clean pages that are not written back are excluded. The whole bar is the migration count from NVM to DRAM plus write back count.

reduces the average total energy consumption by 25.04% compared with VC-HMM, but consumes more energy than AC-CLOCK by 10.22%. TransMigrator consumes 2.5 times energy than THMigrator, but THMigrator fails to provide fast access.

NVM is dominant in energy consumption. Despite the low static power, NVM has big overhead of read and write compared with DRAM, especially in page migrations. The more page migration, the more energy consumption (see Fig. 5). But more page migration may not reduce the access time. On benchmark hmmer and omnetpp, VC-HMM makes much more page migrations than TransMigrator but has higher access time than TransMigrator. VC-HMM has the lowest migrations but the highest energy consumption, because regular accesses of NVM become the majority consumption in this circumstance. AC-CLOCK and Trans-Migrator makes better balance between energy consumption and access time compared with other two approaches.

3.6 Network Overhead

Due to the parallel of prediction part and migration part, the network overhead could be partially hidden. The system will function with or without the network part. The migration part always does its routine. The network affects the system latency more by its prediction accuracy than its inference speed. Considering that the network only commits an inference every multiple memory accesses and all kinds of technics that could be applied to boost the network, a more sophisticate model could be used to achieve better prediction accuracy without inducing notable latency.

4 Related Work

Adavally et al. [1] adjust thresholds of migration by monitoring the number of migrations during a window and average access counts of migrate pages. Besides, it uses a small mapping table and moves some pages to their original positions when the mapping table is almost full. OAM [12], however, migrates data in program object level. It combines access time and energy consumption into one formula, and injects allocation instructions and migration instructions by compiler. For objects that are larger that a page size, they will be split into small chunks.

Kleio's design has three parts [6]. It first selects important pages, and then trains a recurrent neural network per important page. Finally, the predicted access counts are used with a history-based approach to perform migrations. We also use a deep-learning method with a non-deep-learning one, but the two parts both handle all the pages. Besides, we only use one neural network. DeepSwapper [20] uses LSTMs to predict the future address differences from input address differences. It then migrates high frequently written pages to NVM. Whereas our network treat read and write same. Doudali et al. [7] map the page accesses to the pixels of a 256×256 image. And manually mark the area that reflects page access patterns. Pages in the marked area are deemed as important pages, and the same steps are performed on these pages as Kleio's design. TransFetch [24] proposed by Zhang et al. is designed to prefetch data to cache instead of page migration. But they split inputs using the same method as ours and use the transformer as well. Page address and block index are concatenated and split into segments in same bits. But they use a linear layer to get embeddings instead of an embedding dictionary. Besides, each embedding is combined with a classification token and a position embedding. They use bitmaps as outputs and labels, which is also different from us. Long et al. [13] proposed a method to prefetch an additional page when a page fault occurs either on CPU or GPU. Their task is similar to page migration. They model the problem as classification and use transformer encoders to predict the page with the highest probability to be accessed in the near future. Each delta value is a class, so the number of class varies among benchmarks. The input is a vector of 13 features including PC, address of different scales, etc.

5 Conclusion

In this article, we proposed TransMigrator for page migration in hybrid main memory system. We designed an end-to-end neural network using transformer as the backbone to directly predict the hot page in the near future from previous memory accesses. The network achieved 0.7245 average prediction accuracy on different benchmark with 0.804 MB estimated model parameter size. The transformer-based predictor is combined with a fixed threshold migration approach which is a fallback when the prediction accuracy becomes low. These two parts makes migrations accurate, and makes the latency low even if the predictor makes mispredicitons.

TransMigrator achieved high performance on various applications. Our experiments show that TransMigrator reduced average access time over THMigrator, VC-HMM and AC-CLOCK by 38.72%, 26.27% and 5.41% respectively.

Our work also has some insufficiencies. Firstly, the simulator we implemented has no timing, so that some overheads of migration are technically ignored. Secondly, our neural network doesn't distinguish the read and write. Finally, the fallback method is too simple. Our network actually can be used with any other page migration strategies. We leave these problems to our future work.

Acknowledgments. We would like to thank the anonymous reviewers for their invaluable comments. This work was partially funded by the National Natural Science Foundation of China under Grant 61975124, Shanghai Natural Science Foundation (20ZR1438500), State Key Laboratory of Computer Architecture (ICT, CAS) under Grant No. CARCHA202111, and Engineering Research Center of Software/Hardware Co-design Technology and Application, Ministry of Education East China Normal University under Grant No.OP202202. Any opinions, findings and conclusions expressed in this paper are those of the authors and do not necessarily reflect the views of the sponsors.

References

1. Adavally, S., Islam, M., Kavi, K.: Dynamically adapting page migration policies based on applications' memory access behaviors. ACM J. Emerg. Technol. Comput. Syst. **17**(2), 1–24 (2021)
2. Burr, G.W., et al.: Recent progress in phase-change memory technology. IEEE J. Emerg. Sel. Top. Circuits Syst. **6**(2), 146–162 (2016)
3. Cappelletti, P.: Non volatile memory evolution and revolution. In: 2015 IEEE International Electron Devices Meeting (IEDM), pp. 10.1.1–10.1.4 (2015)
4. Chen, A.: A review of emerging non-volatile memory (NVM) technologies and applications. Solid-State Electron. **125**, 25–38 (2016)
5. Dayarathna, M., Wen, Y., Fan, R.: Data center energy consumption modeling: a survey. IEEE Commun. Surv. Tutor. **18**(1), 732–794 (2016)
6. Doudali, T.D., Blagodurov, S., Vishnu, A., Gurumurthi, S., Gavrilovska, A.: Kleio: a hybrid memory page scheduler with machine intelligence. In: Proceedings of the 28th International Symposium on High-Performance Parallel and Distributed Computing, pp. 37–48. HPDC 2019, Association for Computing Machinery, New York, June 2019
7. Doudali, T.D., Gavrilovska, A.: Toward Computer Vision-based Machine Intelligent Hybrid Memory Management. In: The International Symposium on Memory Systems, pp. 1–6. ACM, Washington, DC, USA, September 2021
8. Henning, J.L.: SPEC CPU2006 benchmark descriptions. ACM SIGARCH Comput. Architect. News **34**(4), 1–17 (2006)
9. John Pimo, E.S., Ashok, V., Logeswaran, T., Sri Sai Satyanarayana, D.: A comparative performance analysis of phase change memory as main memory and DRAM. In: Proceedings of Materials Today, February 2021
10. Kim, S., Hwang, S.H., Kwak, J.W.: Adaptive-classification CLOCK: page replacement policy based on read/write access pattern for hybrid DRAM and PCM main memory. Microprocess. Microsyst. **57**, 65–75 (2018)
11. Lee, S., Bahn, H., Noh, S.H.: CLOCK-DWF: a write-history-aware page replacement algorithm for hybrid PCM and DRAM memory architectures. IEEE Trans. Comput. **63**(9), 2187–2200 (2014)

12. Liu, H., Liu, R., Liao, X., Jin, H., He, B., Zhang, Y.: Object-level memory allocation and migration in hybrid memory systems. IEEE Trans. Comput. **69**(9), 1401–1413 (2020)
13. Long, X., Gong, X., Zhou, H.: Deep Learning based Data Prefetching in CPU-GPU Unified Virtual Memory, March 2022
14. Lowe-Power, J., et al.: The gem5 Simulator: Version 20.0+. arXiv:2007.03152, September 2020
15. Mittal, S., Vetter, J.S.: A survey of software techniques for using non-volatile memories for storage and main memory systems. IEEE Trans. Parallel Distrib. Syst. **27**(5), 1537–1550 (2016)
16. Pei, S., Ji, Y., Shen, T., Liu, H.: Migration mechanism of heterogeneous memory pages using a two-way Hash chain list. SCIENTIA SINICA Inform. **49**(9), 1138–1158 (2019)
17. Pei, S., Qian, Y., Ye, X., Liu, H., Kong, L.: DRAM-based victim cache for page migration mechanism on heterogeneous main memory. J. Comput. Res. Develop. **3**, 568–581 (2022)
18. Raoux, S., Xiong, F., Wuttig, M., Pop, E.: Phase change materials and phase change memory. MRS Bull. **39**(8), 703–710 (2014)
19. Tan, Y., Wang, B., Yan, Z., Srisa-an, W., Chen, X., Liu, D.: APMigration: improving performance of hybrid memory performance via an adaptive page migration method. IEEE Trans. Parallel Distrib. Syst. **31**(2), 266–278 (2020)
20. Valad Beigi, M., Pourshirazi, B., Memik, G., Zhu, Z.: DeepSwapper: a deep learning based page swap management scheme for hybrid memory systems. In: Proceedings of the ACM International Conference on Parallel Architectures and Compilation Techniques, pp. 353–354. PACT 2020, Association for Computing Machinery, New York, NY, USA, September 2020
21. Vaswani, A., et al.: Attention Is All You Need, December 2017
22. Vetter, J.S., Mittal, S.: Opportunities for nonvolatile memory systems in extreme-scale high-performance computing. Comput. Sci. Eng. **17**(2), 73–82 (2015)
23. Wang, I.J., et al.: Enabling write-reduction multiversion scheme with efficient dual-range query over NVRAM. IEEE Trans. Very Large Scale Integr. (VLSI) Syst. **29**(6), 1244–1256 (2021)
24. Zhang, P., Srivastava, A., Nori, A.V., Kannan, R., Prasanna, V.K.: Fine-grained address segmentation for attention-based variable-degree prefetching. In: Proceedings of the 19th ACM International Conference on Computing Frontiers, pp. 103–112. CF 2022, Association for Computing Machinery, New York, NY, USA, May 2022

Hardware Acceleration for 1D-CNN Based Real-Time Edge Computing

Xinyu Liu[1], Gaole Sai[2], and Shengyu Duan[1(✉)]

[1] School of Computer Engineering and Science, Shanghai University, Shanghai, China
{croyyin_l,sduan}@shu.edu.cn
[2] Guangdong Provincial Key Lab of Robotics and Intelligent System, Shenzhen Institute of Advanced Technology, Chinese Academy of Sciences, Shenzhen, China
gl.sai@siat.ac.cn

Abstract. One-dimensional convolutional neural network (1D-CNN) has a major advantage of low-cost implementation on edge devices, for time series classification. However, for the edge devices working in real-time computing (RTC) systems, the nonconcurrent availability of input signals leads to a more complex computing process and a bigger challenge to satisfy the resource and timing constraints. In this paper, an energy-efficient high-performance 1D-CNN architecture is proposed for edge inference of RTC systems, which performs 1D-CNN operations element-wisely and simultaneously when the input sequence is streamed. We present a data reuse scheme to maximally reduce the computational and memory resources, based on the generation of 1D-CNN feature maps during RTC. A compiler is developed to generate the hardware architecture in pipeline, for any given 1D-CNN model. We implement our proposed architecture by a 65-nm CMOS technology, and show this design realizes up to 1.72 TOPs/W power efficiency. Regarding computational latency, our design can outperform state-of-the-art CNN accelerators with a reduction of more than one order of magnitude.

Keywords: 1D-CNN · Hardware acceleration · Edge computing · RTC

1 Introduction

The dramatic growth in deep learning has led to a greatly increased demand for larger computing resources. Nevertheless, with the imminent end of Moore's Law, it becomes challenging to continue scaling conventional computer architectures and satisfy the various demands, considering timing, area and power. A push towards deep learning implemented on domain-specific architecture (DSA) is thereby motivated, to provide acceleration while showing superior energy and resource efficiency [3].

One-dimensional convolutional neural network (1D-CNN) has become a widely used deep learning algorithm, due to its state-of-the-art performance in many signal processing applications, specifically for time series classification [7].

S. Liu and X. Wei (Eds.): NPC 2022, LNCS 13615, pp. 192–204, 2022.
https://doi.org/10.1007/978-3-031-21395-3_18

Such applications are usually deployed at edge. The compact structure of 1D-CNNs that only performs 1D convolutions and 1D pooling (Fig. 1) introduces a major advantage of low-cost hardware implementations on edge devices, which generally have limited resources and tight constraints. However, for the edge applications with real-time requirements, data is often streamed in real time to recursively construct the entire time series, which not only imposes a tighter latency constraint due to the nonconcurrent availability of the signals, but also causes high data redundancy among the successive input sequences.

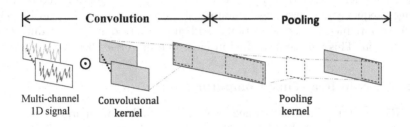

Fig. 1. Convolution and pooling operation in 1D-CNN

In this paper, we propose a 1D-CNN accelerator for edge inference of real-time computing (RTC) systems. Specifically, the computations within the accelerator are performed in an element-wise manner, to realize an immediate computation for the currently available input data. We study the generation of 1D-CNN feature maps constructed by streaming data in RTC systems, and then present a scheme of data reuse to maximally reduce the computational and memory resources. The accelerator is designed in a pipeline architecture for all 1D-CNN layers and a compiler is developed to generate the hardware implementation for the given model and design specifications. Our proposed design can outperform state-of-the-art CNN accelerators with a reduction of more than one order of magnitude, in terms of computational latency.

2   Background

2.1   State-of-the-Art CNN Accelerators

CNN accelerators are realized based on the trade-off between large computational resources and large memory resources, considering the applications, because of the high complexity of CNN computations. For edge computing, it is more challenging to achieve this trade-off due to the limited resources for both computation and storage. So far, only a few works present hardware architectures specifically for 1D-CNN [10, 14].

State-of-the-art designs are mostly proposed based on the assumption that a complete feature map of each layer is concurrently available, for instance a static image, before the computations. However, RTC systems have the fundamental difference: a feature map may be split in frames or elements, streamed in at different time. This feature leads to significantly different computing process and hardware architecture for a CNN accelerator working in RTC systems, as we will further discuss it in Sect. 2.2. Only a few works present CNN accelerations for RTC: Sanchez *et al.* propose AWARE-CNN, which is a framework to convert a given CNN model into a row-wise computing architecture, used for RTC [9]. A similar implementation has been presented in [11]. By definition, these architectures are also applicable for 1D-CNN models. However, the above works fail to consider the relationship between the multiple successively received input images/sequences, where huge amounts of data are shared and can be reused to further reduce the computational and memory resources, according to our observation. This will be described in more detail, in Sect. 3.1.

2.2   CNN in Real-Time Computing

In a RTC system, data is streamed as a certain number of separated frames over time, to produce large batches to be processed. The currently available data is then processed in a strict time limit, often determined by the interval of streaming, to ensure the computation can be immediately initiated, once a stream is received. For a CNN inference in a RTC system, the raw data is treated as an input image, recursively constructed by multiple frames over time. Therefore, the operations, including convolutions and pooling, related to different frames of an input image, are completed at different time. These operations differ from the ones of a conventional CNN, where the entire image can be processed concurrently. Since the result of a CNN is obtained till all frames of a complete input image are streamed and computed, the computing device not only processes the currently received data, but also combines it with the relevant information of the previously received one, to produce the final result. For multiple successive input images, overlapping time windows are usually employed, to prevent important features being eliminated from the borders.

In Fig. 2, we demonstrate the inference process of a 1D-CNN for RTC, where a sequence is streamed as elements over time and each inference is split into multiple phases, performed at different time. There is a great number of elements shared by successive input sequences. We thereby give the key features of a 1D-CNN accelerator for real-time edge computing, as follows:

1) The computation is conducted in an element-wise manner, and the computation of each element has to be completed before a new element is streamed;
2) The successive input sequences may have a large intersection, suggesting a motivation of data reuse to reduce the computational and memory resources.

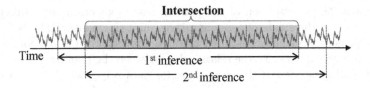

Fig. 2. 1D-CNN inference in RTC

3 Proposed Architecture for 1D-CNN

3.1 Data Reuse

In Sect. 2.2, we demonstrate an input sequence might be element-wisely streamed at different streaming phases, in RTC systems. We hereby give (1) to present the construction of an input sequence with m elements, of which the availability is maintained at the time point t, as $\boldsymbol{F_0}(t)$:

$$\boldsymbol{F_0}(t) = [f_0(t - m + 1), f_0(t - m + 2), \cdots, f_0(t)] \tag{1}$$

where $f_0(t)$ is an element received at t.

For each two successive input sequences, $\boldsymbol{F_0}(t - 1)$ and $\boldsymbol{F_0}(t)$, we assume the intersection includes $m - 1$ elements, for simplicity, which can be further expressed by (2). (2) reveals all elements, except $f_0(t)$, have been covered during the previous streaming phases, for $\boldsymbol{F_0}(t)$. By definition, this common data has been previously processed, and thus the intermediate results can be reused to produce the final result for $\boldsymbol{F_0}(t)$.

$$\boldsymbol{F_0}(t - 1) \cap \boldsymbol{F_0}(t) = [f_0(t - m + 1), f_0(t - m + 2), \cdots, f_0(t - 1)] \tag{2}$$

We then investigate how the intermediate results can be maximally reused, in a single layer 1D-CNN. We denote $\boldsymbol{C_1}(t)$ as the results produced by a convolutional layer for $\boldsymbol{F_0}(t)$, in (3), where $c_{1n}(t)$ is an element, computed by the convolutional operations for multiple elements of $\boldsymbol{F_0}(t)$. Note the size of $\boldsymbol{C_1}(t)$ is determined by the parameters of a specific convolutional layer (*e.g.*, kernel size, stride, padding), and is not defined in (3).

$$\boldsymbol{C_1}(t) = Conv[\boldsymbol{F_0}(t)] = [c_{11}(t), c_{12}(t), c_{13}(t), \cdots] \tag{3}$$

The intersection of the convolutional results generated at different time is dependent on the stride of a convolutional layer. For instance, $\boldsymbol{C_1}(t)$ and $\boldsymbol{C_1}(t-1)$ may not have any data in common, if the stride is not 1, because they are produced by shifting the same convolutional kernel over $\boldsymbol{F_0}(t)$ and $\boldsymbol{F_0}(t - 1)$, respectively. Based on the above observation, we provide (4), to present the relationship between the convolutional results generated at different time, for data reuse, where s_c is the stride of the convolutional layer and $t' \leq s_c$.

$$\boldsymbol{C_1}(t - t') \cap \boldsymbol{C_1}(t) = \begin{cases} = [c_{11}(t), c_{12}(t), \cdots], & t' = s_c \\ \emptyset, & t' \neq s_c \end{cases} \tag{4}$$

Similarly, the intersection of the pooling results generated at different time is dependent on the stride of a pooling layer, in a single layer 1D-CNN. As the input sequence is typically cascaded through convolutional and pooling layers, we give (5) and (6), to show the relationship between the pooling results denoted by $P_1(t)$ and generated at different time, for data reuse, which is related to s_c and the stride of the convolutional layer, s_p, assuming $t' \leq s_c \cdot s_p$.

$$P_1(t) = Pool[C_1(t)] = [p_{11}(t), p_{12}(t), p_{13}(t), \cdots] \tag{5}$$

$$P_1(t - t') \cap P_1(t) = \begin{cases} = [p_{11}(t), p_{12}(t), \cdots], & t' = s_c \cdot s_p \\ \emptyset, & t' \neq s_c \cdot s_p \end{cases} \tag{6}$$

A deep 1D-CNN is composed of multiple convolutional and pooling layers in a cascade. For simplicity, we assume each hidden layer has a convolutional layer cascaded with a pooling layer. Thus, the intermediate results that can be reused to process the currently available input sequence would be given, by recursively performing the above mathematical operations. Assume $C_i(t)$ and $P_i(t)$ are the convolutional and pooling results at the i-th hidden layer, during the computation for the input sequence $F_0(t)$, and $C_i(t)$ and $P_i(t)$ consist of n and l elements, respectively. Assume the strides of the convolutional and pooling layers are s_c^i and s_p^i, respectively. Hence, the data reuse for this layer is shown as follows, in (7) and (8):

$$C_i(t) = [c_{i2}(t - S_c^i), c_{i3}(t - S_c^i), \cdots, c_{in}(t - S_c^i), c_{in}(t)] \tag{7}$$

where

$$S_c^i = \prod_{j=1}^{i} s_c^j \cdot \prod_{j=1}^{i-1} s_p^j$$

$$P_i(t) = [p_{i2}(t - S_p^i), p_{i3}(t - S_p^i), \cdots, p_{il}(t - S_p^i), p_{il}(t)] \tag{8}$$

where

$$S_p^i = \prod_{j=1}^{i} s_c^j \cdot s_p^j$$

We provide Fig. 3 to demonstrate the overall process of (7) and (8). These equations suggest only one element (*i.e.*, $c_{in}(t)$ or $p_{il}(t)$) needs be processed at each 1D-CNN layer during a computing phase, thus in an element-wise manner, while the rest of the data can be reused from the intermediate results of the previous computations, by adjusting S_c^i and S_p^i based on the depth that a layer locates at.

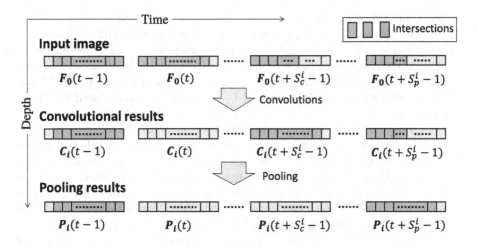

Fig. 3. Reused data of 1D-CNN in RTC

3.2 Accelerated 1D-CNN Architecture

Based on the data reuse scheme, we firstly provide the structures for the typical layers of a 1D-CNN, as follows:

1) 1D convolutional layer (Fig. 4(a)). Assume that the convolutional kernel includes k elements, and thus a processing block (PB) consists of k processing elements (PEs). By definition, the above computation involves the last k elements of the intermediate feature, partially produced by the previous layer. Specifically, assuming this layer receives a feature map produced by a pooling layer and according to (8), all elements, except the last one, have been produced and thus have been stored, during the previous computations. This data, $[p_{i(l-k+2)}(t - S_p^i), \cdots, p_{il}(t - S_p^i)]$, is fetched into the reused data registers, during the present computing phase. The last element, $p_{il}(t)$, is generated by the previous layer, and it is stored in the input register. Each PE of a PB performs the multiplication of one element above by a corresponding weight, and passes the result to another PE. The multiplication results are accumulated for multiple input channels, to produce a partial sum. Note that it is unnecessary to include as many PBs as the number of input channels in a specific convolutional layer, because the final convolutional result can be produced with the accumulations for multiple cycles. Thus, it is possible to flexibly adjust the number of PBs, according to the given design specifications of power, timing, *etc.* The convolutional result is stored, which is then processed immediately by the next layer, and will be reused for future computations.

2) Pooling layer (Fig. 4(b)). The number of the reused data registers is determined by the length of the pooling filter of the layer. In specific, for a pooling filter with k elements, the reused data registers store $k - 1$ elements. Assume that the feature map processed at this layer is produced by a convolutional

layer, and thus the reused data is given as $[c_{i(n-k+2)}(t - S_c^i), \cdots, c_{in}(t - S_c^i)]$. The last element $c_{in}(t)$ is produced by the previous convolutional layer, and saved in the input registers. The pooling result is generated by feeding the k elements into a pooling block. Operations of the pooling block are determined by the pooling methods of a certain CNN model. Like the convolutional layer, the pooling result is both processed by the next layer and stored for future computations.

3) FC layer (Fig. 4(c)). The structure of an FC layer is also mainly composed of PBs. Each PB performs as a neuron, and the number of PBs included is determined by the number of neurons applied in a certain FC layer, often related to the number of classes of a specific classification problem. The number of PEs used in a PB is adjustable from 1 to the number of inputs of a neuron, so that the results are produced through computations of multiple cycles. For an FC layer, we change both the number of PBs and the number of PEs in a PB, to meet the design specifications and balance the latency of each layer.

We provide the overall architecture in a pipeline design, in Fig. 5, where all layers are connected with a RAM. All registers within a layer are controlled by an intra-layer clock with a period of T_{intra}, and the convolutional and FC

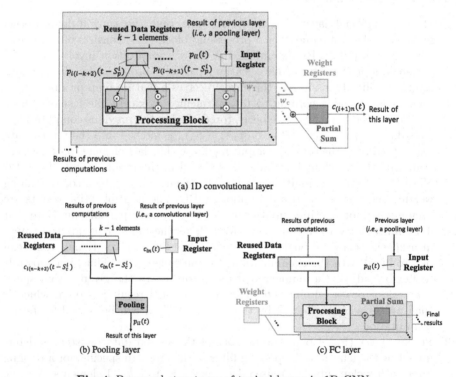

(a) 1D convolutional layer

(b) Pooling layer

(c) FC layer

Fig. 4. Proposed structures of typical layers in 1D-CNN

layers operate in a two-stage pipeline as fetch and compute. Multiple cycles may be required to produce the result of a layer, which are stored in inter-layer registers, inserted between each two layers. The inter-layer registers are controlled by a clock with a period of T_{inter}. By properly adjusting the number of PBs and PEs in each layer, it is possible to ensure that each convolutional or FC layer completes the computation in the similar number of cycles, which will be discussed in Sect. 3.3. We denote the number of cycles to produce the result from a layer as N, and thus T_{inter} is given by $N \cdot T_{intra}$. In this way, all layers can be operated in an inter-layer pipeline. In addition, the intra-layer and inter-layer clocks are used to address the RAM. In specific, the intra-layer and inter-layer clocks determine the frequencies, under which the read and write addresses of the RAM are changed.

3.3   Compiler for 1D-CNN Architecture Generation

The structures presented in Sect. 3.2 are applicable to construct any 1D-CNN networks. In addition, hardware resources need be adjusted, based on the design specifications in terms of power, timing, *etc.* We thereby develop a compiler to generate different architectures, considering the given network and specifications.

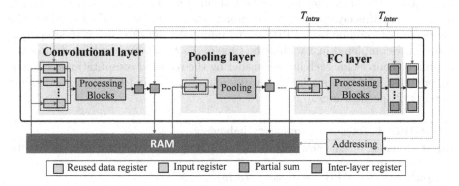

Fig. 5. Inter-layer and intra-layer pipeline architecture

We show the workflow of the compiler, in Fig. 6. The configurations of a certain 1D-CNN are firstly obtained from a PyTorch implementation, where the layer configurations suggest the operations, kernel size and stride of this layer. We separately construct the typical layers given in Fig. 4 by Chisel, and leave their configurations determined by the applied network structure. Meanwhile, we generate the weights and biases from a training process in Python. The network architecture in Chisel is then compiled to a synthesizable behavioral model in Verilog, using FIRRTL [6]. Finally, we exploit Synopsys Design Compiler (DC) to produce and evaluate the structural model.

In order to ensure each convolutional or FC layer produce the result in a similar number of cycles and thus all layers can be operated in pipeline, we further propose Algorithm 1 used with the compiler, to balance the computational latency of each layer, by adjusting the number of PBs included. As each

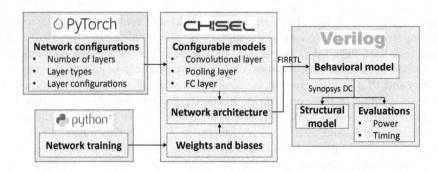

Fig. 6. Workflow for architecture generation

PB performs all multiply-accumulate (MAC) operations of a channel, we firstly obtain the number of channels for all layers, denoted by a set, $\{Q_1, Q_2, ...\}$. For a convolutional layer, it is computed by the multiplication of the number of input channels and that of output channels, while for an FC layer, it is determined by the number of neurons. We then assume the maximal number of PBs that can be accepted to be included in a layer, as q_{max}, which determines the number of PBs used in the layer that has the largest number of channels, and the number of cycles that this layer requires to complete the computation. For the rest of the layers, we set the number of PBs as the minimal values to ensure their computations are completed just within the time of $N \cdot T_{intra}$, which also indicates the minimal resources for each layer considering the required computational latency. Algorithm 1 might be applied with different q_{max} to find the design satisfying the overall specifications.

Algorithm 1. Inter-layer frequency balancing.

Input: Number of channels for all layers, $\{Q_1, Q_2, ...\}$; Maximal number of PBs included in a layer, q_{max};
Output: Number of PBs for all layer, $\{q_1, q_2, ...\}$; N;
1: for $Q_i = max(Q_1, Q_2, ...)$, set $q_i = q_{max}$ and $N = Q_i/q_i$
2: **for** each Q_j in $\{Q_1, Q_2, ...\}$ **do**
3:     set q_j as the minimal value to satisfy $Q_j/q_j <= N$
4: **end for**

---

4   Results

4.1   Setup

To evaluate our proposed architecture, we quantize 1D-CNNs to 8-bit fixed point precision, and implement them by TSMC 65-nm CMOS technology. These designs are synthesized by DC, and we perform static timing and power analysis of DC to measure the clock frequency and power consumption.

Network structures involved in our evaluation are based on the audio processing sub-net of SoundNet [1] with an additional FC layer, trained to solve multiple time series classification problems from UEA datasets [2]. For each utilized dataset, we adjust the number of layers according to the length of the input sequence, and the number of parameters is mostly determined by the number of classes. The classification accuracy of some datasets and the configurations of the corresponding networks are given, in Table 1, where the number of layers is computed by convolutional and FC layers only, as we merge each pooling layer with its previous convolutional layer into one pipeline stage in our designs. Note the classification accuracy of EigenWorms is relatively low, compared with the other cases, while this result is consistent with the existing works [12, 13], so we conclude our evaluated structure is reasonable for such a dataset.

Table 1. Datasets and network structures

Dataset	No. of classes	No. of parameters	No. of layers	Accuracy
ERing	6	4214	2	94.8%
BasicMotions	4	7692	3	97.5%
Epilepsy	4	9052	3	92.7%
ArticularyWordRecognition	25	35757	3	95.7%
Cricket	12	31828	4	95.8%
EigenWorms	5	265505	7	57.2%

4.2 Evaluations of Power, Latency and Bandwidth

We then evaluate how power, latency and bandwidth can be affected by 1D-CNNs with different layer structure and the implementations with different number of PBs. Each PB conducts all MAC operations of an input channel. For the structures demonstrated in Table 1, we utilize the compiler to generate all possible implementations supporting different numbers of MACs, and we show their power, latency and bandwidth in Fig. 7. Proportional increases for power and bandwidth can be observed due to the implementation of more PBs. In each case, the power consumption is relatively low (*i.e.*, in mW) and the required bandwidth is achievable (*i.e.*, in GBps), so the proposed architecture is applicable to be deployed at edge.

It is the most noticeable the latency is dramatically reduced, if more PBs are included in a design, in each case. Here we compute the latency, from the time that a complete input sequence is available until the classification result is produced. Considering a CNN layer with a certain number of MACs, the computational time is inversely proportional to the number of MACs that can be performed by the generated architecture in one cycle, causing this dramatic decrease in latency by implementing more PBs. This observation suggests the computational time can be greatly decreased by implementing a small number of extra PBs in our architecture, leading to a low overhead in power consumption.

Furthermore, comparing the networks with different number of layers, the overall latency largely increases for a network with more layers. This is because the number of input channels exponentially increases for a deeper layer in SoundNet, and thus more clock cycles are required to produce the result, assuming the number of supported MACs is fixed in a certain design. However, even for the case of EigenWorms, classified by a 7-layer structure, the latency can be reduced up to 36.12 μs.

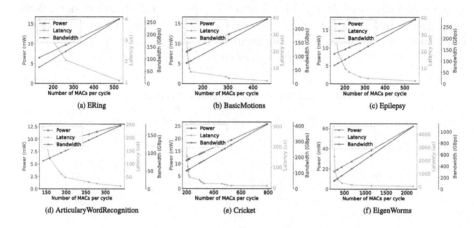

Fig. 7. Power, latency and bandwidth of different 1D-CNN structures

4.3   Comparative Analysis

The proposed architecture with 7-layer used for EigenWorms classification is compared with the existing works, in Table 2. Our proposed architecture operates at a frequency of 62.5 MHz, which is lower than some existing works in the table. According to our simulation, PB of the convolutional layer in our design is the bottleneck limiting a further improvement for the frequency. Thus, it is possible to insert multiple pipeline stages into the PBs for a higher operational frequency.

The power consumption of or design is in the range of 17.49–62.56 mW, generally lower than the existing works, although power is also related to the implementations and models. The power efficiency of our work is in the range of 0.72–1.72 TOPs/W, depending on the total number of MACs supported by a design. Generally, power efficiency is increased if the generated architecture can perform more MACs, by including more PBs in the architecture, according to Fig. 7. The power efficiency of our work is compatible with the existing works.

Finally, the latency is hugely reduced from a few milliseconds for some existing works, to the range of 36.12–4587.8 μs. However, as the compared designs are developed based on different networks, we further compute latency per layer to reveal the efficiency of our architecture. As can be noticed, the latency per layer of our architecture is from 5.16 to 655.4 μs, depending on the number of PBs involved. Specifically compared with the ones implemented in ASIC [5,8], the maximal latency per layer is compatible with those works, while it is noted the minimal latency per layer can be reduced for more than one order of magnitude, with the power efficiency close to those works. This is because the proposed architecture initiates computations simultaneously when the input sequence is streamed, so that it does not rely on the availability of a complete input sequence to initiate the CNN operations.

Table 2. Comparisons between proposed architecture and existing works

Design	DAC19 [8]	DT-CNN [5]	ASAD-CNN [4]	ASICON21 [14]	AWARE-CNN [9]	ISCAS21 [11]	This work
Implementation	ASIC	ASIC	ASIC	FPGA	FPGA	FPGA	ASIC
Tech. node (nm)	28	65	65	28	16	28	65
Model	MTCNN	ENet	AlexNet	1D-CNN	YOLO-HD	YOLO2-tiny	SoundNet**
No. of layers	15	86	7	6	26	9	7
Quantization (bit)	8	8	16	16	16	8	8
Frequency (MHz)	400	200	20–500	200	30–40	200	62.5
Power (mW)	120	196	7–425	470*	15000	NA	17.49–62.56
Power effi. (TOPs/W)	1.17	3.26	0.3–0.8	0.079	0.25–0.49	0.045	0.72–1.72
Latency	6.67 ms	4.74–14.62 ms	NA	170 μs	30.3–45.2 ms	27.78 ms	36.12–4587.8 μs
Latency per layer	444.67 μs	55.11–170 μs	NA	28.3 μs	1.17–1.73 ms	3.09 ms	5.16–655.4 μs

*Estimated based on the DSP and LUT utilization of this work, implemented on Xilinx ZC706
**The audio processing sub-net, with its number of layers adjusted based on the series length of EigenWorms

5 Conclusion

This paper proposes a 1D-CNN accelerator for edge inference of RTC systems. Due to the nonconcurrent availability of the input sequence, we propose to perform element-wise computations to realize an immediate execution for the currently available input data. We present a scheme of data reuse to maximally reduce the computational and memory resources, based on the generation of 1D-CNN feature maps during RTC. The accelerator is constructed in a pipeline architecture, through a developed compiler for any 1D-CNN models. We implement our proposed architecture by a 65-nm technology, and show its maximal power efficiency as 1.72 TOPs/W. We show our design can outperform state-of-the-art CNN accelerators with a reduction of more than one order of magnitude, in terms of latency.

Finally, it is worth noting the proposed architecture is potentially applicable to be used for 2D- and 3D-CNNs, but it may cause a large bandwidth requirement, due to the large amount of reused data transferred between the RAM and the processing blocks. Thus, we only suggest this architecture to be employed for 1D-CNN.

Acknowledgement. The work was supported by State Key Laboratory of Computer Architecture (ICT, CAS) under Grant No. CARCH201909.

References

1. Aytar, Y., Vondrick, C., Torralba, A.: SoundNet: learning sound representations from unlabeled video. In: Advances in Neural Information Processing Systems 29 (2016)
2. Bagnall, A., et al.: The UEA multivariate time series classification archive. arXiv:1811.00075 (2018)
3. Batra, G., Jacobson, Z., Madhav, S., Queirolo, A., Santhanam, N.: Artificial-intelligence hardware: new opportunities for semiconductor companies. McKinsey and Company 2 (2019)
4. Du, Y., Du, L., Li, Y., Su, J., Chang, M.C.F.: A streaming accelerator for deep convolutional neural networks with image and feature decomposition for resource-limited system applications. arXiv:1709.05116 (2017)
5. Im, D., Han, D., Choi, S., Kang, S., Yoo, H.J.: DT-CNN: dilated and transposed convolution neural network accelerator for real-time image segmentation on mobile devices. In: IEEE International Symposium Circuits Systems (ISCAS), pp. 1–5 (2019)
6. Izraelevitz, A., et al.: Reusability is FIRRTL ground: Hardware construction languages, compiler frameworks, and transformations. In: IEEE/ACM International Conference on Computer-Aided Design (ICCAD), pp. 209–216 (2017)
7. Kiranyaz, S., Avci, O., Abdeljaber, O., Ince, T., Gabbouj, M., Inman, D.J.: 1D convolutional neural networks and applications: a survey. Mech. Syst. Signal Process. **151**, 107398 (2021)
8. Mo, H., et al.: A 1.17 TOPS/W, 150fps accelerator for multi-face detection and alignment. In: Proceedings of the 56th Annual Design Automation Conference, pp. 1–6 (2019)
9. Sanchez, J., Sawant, A., Neff, C., Tabkhi, H.: Aware-CNN: automated workflow for application-aware real-time edge acceleration of CNNs. IEEE Internet Things J. **7**(10), 9318–9329 (2020)
10. Wei, L., Liu, D., Lu, J., Zhu, L., Cheng, X.: A low-cost hardware architecture of convolutional neural network for ECG classification. In: 9th International Symposium on Next Generation Electronics (ISNE), pp. 1–4 (2021)
11. Zhang, J., Cheng, L., Li, C., Li, Y., He, G., Xu, N., Lian, Y.: A low-latency FPGA implementation for real-time object detection. In: International Symposium on Circuits and Systems (ISCAS), pp. 1–5 (2021)
12. Zhang, X., Gao, Y., Lin, J., Lu, C.T.: TapNet: multivariate time series classification with attentional prototypical network. In: Proceedings of the AAAI Conference on Artificial Intelligence, vol. 34, pp. 6845–6852 (2020)
13. Zheng, Y., Liu, Q., Chen, E., Ge, Y., Zhao, J.L.: Time series classification using multi-channels deep convolutional neural networks. In: Li, F., Li, G., Hwang, S., Yao, B., Zhang, Z. (eds.) WAIM 2014. LNCS, vol. 8485, pp. 298–310. Springer, Cham (2014). https://doi.org/10.1007/978-3-319-08010-9_33
14. Zhu, L., Liu, D., Li, X., Lu, J., Wei, L., Cheng, X.: An efficient hardware architecture for epileptic seizure detection using EEG signals based on 1D-CNN. In: IEEE 14th International Conference on ASIC (ASICON), pp. 1–4 (2021)

Emerging Applications

DLC: An Optimization Framework
for Full-State Quantum Simulation

Zhikai Qin, Tao Li, and Li Shen[(✉)]

College of Computer, National University of Defense Technology, Changsha, China
{qinzhikai,litao_,lishen}@nudt.edu.cn

Abstract. Quantum simulation on classical computers is one of the main approaches to evaluate quantum computation devices and develop quantum algorithms. Some quantum simulators have been proposed, mainly divided into two categories: full-state simulators and tensor network simulators. The former consumes a lot of memory to hold the quantum state vectors. Therefore, the time overheads cost by calculation are much lower than that cost by memory-accesses and communications. Traditional optimization techniques such as latency hiding are not suitable for quantum simulation, and high-performance devices like GPGPUs cannot be fully utilized. This paper proposes DLC (Data Locality and Communication) optimizer to perform data locality and data layout optimizations. Both optimizations are based on the identification of amplitudes that can be processed by a sequence of quantum gates. They not only increase the data locality on the GPU side, but also reduces the date communication overheads and the times of data exchanges. In addition, layout data dynamically can significantly reduce the memory space on the GPGPU side for data communication. We evaluate our scheme on a small-scale CPU + GPU cluster. Experimental results show that for quantum circuits having 30–34 qubits, the ratio of communication to calculation increases from 12 to 79%, and a performance improvement 1.25–7× is achieved. Theoretically, our optimizations will be more effective as the number of qubits increases.

Keywords: Quantum circuit simulation · Multi-GPU · Heterogeneous CPU + GPU

1 Introduction

Quantum computers employ the properties of quantum physics like superposition and entanglement to perform computation, which makes them have stronger computing abilities that classical computers in some domains such as cryptography [1], artificial intelligence [2, 3], financial modeling, drug development and electronic materials discovery. Some quantum computers have been proposed recently, such as Google's 72-qubit quantum computer Bristlecone [4]. However, quantum computing based on today's Noisy Intermediate Scale Quantum Device (NISQ) [5] cannot replace classical supercomputers yet. One major limitation of today's quantum computation devices is the possible

© IFIP International Federation for Information Processing 2022
Published by Springer Nature Switzerland AG 2022
S. Liu and X. Wei (Eds.): NPC 2022, LNCS 13615, pp. 207–218, 2022.
https://doi.org/10.1007/978-3-031-21395-3_19

errors of quantum states. The quantum states are uncertain of the decoherence of qubits, which influences the quantum computer's practicability. Besides, the stable coherence duration is short because of material limitations on implementing quantum computation devices, at most several seconds, with different error rates and readout fidelity. Researchers cannot directly access the intermediate state of a physical quantum computer, for the quantum superposition state can be destroyed, whenever a measurement is applied to certain qubits.

Simulating quantum computing on classical computers is one of the effective research methodologies currently It can help researchers to understand the functionality of quantum circuits, evaluate quantum computation devices, and develop quantum algorithms. Some simulators have been proposed, and there are mainly two categories of quantum simulators: the full-state simulators [6–10] which record and update the states of all the qubits, and the tensor network simulators [11–15], which represents quantum circuits as tenson networks. In this paper, we restrict ourselves to optimize the full-state simulator.

In the process of simulating a quantum gate, at most two quantum states are interdependent. Thus, the process can be highly parallelized, and massive performance improvement can be achieved by accelerators such as GPUs. However, the quantum state space grows exponentially with the qubits number, it can easily exceed GPU's global memory space, as a result, cannot be accelerated by GPU.

There are generally two approaches to solve this problem. One is to store the quantum state space on the host memory and transfer data to GPU to finish compute tasks. In this way, the calculating time is short, but the amount of data is too large, communication between CPU and the host consumes a lot of time. The other is to use more GPUs to expand memory space. However, the performance of multiple GPUs is also not satisfactory. Communication between GPUs are needed and each communication requires copying all the data on another GPU to the local GPU [7, 16, 17]. While using multiple GPUs can further reduce computing time, communication between multiple GPUs dramatically reduces performance.

We found that for a sequence of quantum gates, the quantum states they updated can be divided into several independent subsets, which can be updated in parallel. Moreover, the size of each state subset can be adjusted via partitioning the quantum gate sequences. Based on these observations, this paper proposes and implements an optimization framework, DLC Optimizer (Data Locality and Communication Optimizer). DLC mainly performs two optimizations, locality enhancement and dynamic data layout. DLC distributes the quantum states to all computation nodes on average. Next, it partitions quantum circuit into a group of gate sequences to ensure that the size of quantum states each sequence updates match the size of GPU's global memory as possible. With this approach, each state can be kept on the GPU side as long as possible, and therefore more temporal locality could be exploited. Then, DLC identifies the quantum states will be exchanged between GPUs in the following gate sequence. The identified states are grouped together and exchanged before next simulation starts. Compared to the original communication schema, this dynamic data layout eliminates unnecessary data communications among GPUs.

DLC has been implemented and evaluated on a small-scale CPU + GPU heterogeneous cluster, which has 4 computation nodes and each node has 2 NVIDIA's

A100 GPUs. Experimental results indicates that for quantum circuits having 30–32 qubits, the calculation to communication ratio increases from 12 to 56%, and a performance improvement 2–3× is achieved. In summary, this paper makes the following contributions:

- We propose the DLC optimizer to exploit more data locality and reduce the communication overheads for full-state quantum simulators.
- We propose a quantum circuit partition algorithm to improve data locality on GPU side. It partitions a quantum circuit into a set of quantum gate sequences, and the quantum states updated by each sequence can be divided into a group of independent sets.
- We propose a dynamic data layout method to eliminate unnecessary data communications between GPUs. Before the simulation of a new quantum gate sequence, the quantum states will be rearranged between GPUs. With this approach, both the communication numbers and the data communicated are reduced.

The rest of this paper is organized as follows. Section 2 introduces the backgrounds and related works. In Sect. 3, we describe our DLC optimizer framework and describe its workflow. In Sect. 4, we detail analyze the data locality between quantum gates and present our quantum circuit partition algorithm. In Sect. 5, we describe our dynamic data layout approach. In Sect. 6, we evaluate our work on a small CPU + GPU cluster, and we conclude this paper in Sect. 7 with a summary and list of our future work.

2 Background and Related Work

2.1 Quantum States and Quantum Circuits

Qubit is the smallest unit of quantum information. A quantum bit can exist in superposition, which means that it can exist in multiple states at once. Compared to a regular bit, which can exist in one of two states, 1 or 0, the quantum bit can exist as a 1, 0 or 1 and 0 at the same time. This allows for very fast computing and the ability to do multitudes of calculations at once, theoretically.

$$|\varphi\rangle = \alpha_0|0\rangle + \alpha_1|1\rangle \tag{1}$$

$$|\varphi\rangle = \begin{bmatrix} \alpha_0 \\ \alpha_1 \end{bmatrix} \tag{2}$$

As shown in formula (1), the state of a qubit, $|\varphi\rangle$, is represented as a superposition of two basis states $|0\rangle$ and $|1\rangle$. Here α_0 and α_1 are both complex numbers, and $|\alpha_0|^2 + |\alpha_1|^2 = 1$. Formula (1) indicates that the probabilities of $|\varphi\rangle$ be $|0\rangle$ and $|1\rangle$ are $|\alpha_0|^2$ and $|\alpha_1|^2$, respectively. α_0 and α_1 are called amplitudes.

The states of multiple qubits can be superimposed too. For example, a two-qubit quantum state can be represented by a group of four complex numbers $\{\alpha_0, \alpha_1, \alpha_2, \alpha_3\}$, and their quadratic sum is 1, as shown in formula (3).

$$|\varphi\rangle = \alpha_0|00\rangle + \alpha_1|01\rangle + \alpha_2|01\rangle + \alpha_3|11\rangle \tag{3}$$

Therefore, a n-qubit quantum state is represented by 2^n complex numbers as following:

$$|\varphi\rangle = \alpha_0|00\ldots0\rangle + \alpha_1|00\ldots1\rangle + \cdots + \alpha_{2^n-1}|11\ldots1\rangle \qquad (4)$$

Obviously, the memory space required to hold all the quantum states grows exponentially with n increases.

Quantum circuits are made up of a group of quantum gates. Each quantum gate describes an operation applied to qubits, and each operation will update all the amplitudes. According to the number of qubits updated by a quantum gate, all the quantum gates can be divided into two groups, single qubit gate and controlled gate.

The single qubit gates can be represented by a 2×2 matrix U_2, and the corresponding operations are implemented by a matrix-vector multiplication $U_2 \times \begin{bmatrix} \alpha_0 \\ \alpha_1 \end{bmatrix}$. For example, the matrixes for PauliX gate and RotateZ gate are $\begin{bmatrix} 0 & 1 \\ 1 & 0 \end{bmatrix}$ and $\begin{bmatrix} e^{-i\theta/2} & 0 \\ 0 & e^{i\theta/2} \end{bmatrix}$, respectively. However, the controlled gates are represented by a 2×2 matrix U_4. For example, the matrix for ControlledNot gate is

$$\begin{bmatrix} 1 & 0 & 0 & 0 \\ 0 & 1 & 0 & 0 \\ 0 & 0 & 0 & 1 \\ 0 & 0 & 1 & 0 \end{bmatrix}$$

2.2 Full-State Quantum Simulator

QuEST [8], a full-state quantum simulator, is chosen as an example to analyze in detail the data dependences and communications in the process of quantum simulation. From the basic quantum computing concept, we can get two characteristics of QuEST: one is huge memory consumption, and the other is heavy calculation overhead. The QuEST stores the whole quantum state, which uses a complex vector to save all the amplitudes. Since each amplitude is composed of two double-precision floating-point numbers, a quantum system with N qubits can consume 2^{N+4} bytes of memory. The amount of calculation also grows exponentially with the number of qubits.

QuEST can use multiple nodes to expand memory space and reduce the calculation overheads further by MPI. The way of implementing a distributed simulation in QuEST is to partition the quantum state equally among processes and each process binds one computing node as shown in Fig. 1. When using 2^m processes to simulate a n-qubit quantum system, a process keeps 2^{n-m} amplitudes. In this situation, for a gate whose target qubit is q, if $q \leq n - m$, the two amplitudes required by one computing task are managed by the same process and can be updated locally; otherwise, communication occurs between processes, and the process needs to exchange all the amplitudes with its pair.

2.3 Related Work

There exist some full-state quantum simulators [6, 7, 9, 10, 16–21], and these simulators propose various optimizations to make good use of the supercomputer to reduce time overheads cost.

In order to reduce runtime overhead, the GPUs [7, 10, 14, 15, 20, 22] are used to perform simulation as GPUs have a stronger computing power. Jones et al. [8] provide a hybrid multithread and distributed, GPU accelerated simulator and show that one Tesla K40m GPU can be 5× faster than a 24-thread CPU.

To improve the performance of GPU simulators, Zhang et al. [21] copy states into shared memory and reduce the expensive exchange of data in shared memory with the global memory. Qulacs [10] combines several gates into one gate, as gate fusion, and achieve better performance by reducing the number of gates. Chen et al. [20] propose two highly optimized methods to improve the performance, which greatly reduces the runtime overhead.

However, the scalability of the simulator is less efficient. Doi et al. [7] proposed a simulator on a heterogeneous HPC System, and their CPU-GPU hybrid design can store more qubits and accelerate simulation on the GPU. But they didn't exploit the data locality between gates and cannot avoid global communication and synchronization per gate, which influences the performance.

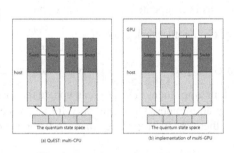

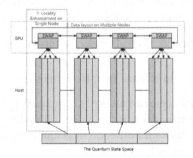

Fig. 1. Implementation of QuEST   **Fig. 2.** Framework of DLC

3 Framework Overview

In the related works, we can see that there are already many optimizations in computing, and the challenge of the simulators becomes the scalability on the GPU. In order to make full use of the computing benefits brought by the GPU, we build a new distributed and CPU + GPU heterogenous framework to optimize the scalability of the simulator as shown in Fig. 2.

Due to the characteristics of quantum simulation, when the simulation consumes more memory than a GPU's memory, it's hard to use the GPU for acceleration because of the global communication and synchronization per gate. We exploit the data locality between gates and change the process of the simulator. DLC store the quantum state on the host and compute on the GPU which highly improve the scalability on the hetero-geneous node. Besides, we propose a communication optimized scheme, which highly reduces the number of communications by exploiting the data locality and reducing the communication traffic by precise data transfer. It's worth to mention that there is no conflict between our framework and the existing computational optimizations.

4 CPU-GPU Locality Enhancement

4.1 Data Dependency Analysis

In order to take advantage of the large host memory to store the quantum state while still benefit from GPU, improving the data reuse on GPU is necessary. We analyze the data dependency between the gates in detail.

From Sect. 2.2, the minimal computational task of simulating the gate G_1, whose target qubit is q, is to finish a multiplication $U_1 \times \begin{bmatrix} \alpha_{m_i} \\ \alpha_{m_i+2^q} \end{bmatrix}$ involved two amplitudes. After finishing the multiplication, the two amplitudes at position m_i and $m_i + 2^q$ are updated. If the target qubit of the next gate G_2 is still q, the computational task of simulating $G_2: U_2 \times \begin{bmatrix} \alpha_{m_i} \\ \alpha_{m_i+2^q} \end{bmatrix}$ can be done advance before G_1 updates other amplitudes. However, if the target qubit of G_2 is not q but p, which is more general, the two related amplitudes are α_{m_i} and $\alpha_{m_i+2^p}$. While α_{m_i} has been updated, $\alpha_{m_i+2^p}$ is not updated by the task of G_1. In order to finish the task of G_2, another task of $G_1: U_1 \times \begin{bmatrix} \alpha_{m_i+2^p} \\ \alpha_{m_i+2^p+2^q} \end{bmatrix}$ should be done first. Here, another task of $G_2: U_2 \times \begin{bmatrix} \alpha_{m_i+2^q} \\ \alpha_{m_i+2^q+2^p} \end{bmatrix}$ is ready. So, we can finish the two tasks of G_1 first and update four amplitudes. Then G_2 can update the four amplitudes advance before G_1 updates other amplitudes. More generally, for a series of gates with t different targetqubit numbers, there are 2^t amplitudes that can be updated repeatedly by these gates.

4.2 CPU-GPU Locality Enhancement

Section 3.2 leads to a conclusion that it is feasible to update only a part of the quantum state with multiple gates, and we can improve the CPU-GPU heterogeneous approach performance by reusing the amplitudes between these gates.

Instead of calculating the gates one by one, we divide the gates into sets with a greedy algorithm, and the quantum state is partitioned into several chunks. For an N-qubit quantum system, and the GPU can contain n qubits, we divide the quantum state into 2^{N-n} chunks. Then transfer each chunk to the GPU and calculate the chunk with the set of gates in turn. In this way, we can calculate a set of gates with a single communication and synchronization. Figure 3 shows a simple example.

We have also made some optimizations with this approach. We set the quantum state on the host to pinned memory to improve the bandwidth between the host and the GPU. Using the pinned memory can save the time of copying from pageable host memory to pagelocked host memory. Besides, at the end of the simulation, when the number of gates in a set is few, we'd like to calculate these few gates on the CPU directly, for the computation time on the CPU is less than the sum of the computation time on the GPU and the communication time between the CPU and the GPU.

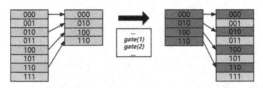

Fig. 3. The four amplitudes can be updated by a set of gates with once communication

5 Communication Optimization Among Multi-GPU

5.1 Challenges of Multi-GPU

Using multiple GPUs can expand memory space and reduce the calculation overheads further. However, it is not suitable to simply partition the quantum states among the GPUs, like the implementation of the multiple CPUs. Since the use of multiple GPUs can further reduce computing time, the performance bottleneck becomes the huge communication overheads between GPUs. In addition, the communication needs lots of additional memory as a buffer, which wastes precious memory on the GPU.

We illustrate the huge communication overhead by the QFT. When simulating the 30-qubit QFT on 8 GPUs, there are 60 times of communication. For each communication, GPU needs to exchange 2GB of data with its pair GPU. The huge gap also makes latency hiding difficult to function.

Except for the large amount of data per communication, there is a hidden reason for the weak scalability of using multiple GPUs. As the number of amplitudes saved in one GPU has an upper limit, communication can be much more frequent with the increase of the qubits. For example, when using multiple A100 40G GPUs, communication occurs that the gates' target qubit(q) is more than $30(n-m)$. The number of such gates is more and more with the growth of the number of qubits.

5.2 Communication Scheme

According to the conclusions in Sect. 4.1, we find a way to reduce the communication overhead of the simulator. Since the quantum circuit has been obtained, it is easy to divide the gates into sets. For a set of gates, the quantum state can be partitioned into several unrelated chunks according to the target qubits of these gates. We can assign a chunk to each GPU so that there is no communication between these gates. After finishing the simulation of a set of gates, we dynamically change the data layout, which significantly reduces communication overhead and improve the scalability.

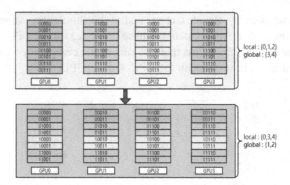

Fig. 4. An example illustrating the data layout on GPUs

The Fig. 4 shows the process of changing the data layout. The GPU0 sends α_{00010} and α_{00011} to the GPU1, sends α_{00100} and α_{00101} to the GPU2, sends α_{00110} and α_{00111} to GPU3. GPU1,2,3 receive the two amplitudes at position 0 and 1. The similar process occurs on other GPUs, too. With our scheme, changing the data layout once after gate(2) enables the gate(3) and gate(4) to be calculate in local, and highly reduce the time of communication.

Because we accurately divide the amplitudes sent to each GPU, the amount of amplitudes that need exchange also reduces. When simulating the 30-qubit QFT with our scheme on 8 GPUs, not only do twice data layout change, but also each GPU exchanges 1.75GB of data.

5.3 Optimization of Communication

Finding the amplitudes to be sent to the same GPU needs to traverse the amplitudes. We traverse them with the step of chunk size, instead of traversing one by one. The chunk size depends on the minimum qubit to be swapped out. We reduce indexing overhead in this way.

When the swapped qubit is at a low position, the amplitudes to be exchanged are dispersed. In this case, changing the data layout leads to frequent small data communication and cannot fully utilize the bandwidth. We set up an additional send buffer and pack the amplitudes which are sent to the same GPU into the buffer to fully utilize the bandwidth. There is a tradeoff in the buffer size, a small buffer can save more memory on GPU while a large buffer can improve the efficiency of communication.

Furthermore, our communication scheme is a N-dimensional communication. To make communication in parallel and improve the communication performance, we manage the order of communication between GPUs. Sending data to the target GPUs and receiving data from other GPUs are at the same time. GPU Direct-RDMA is also used to reduce communication latency.

6 Performance Evaluation

6.1 Environment Setup

We evaluate our scheme on a small-scale heterogenous CPU + GPU cluster. There are four computation nodes and each node has two NVIDIA's Tesla A100 GPUs, which has 40 GB global memory. The CPU in the node is Intel Xeon Gold 6230, 2.1GHz and the memory is 256GB. The CPU and GPU are connected via PCI Express 3.0 and all the nodes are connected via an FDR Infiniband switcher. The software environment includes CentOS 7.0, GCC 7.5.0, OPENMPI 4.0.5, NCCL 2.7.8 and CUDA 11.0.

We choose three common quantum circuits as datasets: QFT, invQFT and shor [10]. QFT and invQFT are the algorithms about quantum fast Fourier transform, and shor is the best-known classical algorithm requires to factor the product of two primes.

6.2 Performance on Single Node

This subsection evaluates the performance of data locality enhancement on a single node. According to the configuration of this node, one GPU can hold at most 31 qubits and one CPU can hold at most 33 qubits.

Figure 5 and Figure 6 shows the simulation time and performance speedup of DLC. The performance of QuEST is used as the baseline. Without DLC, quantum circuits with more than 31 qubits cannot be simulated on one GPU. Figure 7 shows that for the 30 and 31 qubits, GPU achieves 29.69 and 29.73× speedup over CPU. For the 32 and 33 qubits, DLC achieves 10.3 and 17.51× speedup respectively. Simulations using two GPUs are 1.13 and 1.25× faster than only one GPU is used.

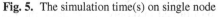

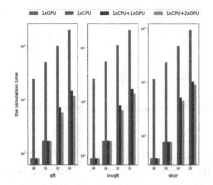 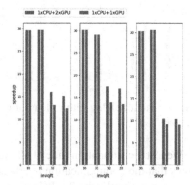

Fig. 5. The simulation time(s) on single node   **Fig. 6.** The performance speedup

As shown in Fig. 7, the communication time accounts for 49.41–79.82% of the total time. The communication overheads are heavy but unavoidable. For example, to simulate a 33-qubit QFT circuit. There are three times of communication during the simulation, and each communication needs to transfer 128GB of data between the host and the GPU twice. Although the communication overhead is heavy, we can get better performance than QuEST.

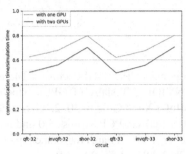
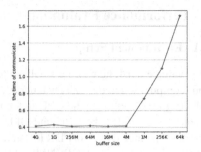

Fig. 7. The ratio of communication and simulation

Fig. 8. The performance of buffer size

6.3 Performance on Multiple Nodes

In this subsection, we evaluate our dynamic data layout scheme on a multi-GPU platform.

A small buffer size can save GPU memory while the bandwidth utilization decreases because of the frequently small message passing. Figure 8 shows that when the buffer size is larger than 4MB, the performance is stable. This means that it is not necessary to set a huge buffer.

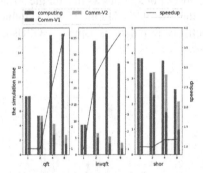

Fig. 9. The scalability with various GPU number

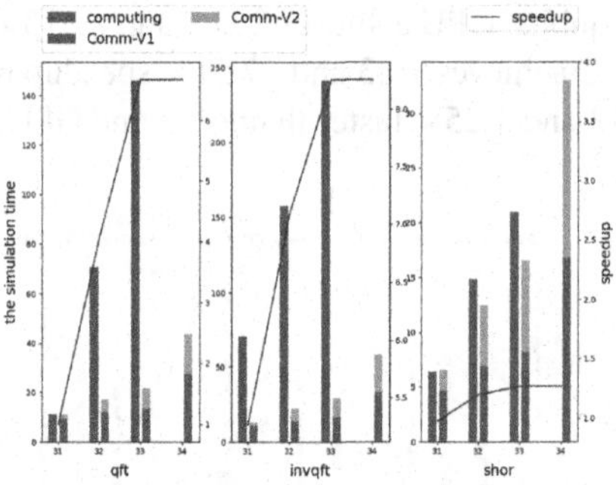

Fig. 10. The scalability of various qubit number

We test the simulation time of all the three circuits with 1, 2, 4, and 8 GPUs. Figure 9 shows that the communication overheads with 2 GPUs is not heavy. There are mainly two reasons. Firstly, the 2 GPUs are in the same node and connected directly via PCI Express. Secondly, as the quantum state is partitioned into only two chunks, the gates which require communication are few.

When using more than 2 GPUs, DLC(Comm-V2) improve the performance a lot. Without DLC(Comm-V1), there are 31 times of communication for the 30-qubit QFT circuit. The time cost by communication is 13.71 s, while the total simulation time is 17.06 s. The Shor circuit consists of about 200 gates and rare gates need communication, but DLC can still reduce some communication overheads.

DLC only need to adjust the data layout twice in the 30-qubit qft when 4 GPUs or 8 GPUs are used. Both the time cost by calculation and the communication overhead are reduced when more GPUs are used.

We simulate circuits having 31, 32 and 33 qubits to evaluate the scalability on the larger simulation scales. Besides, since we reduce the buffer size on the GPU side, our scheme can simulate one more qubit than the original scheme. We use 2 GPUs for 31-qubit quantum simulation, use 4 GPUs for 32-qubit quantum simulation, and use 8 GPUs for 33-qubit and 34-qubit simulation. In this way, we can maximize the utilization of each GPU, and it is also the most reasonable way to expand the number of qubits. With our scheme, the communication over-head is optimized little as the number of the qubits grows com-pared to the original scheme, which enormously improve the scalability. As shown in Fig. 10, DLC achieves about 4–7× speedup for qft and invqft and improves the utilization of GPUs a lot.

7 Conclusion

In this paper, we propose DLC optimizer, which performs two optimizations of the full-state quantum circuit simulation, to effectively improve the scalability on the CPU + GPU heterogeneous platform by exploiting the data locality between gates.

We evaluated the DLC optimizer on a small CPU + GPU cluster. There are four computation nodes and each node has two NVIDIA Tesla A100 GPUs. Our data locality enhancement approach achieves 10.3–17.51× performance speedup on the single node, and our dynamic data layout scheme achieves 4–7× performance speedup on circuit qft and invqft, and improves the utilization of GPUs greatly. In the future, we will utilize the existing computational optimizations to achieve a better performance.

References

1. Biamonte, J., Bergholm, V.: Tensor networks in a nutshell. arXiv pre-print arXiv:1708.00006 (2017)
2. Avila, A., Marqn, A., Reiser, R., Pilla, M., Yamin, A.: GPU-aware distributed quantum simulation. In: Proceedings of the 29th Annual ACM Symposium on Applied Computing, New York, NY, USA, pp. 860–865 (2014). https://doi.org/10.1145/2554850.2554892
3. Kelly, A.: Simulating quantum computers using OpenCL. arXiv preprint arXiv:1805.00988 (2018)
4. A Preview of Bristlecone, Google's New Quantum Processor. [Online]. http://ai.googleblog.com/2018/03/a-preview-of-bristlecone-googles-new.html
5. Villalonga, B., et al.: Establishing the quantum supremacy frontier with a 281 Pflop/s simulation. Quant. Sci. Technol. 5(3), 034003 (2020)
6. Biamonte, J., Wittek, P., Pancotti, N., Rebentrost, P., Wiebe, N., Lloyd, S.: Quantum machine learning. Nature. 549(7671), 195–202 (2017). https://doi.org/10.1038/nature23474
7. Wu, X.-C., et al.: Full-state quantum circuit simulation by using data compression. In: SC '19: Proceedings of the International Conference for High Performance Computing, Networking, Storage and Analysis, New York, NY, USA (2019). https://doi.org/10.1145/3295500.3356155
8. Boixo, S., Isakov, S.V., Smelyanskiy, V.N., Neven, H.: Simulation of low-depth quantum circuits as complex undirected graphical models. arXiv preprint arXiv:1712.05384 (2017)

9. Chen, J., Zhang, F., Huang, C., Newman, M., Shi, Y.: Classical simulation of intermediate-size quantum circuits. arXiv preprint arXiv:1805.01450 (2018)
10. Avila, A., Reiser, R.H., Pilla, M.L., Yamin, A.C.: Optimizing D-GM quantum computing by exploring parallel and distributed quantum simulations under GPUs arquitecture. In: 2016 IEEE Congress on Evolutionary Computation (CEC), pp. 5146–5153 (2016).
11. Preskill, J.: Quantum computing in the NISQ era and beyond. Quantum. **2**, 79 (2018). https://doi.org/10.22331/q-2018-08-06-79
12. Doi, J., Takahashi, H., Raymond, R., Imamichi, T., Horii, H.: Quantum computing simulator on a heterogenous HPC system. In: Proceedings of the 16th ACM International Conference on Computing Frontiers, New York, NY, USA, pp. 85–93 (2019). https://doi.org/10.1145/331 0273.3323053
13. Jones, T., Brown, A., Bush, I., Benjamin, S.C.: QuEST and high performance simulation of quantum computers. Sci. Rep. **9**(1), 1–11 (July 2019). https://doi.org/10.1038/s41598-019-47174-9
14. Markov, I.L., Shi, Y.: Simulating quantum computation by contracting tensor networks. SIAM J. Comput. **38**(3), 963–981 (2008). https://doi.org/10.1137/050644756
15. Pednault, E., et al.: Breaking the 49-qubit barrier in the simulation of quantum circuits. **15**. arXiv preprint arXiv:1710.05867 (2017)
16. Baldonado, M., Chang, C.-C.K., Gravano, L., Paepcke, A.: The Stanford digital library metadata architecture. Int. J. Digit. Libr. **1**, 108–121 (1997)
17. Gisin, N., Ribordy, G., Tittel, W., Zbinden, H.: Quantum cryptography. Rev. Mod. Phys. **74**(1), 145–195 (2002). https://doi.org/10.1103/RevModPhys.74.145
18. Ciliberto, C., et al.: Quantum machine learning: a classical perspective. Proc. R. Soc. A. **474**(2209), 20170551 (2018). https://doi.org/10.1098/rspa.2017.0551
19. Suzuki, Y., et al.: Qulacs: a fast and versatile quantum circuit simulator for research purpose. Quantum. **5**, 559 (2021). https://doi.org/10.22331/q-2021-10-06-559
20. Zhang, C., Song, Z., Wang, H., Rong, K., Zhai, J.: HyQuas: hybrid partitioner based quantum circuit simulation system on GPU. In: Proceedings of the ACM International Conference on Supercomputing, New York, NY, USA, pp. 443–454 (2021). https://doi.org/10.1145/344 7818.3460357
21. Zhang, P., Yuan, J., Lu, X.: Quantum Computer Simulation on Multi-GPU Incorporating Data Locality. In: Wang, G., Zomaya, A., Perez, G.M., Li, K. (eds.) ICA3PP 2015. LNCS, vol. 9528, pp. 241–256. Springer, Cham (2015). https://doi.org/10.1007/978-3-319-27119-4_17
22. Zhang, Y., Ni, Q.: Recent advances in quantum machine learning. Quant. Eng. **2**(1), e34 (2020). https://doi.org/10.1002/que2.34
23. Aleksandrowicz, G., et al.: Qiskit: an open-source framework for quantum computing. **16** (2019). Accessed March

Approximation Algorithms for Reliability-Aware Maximum VoI on AUV-Aided Data Collections

Hao Guo[1], Xiaohui Wei[1(✉)], Xingwang Wang[1], Xiaonan Wang[1], Chenghao Ren[1], and Meikang Qiu[2]

[1] The College of Computer Science and Technology, Jilin University, Changchun 130000, Jilin, China
{guohao17,xnwang19,rench19}@mails.jlu.edu.cn, {weixh,xww}@jlu.edu.cn
[2] The Beacom College of Computer and Cyber Sciences, Dakota State University, Madison, USA

Abstract. Underwater Wireless Sensor Networks (UWSNs) show great potential in ocean exploration on data collection. Recently, with the increasing amount of underwater sensed data, the Autonomous Underwater Vehicle (AUV) is introduced as a mobile sink to collect data from sensors. Existing research mainly regards the Value of Information (VoI) as the metric of real-time value such as data importance and timeliness, and they are committed to finding a path with maximum VoI for efficient collection. However, due to the limitation of AUV energy, partial sensors and their data may be omitted by the optimal path. From the perspective of the integrality dimension, data in the areas not covered by the path are indispensable for UWSN applications, which eventually reduces the reliability of the collection. To maximum VoI and improve reliability simultaneously, in this work, we propose approximate algorithms for reliability-aware AUV-aided data collection framework that extends the definition of VoI as the combination of the real-time VoI and reliability VoI. To find the optimal path under the framework, we first propose a dynamic priority strategy to re-quantify VoI on each sensor. Then we utilize an existing $(2 + \epsilon)$ approximation algorithm to find the optimal path without considering data timeliness which is formulated as the Orienteering Problem (OP). After that, we propose a novel polynomial-factor approximation algorithm to consider the decay of real-time VoI by reducing such variant OP into k-TSP. Finally, simulation results validate the effectiveness of the proposed approximation algorithms.

Keywords: UWSNs · Data collection · AUV · Value of information · Reliability · Approximation algorithm

This research was supported by the National Natural Science Foundation of China (NSFC) (Grants No. U19A2061, No. 61902143), Jilin Scientific and Technological Development Program(No.2020122208JC), the Natural Science Foundation of Jilin Province(No. YDZJ202101ZYTS191) and Sichuan Major R&D Project (Grant No.: 22QYCX0168).

S. Liu and X. Wei (Eds.): NPC 2022, LNCS 13615, pp. 219–230, 2022.
https://doi.org/10.1007/978-3-031-21395-3_20

1   Introduction

The ocean occupies more than seventy percent most of the Earth's surface, yet we know very little about the natural and biological resources in the ocean. Recently, researchers have shown an increased interest in using UWSNs to collect ocean data, which consist of multiple sensors with the capability of sensing, storing and wireless communication. These collected data can be utilized in UWSN applications such as aquaculture, monitoring of oil industry deployments, coastal surveillance and protection [1].

With the increasing requirements of underwater applications and the upgrades of underwater hardware, large amounts of data are produced by sensors such as real-time video and high definition pictures. It is a huge challenge to deliver these data to a sink timely and reliably through wireless communications. To enable these critical applications, some studies recently introduce AUV as a mobile sink to collect data from sensors closely by a judicious combination of acoustic and other communication technologies [2]. Due to the limitation of AUV energy, some existing AUV-based data collection methods like Ref. [3,4] further take the VoI into account to maximize one round's data value. Data in different geographical affinity and sensor's quite different responsibilities lead to inconsistent VoI of sensors. In summary, much of state-of-art researches focus on finding a path with maximum VoI for efficient AUV-aided data collection.

For many applications, the integrality of collected data is also critical, For many applications, the integrality of collected data is also critical, which requires reducing the data loss. However, the trajectory of AUV is unable to cover all sensors with the above metrics of VoI due to its collection capability being limited by speed (roughly $1 - 5knots$ [5]) and endurance capacity. As a result, partial sensors may be omitted by the optimal path. In terrestrial environments, sensors could transmit the omitted data to neighbors or the sink with acceptable cost to meet application requirements [6]. However, it is infeasible to forward such data through acoustic channels in UWSNs. More seriously, the accumulation of omitted data may exceed the sensor's storage capacity and thus have to be dropped or overwritten. Furthermore, in underwater environments, turbidity and light attenuation impede the range of optical sensors, biofouling clouds lenses and underwater housings, and marine species typically range over a large area, far outside of the range of a single camera sensor. Due to these factors, a continuously-recording or time-lapse visual sensor will not be gathering useful data the majority of the time, wasting battery life and filling limited onboard storage with useless images. Thus, dynamic sampling rate is applied in battery-powered networks [7]. The unfixed sampling rate of each sensor further aggravate the data loss. Therefore, it is worth-well to design a reasonable AUV-aided data collection scheme by adding a integrality dimension perspective to improve the reliability of data collection.

In this work, we propose approximate algorithms for reliability-aware AUV-aided data collection framework that extend the definition of VoI from the integrality dimension and new approaches to finding a path for maximum such VoI to enable UWSN applications. With such a perspective, sensors that are omitted for a longer time should have a higher value to be collected by the AUV. To increase AUV's willingness of reaching these sensors, we enable a dynamic priority strategy to re-quantify VoI at each sensor. The re-quantified VoI consists of the real-time VoI and the reliability VoI so that the real-time value and omitted data can be normalized to one optimization objective. Real-time VoI is equivalent to the traditional definition of VoI as mentioned before to distinguish it from reliability VoI.

To find the optimal path with high VoI under the framework, we adopt the approximation algorithm to deal with exponentially large solution spaces. In some UWSN applications without real-time VoI decay, we model the path finding problem into Orienteering Problem (OP) [8]. We further take the real-time VoI decay into consideration by defining a decay factor γ where the real-time VoI collected by an AUV reached at time t is decayed by γ^t. This problem is similar with the Discounted-Reward Traveling Salesman Problems (TSP) [9], but the Discounted-Reward TSP has no length limitation for the path. Facing these variations, our goal is to find a path that maximizes the time-varying VoI from nodes which subjects to a hard limitation on total length. The contributions of this paper are listed as follows:

1. We first formulate a novel framework to the problem of using an AUV to collect sensed data with an objective of maximizing the total VoI collected from sensors. The VoI is re-quantified by a dynamic priority strategy as the combination of real-time VoI and the reliability VoI. To the best of our knowledge, it is the first framework for finding an AUV path that regards VoI from the perspective of integrality dimension.
2. We model path finding problems into variants of OP and prove the defined problems are NP-hard. Then we propose approximation algorithms to tackle these problems. A key technique in the design of approximation algorithms is a nontrivial reduction that reduces each problem into k-TSP problem via the Min-Excess Path problem [9]. Our path finding problem without real-time VoI decay adopts a $(2 + \xi)$ approximation algorithm (for any fixed $\xi > 0$) as a solution. As for the case with real-time VoI decay, we propose a novel polynomial-factor approximation algorithm.
3. We finally evaluate the performance of proposed algorithms through experimental studies. Simulation results reveal that proposed algorithms are promising that could collect VoI at least 76% of the OPT algorithm and effectively reduce data loss.

2 Related Works

2.1 AUV-Aided Data Collection

In AEEDCO [10], an offline strategy is proposed to access each cluster head using the shortest possible path. This is formulated as a Traveling Salesman Problem (TSP) and an Ant Colony Algorithm (ACA) is applied to solve the TSP problem. Similarly, in [4], AUVs travel to all cluster head nodes in a clustered network.

An optimal algorithm based on Branch-and-Bound (BB) method and two near-optimal heuristic algorithms based on the ACA and the Genetic Algorithm (GA) are proposed to solve the problem. Gjanci et al. propose a Greedy and Adaptive AUV Path finding (GAAP [3]) algorithm based on an integer linear programming mathematical model with maximizing VoI as the optimization objective. In this scenario, the AUV moves continuously along a path to collect data, accessing only one node at a time and greedily selecting the node with the highest VoI as the target. However, the algorithm is suitable only for sparse networks. In another VoI-based work, data collectors are fixed with the anchor to collect data from nodes around in [11]. An AUV is deployed to dynamically visit data collectors to maximize the VoI within a given time. The AUV travel time is also taken into consideration in [12]. If the AUV successfully collects data from a sensor node in time, it will obtain a prize, whereas it will incur a penalty if it fails to visit a sensor. This is known as prize collecting TSP (PC-TSP). Unlike in [13], it first adopts the greedy algorithm to make a predetermined trajectory by selecting the next visited node with the smallest distance based on the location of CHs. The ordinary nodes close to the AUV trajectory are then selected as secondary cluster heads to share the workload of cluster heads.

2.2 Orienteering Problem and Variants

The orienteering problem and its variants have attracted a lot of attentions due to their wide applications. The term OP is first introduced in [14]. For solving the OP, Blum et al. propose the first 4-approximation algorithm [9]. Based on this work, [15] and [16] improve the approximation to a 3-approximation and $(2 + \xi)$-approximation separately.

Several variants of the OP have been introduced in [17] such as Team OP, OP with time windows, and the time dependent OP. However, there are rarely works that focus on the time-varying profits of OPs. In [9], it introduces a discounted-reward TSP focus on the time-varying profits but without the length limit. Given a start node, it proposed a $(6.75 + \xi)$-approximation algorithm. In DP-TOP [18], it considers the scenario that multiple vehicles need to serve a number of clients to get profits with a decreasing function of time. The work analyzes a lower bound and upper bound based on a classic mixed integer programs (MIP) formulation. Another work in [19] investigates an OP with arbitrary time-dependent profits. Specifically, it proposes a deterministic integrality representation of the routing topology and computes the solution by employing existing basic sorting and searching algorithms.

3   System Model and Problem Definition

3.1   System Model

We consider the UWSN architecture deployed in an underwater region for environmental monitoring or event detection purpose, which consisting of numerous

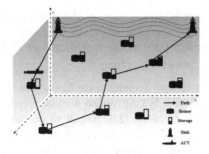

Fig. 1. Example of data collection model for AUV-aided UWSNs.

sensor nodes with unique IDs. Each sensor node performs continuous sensing data from surrounding environment (e.g. video surveillance) and saves these data locally in its limited storage space. An AUV is deployed to collect sensed data from sensor nodes via high-data-rate optical communication. The AUV periodically sails to surface stations to recharge power and offload data. Figure 1 is an illustrative example of data collection via an AUV in UWSN architecture. In the process of collection, the AUV is given a weighted undirected graph $G = (V, E)$ that indicates the network topology of the above UWSN architecture, where V includes two surface station $s, t \in V$ and a set of sensors $v_i \in V$, and $e_{ij} \in E$ denotes the distance between v_i and v_j. After that, the AUV starts from $s \in V$, finds a path among sensors, and then ending at $t \in V$ to complete a cruise cycle. Also, each sensor is equipped a limited storage with capacity B, it will overflow and discard partial data when the value of $\phi_{v_i}(\tau)$ exceeds B. The energy of AUV can not be supplemented underwater and thus it has a limited travel distance D per cruise cycle.

3.2 Problem Definition

Maximize the Total Collected Real-Time VoI: Consider a set of sensors $V^P \in V$ and a set of edges $E^P \in E$ that make up a path P. Suppose the path P starts from $s \in V^P$ at time 0 and ends at $t \in V^P$. For each node v_i along path P, the arrival time of AUV is denoted by τ_i. To calculate the actual real-time VoI collected from sensors, here we introduce a decay factor $\gamma \in (0, 1]$ to express the exponentially decay of it, that is real-time VoI collect at time τ by AUV is decayed by $\gamma^{\tau f_s}$, where f_s is the speed of AUV. Given the initial real-time VoI $\pi(v_i)$ of all sensors along path P, AUV could collect $\pi(v_i)\gamma^{\tau_i f_s}$ from sensor v_i at time τ_i. Then the objective of maximizing the total collected real-time VoI $\rho(P)$ can be defined as: $\max \rho(P) = \max \sum_{v_i \in V^P}(\pi(v_i)\gamma^{\tau_i f_s})$.

Minimize the Total Volume of Data Loss: Suppose that once AUV arrives a sensor along its path P, all the sensed data stored in the sensor will be collected. Correspondingly, sensed data will be accumulated in the sensor who has not been visited yet. Suppose that the volume of data sensed function is given, we can figure out the accumulated data of sensor v_i as $\phi_{v_i}(\tau_i)$ where τ_i is the waiting time for AUV arrival. In the view of the storage capacity at each sensor, data loss will happen once accumulated data in a sensor exceed B. Then the objective of minimizing the total volume of data lost $\Phi(P)$ can be defined as: $\min \Phi(P) = \min \sum_{v_i \in V} (max\{0, \phi_{v_i}(\tau_i) - B\})$.

Dynamic Priority Strategy: To normalize the above two optimization objectives, an alternative approach is to propose a uniform quantification about the priority of the sensor being visited [20]. Recall that, the sampling rate of each sensor is unpredictable and thus the volume of data sensed function is hard to obtain. Fortunately, the omitted sensors can easily be recorded in each cruise cycle, and thus we can figure out them in the integrality dimension and improve their priority. Specifically, we assign a reliability VoI $\theta^{r_{v_i}}$ to each sensor, where r_{v_i} denotes the number of consecutive unvisited cycles about sensor v_i and $\theta > 1$ denotes the priority factor. The value of θ can be adapted to different UWSN applications. Thus, the dynamic priority of each sensor can be denoted as the new definition of VoI: $\Theta(v_i) = \pi(v_i)\gamma^{\tau_i f_s} + \theta^{r_{v_i}}$.

Note that, the new VoI of a sensor is the combination of real-time VoI and the reliability VoI. We then set the path length bound per cycle to $D = f_s T$, where T is the cruise cycle time of the AUV. Let $d^P(s \to t) = \sum_{e \in E^P} d(e)$ denote the path length along P. Finally, the path finding problem converts to construct a certain path $P(s \to t)$ from s to t that traverses nodes with a maximized VoI: $\max_P / \sum_{v_i \in V^P} \Theta(v_i)$, and a bound D for the total length of path: s.t. $d^P(s \to t)/ \leq D$.

Recall that, the definition of OP is a routing problem in which the goal is to determine a s-t path, so that the number of distinct nodes along the path is maximized with a hard limit on the total length of the path. The OP can be seen as a combination between two classical combinatorial problems, the Knapsack Problem and the TSP [8], which are all proved as NP-hard problem. In the path finding problem with $\gamma = 1$, it can be viewed as an OP that the real-time VoI at each sensor is constant. In other case with $\gamma \in (0,1)$, it can not be easily modeled as a traditional OP but an extended OP due to the variable VoI at each sensor. As the OP is NP-hard, the path finding problem above is NP-hard too.

4   Approximation Algorithm for the Path Finding Problem

4.1   Approximation Algorithm for the Path Finding Problem Without Real-Time VoI Decay

In this part, we discuss the approximation algorithm for the case that real-time VoI without decay, where $\gamma = 1$. Consider an optimal path P^* that collects maximized VoI $\Pi(P^*)$ start from s and end at t with total length less than D. Inspired by [16], we break it into $c = \lceil \beta \rceil$ consecutive segments like $P_1^*, P_2^*, ..., P_c^*$, where each segment contains $\Pi(P^*)/c$ VoI. Let s_c and t_c denote the first and last node in P_c^*, and let $\varepsilon(P_c^*)$ express the excess of P_c^* which is the difference between the length of P_c^* and the shortest path from s_c to t_c. And then we find the consecutive segment which has the smallest excess called $\varepsilon(P_j^*)$. Now, we use the min-excess approximation algorithm on P_j^* to find a new $s_j - t_j$ path P_j' that collects $\Pi(P^*)/c$ VoI and with excess at most $\beta\varepsilon(P_j^*)$. Finally, we can construct a path P' that travels directly from s to s_c, then along P_j' from s_c to t_c, and final travels directly from t_c to c. The total length of P' is at most D and collects at least $\Pi(P^*)/c$ VoI. That is, the approximation factor of the approximation algorithm above is $c = \lceil\beta\rceil$ and returns a path of length at most D.

4.2 Approximation Algorithm for the Path Finding Problem with Real-Time VoI Decay

In this section, we further consider a more general model in UWSNs where the collected real-time VoI is decayed with respect to AUV arrival time by a factor $\gamma > 1$. Note that the length of the path is specifically bounded in this problem. However, the usage of Min-Excess path algorithm will generate excess up to β times as the optimal path to achieve the same reward. Thus, we have to give up VoI from part of nodes on the optimal path to assure such constraint. To figure out such a problem, we propose a novel approximation algorithm in the following.

Recall that the decayed VoI collected at node v_i by path P is defined as $\rho_{v_i}(P) = \pi(v_i)\gamma^{d^P(s\to v_i)} + \theta^{r_{v_i}}$. According to the definition above, VoI will lose exponentially by the length of path it takes for arriving at a node. Note that for collecting VoI from node v_i, AUV needs travel $d^P(s \to v_i) = d(s \to v_i) + \varepsilon(P_{v_i})$, where P_{v_i} is the portion of P from s to v_i, and the shortest path from s to v_i is fixed and necessary which is irrelevant to path P. In other world, the upper bound of decayed VoI collected from node v_i is $\pi'(v_i) = \pi(v_i)\gamma^{d(s\to v_i)} + \theta^{r_{v_i}}$ for any path. In such case, we rescale all the original VoI function $\pi(v_i)$ in graph G to $\pi'(v_i)$ and let total VoI collected by path P be at most $\Pi'(P) = \sum\pi'(v_i)$, called rescaled VoI.

Now consider an optimal path P^* from s to t that collects maximized decayed VoI $\rho(P^*)$ with total length less than D. Here we proximate the decayed VoI as $\rho_{v_i}(P) = \gamma^{\varepsilon(P_{v_i})}\pi'(v_i)$, which does not affect the path finding result. Suppose there is a node x on P^* before t where P_x^* express the portion of P^* from s to x with excess $\varepsilon(P_x^*)$. If we abandon collected VoI from P_x^* by taking a shortcut path P' that start from s directly to the next node after x on P^* and then continue along path P^* to t, this path could get VoI upgrade to $(\rho(P^*) - \rho(P_x^*))/\gamma^{\varepsilon(P_x^*)}$. In fact, decayed VoI collects by P' will not exceed the optimal path, thus we have:

$$\rho(P^*) \geq \rho(P')$$
$$\geq (\rho(P^*) - \rho(P_x^*))/\gamma^{\varepsilon(P_x^*)} \tag{1}$$

$$\rho(P_x^*) \geq (1 - \gamma^{\varepsilon(P_x^*)})\rho(P^*) \tag{2}$$

Based on the above lemma, we then turn to approximate $\rho(P_x^*)$ instead of $\rho(P^*)$. Note that path P consist of two parts: the Min-Excess path P' collected the same rescaled VoI $\Pi'(P_x^*)$ as P_x^* with excess at most $\beta\varepsilon(P_x^*)$ and a straight line. We first give the analysis of the possible decayed VoI collected by P. For any node in path P, the excess is at most $\beta\varepsilon(P_x^*)$. That is, compared to rescaled VoI $\pi'(v_i)$ at v_i, the decayed VoI is at least $\gamma^{\beta\varepsilon(P_x^*)}\pi'(v_i)$. Observing $\Pi'(P_x^*) \geq \rho(P_x^*)$, summing over all $(v_i) \in P$ and combining the result in Eq. 2, we have:

$$\rho(P) \geq \sum_{(v_i)\in P} \gamma^{\beta\varepsilon(P_x^*)}\pi'(v_i)$$
$$\geq \gamma^{\beta\varepsilon(P_x^*)}\Pi'(P_x^*) \tag{3}$$
$$\geq \gamma^{\beta\varepsilon(P_x^*)}\rho(P_x^*)$$
$$\geq \gamma^{\beta\varepsilon(P_x^*)}(1 - \gamma^{\varepsilon(P_x^*)})\rho(P^*)$$

Note that given an optimal path $\rho(P^*)$, decay factor γ and the factor of min-excess path approximation β, decayed VoI collected by the approximate path P is a function respect to $\varepsilon(P_x^*)$. Next, we will analyze the effect of different value of $\varepsilon(P_x^*)$ on $\rho(P)$. Let $a = \gamma^{\varepsilon(P_x^*)}$, then the approximation factor in Eq. 3 can be write as $(1 - a)a^\beta$. Let $\psi(a) = (1 - a)a^\beta$, then the derivative of $\psi(a)$ with respect to a is: $\psi'(a) = \beta a^{\beta-1} - (\beta + 1)a^\beta$.

The domain of a is within the range $(0, 1)$ when $0 < \gamma < 1$ and $\varepsilon(P_x^*) > 0$. When we let $\psi'(a) > 0$, we deduce that $\psi(a)$ is monotone increasing if $0 < a < \beta/(\beta + 1)$. Similarly, $\psi(a)$ is monotone decreasing when $\beta/(\beta + 1) < a < 1$. Therefore, the best approximation factor δ^* at $a = \beta/(\beta + 1)$, that $\varepsilon(P_{x^*}^*) = \log_\gamma(\beta/(\beta + 1))$ at x^* is: $\delta^* = (\frac{1}{\beta+1})(\frac{\beta}{\beta+1})^\beta$.

However, the value of excess $\varepsilon(P_x^*)$ has an upper bound caused by the deadline in our problem and thus may not reach the optimal value to maximize the approximation factor. Next, we discuss the upper bound in different scenarios with respect to different network topology and deadline. Recall that the length of approximate path P is $d(s \to x) + d(x \to t) + \beta\varepsilon(P_x^*)$ and we hope it less than the length bound D. Compared to the optimal path, the approximate path prolongs the prefix of P^* with the Min-Excess algorithm by $(\beta - 1)\varepsilon(P_x^*)$ and reduces the suffix of P^* by $\varepsilon(P^*) - \varepsilon(P_x^*)$ through a straight path. To make the total length of approximate path less than D, we have to let the prolonged part shorter than the reduced part and derive as follows: $\varepsilon(P_x^*) \leq \varepsilon(P^*)/\beta$.

Given the network topology G and length bound calculated from deadline D, we have the fix optimal excess of path $\varepsilon(P^*) = D - d(s \to t)$ and thus the domain of $\varepsilon(P_x^*)$ is within the range $[0, \varepsilon(P^*)/\beta]$. In the case $\varepsilon(P^*)/\beta < \log_\gamma(\beta/(\beta+1))$, the theoretical maximum value δ^* cannot be achieved and will be replaced by: $\delta^* = \gamma^{\varepsilon(P^*)}(1 - \gamma^{\varepsilon(P^*)/\beta})$.

In summary, The explicit expression of the best approximation factor is:

$$\delta^* = \begin{cases} \gamma^{\varepsilon(P^*)}(1 - \gamma^{\varepsilon(P^*)/\beta}), & \varepsilon(P^*)/\beta < \log_\gamma(\beta/(\beta + 1)) \\ (\frac{1}{\beta+1})(\frac{\beta}{\beta+1})^\beta, & \varepsilon(P^*)/\beta \geq \log_\gamma(\beta/(\beta + 1)) \end{cases} \tag{4}$$

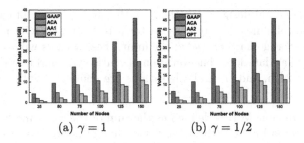

(a) $\gamma = 1$ (b) $\gamma = 1/2$

Fig. 2. The total volume of data loss generated by different algorithm.

5   Simulation and Performance Evaluation

In this section, we present the results of a simulation-based performance evaluation with the help of Aquasim [21] in NS2 simulator. We consider the cases that there exist $|N| = \{25, 50, 75, 100, 125, 150\}$ underwater sensor nodes randomly deployed over a $2\,\mathrm{km} \times 2\,\mathrm{km}$ square area with depth $200\,\mathrm{m}$. Consistent with the previous system model, sensor nodes in the network are assumed to be stable and thus will not affect by the turbulence of the flow. We set an AUV cruising among these nodes to collect sensed data with speed $2\,\mathrm{m/s}$, to match that of the existing AUV *Remus* 100 [5]. Each node sends short control packets over the acoustic channel and waits for the arrival of AUV. The size of short control packets is set to $10\,\mathrm{B}$ and the acoustic channel data rate is set to $4\,\mathrm{Kbps}$ by using the flooding routing algorithm implemented in Aquasim. For acoustic communications the transmission power is set to $3.3\,\mathrm{W}$ and its reception power is set to $0.5\,\mathrm{W}$. When AUV cruises within $10\,\mathrm{m}$ of a node [22], we set the optical data transfer rate to $1\,\mathrm{Gbps}$. Power consumption for optical data exchange is set to $3\,\mathrm{W}$ [23].

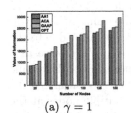 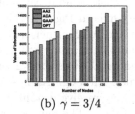 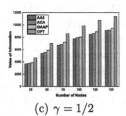

(a) $\gamma = 1$ (b) $\gamma = 3/4$ (c) $\gamma = 1/2$

Fig. 3. The total real-time VoI collected by different algorithms

We consider a scenario where the sensors use cameras to take videos. Surveillance data generates as $1080p$ high-definition videos at random between $[1, 10]$ GB per hour. Each node generates these data with random initial real-time VoI per hour which is represented by an integer value chosen from $[1, 100]$. The real-time VoI of these data decays by a decay factor γ which varying in different experimental designs. We then set the storage space of each sensor to 30 GB and the reliability VoI priority factor θ to 2. If AUV can not arrive the sensors whose storage have exceeded the limit, these sensors will discard part of data and record as data loss. The duration of cruise cycle and network operation is set to 1 and 24 h, and then all algorithms are compared with respect to the following metrics:

1. Collected real-time VoI: Is defined as the sum of the real-time VoI of all data chunks collected by AUV throughout the time of network operations.
2. Volume of data loss: Is defined as the sum of the volume of data loss when AUV missed the sensors whose storage have exceeded the limit.
3. Running time of algorithms: Is defined as the statistics of practical running time of algorithms for determining each cruise cycle.

For the following set of experiments we consider the above metrics under the different combinations of node numbers and decay factor and analysis the reasons. The simulation uses a Monte Carlo method that all numerical results are obtained after 100 calculations.

We then show results on the performance of our proposed approximation algorithms termed AA1 (Algorithm in Sect. 4.1) and AA2 (Algorithm Algorithm in Sect. 4.2) by comparing with the optimal algorithm (termed OPT), GAAP [3] and ACA [4]. Although the considered scenario in GAAP and ACA is different from our work, we adopted the core idea of them in the simulation that AUV chooses the node with greatest contribution to the real-time VoI as next hop at every decision point. The results of OPT is obtained by solving the path planning problem formulated into ILP by using a freely available software Gurobi [24] as a benchmark.

Results for our approximation algorithms (AA1, AA2), GAAP, ACA and OPT about their data loss are shown in Fig. 2(a) and Fig. 2(b). This set of experiments is aimed at measuring the reliability of data collection on the performance of AUV path planning algorithms. Figure 2(a) and Fig. 2(b) shows the total volume of data loss when there is no decay and with decay factor $\gamma = 1/2$ respectively. The unit of the y-axis in Fig. 2 is the absolute value of data volume (GB). As expected, AA1 and AA2 outperform GAAP and ACA due to the consideration of deadline requirement from each sensor node. We observe that GAAP loss data 3–4 times and ACA loss data 2 times more than OPT while AA1 and AA2 at most 1.5 times. Although AA1, AA2 and OPT guaranteed the total length constraint, AUV may receive deadlines from multiple nodes at the same time and thus lost some data. The gap between OPT and AA1, AA2 is due to the fact that AUV visit less sensors with AA1 and AA2 than OPT under the same path length constraint.

Figure 2(b), 3(a) and 3(b) concerns the total real-time VoI collected by AUV in different algorithms. When the real-time VoI has no decay in Fig. 2(b), AA1 collects at least 76% real-time VoI compare to OPT at any network topology. As for GAAP and ACA, it collects real-time VoI about 83 and 80% of that in OPT. GAAP collects more real-time VoI than AA1 is mainly because GAAP has no interest in visiting the sensors with low real-time VoI yet AA1 have to visit these sensors for avoiding data loss. Likewise, ACA also prefers such sensor nodes. For the same reason, GAAP and ACA collects more real-time VoI than AA2 when it has decay in Fig. 3(a) and Fig. 3(b), about 85% (GAAP), 82% (ACA) and 80% (AA2) of OPT. Note that different γ has little effect when AA1, GAAP and ACA compare to OPT. The reason is that different γ can be unified by rescaling the edge length when construct the network graph. Combining the above experimental results, it validates the superiority of our proposed algorithms AA1 and AA2 when considering both real-time VoI and data loss.

6   Conclusion

In this article, we studied the AUV-aided data collection problem in UWSNs. The aim is to find the path for the AUV that maximize the real-time and reliability VoI of the collected data. Specifically, we enabled a dynamic priority strategy to re-quantify VoI and design two approximation algorithms based on the Min-excess path algorithm for the case with or without real-time VoI decay respectively. After a series of derivations, we proved that the approximation algorithm without decay achieves a constant-factor approximation and another algorithm obtains a polynomial-factor approximation with respect to the excess of the optimal path. Simulation results showed that our approximation algorithms collect VoI at least 76% of the OPT algorithm and effectively reduced data loss.

References

1. Heidemann, J., Stojanovic, M., Zorzi, M.: Underwater sensor networks: applications, advances and challenges. Philos. Trans. **370**(1958), 158–175 (2012)
2. Khan, M.T.R., Ahmed, S.H., Kim, D.: AUV-aided energy-efficient clustering in the internet of underwater things. IEEE Trans. Green Commun. Netw. **3**(4), 1132–1141 (2019)
3. Gjanci, P., Petrioli, C., Basagni, S., Phillips, C.A., Bölöni, L., Turgut, D.: Path finding for maximum value of information in multi-modal underwater wireless sensor networks. IEEE Trans. Mob. Comput. **17**(2), 404–418 (2018)
4. Duan, R., Jun, D., Jiang, C., Ren, Y.: Value-based hierarchical information collection for AUV-enabled internet of underwater things. IEEE Internet Things J. **7**(10), 9870–9883 (2020)
5. Zeng, Z., Lian, L., Sammut, K., He, F., Tang, Y., Lammas, A.: A survey on path planning for persistent autonomy of autonomous underwater vehicles. Ocean Eng. **110**, 303–313 (2015)
6. Qiu, M., Ming, Z., Li, J., Liu, J., Quan, G., Zhu, Y.: Informer homed routing fault tolerance mechanism for wireless sensor networks. J. Syst. Archit. **59**(4–5), 260–270 (2013)
7. Wei, X., Yan, S., Wang, X., Guizani, M., Du, X.: STAC: a spatio-temporal approximate method in data collection applications. Pervasive Mob. Comput. **73**(1), 101371 (2021)
8. Vansteenwegen, P., Souffriau, W., Van Oudheusden, D.: The orienteering problem: a survey. Eur. J. Oper. Res. **209**(1), 1–10 (2011)

9. Blum, A., Chawla, S., Karger, D.R., Lane, T., Meyerson, A., Minkoff, M.: Approximation algorithms for orienteering and discounted-reward TSP. SIAM J. Comput. **37**(2), 653–670 (2007)
10. Zhuo, X., Liu, M., Wei, Y., Guanding, Yu., Fengzhong, Q., Sun, R.: AUV-aided energy-efficient data collection in underwater acoustic sensor networks. IEEE Internet Things J. **7**(10), 10010–10022 (2020)
11. Yan, J., Yang, X., Luo, X., Chen, C.: Energy-efficient data collection over AUV-assisted underwater acoustic sensor network. IEEE Syst. J. **12**(4), 3519–3530 (2018)
12. Hollinger, G.A., et al.: Underwater data collection using robotic sensor networks. IEEE J. Sel. Areas Commun. **30**(5), 899–911 (2012)
13. Huang, M., Zhang, K., Zeng, Z., Wang, T., Liu, Y.: An AUV-assisted data gathering scheme based on clustering and matrix completion for smart ocean. IEEE Internet Things J. **7**(10), 9904–9918 (2020)
14. Golden, B.L., Levy, L., Vohra, R.: The orienteering problem. Nav. Res. Logist. **34**(3), 307–318 (1987)
15. Bansal, N., Blum, A., Chawla, S., Meyerson, A.: Approximation algorithms for deadline-TSP and vehicle routing with time-windows. In: Babai, L. (ed.) Proceedings of the 36th Annual ACM Symposium on Theory of Computing, Chicago, IL, USA, 13–16 June 2004, pp. 166–174. ACM (2004)
16. Chekuri, C., Korula, N., Pál, M.: Improved algorithms for orienteering and related problems. ACM Trans. Algorithms **8**(3), 23:1–23:27 (2012)
17. Gunawan, A., Lau, H.C., Vansteenwegen, P.: Orienteering problem: a survey of recent variants, solution approaches and applications. Eur. J. Oper. Res. **255**(2), 315–332 (2016)
18. Murat Afsar, H., Labadie, N.: Team orienteering problem with decreasing profits. Electron. Notes Discret. Math. **41**, 285–293 (2013)
19. Ma, Z., Yin, K., Liu, L., Sukhatme, G.S.: A spatio-temporal representation for the orienteering problem with time-varying profits. In: 2017 IEEE/RSJ International Conference on Intelligent Robots and Systems, IROS 2017, Vancouver, BC, Canada, 24–28 September 2017, pp. 6785–6792. IEEE (2017)
20. Tang, X., Li, K., Qiu, M., Sha, E.H.M.: A hierarchical reliability-driven scheduling algorithm in grid systems. J. Parallel Distrib. Comput. **72**(4), 525–535 (2012)
21. Xie, P., et al.: Aqua-Sim: an NS-2 based simulator for underwater sensor networks. In: OCEANS 2009, pp. 1–7 (2009)
22. Hanson, F., Radic, S.: High bandwidth underwater optical communication. Appl. Opt. **47**(2), 277–283 (2008)
23. Anguita, D., Brizzolara, D., Parodi, G.: Prospects and problems of optical diffuse wireless communication for underwater wireless sensor networks. InTech (2010)
24. Gurobi Optimization, LLC: Gurobi optimizer reference manual (2014)

CCSBD: A Cost Control System Based on Blockchain and DRG Mechanism

Weiqi Dai[1] , Yan Yu[2], Xia Xie[3] , Dezhong Yao[2]([⊠]) , and Hai Jin[2]

[1] National Engineering Research Center for Big Data Technology and System, Services Computing Technology and System Lab, Hubei Engineering Research Center on Big Data Security, School of Cyber Science and Engineering, Huazhong University of Science and Technology, Wuhan 430074, China

[2] National Engineering Research Center for Big Data Technology and System, Services Computing Technology and System Lab, Cluster and Grid Computing Lab, School of Computer Science and Technology, Huazhong University of Science and Technology, Wuhan 430074, China
dyao@hust.edu.cn

[3] School of Computer Science and Technology, Hainan University, Haikou 570228, China

Abstract. *Diagnosis Related Group* (DRG) allows patients to be grouped according to the initial diagnosis and to be prepaid within the group. Actual costs in follow-up treatment cannot exceed the prepaid value, achieving the purpose of medical cost control. Three problems exist in the process. First, some treatment operations are highly overlapping and therefore cannot be accurately classified. Second, classification data cannot be credibly shared across hospitals. Third problem is the historical payment path required to predict costs cannot be fully traced. To address these problems, we design a *Cost Control System Based on Blockchain and DRG Mechanism* (CCSBD). We proposes a fusion classification model to realize the contribution assessment of the important feature factors, leading to accurate classification. In order to ensure the security and consistency of shared information, We establish a hyper-ledger blockchain architecture for secure sharing of medical data. Through smart contract, the architecture realizes dynamic consensus endorsement of data and cross-chain cross-authentication of departmental attributes. We realize value data screening and clinical path tracking through logical chain code to generate reasonable cost metrics to predict expenses, and implement CCSBD on the Fabric consortium-chain platform. Through comparative analysis with three single classification models, we prove that CCSBD improves classification accuracy by 7%. Furthermore, the security and efficiency of the shared structure are demonstrated by smart contract latency tests and consistency attack tests.

Keywords: Consortium chain · DRG · Cross certification · Dynamic endorsement · Fusion classification

© IFIP International Federation for Information Processing 2022
Published by Springer Nature Switzerland AG 2022
S. Liu and X. Wei (Eds.): NPC 2022, LNCS 13615, pp. 231–242, 2022.
https://doi.org/10.1007/978-3-031-21395-3_21

1   Introduction

Diagnosis Related Group (DRG) method uses historical data to forecast clinical diagnosis and treatment paths, so as to form a classification of diagnostic and treatment plans through exhaustive enumeration and clustering [1]. The DRG cost control management pattern requires the establishment of quantitative standards for clinical indicators, and set a uniform cost pricing strategy within each category. Patients then pay the corresponding costs in advance [2]. The DRG classification process requires a high level of information technology, because it requires a large amount of collection of historical treatment data and the setting of reasonable classification criteria based on historical experience. However, today's *Hospital Information System* (HIS) has been developed more mature [3], the design of a more flexible DRG classification algorithm is still a key concern for many hospitals, but the results are not satisfactory. Smarter grouping systems and more reliable category cost forecasting systems are the top priorities to make DRG categorization and cost control truly effective [4]. Furthermore, it is a necessary prerequisite for training a reasonable classifier so that clinical consultation data can be credibly shared within the medical society [5]. To solve the problem of low value of these classification training data, the main research direction is to find a more secure and trustworthy shared storage mechanism for clinical data.

The main objective of this study is to investigate the solutions to some technical bottlenecks in the classification and cost control process. Challenges include poor accuracy of classification algorithms and incomplete tracking of historical clinical pathways used for cost measurement [6], as well as research gaps in distributable and secure sharing mechanism for classification data. Firstly, when classifying the features of highly overlapping treatment, there is no automated DRG classification grouping mechanism with satisfying fitting degree and accuracy, satisfying the requirements of DRG indicators. The process does not reasonably evaluate the classification feature factors with high overlap, and thus cannot accurately extract the classification feature indicators, resulting in an unreasonable structure of the finally obtained disease class groups. Secondly, the data used for training the classification algorithm is the historical treatment path attribute data set of each hospital in the medical association, but the current cross-hospital data sharing mechanism does not guarantee the privacy and security of the attributes of the participating departments [7], nor the consistency of the treatment information. Accordingly, a trusted distributed storage solution is needed, which should also guarantee that the shared data cannot be changed by external unauthorized users. Finally, when the cost prediction is performed, the complete tracking analysis of historical patient payment paths and the extraction of high-value path information is not achieved, thus preventing the training of reasonable rate indicators for predicted cost generation [8].

To achieve the above mentioned aims, we have developed a *Cost Control System Based on Blockchain and DRG Mechanism* (CCSBD), which improves the classification precision by designing a more reasonable classifier. It generates DRG class groups using an optimized fusion classification training model.

Separately, we propose a federated blockchain deposition architecture to achieve high-value data filtering, tamper-evident storage and consistent communication of data, cross-chain confirmation of shared nodes, complete tracking of path data.

The key steps of the CCSBD scheme are as follow: Fusion of classification learning algorithms with weights [9], and then output the final disease class group number to complete the classification process [10]. The two-stage smart contract strategy guarantees the security and consistency of the data sharing of treatment process attributes in the distributed ledger federated chain architecture [11]. The logical chain code is used to realize payment path tracking and heterogeneous path data annotation, and then, complete total cost prediction based on reliable tracking results.

2   Related Work

This section provides an overview of the blockchain literature related to decentralized identity authentication, and distributed ledger storage. Public Key Infrastructure mainly consists of hardware and software support platforms together with pre-defined secure communication policies. It is a complete set of security mechanisms, which are mechanisms widely used in identity authentication demand systems and distributed systems [12]. Relevant organizations can use the distributed public key technology and X.509 certificate security services provided by PKI-related products to establish their own security domains, realize the whole process of key and certificate management through PKI within the domain, and establish a secure association relationship with security domains of other organizations by cross-certification between domains [13]. The classical PKI system mainly includes the *Certificate Authority* (CA) and issuance system, *Registration Authority* (RA), which are supported by relevant built-in policies and software and hardware platforms. The CA component has been built into the Fabric system for PKI security services to issue verifiable ID certificates, and certificates are used to determine the membership of a particular organization in the blockchain network through the built-in *Membership Service Provider* (MSP) [14]. MSP provides identity permission forms which are added to each channel configuration, it confirms the identity of the organizational members internally, and externally, it confirms the permission of other organization's members to perform operations in that channel.

3   System Design

3.1   System Overview

CCSBD focuses on designing solutions for the three problem scenarios of classification accuracy, trusted sharing of classification data, and intra-class cost prediction in the DRG diagnosis classification and cost control process proposed in the introduction.

For the classification accuracy problem, a generalized fusion classification model is designed which is trained to output a high coverage classifier. For the data trustworthy sharing, we build an on-chain storage architecture for clinical diagnosis and treatment data. Smart contract strategy of federation blockchain is used in the architecture to annotate and clean heterogeneous data to aggregate high-value information, establish a pathway for cross-domain sharing and validation of medical associations, and build an endorsement voting mechanism for data consistency certification on the blockchain. For the problem of intra-category prepayment measurement, the block traceability of the historical path is completed by using logical chain code, and the rate index factor is rewritten according to the traceability result, so as to reasonably predict the category fee. Combining the above three mechanisms into a complete DRG charge control decision system, we can realize the whole classification and charge measurement process. Their detailed algorithm design is discussed separately below.

3.2   Medical Evidence-Based Classification Model

The classification index is obtained through chain code information collection, mainly by polling the case diagnosis and treatment path information of discharged patients deposited in the alliance chain, and applying blockchain transaction evidence to obtain the aggregated specification history knowledge base, and parse out the required metric values from the knowledge base. Meanwhile, all information collection process operations are renewed in the distributed ledger and broadcast to the nodes of medical entities in the whole domain, so as to complete the tamper-proof deposition and probing operations. In order to accelerate indicator acquisition, a record traceability rollback function for future clinical diagnosis and treatment sample analysis and quality control assessment is designed. When a certain query is made, if the records fitted by indicator screening have been bound to patient information stored in the chain, the complete operation information chain is directly traced back for use afterward to reduce the repeated indicator screening process. Single query process operation left by the distributed ledger records, in the future data leakage risk can be used to trace the DRG operation information for accurate attribution.

The segmentation strategy chosen here is mainly obtained from the secondary diagnostic information of the disease. The acquisition process is performed by initiating a "get transaction" request to poll the publicly shared clinical cases in the blockchain network of the medical association. After acquiring and analyzing the cases, we analyzed and filtered the information obtained on the medical prescriptions of patients with chronic diseases, sorted the payment details of each patient to extract the high-rate indicators and summarized them. Thereby, four major categories of characteristic indicators to be considered for systematic classification were identified, including age classification, length of treatment cycles, definition of care specifications, and the development index of comorbidity/complication complexity used to measure the development of treatment pathways. These metrics are used to comprehensively assess individual patient factors, and in the subsequent decision algorithm design, it will tell how to aggregate their data and distill pathway expansion cost information and in-hospital non-disease targeted universal treatment cost information to pinpoint the full cost. The four metrics and their values for DRG segmentation generated after the above metric design are shown in Table 1. The segmentation design shown in the table can cover the effects of path complexity, universal treatment, duration, and individual factors on DRG. There is also a correlation between these indicators, using several parameters in this table for hierarchical classification, a more adaptive classifier can be obtained.

Table 1. Sub-indicator value table

Age	PCCL	Nursing type	Treatment period
<18	Level 1	Grade I	Emergency temporary observation
18–50	Level 2	Grade II	Short-term
50–80	Level 3	Grade III	Mid-term
>80	Level 4	Grade IIV	Emergency long-term

Single decision algorithms here are designed to reduce data confusion and complexity as quickly as possible and take into account that the different features are not entirely independent. The empirical entropy is used as the basis for measuring the degree of confusion and uncertainty reduction, and higher entropy proves that the uncertainty of the data set is stronger. The conditional empirical entropy is mainly used here, because it is necessary to measure and compare the choices separately according to different situations and conditions of different features, and the conditional empirical entropy is calculated as shown in Eq. 1.

$$H(D \mid M) = -\sum_{t}^{m} \frac{|D_t|}{|D|} \sum_{k=1}^{K} \frac{|D_{tk}|}{|D_t|} \mid \log 2 \frac{|D_{tk}|}{|D_t|} \tag{1}$$

It represents the information uncertainty conditional entropy of the data set D when the classification of the feature indicator M has been determined, and D_t represents that the feature indicator M can be divided into m classification values, and D_t is the capacity of the data set in one of the classifications. This is used in order to calculate the probability value when the feature value M is set to t. Then it is set that the final decision algorithm generates the completed classification with K classes, and the latter D_{tk} represents the number of sample sets that finally belong to the kth class in D_t. The latter summation part of the calculation process is the empirical entropy of the sample data set, with the classification probability of the feature value M attached earlier, combined to become the conditional empirical entropy value when determining the feature indicator selected in this layer as M.

The most basic algorithm is an algorithm for gain contribution assessment with reduced information confusion. The medical insurance cost control scenario requires a high degree of result fitting, so the first choice is to use the ID3 algorithm with a very high degree of fitting to process some discrete and unrelated feature value data of treatment-related groupings similar to age, treatment complexity, etc. Based on the empirical entropy with conditions to evaluate the contribution of uncertainties in the feature conditions, finally the information gain value is used to compare the contribution of different feature groups to the differentiation of the data set. The information gain is calculated as shown in Eq. 2.

$$g(D, M) = H(D) - H(D \mid M) \tag{2}$$

Algorithm design considers that if the greater information gain proves that by classifying according to feature M, the grouping obtained is less confusing and the grouping effect is better, so the algorithm is designed to recursively perform information gain comparison, and the information gain is calculated separately for the unselected feature metrics in each round of execution, the highest of which is selected as the classification metric in this layer.

The next step is to implement the information gain boosting algorithm. Although the above method can ensure a more detailed division of data matching branches, there is a risk of producing over-fitting results. As the above method is to judge the contribution of information features to the grouped chaos reduction situation by the empirical entropy of information and the empirical entropy under conditional probability, it will cause unreasonable feature selection when the number of values taken for a feature class is too large and causes a large contribution to the information gain rather than the information gain because of its content contribution. It so happens that among the feature values selected for clinical segmentation, similar indicators such as PCCLs exist with a high number of takes. Thus, an algorithmic model for quantitative impact elimination penalty is introduced here for some features with overly disparate quantitative differences in metric values, addressing both the impact of quantitative differences in the values taken by different features and the impact of capacity differences in the set of values taken within the same feature. The algorithm corrects the problem of information gain training by incorporating unconditional empirical entropy. The realized information gain ratio gr(D,M) is calculated as shown in Eq. 3.

$$g_r(D, M) = \frac{-\sum_{k=1}^{K} \frac{|D_k|}{|D|} log_2 \frac{|D_k|}{|D|} - \left(-\sum_{t}^{m} \frac{|D_t|}{|D|} \sum_{k=1}^{K} \frac{|D_t|}{|D_t|} log_2 \frac{|D_t|}{|D_t|} \right)}{-\sum_{t=1}^{m} \frac{|D_t|}{|D|} log_2 \frac{|D_t|}{|D|}} \tag{3}$$

K represents the classification categories of all tree-like leaf nodes. The overall empirical entropy of the dataset D is calculated, and thus the calculated value of the information gain based on feature M is generated at the numerator. The m in the denominator represents that the features M can be divided into a total of m classes, and the empirical entropy of the classification based on the features

M is calculated as the elimination factor in the denominator. The gain ratio formed so far can eliminate the influence of the number of classifications on the complexity judgment, and for such discrete data as the care category in DRG grouping, it is also necessary to use this algorithmic model that is more adapted to discrete grouping.

Finally, a dichotomous feature-friendly algorithm is proposed. For continuous data such as cycle time in DRG requirements, the above conditional information gain requires greater computational resource consumption than continuous scan computation, so it is necessary to choose a simplified algorithm with fewer repeated scans per iteration round, each round of execution is to generate two subdivisions, and the dichotomous strategy is also more adapted to computer execution language with later rule understanding. In addition, there are sometimes grouping correlations between DRG classification features such as age metrics and complication complexity PCCL metrics, so it is not feasible to directly divide at a level exactly according to one of them. The algorithm chosen here tries to preserve the connotations of the associated features when branching down, and ensures that the connotations continue to contribute later.

Gini coefficient is chosen as the judgment criterion of classification uncertainty. It is calculated separately for different values of a DRG feature indicator in the algorithm, and then the smallest Gini coefficient among the calculated values is selected as the Gini coefficient of the feature indicator. By selecting the feature with the lowest Gini index in all features, that is, the feature with the greatest improvement in the purity of the sample obtained after classification, as the forked indicator in this layer, the dichotomous decision is made after selecting the forked feature. The Gini coefficient is calculated as shown in Eq. 4.

$$
\begin{aligned}
&\mathrm{Gini}(D, M = m1) \\
&= \frac{|D_a|}{|D|}\left[1 - \sum_{k=1}^{K}\left(\frac{|D_{ak}|}{|D|}\right)^2\right] + \frac{|D_b|}{|D|}\left[1 - \sum_{k=1}^{K}\left(\frac{|D_{bk}|}{|D|}\right)^2\right]
\end{aligned}
\tag{4}
$$

It shows the Gini coefficient based on the dataset D when calculating the feature M taking value m1. A and b mean that the values of the feature values M in the dataset are sorted and then m1 is used as the dividing line to classify the sorted results into two categories a and b. The number of final categories of the tree structure is denoted by K. The final calculation is obtained by summing the Gini coefficients of a and b after binding the frequency weights of the categories.

The fusion of the models is performed after completing three base cases. The algorithm of this system here generates regression criteria through a preconfigured target loss function used for learning, and the function regression calculation process uses a cyclic iteration based on dynamic batch gradient descent. The contribution weights obtained when the loss rate reaches the target error are used as the final per-model contribution weights, from which the model fusion is then completed. The loss function is shown in Eq. 5, where y of the data sample represents the true grouping value and F is the predicted value, while the batch gradient descent method reduces the loss rate to the threshold criterion to obtain the final contribution coefficient.

$$\text{Loss} = \frac{1}{2n} \sum_{i=1}^{n} (y_i - F(x_i))^2 \tag{5}$$

Implementation of the fusion proposes a major contribution update generation diffusion method to generate an array of validity values in each iteration round. The input to the method is the DRG group coding values and the information matrix of the clinical case for the patient, which has been previously generated by the three base models at the end of the training, and the input values are later used as independent variables for the generation of the fusion classification value coefficients. The contribution validity array generated after the previous round of fusion iterations is also entered as the starting point for the current performance data update. Each iteration round will use all the decomposition in the information base, and finally a new contribution degree matrix will be output.

3.3   Contract Strategy for Clinical Data Sharing

The learning rate steps are dynamically decayed for each decrease in the function training process, in order to improve the efficiency of the initial learning and to ensure the learning accuracy at the end. The initial learning rate is set to 0.01, and then each cycle adds a decay number with the number of diffraction rounds as the denominator. In addition, when the function is executed in each round, it does not follow the coding order in the information base, but generates a random order to update the validity values to ensure the accuracy of the resultant metric update. The execution process also performs error threshold judgment and does not continue training when the threshold value is reached, thus improving the efficiency of the resulting output.

Cleansed speciated data needs to enter the blockchain depository architecture, and the next step is to provide cross-domain peer-to-peer authentication for the entities that provide this data. The access mechanism of the federated chain is used to realize the peer-to-peer authentication of node identity in the medical association, so as to reduce the possibility of a threat to the business system caused by the single point of failure in the certification authority. The system uses the built-in Fabric CA of the federated chain network to realize the access to the medical federation network, issues the ID card through the distributed *Public Key Infrastructure* (PKI), and confirms the identity belonging to the organizations in the domain through the *Membership Service Provider* (MSP). Thus, the trustworthy network of the medical association is completed. The overall identity authentication and authorization architecture is shown in Fig. 1.

Between two separated entities within a health care consortium, cascading CA authentication links are automatically constructed within each organization and cross-identity authentication between different organizations is achieved through smart contracts in the top-level blockchain network. This process achieves the construction of a trust bridge for the medical association, thus opening up the identity trust chain across hospitals in a distributed medical community.

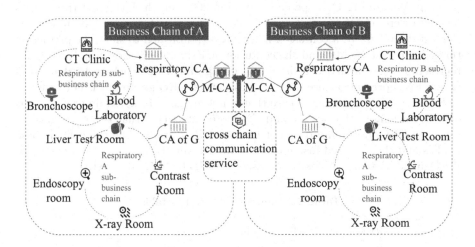

Fig. 1. Cross-domain confirmation network of medical consortium chain

To achieve a complete identity verification of a medical association, cross-certification between master CAs given by two medical entity organizations is required to establish the association between organizations. In order to solve the problem of establishing trust between CAs at the same level as described in the previous problem by relying on customized past proof templates, an evaluation criterion is designed to generate a score in the range of 0 to 1 according to the attributes. The score is mainly calculated based on the attributes related to identity security. The system calculates the percentage of the grading criteria according to three parameters, including the complexity of the identification algorithm with a weight of 60%, the complexity of the encryption algorithm with a weight of 20%, and the validity of the certificate with a weight of 20%. After the scores are calculated according to the rules, the trust relationship can be established only when the requested party has a higher score than the requesting party. The canonical policy generated by the rating criteria is written into the system deployment chain code of the distributed ledger through block transactions.

The next designed chain code strategies are the strategies related to distributed medical entity node endorsement voting. Consistency of on-chain deposited data can be guaranteed using these strategies, these strategies need to be used when clinical processing operations are performed on-chain by submitting transactions. The attack cost at this stage is low and different hospitals may choose inconsistent endorsement strategies, which may lead to confusing transaction results or passive termination of transactions. This is one of the most important security scenarios for hospitals to focus on.

4   Evaluation

The test dataset of the learning model was the clinical pathway dataset completed in Wuhan 672 Orthopedic Hospital in 2021, in which the first three quarters data were selected as the training set and the fourth quarter patient data as the test data. Firstly, a confusion matrix was established to show the prediction through the test results, and the confusion matrix style is shown in Table 2. TP represents a case assigned to a certain group and it does belong to that DRG group, FN represents a case that belongs to that DRG group but is not assigned to that class, FP represents a case that is not assigned to a certain group and it does not belong to that group, and TN represents a case that is not assigned to a certain DRG group and does not belong to that group. The three single base models and the designed fusion decision model were trained separately, and the three single base models for comparison were ID3, C4.5, and CART.

Table 2. Confusion matrix style table

True value	Predictive value	
True	True Positives (TP)	True Negatives (TN)
False	False Positives (FP)	False Negatives (FN)

Further, the classification efficacy was compared based on the accuracy rate, precision rate, recall rate, and F1 score of the comprehensive evaluation for the three basic decision models and the generalized fusion decision model, and the measurement results are shown in Table 3. The accuracy rate indicates the proportion of correctly classified test data, the precision rate indicates TP/(TP+FP), and the recall rate indicates TP/(TP+FN), and the F1 score indicates the summed average of the check-all rate and precision rate.

Table 3. Model evaluation indicators comparison table

Algorithm model	Accuracy	Precision	Recall	F1 score
ID3	81.4%	84.7%	89.7%	87.1%
C4.5	76.8%	81.1%	88.2%	84.5%
CART	85.3%	89.2%	91.7%	90.4%
CCSBD	89.2%	93.2%	93.3%	93.2%

The final results show that the fusion model achieves more than 90% precision rate and completeness rate, and its F1 score is improved by more than 3%. Our results demonstrate that the system has improved the accuracy and comprehensiveness of enrollment, and thus the fusion model is adapted to the overall variance reduction factor requirement of the clinical disease data categorization entry path.

5   Discussion

The currently designed federation chain is completely tamper-proof, but different roles in the medical federation need to have different control rights, so it is necessary to design different permission strategies for different roles in the interaction between the hospital HIS system and the blockchain, so as to provide different roles with hierarchical management operation rights for the deposition in the future.

6   Conclusion

This paper focuses on the completion of a more adaptive classification model, and the customization of a federated chain level contract strategy for clinical sharing needs. We design a DRG fusion classification decision model, propose a high-accuracy classification decision model for DRG, and complete the regression fusion of multiple models, and implement a high-fit and dichotomous feature-friendly implication-preserving learning algorithm, which can accurately evaluate the overlapping classification impact factors to obtain a classification mechanism adapted to clinical needs. A blockchain contract deposition strategy is proposed for the demand of trustworthy sharing of data in the treatment process. Through cross-channel decentralized cross-certification contracts, we construct peer-to-peer rules for the authentication of departmental entities involved in cross-hospital sharing and accelerate the flow of identification cards, thus securing the attributes of the departmental entities involved in sharing. Through anonymous unbiased endorsement contracts, it hides the private attributes of nodes and dynamically selects the set of endorsement nodes, which improves the difficulty for attackers to control the endorsement voting process, thus enhancing the attack resistance of the consistent voting process and the recoverability of the endorsement system, ensuring the consistency of shared data.

Acknowledgement. This work is supported by the National Key R&D Program of China (Grant No. 2019YFB2101700), and the National Natural Science Foundation of China (Grant No. 62072202). Dezhong Yao is supported in part by National Natural Science Foundation of China under grand (Grant No. 62072204).

References

1. Zlotnik, A., Alfaro, M.C., Pérez, M.C.: Lifting the weight of a diagnosis-related groups family change: a comparison between refined and non-refined DRG systems for top-down cost accounting and efficiency indicators. Health Inf. Manag. J. **44**(2), 11–19 (2018)
2. Eugenio, A.P., Luciano, N., Giovanni, R.M.: Does DRG funding encourage hospital specialization? Evidence from the Italian national health service. Int. J. Health Plann. Manag. **34**(2), 534–552 (2019)

3. Tobias, F., Patrick, A., Dirk, B., Dirk, B., Sascha, K., Gerd, M.U.: MpMRI of the prostate (MR-Prostatography): updated recommendations of the DRG and BDR on patient preparation and scanning protocol. RoFo: Fortschritte Auf Dem Gebiete Der Rontgenstrahlen Und Der Nuklearmedizin **193**(7), 763–777 (2021)

4. Wang, Z.: Innovation of corporate governance: a discussion based on blockchain technology. In: Proceedings of the 2nd International Symposium on Economics, Management, and Sustainable Development, Hangzhou, China, pp. 9–19 (2021)

5. Gao, F., Wang, H., Wang, H.: Study on the effect of one-stop service combined with clinical nursing path on patients with acute bronchial asthma. Am. J. Transl. Res. **13**(4), 3773–3779 (2021)

6. Chang, M.C., Hsiao, M., Mathieu, B.: Blockchain technology: efficiently managing medical information in the pain management field. Pain Med. **21**(7), 1512–1513 (2020)

7. Hau, Y.S., Chang, M.C.: A quantitative and qualitative review on the main research streams regarding blockchain technology in healthcare. Healthcare **9**(3), 247–262 (2021)

8. Long, J., Wang, H.: Design of blockchain system in BDCP using hyperledger fabric. In: Proceedings of the 2019 the World Symposium on Software Engineering, Wuhan, China, pp. 79–83 (2019)

9. Miyamae, T., Honda, T., Tamura, M., Kawaba, M.: Performance improvement of the consortium blockchain for financial business applications. J. Digit. Bank. **2**(4), 369–378 (2018)

10. Singh, K., Dib, O., Huyart, C., Toumi, K.: A novel credential protocol for protecting personal attributes in blockchain. Comput. Electr. Eng. **83**(4), 10586–10598 (2020)

11. Dhagarra, D., Goswami, M., Choudhury, A.: Big data and blockchain supported conceptual model for enhanced healthcare coverage. Bus. Process. Manag. J. **25**(7), 1612–1632 (2019)

12. Barouni, M., Ahmadian, L., Anari, H.S., Mohsenbeigi, E.: Investigation of the impact of DRG based reimbursement mechanisms on quality of care, capacity utilization, and systematic review. Int. J. Healthc. Manag. **14**(4), 1–12 (2020)

13. Sarheim, A.K., Håkon, B.J., Jon, M.: Economic incentives and diagnostic coding in a public health care system. Int. J. Health Econ. Manag. **17**(1), 83–101 (2017)

14. Sheaff, R., et al.: Managerial workarounds in three European DRG systems. J. Health Organ. Manag. **34**(3), 295–311 (2020)

Number of UAVs and Mission Completion Time Minimization in Multi-UAV-Enabled IoT Networks

Xingxia Gao, Xiumin Zhu, and Linbo Zhai[✉]

School of Information Science and Engineering, Shandong Normal University, Jinan, Shandong, China
zhai@mail.sdu.edu.cn

Abstract. The application of unmanned aerial vehicles (UAVs) in IoT networks, especially data collection, has received extensive attention. Due to the urgency of the mission and the limitation of the network cost, the number and the mission completion time of UAVs are research hotspots. Most studies mainly focus on the trajectory optimization of the UAV to shorten the mission completion time. However, under different data collection modes, the collection time will also greatly affect the mission completion time. This paper studies the data collection of ground IoT devices (GIDs) in Multi-UAV enabled IoT networks. The problem of data collection is formulated to minimize the number and the maximum mission completion time of UAVs by jointly optimizing the mission allocation of UAVs, hovering location, and the UAV trajectory. In view of the complexity and non-convexity of the formulated problem, we design improved ant colony optimization (IACO) algorithm to determine the number of UAVs by the mission allocation. Then, based on the data collection scheme combining flying mode (FM) and hovering mode (HM), a joint optimization algorithm (JOATC) is proposed to minimize flight time and collection time by optimizing the trajectory of the UAV. Simulation results show that our scheme achieves excellent performance.

Keywords: Multi-UAV iot networks · Mission allocation · Flying mode · Hovering mode

1 Introduction

The Internet of things plays an important role in mobile detection application scenarios [1]. In these IoT networks, many ground IoT devices (GIDs) are deployed in areas to monitor information. The wide distribution and diverse demands of GIDs have also brought new challenges about the data collection in the IoT networks. Fortunately, unmanned aerial vehicle (UAV) plays an important role in the communication network associated with GIDs because of its mobility and flexibility.

The UAV, also known as drone, is a new mobile platform. In some emergency situations, such as disaster rescue, there is a strict deadline for the completion of

© IFIP International Federation for Information Processing 2022
Published by Springer Nature Switzerland AG 2022
S. Liu and X. Wei (Eds.): NPC 2022, LNCS 13615, pp. 243–254, 2022.
https://doi.org/10.1007/978-3-031-21395-3_22

data collection missions of UAVs [2]. In addition, the limited energy also poses new challenges for the data collection of UAVs. Hence, it is an important issue to optimize the trajectory of the UAV to minimize the mission completion time of UAV.

Another challenging problem is how to set the appropriate number of UAVs in the Internet of things network. Due to the uncertainty of data size and the limitation of the UAV power, a fixed number of UAVs [3] may not be able to complete the data collection mission. Therefore, it is significant to determine the appropriate number of UAVs.

Based on the above two challenges, we study the data collection problem in multi-UAV enabled IoT networks. To meet the needs of shortening the maximum mission completion time of UAVs and reducing network costs, we jointly optimize the mission allocation, hovering location, and trajectory of UAVs to minimize the number of UAVs and the maximum mission completion time. The main contributions of this paper are summarized as follows:

(1) Considering the energy budget of the UAV and the association between the UAV and the GID, we formulate the problem for data collection in multi-UAV enabled IoT networks. Our goal is to minimize the number of UAVs and the maximum mission completion time.
(2) To balance the mission load of each UAV, we design the improved ant colony optimization algorithm (IACO) to determine the number and mission allocation of the UAVs by optimizing the association between the UAV and the GID.
(3) We prove the efficiency of the data collection on flying mode (FM) and hovering mode (HM) with mathematical analysis. Since the interaction between the flight service time and collection service time of each GID, we propose a joint optimization algorithm (JOATC) for the flying into point, hovering point and flying out point in the transmission area of GIDs to optimize the trajectories of all UAVs and minimize mission completion time of the UAV.
(4) Extensive simulations illustrate the effectiveness of our proposed scheme in the data collection scenario with many actual parameter settings.

2   Related Work

Most of the existing work studies the correct deployment location and coverage efficiency of the UAV to improve the efficiency of the whole system in processing missions [4]. However, in large-scale wireless communication networks, the flight time of the UAV accounts for the largest proportion of the total time cost. Therefore, the trajectory optimization of the UAV is particularly important to improve the overall energy consumption of the system.

There are a lot of literatures for the data collection of multi-UAV-enabled IoT networks. Two kinds of data collection schemes assisted by the UAV are mainly adopted: FM and HM. In order to shorten the mission completion time of the UAV data collection, authors have conducted many related studies on this basis [5]. In

[6], based on the mathematical analysis of the collection time on FM and HM, the authors propose a V-shaped trajectory to minimize the data collection time.

Besides, it is also necessary to find the appropriate number of UAVs. In most of the literatures, the number of UAVs is fixed to solve the problem of the UAV data collection. In the single UAV system, the authors of [7] propose a new trajectory search algorithm based on spatial pruning (SPTs) to minimize the overall mission completion time. In the multi-UAV system, the authors select two UAVs to complete data collection, and jointly optimize the UAV trajectory, wake-up time allocation and the transmit power of SNs to minimize the mission completion time [8].

Different from the above work, we study a data collection problem that simultaneously minimizes the number of UAVs and the maximum mission completion time. We design the IACO algorithm to achieve mission allocation and determine the number of UAVs. In order to minimize the flight time and collection time of each UAV, we design the JOATC algorithm for the flying into point (FIP), hovering point (OH) and the flying out point (FOP) on the UAV trajectory.

3   System Model and Problem Formulation

3.1   System Model

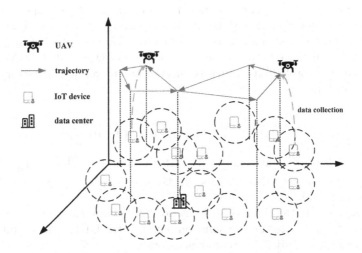

Fig. 1. Multi-UAV enabled data collection system in remote IoT scenarios.

System Architecture. As shown in Fig. 1, we consider a wireless communication network with multiple UAVs for data collection, which consists of several UAVs, denoted by $\mathcal{N} \triangleq \{1, 2, \cdots, N\}$. We assume N is a sufficiently large integer, which is greater than or equal to the number of UAVs put into scheduling.

In addition, there are M GIDs, represented as $\mathcal{M} \triangleq \{1, 2, \cdots, M\}$. All UAVs fly at the same altitude h. Each GID corresponds to a dotted circle. When the UAV flies into this circle, it can continuously collect the data of the corresponding GID. We establish a three-dimensional Cartesian coordinate system, where the coordinate of the UAV n is expressed as $UAV_n = (UAV_{n_x}, UAV_{n_y}, h)$, and the coordinate of the GID m is denoted by $GID_m = (GID_{m_x}, GID_{m_y})$. Each GID corresponds to one hovering point (OH). In the process of data collection, the association and scheduling status of the UAV n among the adjacent GIDs is expressed as $\alpha_{m,k}[n]$. If the UAV n flies from the OH m to the OH k, $\alpha_{m,k}[n] = 1$. Otherwise, $\alpha_{m,k}[n] = 0$. The index of the data center is expressed as 0. $\alpha_{0,k}[n] = 1$ means that the UAV n starts from the data center to the adjacent OH k. Hence, $Nu = \sum_{n=1}^{N} \sum_{k=1}^{M} \alpha_{0,k}[n]$ indicates the number of UAVs.

Channel Model and Transmission Model. The signal transmission channel between the UAV and the GID considers the Los link and the non-Los link. The relevant path losses are as follows:

$$L_\xi(d_{m,n}) = \begin{cases} \left(\frac{4\pi f d_{m,n}}{c}\right)^2 \eta_0 & , \xi = 0 \\ \left(\frac{4\pi f d_{m,n}}{c}\right)^2 \eta_1 & , \xi = 1 \end{cases} \tag{1}$$

where $\xi = 0$ and $\xi = 1$ represent Los link and non-Los link, respectively, f is the carrier frequency, and c is the speed of light. η_0 and η_1 are the path loss parameters for the Los link and the non-Los link, respectively. Let $d_{m,n}$ denote the Euclidean distance between the scheduled the GID m and the UAV n.

The Los link probability which is affected by environmental factors can be expressed as follows:

$$p_0(d_{m,n}, h) = \frac{1}{1 + a \exp(-b(\theta - a))} \tag{2}$$

where a and b are the environmental constants, and $\theta = \frac{180}{\pi} arcsin(\frac{h}{d_{m,n}})$ is the elevation angle between the UAV and the GID. $1 - p_0(d_{m,n}, h)$ is the probability of the non-Los link.

Let γ_{mn} denote the signal-to-noise ratio (SNR) between the GID m and the UAV n, and P_m denote the transmission power of the GID m. According to the SNR formula, the SNR is calculated as follows:

$$\gamma_{mn} = \frac{\beta P_m}{\sigma^2 L_\xi(d_{m,n})} \tag{3}$$

where β is the channel power gain at the reference distance of $1\,\mathrm{m}$, and σ^2 means the noise power of the UAV receiver. All UAVs operate in non-overlapping frequency channel through frequency division multiplexing (FDM). Since the total bandwidth B is fixed and each UAV occupies the same bandwidth, the bandwidth of each UAV is B/Nu. The transmission rate from the GID m to the UAV n is shown as follows:

$$R_{mn} = \frac{B}{Nu} log_2(1 + \gamma_{mn}) \tag{4}$$

Data Collection Model. The data collection process of the UAV are divided into two modes, flying mode (FM) and hovering mode (HM). FM indicates the mode of collecting data when UAVs are flying. HM represents the mode of data collection when UAVs are hovering at a certain point. During the data collection of the GID m, the UAV n enters the signal transmission range of the GID m from the flying into point FIP_m, passes through the point OH_m, and hovers at it for a period, then leaves the signal transmission range of the GID m from the flying out point FOP_m. The UAV n hovers at the point OH_m to collect data on HM. From FIP_m to OH_m and OH_m to FOP_m, the UAV n fights and collects data on FM. Within the signal transmission radius R, the UAV can successfully receive data from GIDs. If the distance between GIDs is less than 2R, the signal transmission range overlaps. Otherwise, it does not overlap. The coordinates of the passing points of the UAV in the data collection area are expressed as $FIP_m\left(FIP_{m_x}, FIP_{m_y}\right)$, $FOP_m\left(FOP_{m_x}, FOP_{m_y}\right)$, $OH_m\left(OH_{m_x}, OH_{m_y}\right)$.

We define t^c_{hm} as the collection time on HM and t^c_{fm} as the collection time on FM. Let C_m be the data size of the GID m. The distance between FIP and OH in the transmission area of the GID m is $\|FIP_m - OH_m\|$, and the distance between OH and FOP is $\|OH_m - FOP_m\|$. All UAVs fly at the optimal flight speed v_{opt}. On FM, the collection time of the UAV in the transmission area of the GID m is $t^c_{fm} = \frac{\|FIP_m - OH_m\|}{v_{opt}} + \frac{\|OH_m - FOP_m\|}{v_{opt}}$. On HM, the collection time of the UAV in the transmission area of the GID m is $t^c_{hm} = \frac{C_m - \int_0^{t^c_{fm}} R_{mn}(t)dt}{R_h}$, where R_h is the transmission rate from the GID m to the UAV n in hovering state. Hence, the collection time t^c_m of data collected by the UAV n from the GID m can be expressed as

$$t^c_m = t^c_{fm} + t^c_{hm} = \frac{\|FIP_m - OH_m\|}{v_{opt}} + \frac{\|OH_m - FOP_m\|}{v_{opt}} + \frac{C_m - \int_0^{t^c_{fm}} R_{mn}(t)dt}{R_h} \tag{5}$$

For the distance between FOP_{m-1} and FIP_m, the flight time t^f_m of the UAV can be expressed as

$$t^f_m = \begin{cases} \frac{d_{m1}}{v_{opt}} & , in\ non-overlapped\ scenario \\ 0 & , in\ overlapped\ scenario \end{cases} \tag{6}$$

where $d_{m1} = \sqrt{\left(FOP_{m-1_x} - FIP_{m_x}\right)^2 + \left(FOP_{m-1_y} - FIP_{m_y}\right)^2}$.

Energy Consumption Model. The power consumption of the UAV mainly includes the related power consumption during data collection and flight. The flying power can be given by $P^f = P(v_{opt})$. Then, the hovering power can be expressed as $P^h = P(0)$. Therefore, the energy consumption of the UAV n to complete the data collection mission can be calculated as follows:

$$
\begin{aligned}
E_n &= \int_0^{T_n^f} P^f dt + \int_0^{T_f^c} (P^f + P^c)dt + \int_0^{T_h^c} (P^h + P^c)dt \\
&= \sum_{m=1}^{M_n} \int_0^{t_m^f} P^f dt + \int_0^{t_0^f} P^f dt + \sum_{m=1}^{M_n} \int_0^{t_{fm}^c} \left(P^f + P^c \right) dt \\
&\quad + \sum_{m=1}^{M_n} \int_0^{t_{hm}^c} (P^h + P^c)dt
\end{aligned} \tag{7}
$$

where M_n means the number of GIDs visited by the UAV n, T_n^f represents the total flight time of the UAV n outside the transmission area of GIDs, T_f^c indicates the total data collection time on FM, T_h^c indicates the total data collection time on HM. t_0^f denotes the flight time from the last collected GID by the UAV to the data center. P^c is the circuit power in the process of the UAV data collection.

3.2 Problem Formulation

The UAV n completes the data collection on the planned trajectory $U_n(t)$. The $U_n(t)$ and M_n affect the mission completion time of UAVs. $\Lambda \triangleq \{\alpha_{m,k}[n]|m,k \in \mathcal{M}, n \in \mathcal{N}\}$ is the association status and sequence among the GIDs. The set Λ affects the number of UAVs.

The mission completion time of a single UAV is the sum of all flight time and data collection time on its trajectory. Therefore, minimizing the number of UAVs and the maximum completion time of UAVs can be formulated as follows:

$$
P_1: \min_{U_n(t), \Lambda, M_n} F_1 Nu + F_2 \max_{n \in \mathcal{N}} \left(\sum_{m=0}^{M_n} \sum_{k=1}^{M_n} \alpha_{m,k}[n] t_{m,k}^f + \sum_{m=1}^{M_n} \alpha_{m,0}[n] t_{m,0}^f + \sum_{m=1}^{M_n} t_m^c \right)
\tag{8}
$$

$$
s.t. \quad C_1: \gamma_{mn}(t) \geq \gamma_{th}
$$

$$
C_2: \sum_{n=1}^{Nu} M_n = M
$$

$$
C_3: E_n \leq E_{th}
$$

$$
C_4: M_n = \sum_{m=0}^{M} \sum_{k=1}^{M} \alpha_{m,k}[n] \leq M_{max}
$$

$$
C_5: \sum_{n \in \mathcal{N}} \left(\sum_{m=0}^{M_n} \sum_{k=1}^{M_n} \alpha_{m,k}[n] t_{m,k}^f + \sum_{m=1}^{M_n} \alpha_{m,0}[n] t_{m,0}^f + \sum_{m=1}^{M_n} t_m^c \right) \leq D_n
$$

$$
C_6: \sum_{n=1}^{N} \sum_{m=0}^{M} \alpha_{m,k}[n] = 1, \forall k \in \mathcal{M}
$$

where F_1 and F_2 denote the weight coefficients of the number of UAVs and the maximum completion time of UAVs, respectively. $t_{m,k}^f$ denotes the flight time between the FOP_m and the FIP_k. $t_{m,0}^f$ indicates the flight time between the FOP_m and the data center. D_n represents the total mission completion delay. Constraint C_1 indicates that, within the transmission range, the real SNR is higher than γ_{th} and the UAV can continuously collect data from the GIDs. Constraint C_2 means that the data collection mission of M GIDs is assigned to several UAVs. Constraint C_3 gives the energy budget E_{th} of the UAV. Constraint C_4 represents the maximum number of GIDs that can be served of the UAV n. Constraint C_5 ensures that the mission completion time of all UAVs cannot exceed the total mission completion time delay. Constraint C_6 states that each GID only transmits its data to one UAV.

4   Algorithm Design

In this section, we will optimize problem P_1. At first, we assign the data collection mission of M GIDs to several UAVs. Then, we will optimize the UAV's FIP, FOP and OH in the transmission area of each GID and the optimal flight trajectory of the UAV.

4.1   Optimization of UAV Number and Mission Allocation

We assume that the nominal values of the number of UAVs and the maximum mission completion time of UAVs are expressed as $(\widetilde{N}, \widetilde{T})$. Under the condition of $w^{Nu} + w^T = 1$, by combining a group of weight factors $\{w^{Nu}, w^T\}$, the relative importance of the number of UAVs and the maximum mission completion time of UAVs can be reflected respectively. Consequently, problem P_1 is transformed into optimization problem P_2 denoted by

$$P_2 : \min_{S_n \in S, M_n} \Psi \triangleq \frac{w^{Nu}}{\widetilde{N}} Nu + \frac{w^T}{\widetilde{T}} (\max_{n \in \mathcal{N}} (\sum_{m=1}^{M_n} T_{mn})) \qquad (9)$$

$$s.t. \quad C_1 - C_6$$

where S is the set of the UAV collection sequences, S_n is the collection sequence of the UAV n. T_{mn} is the service time of the UAV n to the GID m.

We propose an improved ant colony optimization algorithm (IACO) to obtain the optimal solution of problem P_2. The initial OH is just right above the associated GID m. The first part is to find the allocation sequence of each UAV. The process of this algorithm after initializing pheromones is summarized as follows:

– *Step*1-1: From the set of GIDs that have data collection missions and have not been visited, select the GIDs that make constraints C_1 and C_3 satisfied.
– *Step*1-2: If there is no GID that meets the above requirements, add the initial point to the end of the current trajectory. This search process is completed.

- *Step*1-3: Calculate the heuristic information and the transition probability of each satisfied GID based on the pheromone.

The heuristic information $\phi_{mk}(t+1)$ reflects the predetermined factors on the sub path $\alpha_{m,k}[n]$ in the hover point search process of the $(t+1)$−th iteration and can be calculated as follows:

$$\phi_{mk}(t+1) = \varpi \cdot \frac{e^{-\sum_{k=1}^{M_n} E_{kn}}}{(dis(m,k)+1) \cdot lnNu} \quad Nu \geq 1 \quad (10)$$

where ϖ is used to adjust the value of $\phi_{mk}(t+1)$, $dis(m,k)$ is the shortest path length between OHs, and $\sum_{k=1}^{M_n} E_{kn}$ is the total energy consumption from departure to the next OH k.

We use $R_{mk}(t+1)$ to describe the probability of selecting a certain OH k as the next OH of the current OH m in the hover point search process of the $(t+1)$-th iteration. Let $\tau_{mk}(t+1)$ denote the rule of pheromone update. α and β describe the importance of pheromone concentration $\tau_{mk}(t+1)$ and heuristic information $\phi_{mk}(t+1)$ respectively. The transition probability is defined as follows:

$$R_{mk}(t+1) = \frac{(\tau_{mk}(t+1))^{\alpha} \cdot (\phi_{mk}(t+1))^{\beta}}{\sum_{k \in M_n} (\tau_{mk}(t+1))^{\alpha} \cdot (\phi_{mk}(t+1))^{\beta}} \quad (11)$$

- *Step*1-4: Ants choose the next GID according to (11), then go to *Step*1-1:.

The second part of this algorithm is to optimize the number of UAVs. The main steps in this section are summarized as follows:

- *Step*2-1: Each ant will search the trajectory of the current UAV in sequence. If there are still GIDs that have not been visited, go to *Step*2-3.
- *Step*2-2: If there is no GID that meets the requirements of C_1 and C_3, add one UAV and recalculate the transmission rate of each GID, then go to *Step*2-1.
- *Step*2-3: At the end of each iteration, we update the global optimal solution and the pheromone value. The rules for updating pheromones are defined as:

$$\tau_{mk}(t+1) = (1-\rho)(\tau_{mk}(t)) + \Delta\tau_{mk}(t) \quad (12)$$

where ρ is pheromone evaporation coefficient, and $\Delta\tau_{mk}(t)$ is the pheromone update value based on the feedback.

- *Step*2-4: Update the global pheromone until the number of iterations is reached, and then go to *Step*2-1.

Algorithm 1. Joint optimization algorithm of mission completion time on HM and FM (JOATC).

Input: the coordinates of the data center and GIDs; the transmission radius R; the data size of the GID C_m; the optimal speed of the UAV v_{opt}; the data size C_n collected by the UAV n in the GID m.

1: $l_{min} = ||FIP_m - FOP_m||$, $l_{max} = ||FIP_m - GID_m|| + ||FOP_m - GID_m||$; calculate d_{1min} and d_{1max}, d_{2min} and d_{2max};

2: Divide l, d_{m1}, and d_{m2} into $\Delta_1 = l_{min} : k : l_{max}$, $\Delta_2 = d_{1min} : k : d_{1max}$, and $\Delta_3 = d_{2min} : k : d_{2max}$, and establish matrix A and B.

3: **while** $C_n \neq C_m$ and $E_n < E_{th}$ **do**

4:    **if** $(||FOP_{m-1} - GID_m|| \leq R) \cap (||GID_m - FIP_{m+1}|| \leq R)$ **then**

5:      **else if** $||FOP_{m-1} - GID_m|| \leq R$ **then**

6:        **while** Δ_3 is not empty C_1 and C_5 **do**

7:          Calculate $t_m^f + t_m^c$, store in the matrix B.

8:        **end while**

9:        Calculate d_{m2} of the minimum value in matrix B.

10:     **else if** $||GID_m - FIP_{m+1}|| \leq R$ **then**

11:       **while** Δ_2 is not empty **do**

12:         Calculate $t_m^f + t_m^c$, store in the matrix B.

13:       **end while**

14:       Calculate d_{m1} of the minimum value in matrix B.

15:       Calculate the FIP_m, FOP_m based on the d_{m1} and the d_{m2}.

16:       **while** Δ_1 is not empty **do**

17:         Calculate data collection time t_m^c of the GID m, store in the matrix A.

18:       **end while**

19:       Calculate l_{min} of the minimum value in matrix A.

20:       Calculate OH_m of l_{min}.

21:     **else**

22:       **while** Δ_2 is not empty **do**

23:         **for** each Δ_3 **do**

24:           Calculate $t^f + t_m^c$, store in the matrix B.

25:         **end for**

26:       **end while**

27:       Calculate d_{m1} and d_{m2} of the minimum value in matrix B.

28:       Calculate the FIP_m, FOP_m based on d_{m1} and d_{m2}.

29:       Calculate OH_m.

30:     **end if**

31: **end while**

Output: The coordinates of FIP_m, FOP_m, OH_m, the number of UAVs; the mission completion time of the UAV n.

4.2 Joint Optimization of Flight Time and Data Collection Time of UAV

In this section, we redefine the flight time t_m^f of the UAV n as the flight time of two adjacent GIDs, $t_m^f = \frac{d_{m1}}{v_{opt}} + \frac{d_{m2}}{v_{opt}}$, where d_{m1} and d_{m2} are the flight distances of the UAV for the GID m and the GID $m+1$ respectively. When the transmission areas of the former or the latter overlap, FOP_{m-1} and FIP_m may overlap. Then, d_{m1} or d_{m2} equals 0.

We redefine the total mission completion time of the UAV n on the predetermined trajectory as

$$\min_{FIP_m, FOP_m, OH_m} \left(\frac{\sum_{m=0}^{M_n} d_{m1}}{v_{opt}} + \sum_{m=1}^{M_n} t_m^c \right) \tag{13}$$

$$s.t. \quad C_1, \ C_3, \ C_5$$
$$d_{1min} \leq d_{m1} \leq d_{1max}$$

$$d_{1min} = \begin{cases} ||FOP_{m-1} - GID_m|| - R, & ||FOP_{m-1} - GID_m|| > R \\ 0, & ||FOP_{m-1} - GID_m|| \leq R \end{cases}$$

$$d_{1max} = \begin{cases} \sqrt{(||FOP_{m-1} - GID_m||)^2 - R^2}, & ||FOP_{m-1} - GID_m|| > R \\ 0, & ||FOP_{m-1} - GID_m|| \leq R \end{cases}$$

When the transmission areas of GIDs overlap, if GID m overlaps GID $m - 1$, we only calculate the FOP of GID m. If GID m overlaps GID $m + 1$, we only calculate the FIP of GID m. Then, we find the OH in the non-isosceles triangle region, which is described in Algorithm 1. When the transmission areas of GIDs do not overlap, we optimize the collection trajectory of UAV based on the Fermat points in the triangle. According to the properties of isosceles triangle, the Fermat point of isosceles triangle is on the midperpendicular of the triangle with the three points of the FIP, FOP and OH as the vertices.

5   Simulation Results

To demonstrate the performance of our proposed scheme, we compare our scheme with the other three schemes: improved fly-hover-fly trajectory planning algorithm (IFTPA) [9], FM or HM scheme based on partition algorithm for fixed trajectory (FHSPF) [10], and joint optimization algorithm for flight trajectory and collection trajectory (JOFC) [6]. In IFTPA, the OHs are optimized by clustering GIDs obtain the trajectory of each UAV. The FHSPF compares the two data collection modes. On FM, the optimal flight speed, and the optimal collection point (OCP) of the UAV are optimized. On HM, the UAV collects data only when hovering over GID. JOFC applies two collection modes to the V-shaped trajectory.

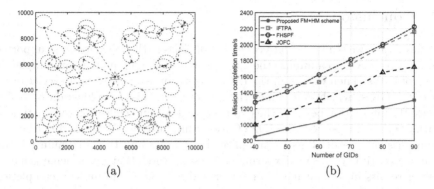

(a)   (b)

Fig. 2. (a): The final trajectory of the proposed scheme of combining FM with HM. (b): The mission completion time with diverse number of UAVs.

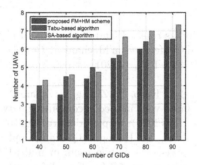

Fig. 3. The mission completion time with diverse number of UAVs.

Figure 2(a) shows the final collection trajectory obtained by using the scheme of combining FM and HM. The OH of the UAV within the transmission range of the GID deviates right above the GID, which shortens the overall length of the UAV trajectory and reduces the collection time on FM and HM, to achieve less mission completion time. Our scheme can achieve a compromise between the collection time on FM and that on HM by adjusting the flight distance of the UAV within the transmission range of the GID.

The overlap between GIDs is affected by the number of GIDs. Thus, in Fig. 2(b), we further test the impact of the number of GIDs on the mission completion time, including three UAVs, $C = 190Mbit$. Overall, our scheme achieves the best results. In FHSPF, the trajectory of the UAV is optimized, which may lead to longer transmission time of the UAV. On the contrary, in IFTPA, the trajectory of UAV can be shorter by combining the clustering method.

Next, we will compare the proposed algorithm with simulated annealing algorithm and tabu search algorithm, where $C = 95\,Mbit$. The results of more than 10 runs are averaged, resulting in that the results in Fig. 3 are not integers. The proposed algorithm searches the trajectory more comprehensively, obtaining better performance.

6   Conclusion

In this paper, we study the data collection of GIDs in the IoT networks supported by multiple UAVs to minimize the number and the maximum mission completion time of UAVs. Then we design the IACO algorithm to find the best service order between GIDs, which determines the number and mission allocation of UAVs. Since the interaction between the flight service time and collection service time of various GIDs, we propose the JOATC algorithm for the FIP, OH and FOP in the transmission area of GIDs to minimize the number and the maximum mission completion time of UAVs. Experimental results show that our scheme achieves better results in minimizing the number and the maximum mission completion time of UAVs.

References

1. Xia, X.: Internet of things research and application of information technology. In: 2020 5th International Conference on Mechanical, Control and Computer Engineering (ICMCCE), pp. 1818–1821 (2020). https://doi.org/10.1109/ICMCCE51767.2020.00399
2. Liu, J., Guo, H., Xiong, J., Kato, N., Zhang, J., Zhang, Y.: Smart and resilient EV charging in SDN-enhanced vehicular edge computing networks. IEEE J. Sel. Areas Commun. **38**(1), 217–228 (2020). https://doi.org/10.1109/JSAC.2019.2951966
3. Wang, Y., Ru, Z.Y., Wang, K., Huang, P.Q.: Joint deployment and task scheduling optimization for large-scale mobile users in multi-UAV-enabled mobile edge computing. IEEE Trans. Cybern. **50**(9), 3984–3997 (2019)
4. Yang, L., Yao, H., Wang, J., Jiang, C., Benslimane, A., Liu, Y.: Multi-UAV-enabled load-balance mobile-edge computing for IoT networks. IEEE Internet Things J. **7**(8), 6898–6908 (2020)
5. Zhao, H., Wang, H., Wu, W., Wei, J.: Deployment algorithms for UAV airborne networks toward on-demand coverage. IEEE J. Sel. Areas Commun. **36**(9), 2015–2031 (2018). https://doi.org/10.1109/JSAC.2018.2864376
6. Li, M., He, S., Li, H.: Minimizing mission completion time of UAVs by jointly optimizing the flight and data collection trajectory in UAV-enabled WSNs. IEEE Internet Things J. **9**(15), 13498–13510 (2022). https://doi.org/10.1109/JIOT.2022.3142764
7. Meng, K., Li, D., He, X., Liu, M.: Space pruning based time minimization in delay constrained multi-task UAV-based sensing. IEEE Trans. Veh. Technol. **70**(3), 2836–2849 (2021). https://doi.org/10.1109/TVT.2021.3061243
8. Zhu, G., Guo, L., Dong, C., Mu, X.: Mission time minimization for multi-UAV-enabled data collection with interference. In: 2021 IEEE Wireless Communications and Networking Conference (WCNC). pp. 1–6. IEEE (2021)
9. Qin, Z., Li, A., Dong, C., Dai, H., Xu, Z.: Completion time minimization for multi-UAV information collection via trajectory planning. Sensors **19**(18), 4032 (2019)
10. Wang, Y., Hu, Z., Wen, X., Lu, Z., Miao, J.: Minimizing data collection time with collaborative UAVs in wireless sensor networks. IEEE Access **8**, 98659–98669 (2020). https://doi.org/10.1109/ACCESS.2020.2996665

A Spatial-Temporal Similarity-Based Cooperative Surveillance Framework by Edge

Jie Tang[1], Yuxuan Zhao[1], and Rui Huang[2(✉)]

[1] South China University of Technology, Guangzhou, China
cstangjie@scut.edu.cn, 202121045373@mail.scut.edu.cn
[2] Sun Yat-Sen University, Guangzhou, China
huangr257@mail2.sysu.edu.cn

Abstract. Most of the current video cooperative surveillance strategies upload all video clips the camera takes, which will cause great data redundancy and bandwidth waste. In this paper, we combine temporal similarity with spatial similarity and introduce the concept of spatiotemporal similarity. In particular, we design a framework to calculate spatial-temporal similarity to reduce the complexity of the collection and the transmission of source data. Besides, we model the problem of minimum spatiotemporal similarity with the bandwidth limitation into a knapsack problem and propose a dynamic programming-based algorithm to determine the selection of video uploading. The results show the framework can make a 10% data redundancy reduction and bandwidth saving.

Keywords: Edge computing · Cooperatives surveillance · Data similarity

1 Introduction

The past decade has witnessed explosive growth in live video streaming and one of its major applications is real-time surveillance [1]. Nowadays, cameras are widely distributed as a kind of infrastructure and these stationary or mobile devices can work together to accomplish surveillance for a large area. On top of non-stop and full-covered monitoring, cooperative surveillance can fulfill the great demands on the real-time discovery and tracking of individual targets.

With the application of edge computing, edge servers can be deployed for surveillance data collection, storage, and real-time processing. As shown in Fig. 1, it gives a typical setup for an in-vehicle camera based surveillance system. Within the coverage of an edge server, multiple cameras are working for video streaming. Each of them only takes care of an area section within its field of view. Thus, they can make full-scale monitoring only if they work cooperatively.

We find that cooperative surveillance is challenging due to the limitations of each participating camera's coverage. It is hard to form a comprehensive environment update with limited video sources. On the other hand, if we over-select data sources, serious bandwidth contention will lead to a great delay in data transmission.

S. Liu and X. Wei (Eds.): NPC 2022, LNCS 13615, pp. 255–260, 2022.
https://doi.org/10.1007/978-3-031-21395-3_23

To solve this problem, we propose a cooperative video surveillance framework, which uses the spatial-temporal similarity in video filtering and selection. This framework aims to minimize the redundancy between multiple uploaded videos and effectively complete the selection of crowdsourcing data objects under the condition of ensuring real-time perceptual coverage.

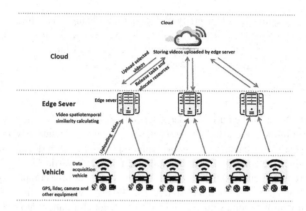

Fig. 1. The system architecture for mobile-sensor-based surveillance

This study made the following contributions:

1. We redefine the temporal and spatial similarity of the sensor data and apply these two concepts to video metadata.
2. We model the problem of spatiotemporal similarity minimization under bandwidth limitation into a 0-1 knapsack problem and design a dynamic programming-based algorithm as a real-time solution.
3. We compare the video selection algorithm based on time coverage length with the one based on-location coverage both in coverage and upload efficiency.

2 The Problem in Application

The edge server is responsible for processing the data from nearby selected vehicles. It should select the data with the minimum redundancy to meet the requirements for data uploading. Here, the selection is made by the video metadata, $\left(t_s, t_e, l_j, r_j, \phi_j, \overrightarrow{d_j}\right)$. The metadata includes the start time and end time of the video, which are denoted as t_s and t_e, respectively. Between t_s and t_e, there are countless timestamps t_i, each timestamp is associated with quadruples $\left(l_j, r_j, \phi_j, \overrightarrow{d_j}\right)$ in the image metadata. Those four parameters can be obtained directly from cameras and sensors 1. Here, l_j is where the location. r_j and ϕ_j are two internal parameters of the camera which are used to take pictures 2. r_j is the effective range of the camera. ϕ_j is the field of view of the camera lens. $\overrightarrow{d_j}$ is the direction of the camera when the photo is taken, measured by the direction of gravity and the surrounding geomagnetic field 4.

2.1 Spatial Similarity

The spatial similarity is represented by *Ssem* which includes three measurement standards, topological relationship, measurement relationship and orientation relationship. It can be calculated from the quadruples $(l_j, r_j, \phi_j, \overrightarrow{d_j})$ defined in this article.

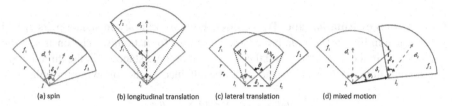

(a) spin   (b) longitudinal translation   (c) lateral translation   (d) mixed motion

Fig. 2. Several cases of rigid body motion

The respective angle ranges of the two different video frame metadata f_1 and f_2 are φ_1 and φ_2. δ_l represents the distance between the locations of two different video frames, and δ_φ represents the difference in direction. So, we have:

$$\delta_l = \left|\overrightarrow{l_1 l_2}\right|, \delta_\varphi = \min(|\varphi_2 - \varphi_1|, 2\pi - |\varphi_2 - \varphi_1|) \tag{1}$$

Any rigid body motion can be divided into translation and rotation. Therefore, we can calculate the similarity between frames by combining these two movements 3.

Rotation: As shown in Fig. 2(a). It's obvious that the similarity of rotation is only related to the difference in direction. Intuitively, we define the overlay intersection as the similarity between two metadata:

$$Ssem_{R(f1,f2)} = \frac{|\varphi_1 \cap \varphi_2|}{|\varphi|} = \begin{cases} \frac{\varphi - \delta_\varphi}{\varphi} & \delta_\varphi < \varphi \\ 0 & otherwise \end{cases} \tag{2}$$

Translation: Translation only changes the position of the object without changing the angle. In this case, f_1 and f_2 maintain the same direction φ and f_2 can be regarded as f_1 with distance translation δ_l. For f_1 and f_2, by means of orthogonal decomposition, the translations can be divided into two different situations: parallel translation and vertical translation. Figure 2(b) shows the translation of f_2 in the vertical direction of δ_l. The similarity in the vertical direction $Ssem_\perp$ can be obtained by the following transformation:

$$Ssem_\perp = \frac{(r - \delta_l)^2}{r^2} \tag{3}$$

Figure 2(c) shows the case of parallel translation, where the translation of f_2 is in the same direction as φ. r_j represents the radius of the camera range as well as δ_l represents the translation distance. The horizontal similarity can be calculated by the formula (4):

$$Ssem_\parallel = \frac{r_\theta^2}{r^2} = \frac{\left(r - \frac{\delta_l}{2cos\alpha}\right)^2}{r^2} \tag{4}$$

where $r_\theta = r - \frac{\delta_l}{2cos\alpha}$ and $\alpha = \frac{\pi - \varphi}{2}$.

According to mathematical calculations, we have the following expressions for $Ssem_{\parallel}$ and $Ssem_{\perp}$:

$$Ssem_{T(f1,f2)} = \left(1 - \frac{4\delta_\varphi}{\pi}\right)Ssem_{\parallel} + \frac{4\delta_\varphi}{\pi}Ssem_{\perp} \tag{5}$$

Combination of Rotation and Translation: For two arbitrary metadata pairs f_1 and f_2, as shown in Fig. 2(d), f_2 can be regarded as a transformation, which consists of the rotation of f_1 in the direction δ_φ and the translation of the distance δ_l in the direction φ_l. The spatial similarity between f_1 and f_2 can be obtained by the following formula:

$$Ssem_{(f_1,f_2)} = Ssem_R \times Ssem_T \tag{6}$$

2.2 Time Similarity

Time similarity is represented by *Tsem*, which includes two measurement standards, topological relationship and measurement relationship. They can be directly obtained from the start time t_s and the end time t_e in the metadata. There are 13 kinds of temporal relationships recognized in the literature today 6. Each time the topology relationship has corresponding basic weight (W_{T_1min}) and control weight (W_{T_1max}).

$$T_{measure} = W_{T_{overlap}}T_{overlap} + W_{T_{gap}}T_{gap} \tag{7}$$

The correlation of the time measurement relationship is calculated as Eq. 7. $T_{measure}$ is the correlation degree of the time measurement relationship; $T_{overlap}$ is the mean value of the proportion of time overlap in the proportion of time A and time B; T_{gap} is the time distance between time period A and time period B; $W_{T_{overlap}}$ and $W_{T_{gap}}$ are the weights of the corresponding indicators and satisfy $W_{T_{overlap}} + W_{T_{gap}} = 1$ and we set them to 0.5. The time correlation calculation model can be expressed as:

$$Tsem = W_{T_1min} + \left(W_{T_1max} - W_{T_1min}\right)T_{measure} \tag{8}$$

W_{T_1min} and W_{T_1max} are the minimum correlation weight and the maximum correlation weight of the corresponding time topological relationship, where the correlation weight refers to the ratio of the union of the period of time A and B respectively.

2.3 Spatiotemporal Similarity

When comparing two videos, we directly compare the spatiotemporal similarity. It integrates the area covered by each frame of the video in time and the similarity of the total video area. The spatiotemporal similarity $Stsem_{s(f_1,f_2)}$ is the integral of the area S along the l_j curve, calculated by the following formula:

$$Stsem_{s(f_1,f_2)} = \left| \int_{l_{jf_1 start}}^{l_{jf_1 end}} S dt - \int_{l_{jf_2 start}}^{l_{jf_2 end}} S dt \right| \tag{9}$$

The calculation of the total video topology and the orientation relationship is to directly obtain $Ssem_{TA(f_1,f_2)}$ and then associate with the time similarity, namely:

$$Stsem_{TA(f_1,f_2)} = Tsem \times Ssem_{(f_1,f_2)} \tag{10}$$

Therefore, the total spatiotemporal similarity can be calculated below. Here, *Stsem* is the total spatiotemporal similarity; W_{ts} and W_{tta} are the spatiotemporal correlation weight valuesrespectively and satisfies $W_{ts} + W_{tta} = 1$.

$$Stsem = W_{ts}Stsem_{s(f_1,f_2)} + W_{tta}Stsem_{TA(f_1,f_2)} \tag{11}$$

3   Diversity Maximization Based on Spatiotemporal Similarity

Here, it assumes that the numbers of cars involved in the collection are $d_1, d_2, \ldots, d_i$, the bandwidth allocated by the cloud is B, the coverage requirement is S_{cov}, and the set of video segments which are collected in the cycle are $V_1, V_2, \ldots V_n$. Each segment has a start time $ts(V_i)$, an end time $te(V_i)$ and a size of $s(V_i)$. Given the upload time limit t, each device can upload its video in the form of V_i within the time limit and meet the bandwidth limit, that is, $s(V_i) \leq B$. The collection of all segments should have the smallest spatiotemporal similarity, or the largest coverage diversification.

We reduce the maximum diversification problem based on spatiotemporal similarity to a known NP-hard problem, the 0–1 knapsack problem 3. To solve it, we randomly select a mobile device d_i, where the network bandwidth B is set as the weight limit of the knapsack and the number of videos uploaded by the mobile device n_i is set as the number of items. We set the initial spatiotemporal similarity *Stsem* to 0. For the *j-th* segment V_j, the sum of similarity $\sum Stsem(V_j)$ with the selected video metadata is set to the value of the *j-th* item and V is to meet the weight limit and minimize the total value of the subset of items. Therefore, the biggest diversification problem based on spatiotemporal similarity is the NP-hard problem.

4   Experiment

The experimental is made by using BDD100k Dataset [5]. The proposed video selection algorithm is named as **S-TBS**. It is compared with the algorithm named **TBS** solely working on maximizing the length of time coverage and the algorithm named **LBS** solely working on maximizing the location coverage in practical applications.

The Fig. 3(a) shows how the increase of selected video sections on improving the spatial coverage of video. The Fig. 3(b) shows how the increase of selected video sections working improves the time coverage of video. When the coverage required by the system remains unchanged and the coverage area increases, it can be directly seen from the figure that when the area is small, the effect of **LBS** algorithm is best, our **S-TBS** algorithm is second, and **TBS** algorithm is weak. This is because **LBS** algorithm takes the coverage area as the priority condition for video selection. With the increase of the area, the coverage of our algorithm is better than the other two methods. This is because our algorithm takes into account both time and space coverage, when the coverage area is increased, it can still guarantee the coverage in time and space. Similarly, when the coverage area is increased, the number of videos selected by our algorithm is the least. It shows that our **S-TBS** algorithm can guarantee as few choices as possible when the single variable is improved, which clearly reflects the superiority of **S-TBS**.

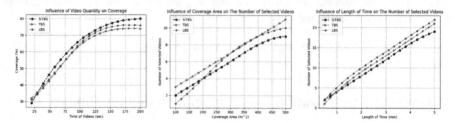

Fig. 3. The experiment results (a. The Influence of Video Duration. b. The Influence of Coverage Area. c. The Influence of Length of Time)

5 Conclusion

In this paper, we studied how to select appropriate video metadata to minimize the similarity of all metadata to maximize the coverage. In future, we will discuss how the content of the frame can decide the video selections.

Acknowledgement. This work is supported by Guangdong Natural Science Foundation under Grant No. 2021A1515011755. Rui Huang is the corresponding author of this paper.

References

1. Bagheri, H., et al.: 5G NR-V2X: toward connected and cooperative autonomous driving. IEEE Commun. Stand. Mag. **5**(1), 48–54 (2021)
2. Wu, Y., Wang, Y., Hu, W., et al.: Resource-aware photo crowdsourcing through disruption tolerant networks. In: IEEE International Conference on Distributed Computing Systems. IEEE (2016)
3. Wu, Y., Wang, Y., Cao, G.: Photo crowdsourcing for area coverage in resource- constrained environments. In: IEEE INFOCOM 2017 - IEEE Conference on Computer Communications. IEEE (2017)
4. Wu, Y., Wang, Y., Hu, W., et al.: SmartPhoto: a resource-aware crowdsourcing approach for image sensing with smartphones. IEEE Trans. Mob. Comput. **15**(5), 1249–1263 (2016)
5. Yu, F., Chen, H., Wang, X., et al.: BDD100K: a diverse driving dataset for heterogeneous multitask learning (2018)
6. Chen, Y., Li, B., Zhang, Q.: Incentivizing crowdsourcing systems with network effects. In: IEEE Infocom -the IEEE International Conference on Computer Communications. IEEE (2016)

A Progressive Transmission Method of Cloud Point Data for HD Map in Autonomous Driving

Jie Tang[1], Kai Jiang[1], and Rui Huang[2（✉）]

[1] South China University of Technology, Guangzhou, China
cstangjie@scut.edu.cn, mecsjiangkai@mail.scut.edu.cn
[2] Sun Yat-Sen University, Guangzhou, China
huangr257@mail2.sysu.edu.cn

Abstract. The High-Definition map (HD map) is an indispensable part of autonomous driving vehicle positioning and navigation. Because of its high accuracy, the general high-precision map has a very large data volume, and the existing network cannot meet the requirements of high-speed transmission. It will result in significant time delay and greatly threaten driving safety. Therefore, we propose a progressive cloud point data transmission model for HD map applications. It consists of three-level modeling of data compression, transmission time, and delivered data restoration. It can also adjust the data transmission accuracy to get a better transmission time delay according to different application demands. Experiments show that with map data being progressively delivered, autonomous driving can get a more fluent HD map service even though when the network is unstable.

Keywords: HD map · Cloud point data · Data transmission

1 Introduction

Compared with traditional driving, the autonomous driving vehicle can greatly enhance driving safety. As an important part of autonomous driving, HD map offers far-beyond sensor ability as well as more assistance for planning and control [1]. The HD map is composed of a variety of formats of data, including point cloud data, semantic data of traffic entities, traffic condition data and etc. Within them, the point cloud data in the high-precision map is a kind of data collected by the data acquisition vehicle through laser LiDAR. It records and organizes images in the form of points. Through this method, we can obtain the coordinates of each point in the surrounding environment and then form the whole point cloud data map [2]. Compared to the abstraction of the surrounding environment in the traditional map as a point-line representation, the point cloud data can obtain a more accurate and comprehensive representation of various road conditions and obstacles in the environment [3]. Therefore, it is the most important basic data for autonomous driving safety.

However, due to the huge data amount of point cloud data, point cloud data compression is a difficult problem in the high-precision map's transmission and application. In

© IFIP International Federation for Information Processing 2022
Published by Springer Nature Switzerland AG 2022
S. Liu and X. Wei (Eds.): NPC 2022, LNCS 13615, pp. 261–266, 2022.
https://doi.org/10.1007/978-3-031-21395-3_24

order to guarantee the transmission of HD maps, we construct a progressive transmission model, including data compression, transmission time, and data restoration mathematical model and corresponding algorithms.

In this paper, we have completed the following work:

1. We introduce the octree structure into our model of progressive transmission. We construct a detailed mathematical model which is established by three steps of data compression, transmission, and data reduction.
2. We build the algorithms to progressively trigger the point cloud data transmission with the network conditions.
3. We prove the feasibility and superiority of our progressive transmission model with the traditional direct transmission method.

2 Progressive Transmission of Point Cloud Data

2.1 Data Compression for Progressive Transmission

We introduce the octree structure coded by Morton code into our model of progressive transmission. Using an octree to compress point cloud data can better retain the feature points and compress as many points as possible while ensuring the characteristics of the object. It is very convenient for our subsequent data restoration. Therefore, we can use it to realize the progressive transmission of point cloud data.

In order to improve efficiency and save space, we can set up a flag. For cubes (containing no point), we set a flag to 0 and discard them. For cubes with a point, we set the flag to 1. The bounding box with only one point is represented by its center point, but for the bounding box containing more than one point of the cloud data, we have to represent its center point, and also store the vector relationship between each data and the center point, so that we can more conveniently and accurately represent the dense and large curvature data. This split model is also suitable for areas with high point density which can well retain its density characteristics [4].

Due to the characteristics of the octree, the minimum multiple that the Morton code [5] can be reduced must be a multiple of 8. We denote the original uncompressed point cloud data as G_0. Assuming that there are s point objects in the original point cloud data G_0, we denote G_0 as $G_0 = \bigcup_{i=0}^{s-1} point_i$. The data after n-level compression G_n going through the octree has s' points, and we denote it as $G_n = \bigcup_{i=0}^{s'-1} point_i$. We record the difference in the number of points between the two adjacent levels G_j and G_{j+1} as $\Delta\alpha_j$, where $\Delta\alpha_j = G_j - G_{j+1} = \bigcup_{r=0}^{k} point_r$, $\Delta\alpha_j$ is the points we condensed at the j-th level. In the uniform distribution model in the ideal state, G_j has the number of points G_{j+1} after being compressed one level which is $\frac{1}{8} \times G_j$, and the number of points being simplified is $\Delta\alpha_j = G_j - G_{j+1} = \frac{7}{8} \times G_j$. For the distortion ΔR_i caused by the simplification of each layer, we perform the following calculation to obtain: Comparing the compressed point cloud to the original model to calculate the mean square error of the distance between all compressed points and the original model, that is, $\Delta R_i = \sqrt{\frac{\prod_{k=1}^{i}(\Delta d_k)^2}{i}}$, where Δd_k is the distance between the points.

In the progressive transmission process, we first compress the points, and the sum of the compressed points at each stage is

$$\sum_{i=1}^{n} \Delta\alpha_i = \frac{7}{8}(G_1 + G_2 + \cdots + G_n) = G_1(1 - (\frac{1}{8})^n) \tag{1}$$

This is the number of points we have reduced after the final compression. The number of points we compressed for each layer is $(\frac{7}{8})^{i-1}G_1$, and these data can be used in the subsequent establishment of a progressive transmission model.

In the actual situation, the point cloud distribution cannot be uniformly distributed. The above mathematical model cannot be simply applied to the general situation. Actually, the number of point reductions is different due to the distinct point density of the model. Therefore, we can't make specific model settings for them, and use abstract functions to express the simplification of points at each level. We can get a simplified abstract model for each level:

$$\sum_{i=1}^{n} \Delta\alpha_i = f_1(G_1) + \cdots + f_{n-1}(G_{n-1}) \tag{2}$$

where $G_{i-1} = G_{i-2} - f_{i-2}(G_{i-2})$ and $\Delta\alpha_i = f_{i-1}(G_{i-1})$.

2.2 Transfer Data and Restore Process

The progressive transmission process of data is as follows:

We can establish a general framework for the progressive transmission of the point cloud data. The restoration process is repeated until the data is as refined as required by the system. Since there will be some errors between the data after the transmission and the data at the beginning of the transmission, it cannot be regarded as the original data. We will represent the restored data as G_0'.

At the beginning of the transmission, we first transmit the simplest data G_n obtained through the above compression process, and then slowly complete it in need. The amount of the data obtained is $G_i = G_n + \Delta\alpha_n + \Delta\alpha_{n-1} + \ldots \Delta\alpha_i$. We use the top data of the stack to save the octree structure. After the inverse transformation of the MD code, the number of each grid can be calculated. At this time, we assign the MD code and attribute value of the top of the stack to this grid data. According to our data compression rules above, the difference between the MD code of the top of the stack and the MD code of the next data is the sum of simplified data among the process. Therefore, we can repeat the assignment of these data to facilitate the recovery of them, and then the MD code of the next data on the top of the stack plus one. We integrate the restoration of the data by completing the condensed data of each layer, that is, $G_{i+1} = G_i + \Delta\alpha_i$. The selection of the subsequent completed data of each layer is also selected by the Morton code. During the transmission process, the transmission accuracy of each layer is gradually increased, and the selection queue of the point cloud data within the accuracy interval is transmitted in each round to complete the data, repeat this process, and finally the receiving end can get the most complete data G_0', with $G_0' = G_n + \Delta\alpha_1 + \cdots + \Delta\alpha_{n-1}$.

2.3 Progressive Transmission Time Model

In order to obtain the transmission time model, according to the above transmission process, we need to make the following further settings:

We set a compression ratio λ according to the required situation and calculate $\Delta\alpha_i = (1-\lambda)G_{i-1} = (1-\lambda)\lambda^{n-i+1}G_0$, therefore:

$$G_0' = \lambda^{n-1}G_0 + (1-\lambda)\lambda^{n-2}G_1 + \cdots + (1-\lambda)G_{n-1} \tag{3}$$

During the transmission process, the transmission rate v_1 of the first layer is determined by detecting the bandwidth B, and then we use the following expression to calculate each subsequent layer:

$$v(n+1) = \begin{cases} \alpha v(n), t(n) > s_2 \\ v(n) + \beta, t(n) \le s_1 \end{cases} \quad (0 \le \alpha < 1, \beta \ge 0) \tag{4}$$

where $t(n)$ is the packet loss rate per unit time, s_1 and s_2 are the two thresholds of the loss rate, α can be determined by the packet loss rate $t(n)$, and β can be calculated by α:

$$\alpha = (1 - t(n))(0 \le t(n) < 1) \tag{5}$$

$$\beta = \frac{4(1-\alpha^2)}{3} \tag{6}$$

The transmission time of each layer T_i can be calculated from the above two models:

$$\begin{cases} T_1 = \frac{G_n}{v(1)} = \frac{\lambda^{n-1}G_0}{v(1)}, i = 1 \\ T_i = \frac{\Delta\alpha_i}{v(i)} = \frac{(1-\lambda)\lambda^{n-i+1}G_0}{v(i)}, i \ne 1 \end{cases} \tag{7}$$

Total transmission time $\sum_{i=1}^{n} T_i$:

$$\sum_{i=1}^{n} T_i = T_1 + \cdots + T_n = \frac{\lambda^{n-1}G_0}{v(1)} + \cdots + \frac{(1-\lambda)\lambda^{n-i+1}G_0}{v(n)} \tag{8}$$

Assuming that the bandwidth of the transmission is B, under ideal conditions we can get the first layer of transmission time $t_1 = \frac{G_n}{B}$, and then for the completion of each layer of data, we can calculate the transmission time $t_i = \frac{\Delta\alpha_i}{B}$, in the uniformly distributed point cloud model the transmission time presents $t_i = \frac{(\frac{7}{8})^{i-1}G_1}{B}$. The total transmission time is $\sum_{i=1}^{n} t_i = \frac{G_1(1-(\frac{1}{8})^n)}{B} + t_1$, we can calculate f as long as we know the total data volume and bandwidth, but in actual situations, if we know the number of reductions in each layer and the number of points in the first layer, we can also calculate the total transmission time $\sum_{i=1}^{n} t_i = \frac{G_n + \Delta\alpha_1 + \ldots \Delta\alpha_{n-1}}{B}$.

Repeat the above steps and loop until the degree of recovery reaches the level we need. At this time, we have completed the progressive transmission of point cloud data.

3   Experiment

3.1   Experimental Set up

The point cloud data format used in our study is PCD. The point cloud files in this format contain a header encoded with ASCII code to determine and declare the characteristics of the point cloud data stored in the file. Compared with other formats of point cloud data, PCD file format has the ability to store and process ordered point cloud data sets. As it can control the file format, we can maximize the best performance of the application.

3.2   Comparison of Transmission Experiment Results

In this section, the time required for progressive transmission is compared with that of traditional direct transmission. The transmission files are point cloud images of different sizes. The transmission bandwidth in the experiment is set to be 20 kpbs.

Table 1. The time required for transmitting.

Document size (KB)	Time for progressive transmission (s)	Time for direct transmission (s)
1114	0.1	62
2788	0.3	112
5965	0.8	198
11983	2.2	378

Table 1 shows the time required for transmitting the same file under the same bandwidth. It can be seen from the table that the time required for progressive transmission is much shorter than that for direct transmission. This is because the progressive transmission does not transfer complete data in the transmission process, but first transfers the reduced data to the other end and then restores the data on the receiving device, which greatly reduces the time and bandwidth required in the transmission diagram, proving that the progressive transmission is more progressive and suitable for HD map transmission because of its better real-time performance and less bandwidth requirement.

Table 2 summarizes the number of points in files obtained by the two methods when transferring the same file. It can be seen that with the increase of the number of points, although the number of points lost in progressive transmission will increase correspondingly, the distortion ratio still fluctuates very little, which is not different from the result of direct transmission.

From the above experimental results, progressive transmission has great advantages over direct transmission, especially in the unmanned environment, progressive transmission is obviously more suitable for the generation and transmission of HD maps.

Table 2. The number of points obtained by two methods.

Original file points	Progressive transfer of final restoration points	File points obtained by direct transfer
11983	10783	11983
24756	22384	24756
93039	91206	93039
207846	203774	207846

4 Conclusion

The research on HD maps in autonomous driving is getting more and more focus. In the next step of the research process, we can optimize the restoration algorithm to speed up the speed of restoration, we hope to find a more accurate method to predict the restoration point.

Acknowledgements. This work is supported by Guangdong Natural Science Foundation under Grant No. 2021A1515011755. Rui Huang is the corresponding author of this paper.

References

1. Ghallabi, F., Nashashibi, F., elhajshhade, G., et al.: LIDAR-based lane marking detection for vehicle positioning in an HD map. In: 2018 21st IEEE International Conference on Intelligent Transportation Systems (ITSC) (2018)
2. Potó, V., Somogyi, Á., Lovas, T., et al.: Creating HD map for autonomous vehicles – a pilot study. In: Advanced Manufacturing and Repairing Technologies in Vehicle Industry (2017)
3. Elhousni, M., Huang, X.: A survey on 3D LiDAR localization for autonomous vehicles. In: 2020 IEEE Intelligent Vehicles Symposium (IV). IEEE (2020)
4. Samet, H., Kochut, A.: Octree approximation and compression methods. In: International Symposium on 3d Data Processing Visualization & Transmission. DBLP (2002)
5. Cheng-Qiu, D., Min, C., Xiao-Yong, F.: Compression algorithm of 3D point cloud data based on Octree. Open Autom. Control Syst. J. **7**(1), 879883 (2015)

IMRSim: A Disk Simulator for Interlaced Magnetic Recording Technology

Zhimin Zeng⬨, Xinyu Chen, Laurence T. Yang⬨, and Jinhua Cui(✉)⬨

Huazhong University of Science and Technology, Wuhan, China
csjhcui@gmail.com

Abstract. The emerging interlaced magnetic recording (IMR) technology achieves a higher areal density for hard disk drive (HDD) over the conventional magnetic recording (CMR) technology. Unfortunately, there has been no related disk simulator and product available to the public. So, in this work, we implement the first public IMR disk simulator, called IMRSim, simulating the interlaced tracks and implementing many state-of-the-art data placement strategies. IMRSim is built on the actual CMR-based HDD to precisely simulate the I/O performance of IMR drives. We release IMRSim as an open-source IMR disk simulation tool and hope to provide a platform for related research.

Keywords: Hard device driver · Interlaced magnetic recording · Disk simulator

1 Introduction

With the advent of the big data era and the limitations of the superparamagnetic effect, enterprises and industries need storage systems with larger capacity and lower costs. As a result, some new technologies and methodologies have emerged, including shingled magnetic recording (SMR) [6] and interlaced magnetic recording (IMR) [2,3].

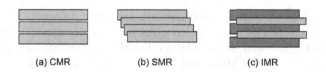

(a) CMR   (b) SMR   (c) IMR

Fig. 1. The different track layouts in HDDs.

As shown in Fig. 1(b), SMR overlaps tracks like roof tiles to shorten the track gap. However, random writes may corrupt data on the subsequent tracks. To protect the data, all subsequent tracks must be backed up before randomly

S. Liu and X. Wei (Eds.): NPC 2022, LNCS 13615, pp. 267–273, 2022.
https://doi.org/10.1007/978-3-031-21395-3_25

writing a track, and then rewritten after randomly writing the track. This time-consuming phenomenon is known as read-modify-write (RMW). Compared to SMR, the alternative IMR technique (Fig. 1(c)) organizes the tracks in an interlaced fashion rather than the tiled coverage, thus the random write process will only affect at most two adjacent tracks.

The essences of the IMR technique are energy-assisted recording and track overlapping. In IMR, the bottom track is wider than the top track [2,8] and requires higher energy intensity than the narrower top track. Therefore, data updating on one top track requires a lower energy intensity that is not enough to destroy the adjacent bottom tracks. As a result, IMR can perform update-in-place updating on top track without the additional rewriting overhead. Unfortunately, higher energy intensity is required to update data on a bottom track. This will destroy data from the adjacent top tracks. To avoid data corruption on the top tracks, a time-consuming update mechanism (e.g., RMW) is required [2]. Anyway, compared with SMR, the theoretical performance of IMR technology is outstanding. However, at present, there is no publicly available IMR simulator.

Therefore, we propose an open-source IMR disk simulator, called IMRSim [4], as a block device driver in the Linux kernel. *To the best of our knowledge, this is the first public IMR disk simulator.* The main contributions are summarized as follows:

- We implement the first public IMR disk simulator, IMRSim. IMRSim can effectively capture the key characteristics of IMR and support many state-of-the-art data placement schemes. It should be noted that we have to ignore some special physical factors of IMR since there are currently no IMR-based HDD products on the market.
- IMRSim is scalable. IMRSim provides an extensible user interface for adjusting the simulator behavior flexibly.

We test IMRSim against CMR-based HDD on some real workloads to evaluate the I/O performance of the IMR-based HDD. The results show that IMR's update strategy brings significant performance loss which meets the expectation of the evaluation.

2   IMR Simulation

We use the device-mapper (DM) framework to export a pseudo block device in user-space that acts like an IMR drive. As we build the device target directly on top of the CMR-based HDD, IMRSim has the same rotational speed and the head switch time as the CMR-based HDD [5]. Only, the logical arrangement of the tracks is different. Specifically, IMRSim includes two parts: kernel module and user interface.

2.1   IMRSim Kernel Module

Figure 2 depicts the architectural overview of IMRSim. The IMRSim kernel module contains the data layout and management, data placement, address translation and I/O mapping, and availability and statistics collection.

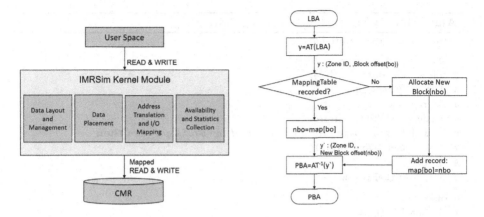

Fig. 2. The architecture of IMRSim.   **Fig. 3.** The I/O Mapping process.

Data Layout and Management. The data is organized in zones ("zone" is similar to "TG" [9]), which are clusters of several continuous interlaced tracks. According to previous research [3], the data density of the bottom track in IMR-Sim is about 1.25 times that of the top track. IMR can consist of one or more zones. Such a partition method can maintain the spatial locality of application data inside the zone to increase data access efficiency.

Data Placement. The RMW process of data read, write and update operations is shown in Algorithm 1. Read operation is similar to CMR. For updating on the top track, there is no cost. For updating on the bottom track, to avoid data loss or damage, the RMW process is required. In our implementation, we use pages to keep data that needs to be backed up in memory.

Recently, more and more different update strategies have emerged, such as read-swap-write (RSW) [5], etc. IMRSim can easily extend these strategies, here for simplicity, IMRSim applies the classic RMW update strategy.

Address Translation and I/O Mapping. For traditional CMR, LBA (logical block address) is equal to PBA (physical block address) and it can write randomly. However, to decrease write amplification, we let the IMR allocate from the bottom tracks, and then allocate top tracks. In this way, IMR needs to keep a mapping table (MT) to map the LBA to PBA.

Here, we define two helpful functions. The address translation function (AT, e.g., $y = AT(x)$) and its inverse function (denoted as AT^{-1}). The x represents LBA or PBA, and y represents the relative block address, which is represented by a triple ($Zone\,ID$, $Track\,Offset$, $Block\,Offset$).

Algorithm 1: The process of reading/writing.

---

   input: A bio structure *bio*.

1 lba ← bio.bi_sector;
2 cdir ← bio_data_dir(bio);
3 **if** lba *is illegal* **then**
4 | *report error*;
5 **if** cdir == WRITE **then**
6 | **if** lba *is on bottom track and adjacent top blocks are valid* **then**
7 | | RMWStrategy(bio);
8 | **else**
9 | | WriteBio(bio);
10 **else**
11 | ReadBio(bio);

As illustrated in Fig. 3, IMRSim uses AT to convert the LBA to get the zone ID and block offset (*bo*). Then, there will be two cases: (1) The *bo* is not recorded in the MT, which means a new write operation. IMRSim will allocate a free block (with the new block offset, i.e. *nbo*) according to the specific track allocation scheme, and then record *bo* to *nbo* in the MT. (2) The *bo* is recorded in the MT, which means an update operation. Thus, the *nbo* can be obtained by querying the MT.

Finally, the PBA can be obtained by using AT^{-1}.

Note that, the mapping table may be utilized to implement some strategies such as track caching, hot and cold data swap, and track flipping [9].

Availability and Statistics Collection. This sub-module provides a certain level of availability for disks and collects some simulator status information. We record the behavior information of the simulator (e.g., the extra write times) into memory, and open a persistent thread to periodically flush the collected statistics to the disk.

2.2 User Interface

We use ioctl system calls to design a command-line user interface, which makes IMRSim highly extensible. The user can use such system calls to flexibly adjust the design parameters and control the behavior of the simulator according to their needs.

3 Simulation Analysis

3.1 Experimental Methodology

This section evaluates the performance of simulated IMR-based HDD. We created IMRSim on a Western Digital's pure CMR drive (see Table 1 and 2). Also, we test IMR with two-stage allocation strategy (denoted as two-stage IMR) and three-stage allocation strategy (denoted as three-stage IMR).

We conduct all the experiments on 64-bit Ubuntu 14.10, and use fio to replay and evaluate four real write-intensive workloads, i.e., hm_0, proj_0, src1_2 and src2_2, collected by Microsoft Research Cambridge. In addition, we use direct I/O to avoid the impact of kernel cache on the simulator performance.

Table 1. The info for tested HDD.

HDD details	
HDD model	WD20EJRx
Drive cache size	64 MB
Rotational speed	5400 rpm

Table 2. The info for IMRSim.

IMRSim parameters	
Top track size	456 blocks
Bottom track size	568 blocks
Capacity	128 GB

3.2 Experimental Results

1) *Write Amplification under Different Space Usages:* As shown in Fig. 4a, under the src1_2 workload, the WA increases as the space usage increases. Also, the WA of two-stage IMR is slightly larger than that of three-stage IMR.

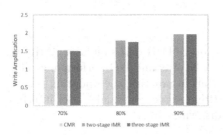

(a) WA under the src1_2 workload.

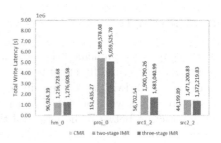

(b) Write latency under 80% usage.

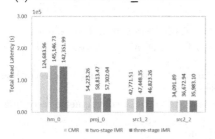

(c) Read latency under 80% usage.

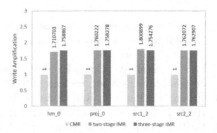

(d) WA under 80% usage.

Fig. 4. Performance results under different situations.

2) *Performance results under different workloads:* As shown in Fig. 4b–4d, we evaluate total write and read latency and write amplification with different workloads under 80% space usage.

Write Performance. Figure 4b demonstrates the write performance of three simulated devices under 80% space usage. Also, as shown in Fig. 4d, the additional writes of IMR are at most 1.8x that of CMR. However, a mere 1.8x difference in write times results in a 28x difference in write performance. This is mainly because mechanical disks consume time in seek and rotation delays, and the RMW process needs to spend extra time on these positioning operations.

Read Performance. As shown in Fig. 4c, IMR exhibit read performance close to CMR, as expected.

4   Related Works

DiskSim [1] is a disk simulator to accurately simulate the performance of traditional hard disks. Tan et al. [7] designed the SMR simulation platform for the analysis of shingled translation layer designs. Pitchumani et al. [6] developed a tool to imitate SMR disk by implementing a shingled device-mapper target on top of the Linux kernel's block devices.

5   Conclusion

In this paper, we implement the first open-source IMR disk simulator, IMRSim, to simulate several different interlaced track layouts and I/O performance. The performance of IMR is excellent in theory, but in practice, the updating process costs more than we expected. Further, IMRSim exposes a scalable user interface for interaction between the user and the disk simulator.

References

1. Bucy, J.S., Schindler, J., Schlosser, S.W.: The Disksim Simulation Environment Version 4.0 Reference Manual (cmu-pdl-08-101). Carnegie Mellon University: Parallel Data Laboratory (2008)
2. Gao, K., Zhu, W., Gage, E.: Write management for interlaced magnetic recording devices (Nov 29 2016), uS Patent 9,508,362
3. Hwang, E., Park, J., Rauschmayer, R., Wilson, B.: Interlaced magnetic recording. IEEE Trans. Magn. **53**(4), 1–7 (2016)
4. IMRSim. https://github.com/AlieZ22/IMRSim
5. Liang, Y., Yang, M.C., Chen, S.H.: Magic: making IMR-based HDD perform like CMR-based HDD. IEEE Trans. Comput. **71**(3), 643–657 (2022)
6. Pitchumani, R., Hospodor, A., Amer, A., Kang, Y., Miller, E.L., Long, D.D.: Emulating a shingled write disk. In: 2012 IEEE 20th International Symposium on Modeling, Analysis and Simulation of Computer and Telecommunication Systems, pp. 339–346. IEEE (2012)

7. Tan, S., Xi, W., Ching, Z.Y., Jin, C., Lim, C.T.: Simulation for a shingled magnetic recording disk. IEEE Trans. Manage. **49**(6), 2677–2681 (2013)
8. Wang, G., David, H.C.D., Wu, F., Liu, S.: Survey on high density magnetic recording technology. J. Comput. Res. Dev. **55**(9), 2016 (2018)
9. Wu, F., et al.: Tracklace: data management for interlaced magnetic recording. IEEE Trans. Comput. **70**(3), 347–358 (2020)

Storage and I/O

Alleviating Performance Interference Through Intra-Queue I/O Isolation for NVMe-over-Fabrics

Wenhao Gu, Xuchao Xie$^{(\boxtimes)}$, and Dezun Dong$^{(\boxtimes)}$

College of Computer, National University of Defense Technology,
Changsha 410073, China
{guwenhao16,xiexuchao,dong}@nudt.edu.cn

Abstract. The NVMe-over-Fabrics (NVMeoF) protocol enables high-performance Protocol Data Units (PDUs) exchanges between hosts and remote NVMe controllers. The performance benefits of NVMeoF are mainly derived from the multiple deep queue pairs for parallel PDUs transfers. NVMeoF has significantly facilitated NVMe SSD disaggregation from compute nodes for better resource utilization and scaling independence. However, as the performance of NVMe SSD and network infrastructure increases, the near-perfect performance delivery of NVMeoF is harder to achieve. The primary reason is the increased CPU interrupts and performance interference originated from the I/O requests served by the same NVMeoF queue pair.

In this paper, we investigate how intra-queue requests are mutually affected, and propose PINoF, a Performance Isolated remote storage access mechanism for NVMe-over-Fabrics. PINoF separates CMD and Data PDUs resources in each NVMeoF queue pair to achieve intra-queue I/O isolation, transfers PDUs in batch along with read or write specific I/O path to achieve isolated interrupt-coalescing, and introduces differentiated PDU reordering schemes to achieve isolated scheduling. Our experimental results demonstrate that compared with state-of-the-art NVMeoF implementations, PINoF achieves 23.92% lower latency, increases bandwidth by up to 19.59%, and improves IOPS by 12.41% on average.

Keywords: NVMeoF · Performance interference · I/O Isolation

1 Introduction

Resource disaggregation architecture has been significantly facilitated by recent advances in high-speed network technologies [7]. Meanwhile, various resource-specific interconnection protocols have been developing for ultra-low latency and high throughput communication between different kinds of disaggregated resources. In terms of storage disaggregation, as NVMe SSDs perform much faster than SAS/SATA SSDs and Hard Disk Drives (HDDs) [20], the software overheads in the I/O path to NVMe SSDs become much more pronounced [2].

© IFIP International Federation for Information Processing 2022
Published by Springer Nature Switzerland AG 2022
S. Liu and X. Wei (Eds.): NPC 2022, LNCS 13615, pp. 277–289, 2022.
https://doi.org/10.1007/978-3-031-21395-3_26

Recently, the NVMe-over-Fabrics (NVMeoF) protocol [15] reclaims that it can dramatically reduce network and processing overheads [8], thus achieving negligible performance degradation for remote storage access through RDMA, FC, and TCP networks [6]. Compared with the iSCSI protocol that was originally designed for disaggregating HDDs, the performance benefits of NVMeoF are mainly derived from the multiple deep queue pairs for parallel PDUs (Protocol Data Units) transfers that can fully utilize the internal parallelism of SSDs [18].

Unlike NVMe-over-RDMA that builds on the basis of large-scale RDMA-enabled specific network infrastructures, NVMe-over-TCP (NoT) is a recent transport extension of NVMeoF that can be implemented on top of commodity Ethernet hardware and standard TCP/IP protocol stack [11,17]. NoT promotes NVMeoF deployment scenarios to the most common network infrastructure in datacenters without building out separate storage networks. Specifically, NoT defines how NVMe command (CMD) and data are encapsulated within TCP PDUs and provides regulations of how the queue pairs of host and remote NVMe controller are mapped to TCP connections and CPU cores.

As NoT inherits the superiorities of both NVMe and TCP/IP protocols, it comes at a cost of the flaws of TCP/IP software stack, such as additional memory copies and more CPU overhead compared with NVMe-over-RDMA [4, 5,13]. Therefore, as the performance of NVMe SSD and network infrastructure increases, NoT has to cost more CPU processing overhead on both host and target sides to achieve full performance delivery of NVMe SSDs. The primary reason is the increased CPU interrupts and performance interference originated from the CMD and Data PDUs served by the same queue pair [1]. Hwang et al. have proposed i10 [9,10] to delay ringing doorbells to accumulate requests and process the requests in batch to amortize network and software overhead. However, accumulating requests further exacerbates performance interference issues of the PDUs processed in the same batch.

As the performance interference issue caused by the diverse PDUs of requests in NoT implementation has not been paid sufficient attention and is rarely studied, in this work, we investigate how intra-queue requests are mutually affected in current NoT implementation and propose PINoF, a Performance Isolated remote storage access mechanism for NVMe-over-Fabrics. Overall, our main contributions in this paper can be summarized in three aspects as below.

- Intra-Queue I/O Isolation. We propose to separate data structures and resources of CMD and Data PDUs in each PINoF queue pair to isolate the PDUs generated by read and write I/O, thus PINoF can greatly mitigate the performance interference between CMD and Data PDUs and manage CMD and Data PDUs with the same kind of operation independently.
- Specific I/O Paths. PINoF always transfers NoT PDUs in batch along with specific read or write I/O path that uses specially designed interrupt-coalescing strategy, thus the performance interference among the PDUs generated from the requests processed in a same batch can be further mitigated.
- Isolated Scheduling. PINoF further introduces differentiated PDU reordering schemes by offering different priorities for different types of PDUs. In this case,

the waiting latency of the PDUs that potentially affect subsequent PDUs can be significantly reduced.

We implemented PINoF in Linux kernel and evaluated it by FIO and RocksDB benchmarks. Our experimental results demonstrate that compared with state-of-the-art NVMeoF implementations, PINoF can achieve 23.92% lower latency, increase bandwidth by up to 19.59%, and improve IOPS by 12.41% on average.

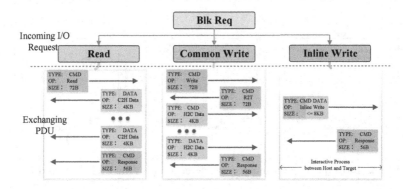

Fig. 1. NoT PDUs generated by the I/O requests with different types and sizes

2   Background and Motivation

2.1   NVMe-over-TCP

NoT host needs to establish a connection to remote NVMe controller in target to enable transfers. The process of connection is to create multiple one-to-one mappings between host queues and controller queues. Each host queue and its associated controller queue will be mapped to a specific TCP connection and a separate CPU core. As long as a NoT connection is established, NoT drivers will encapsulate the NVMe command, response, and data into TCP PDUs, transferred along standard TCP/IP protocol stack [14,19]. Generally, there are five kinds of PDUs used in NoT implementation, i.e., Read/Write CMD PDU, R2T (Ready to Transfer Command) PDU, H2CData (Host to Controller Data) PDU, C2HData (Controller to Host Data) PDU, and Resp (Response) PDU.

The detailed NoT workflows of the I/O requests with different types and sizes can be characterized in Fig. 1. Take common write I/O as an example, for the write request that is larger than 8KB, its data to write has to be transferred by at least two H2CData PDUs. Specifically, when target receives a CMD PDU of a large-size write request, target driver will determine the size of data it can receive in the next transfer and pass the information to host via R2T PDU. Host driver will always send H2CData PDUs following the requirement in R2T PDUs. Target driver will execute the write request only if all the data to write has been transferred by H2CData PDUs. The Resp PDU will be sent to host when the write request is executed successfully on target side.

2.2 Intra-Queue Performance Interference

In this paper, we further investigate the performance interference issue [3,12,16] in NoT from a microscopic point of view. The performance interference mainly comes from the I/O requests with different types and sizes that are handled in a same NoT queue. These I/O requests will finally generate a large number of NoT PDUs with different attributes in terms of types, sizes, relevance, and urgencies. Thus the common unified transceiver strategy should be carefully reconsidered, especially when multiple PDUs are accumulated for transferring in batch.

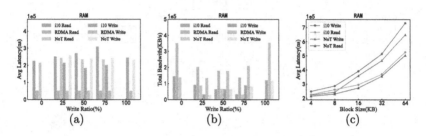

Fig. 2. Intra-queue performance interference in NVMe over TCP and i10.

For a read request, NoT host first sends a CMD PDU of 72B to target, then NoT target returns many C2HData PDUs that contains data typically 4KB. In the case of an application with read-intensive I/O workloads, such as reading data sets from remote NVMe SSDs for machine learning, both NoT and i10 hosts will continuously process PDUs with short flow data while targets always return PDUs with long flow data. Apparently, PDUs on the host side are latency-sensitive and need to be sent out in time for processing. Meanwhile, PDUs on the target side are more suitable for gathering and transferring in batch to achieve high throughput. However, the desired PDU sending strategies of read and write requests are diametrically opposite as Fig. 1. Therefore, once these PDUs with different desires are accumulated together as i10 does, both the read and write requests have to endure severer intra-queue performance interference caused by their uncompromising PDUs.

As read and write mixed I/O workload is common in production storage systems, simply designing different NoT PDU accumulation and sending strategies on host and target sides can hardly adapt to the dynamic needs of read and write requests, and the performance interference is inevitable. As shown in Fig. 2, the read/write latency and bandwidth performance of NVMe-over-RDMA keeps stable and basically proportional respectively with the read/write ratio, while the performances of NoT and i10 are significantly interfered especially when read and write mixed. Thus, managing PDUs from read and write requests separately on both host and target sides is essential to accurately provide the most appropriate PDU accumulation and sending strategies.

Besides type and size, NoT PDUs may present significant differences in relevance and urgency. For example, even if the CMD PDU of a write request is transferred to target in time, the data of the write request cannot be transferred until its associated R2T PDU returns back. For both read and write requests, even if their data have been transferred, NoT will not signal blk-mq (multiple per-core block queues) the finish of these I/O requests since not received their Resp PDUs. Thus, R2T and Resp PDUs need to be prioritized to transfer for their relevance to H2CData PDU and urgency to finish an I/O request to further mitigate the performance interference. As shown in Fig. 2(c), the write request latency increases significantly after the block size is 16 compared with read, due to the R2T PDU transmission.

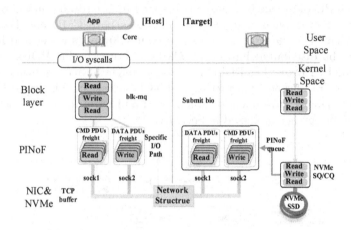

Fig. 3. System overview of PINoF.

2.3 Motivation

In this paper, we propose intra-queue I/O isolation to alleviate the performance interference in NoT. Our work is motivated by the observations below.

- Performance overhead can be amortized. Aggregating multiple requests for batch processing can amortize the overheads from network processing and TCP /IP software stack, thus the performance of NoT can be improved.
- PDU attribute should be distinguished. I/O requests with different types and sizes will generate PDUs with different attributes in terms of type, size, relevance, and urgency, which inspires differentiated PDU batch processing mechanisms.
- PDU dependency should be considered. R2T and Resp PDUs show significant relevance to H2CData PDU and urgency to finish an I/O request. Prioritizing R2T and Resp PDUs while accumulating H2CData and C2HData PDUs can achieve high throughput and mitigate I/O latency amplification simultaneously.

3   System Overview

PINoF is a modified implementation of standard NoT and works as a shim NVMe capsule and data forwarding layer between the Linux blk-mq layer and TCP/IP software stack. As shown in Fig. 3, different from standard NoT implementation, PINoF isolates both resources and strategies of CMD and Data PDUs while separating read and write requests. Specifically, the isolated resources include spatial resource "freight" and temporal resource "hrtimer". freight is the newly established container for accumulating PDUs while hrtimer leverages the kernel high-precision timer for controlling PDU aggregation processes.

As each PINoF queue is one-to-one mapped to a hardware queue in the blk-mq layer, for each queue pair, PINoF maintains both CMD and Data PDUs freights. The PDUs generated by an I/O request from its associated hardware queue will be distributed into either CMD or Data specific PDUs freight for aggregation by PINoF. The PDUs in the same freight have the same destination, thus can be transferred by a preassigned TCP socket. In this way, PINoF can separately manage intra-queue PDUs of read and write requests. The detailed design will be further discussed in Sect. 4.1.

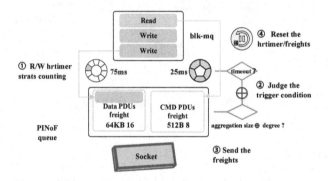

Fig. 4. Isolated resources on the host side of PINoF.

The time when a freight can be sent to the remote side is cooperatively controlled by its size and the hrtimer. In PINoF, there is a trade-off between the long-time aggregation to accumulate more PDUs in a single freight and the short-time aggregation for less delays of the accumulated PDUs in the freight. To this end, PINoF separates intra-queue PDUs into different I/O paths, i.e., read specific I/O path and write specific I/O path, to achieve a good balance between interrupt-coalescing and extra delays for both read and write I/O requests. We will particularly describe the specific I/O paths in detail in Sect. 4.2.

With isolated resources and I/O paths, PINoF can achieve isolated scheduling to flexibly tune the transfer priorities of intra-queue PDUs. Besides, in PINoF, we always prioritize R2T PDUs in write specific I/O path to alleviate the PDU dependency issue, which will be discussed in Sect. 4.3.

4   PINoF Design

4.1   Intra-queue I/O Isolation

PINoF implements intra-queue I/O isolation by introducing two kinds of dedicated resources, freight and hrtimer. Both freight and hrtimer are allocated separately for the CMD and Data PDUs served by the same queue pair. Each freight is considered as a PDU container where multiple PDUs to the same destination are gathered and will be transferred along the I/O path in PINoF together. Compared with standard NoT, PINoF can significantly reduce the overhead from frequent context switches caused by fragmented PDU transmission and fully utilize the TCP acceleration technologies such as TCP segmentation offload (TSO) and generic receive offload (GRO).

As shown in Fig. 4, PINoF uses both spatial and temporal measurements to determine whether a freight should be transferred or not. Spatial measurements include aggregation size and aggregation degree. When the allocated memory size for a freight cannot accommodate the next PDU, the freight will incur an aggregation size triggered freight send operation. Similarly, a freight will incur an aggregation degree triggered send operation when the number of its accommodated PDUs exceeds the predefined threshold. PINoF introduces hrtimer as the temporal measurement of freight. Each hrtimer is used to record how much time its associated freight has spent to accumulate PDUs and has a predefined threshold to indicate the freight should be sent out. In PINoF, once a freight receives its first request, its associated hrtimer will wake up. As the hrtimer reaches its threshold, its associated freight will incur an hrtimer triggered send operation. Note that no matter whether a freight send operation is triggered by hrtimer or other spatial measurements, its hrtimer will always be reset.

4.2   Specific I/O Paths

Due to the different attributes of the PDUs generated by read and write requests, as shown in Figs. 3 and 4, the freights for read and write requests are organized and managed differently. Take read requests as an example, PINoF first prepares all the data structures needed by freights in each PINoF queue pair on both host and target sides. On host side, once a CMD PDU generated by a read request arrives, it is simply linked to the send list of the PINoF queue rather than rings the doorbell to wake up send thread directly. All the following PDUs from read requests will repeat this step until the sending condition is triggered and the freight is sent to the remote PINoF queue through socket. On the remote target side, PINoF caches freight in buffer and receives the fixed-length header to parse the header information, analyze the length of subsequent data, and receive data accordingly. This process will be repeatedly processed to realize the unpacking of the freight and parse each read request. Subsequently, the request gets off the specific I/O path, transferred to other layers for processing. The workflow of the write path is similar to that of the read, yet they mainly differ in the predetermined parameters of dedicated resources in Sect. 4.1.

kernel_sendpage() can avoid data replication on the transmission side when sending data per page, but leads to a weak batch processing capacity. While kernel_sendmsg() can copy the kernel I/O vector to the socket buffer as a function parameter, thus significantly improves the throughput at high load. Therefore, we always call kernel_sendmsg() for sending the bandwidth-intensive Data PDUs of which host write requests and target read requests mainly composed. Conversely, the CMD PDUs generated by read requests and the Resp and R2T PDUs generated by write requests are always regarded as latency-sensitive PDUs and sent by calling kernel_sendpage().

4.3 Isolated Scheduling

During the whole I/O workflow in PINoF, CMD PDUs are the initiator of all the interactions between host and target sides. Apparently, sending CMD PDUs for processing as soon as possible can significantly reduce I/O waiting latency.

As the PDUs handled on host and target sides are different, we introduce isolated scheduling mechanism in PINoF to schedule freights on host and target sides. Our basic strategy is to set different threshold for the dedicated resources of host and target. The timeout threshold of the CMD PDUs hrtimer is set to 25 ms and that of the Data PDUs hrtimer is set to 75 ms in PINoF. The PDUs on host side in read specific I/O path and target side in write specific I/O path are all CMD PDUs smaller than 72 B, hence we heuristically set the size of CMD PDUs freight to 512 B and the degree of aggregation to 8. As the Data PDUs are no less than one physical page, the Data PDUs freight size and aggregation degree are set to 64 KB and 16 respectively, since 64 KB is the partition upper limit of TSO technology.

Besides, we manually set the weight of R2T PDU to 3 and Resp PDU to 2 to trigger the aggregation size preferentially. Thus, the freights that contain R2T and Resp PDUs on target side will achieve highest priority to transfer in PINoF, while the freights that contain H2CData or C2HData PDUs have to endure a longer accumulation time. Consequently, the PDUs show significant relevance to H2CData PDU and urgency to finish an I/O request can be transferred in time while the H2CData and C2HData PDUs can be fully accumulated to achieve high throughput in PINoF. These parameters (high-quality setting obtained from experiments) are set loosely to prove the effectiveness of isolated scheduling.

5   Performance Evaluation

5.1   Experimental Setup

Table 1. Hardware and software configurations

	Host	Target
CPU	2-socket Intel (R) Xeon (R) CPU E5-2692v2@2.20 GHz 12cores per socket, NUMA enabled (2 nodes)	2-socket Intel (R) Xeon (R) CPU E5-2660v2@2.60 GHz 10cores per socket, NUMA enabled (2 nodes)
MEM	125 GB of DRAM	64 GB of DRAM
NIC	Mellanox CX-5 EX (100G) TSO/GRO = on, LRO = off, DIM disabled Jumbo frame enabled (4096 B)	
SSD	N/A	1.6TB DERA D5457 NVMe SSD
IRQ	N/A	irqbalance enabled
OS	Centos 7 (kernel 5.4.43)	
FIO	version = fio–3.7, rw = randrw, size = 15 G cpus_allowed = 0–23, runtime = 300, engine = libaio iodepth = 8, Direct I/O = on CPU affinity enabled, block size = 4 KB	

We implement PINoF as a loadable kernel module of Linux 5.4.43 by adding 723 lines of C codes on the basis of the standard NoT implementation, which can be reached at https://github.com/jackey-gu/PINoF. We build a PINoF prototype using the hardware and software configurations described in Table 1.

5.2   Evaluation Results

Performance with Varying Read/write Ratios. We evaluate the impact of intra-queue PDU isolation by setting different read/write IO request ratios in FIO benchmarks. As shown in Fig. 5, compared with NoT and i10, PINoF shows obvious advantages in average latency, tail latency, and bandwidth. When evaluated using RAM, compared with i10, PINoF decreases the average latency and tail latency by 31.94% and 20.45% respectively in the read-only condition. Meanwhile, PINoF provides 33.58% bandwidth growth than i10. In the write-only condition, PINoF shows about 13.52% performance improvement in terms of latency and bandwidth, which is a little bit lower than that of the read-only workload. In the condition of mixed read and write requests, PINoF presents by up to 20.57% latency reduction and 18.92% bandwidth improvement than i10.

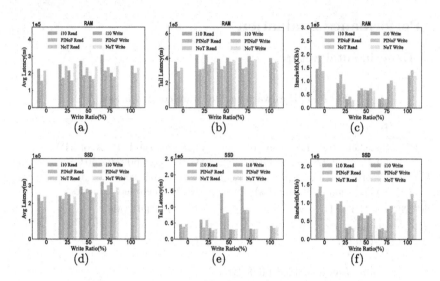

Fig. 5. Latency comparison with varying write ratio.

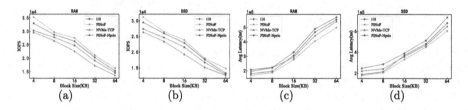

Fig. 6. IOPS and latency comparison with varying block sizes.

PINoF achieves similar performance trends when evaluated using NVMe SSDs, as shown in Fig. 5. However, the overall performance improvements are lower than that of RAM. This is because the bandwidth of a single NVMe SSD can be easily saturated in the experiments, which limits the demonstration of the performance benefits of PINoF. Nevertheless, PINoF still has an 12.82% bandwidth improvement than i10 at least. As intra-queue PDU isolation can give play to the advantages of precise resource allocation and dedicated processing of read and write specific paths, it can significantly alleviate the performance interference of the aggregated PDUs no matter works alone or collaboratively with other PDU management strategies.

Performance with Varying Block Sizes. In this experiment, we choose the write-intensive workloads with different block sizes to comprehensively evaluate the impact of the isolated scheduling design because the requests will generate a large number of R2T PDUs, which can activate the isolated scheduling in I/O path. By setting all CMD and Data PDUs aggregation conditions to 16 64 KB

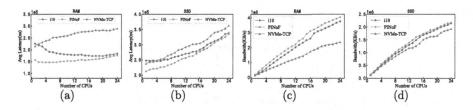

Fig. 7. Latency and bandwidth comparison with varying number of CPU cores.

and cancelling PDUs weight design, we enable a PINoF_Nprio system without a isolation scheduling function, so as to compare with PINoF to prove its effect.

Figure 6 shows the IOPS and latency comparisons with varying I/O request sizes to access remote NVMe SSD and RAM block devices. Apparently, the performance of PINoF is much better than NoT and i10 no matter to access remote RAM or NVMe SSDs. PINoF can provide an IOPS improvement of 9.15% than that without designing isolated scheduling for R2T PDUs. Notably, as shown in Fig. 6(c) and (d), 16K block size is a dividing point of latency performance, where the trend lines of the four tested systems change dramatically. This is because when write remote storage with 4K and 8K requests, all the write requests issued from host are inline write requests that will not generate R2T PDUs. For the write requests larger than 8 KB, R2T PDUs are necessary for these write requests. Besides, all the R2T PDUs are highly relevant to H2CData PDUs and considered more urgent for transferring in PINoF. In this case, the isolated scheduling design in PINoF can significantly mitigate the system performance loss caused by aggregating PDUs.

Scalability with Number of Cores. To further understand the performance scalability of PINoF in the systems with multiple CPU cores, we evaluate the performance of PINoF with different number of CPU cores from 1 to 24. As shown in Fig. 7, both i10 and PINoF present better performance than NoT as the number of PINoF queues increases. Besides, for a fixed number of CPU cores involved in this experiment, PINoF always performs better than i10 and NoT in both latency and bandwidth. This indicates that all the designed strategies in PINoF do not incur any performance scalability loss.

As shown in Fig. 7(c), when accessing remote RAM, the bandwidth of PINoF is steadily improved as the number of CPU cores increases and is roughly proportional to the number of CPU cores. This trend does not appear in Fig. 7(d) is mainly because the performance of NVMe SSD cannot saturate the high performance of PINoF. Different from bandwidth, the average latencies of i10 and PINoF are obviously reduced compared with NoT as the number of CPU cores are used in this experiment while the average latency of PINoF increases. This is because both i10 and PINoF can benefit from the increase of CPU cores that accelerate the trigger of threshold for batch transfer, i.e., ring the doorbell with a shorter waiting time. As the average waiting time of the PDUs aggregated in freight is shorten, PINoF finally achieves lower average I/O latency.

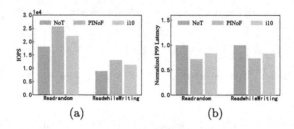

Fig. 8. IOPS and latency comparison with RocksDB.

RocksDB Performance. We use RocksDB, a widely-deployed key-value storage system, as a real application to evaluate the performance of PINoF. With Ext4 filesystem to format the SSD block device and the default db_bench tool, we populate a 43 GB database containing 1,000,000,000 pieces of data.

Figure 8 shows the evaluation results of P99 tail latency and IOPS performance. Compared with the FIO tests, due to the high application layer overhead of RocksDB, the performance improvement of PINoF slightly reduces. The throughput of PINoF is almost 0.44 times higher than that of NoT, while it is about 15.66% higher than that of i10. In terms of latency performance, since the total number of operations is fixed, the average latency is inversely proportional to IOPS, so we use P99 tail latency to represent the system latency performance. PINoF gains about a 12.91% improvement than i10, and has a greater improvement compared with NoT. As RocksDB test is to operate on the file system while FIO is to directly read the block device, thus the additional operation overhead in RocksDB leads to this performance difference. Since the application layer and filesystem occupy more latency and limit the bandwidth, the benefits obtained from the modification of the kernel software layer are partially overshadowed.

6   Conclusion

This paper introduces the design, implementation and evaluation of PINoF, a performance isolated NVMeoF design that follows the standard NoT protocol. The experimental results show that PINoF can achieve better performance in latency, bandwidth, and throughput compared with NoT and i10.

Acknowledgements. We would like to thank the NPC reviewers for their insightful feedback. This work was supported in part by Excellent Youth Foundation of Hunan Province under Grant No.2021JJ10050 and the Science Foundation of NUDT under grant ZK21-03. Dezun Dong and Xuchao Xie are the corresponding authors.

References

1. Ahmad, I., Gulati, A., Mashtizadeh, A.: vIC: interrupt coalescing for virtual machine storage device IO. In: 2011 USENIX Annual Technical Conference, pp. 45–58 (2011)

2. Bjørling, M., Axboe, J., Nellans, D., Bonnet, P.: Linux block IO: introducing multi-queue SSD access on multi-core systems. In: Proceedings of the 6th international systems and storage conference, pp. 1–10 (2013)
3. Cheng, L., Wang, C.L.: Network performance isolation for latency-sensitive cloud applications. Future Gener. Comput. Syst. **29**(4), 1073–1084 (2013)
4. Cobb, D., Huffman, A.: Nvm express and the PCI express SSD revolution. In: Intel Developer Forum (2012)
5. Cohen, D., Talpey, T., Kanevsky, A., Cummings, U., Krause, M.: Remote direct memory access over the converged enhanced ethernet fabric: evaluating the options. In: 2009 17th IEEE Symposium on High Performance Interconnects, pp. 123–130 (2009)
6. Dragojević, A., Narayanan, D., Castro, M., Hodson, O.: Farm: fast remote memory. In: 11th USENIX Symposium on Networked Systems Design and Implementation, pp. 401–414 (2014)
7. Gao, P.X., Narayan, A., Karandikar, S., Carreira, J., HAN: network requirements for resource disaggregation. In: 12th USENIX Symposium on Operating Systems Design and Implementation, pp. 249–264 (2016)
8. Guz, Z., Li, H., Shayesteh, A., Balakrishnan, V.: Performance characterization of NVMe-over-fabrics storage disaggregation. ACM Trans. Storage **14**(4), 1–18 (2018)
9. Hwang, J., Cai, Q., Tang, A., Agarwal, R.: Tcp≈rdma: CPU-efficient remote storage access with i10. In: 17th USENIX Symposium on Networked Systems Design and Implementation, pp. 127–140 (2020)
10. Hwang, J., Vuppalapati, M., Peter, S., Agarwal, R.: Rearchitecting linux storage stack for μs latency and high throughput (2021)
11. Kaufmann, A., Stamler, T., Peter, S., Sharma, N.: TAS: TCP acceleration as an OS service. In: Proceedings of the Fourteenth EuroSys Conference, pp. 1–16 (2019)
12. Lee, M., Kang, D.H., Lee, M., Eom, Y.I.: Improving read performance by isolating multiple queues in NVMe SSDs. In: International Conference on Ubiquitous Information Management and Communication, p. 36 (2017)
13. Li, Y.T., Leith, D., Shorten, R.N.: Experimental evaluation of TCP protocols for high-speed networks. IEEE/ACM Trans. Netw. **15**(5), 1109–1122 (2007)
14. Marinos, I., Watson, R.N., Handley, M.: Network stack specialization for performance. ACM SIGCOMM Comput. Commun. Rev. **44**(4), 175–186 (2014)
15. Minturn, D.: Nvm express over fabrics. In: 11th Annual OpenFabrics International OFS Developers' Workshop (2015)
16. Nguyen, et al.: Reducing smartphone application delay through read/write isolation. In: the 13th Annual International Conference (MobiSys 15), pp. 287–300 (2015)
17. Qiao, X., Xie, X., Xiao, L.: Load-aware transmission mechanism for NVMeoF storage networks. In: International Conference on High Performance Computing and Communication (HPCCE 2021), pp. 105–112 (2022)
18. Son, Y., Kang, H., Han, H., Yeom, H.Y.: An empirical evaluation of nvm express SSD. In: International Conference on Cloud & Autonomic Computing (ICCAC 15), pp. 275–282 (2015)
19. Tai, A., Smolyar, I., Wei, M., Tsafrir, D.: Optimizing storage performance with calibrated interrupts. In: Proceedings of the 15th USENIX Symposium on Operating Systems Design and Implementation, pp. 129–145 (2021)
20. Zheng, S., Hoseinzadeh, M., Swanson, S.: Ziggurat: a tiered file system for non-volatile main memories and disks. In: 17th USENIX Conference on File and Storage Technologies, pp. 207–219 (2019)

WALOR: Workload-Driven Adaptive Layout Optimization of Raft Groups for Heterogeneous Distributed Key-Value Stores

Yangyang Wang[1,2], Yunpeng Chai[1,2(✉)], and Qingpeng Zhang[3]

[1] Key Laboratory of Data Engineering and Knowledge Engineering, MOE,
Beijing, China
ypchai@ruc.edu.cn
[2] School of Information, Renmin University of China, Beijing, China
[3] School of Data Science, City University of Hong Kong, Hong Kong, China

Abstract. In a heterogeneous cluster based on the Raft protocol, in order to solve the problem of slow performance caused by the leader on a slow node, someone proposed ALOR. However, the leader distribution of ALOR is not optimal. In this paper, we propose *Workload-driven Adaptive Layout Optimization of Raft groups* (WALOR), which changes the leader distribution of ALOR to promote the performance further by more fitting the read-write request ratio of the system's workload. Our experiments on an actual heterogeneous cluster show that, on average, WALOR improves throughput by 82.96% and 32.42% compared to the even distribution (ED) solution and ALOR, respectively.

1 Introduction

The consensus protocol ensures data consistency. As a consensus protocol, Raft [1, 2] is widely used in many distributed systems due to its ease of understanding and implementation. In a Raft group, one node will be selected as the leader, and the other nodes will be the followers. To ensure data consistency, the leader processes all read and write requests, and write requests are also sent to other followers for replication. In a Raft-based heterogeneous distributed system, if many leaders are located on slow nodes, the system's performance will be slowed down.

In order to solve this problem, ALOR [3] migrates the leader to the node with the best performance in the Raft group. However, the leader distribution of ALOR [3] is not optimal (see Sect. 2.2 for more details). In this paper, we propose *Workload-driven Adaptive Layout Optimization of Raft groups* (WALOR) based on ALOR. WALOR changes the leader distribution of ALOR to promote the performance further by more fitting the read-write request ratio of the system's workload.

We have implemented our proposed WALOR in an enterprise-grade open source distributed system (i.e. TiKV [4]) and evaluated it under the YCSB benchmark [5]. Experiments based on real heterogeneous clusters show that, on average, WALOR improves throughput by 82.96% and 32.42% compared to the even distribution (ED) solution and ALOR [3], respectively.

S. Liu and X. Wei (Eds.): NPC 2022, LNCS 13615, pp. 290–301, 2022.
https://doi.org/10.1007/978-3-031-21395-3_27

The rest of this paper is organized as follows. Section 2 introduces the background and motivation. In Sect. 3, we elaborate on our proposed WALOR in detail. Section 4 presents the evaluations, accompanied by the related work outlined in Sect. 5. Finally, we conclude this paper in Sect. 6.

2 Background and Motivation

2.1 Background

The Raft Protocol. In the previous distributed systems, the Paxos [6,7] protocol was generally used to ensure data consistency, but the Paxos protocol was particularly difficult to understand and could not be used as a good foundation for building practical systems. Until the Raft [1,2] protocol was proposed in 2014, the Raft protocol is easy to understand and adapt to the actual system. Many systems (see the website [8] for details) such as Etcd [9] and TiKV [4] use the Raft protocol.

The process of processing the read and write requests by the Raft protocol is shown in Fig. 1. In a Raft group, one node will be selected as the leader, and the other nodes will be the followers. The leader is responsible for processing read and write requests.

When a write request arrives at the leader from the user, the leader will write the request append to the local log and distribute it to the followers. When more than half of the nodes append the request log successfully, the leader will apply the request log. When the leader apply request log is completed, the result is returned to the client. Additionally, all read requests are handled by the leader to ensure data consistency. Nowadays, many distributed systems such as Spanner [10], TiDB [11], Etcd [9], and PolarDB [12] are considered in the homogeneous background, but this paper will be considered in the heterogeneous cluster.

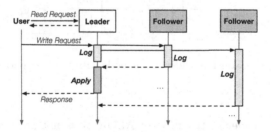

Fig. 1. The read and write process of Raft.

Multiple Raft Groups. If all data has only one Raft group to ensure data consistency, this will lack scalability, because only N nodes are needed for N copies, and more nodes will not be used. At the same time, Raft's operations are executed sequentially, without parallelism. Therefore, there are multiple Raft groups. The data is divided into many segments. Each data segment is a Raft group, and the Raft groups do not affect each other and operate in parallel. Multiple Raft groups lead to better scalability, it is no longer limited by the N-copies only N nodes. Figure 2 is an example of multiple Raft groups, which are 6 nodes, 3 copies, and 4 Raft groups. All experiments in this paper are based on multiple Raft groups, each of which is usually around 100MB in size.

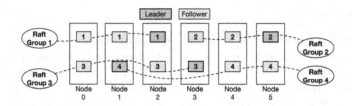

Fig. 2. An example of multiple Raft groups.

2.2 Motivation

In a heterogeneous cluster, if many leaders are located on slow nodes, the system's performance will be slowed down. To solve this problem, ALOR [3] migrates the leader to the node with the best performance in a Raft group, as shown in Fig. 3.

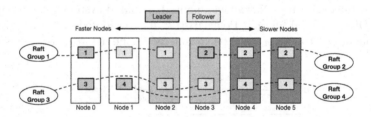

Fig. 3. ALOR [3] migrates the leader to the node with the best performance in a Raft group.

However, the leader distribution of ALOR [3] is not optimal. For example, in the case of a read-only workload, suppose the read performance of the three nodes is 40 MB/s, 30 MB/s, and 10 MB/s, respectively. ALOR will migrate all leaders to the node with the best performance, and finally get the performance of 40 MB/s. However, for the read-only workload, the optimal situation should be that the leaders should be distributed according to the proportion of read performance (i.e., 4/8, 3/8, 1/8), and finally the performance of 80 MB/s can be obtained.

3   WALOR

In this section, we propose *Workload-driven Adaptive Layout Optimization of Raft groups* (WALOR) based on ALOR. WALOR changes the leader distribution of ALOR to promote the performance further by more fitting the read-write request ratio of the system's workload.

In order to obtain the optimal leader distribution, we need to estimate the performance of the system under different system's workloads. The symbols used in the following part are summarized in Table 1.

Table 1. Symbols used in the system performance model.

Symbols	Descriptions
C_s	Concurrency of the system's workload
T_s	Throughput of the system
L_s	Average latency of the system
R_w	Ratio of write requests in the system
L_w	Average latency of write requests
L_r	Average latency of read requests
N	Number of nodes in the system
P_i	Proportion of the leader data volume of node i to the leader data volume of all nodes
L_w^i	Average write latency of node i
C_w^i	Write concurrency of node i
T_w^i	Write throughput of node i
V_i	Data volume of node i
V_s	Data volume of the system (excluding redundant replicas)
T_r	Read throughput of the system
RR	Number of read requests
$Time$	Processing time
T_r^i	Read throughput of node i
C_r	Concurrency of read requests

Little's Law [13,14] shows the relationship between throughput, latency and concurrency, as shown in Eq. (1) [15,16].

$$Concurrency = Latency \times Throughput \tag{1}$$

When the concurrency of the system's workload (i.e., C_s) is given, in order to maximize the throughput of the system (i.e., T_s), we only need to minimize the average latency of the system (i.e., L_s). Assuming R_w is the ratio of write requests in the system, the average latency of the system (i.e., L_s) is shown as

Eq. (2), where L_w is the average latency of write requests and L_r is the average latency of read requests.

$$L_s = L_w * R_w + L_r * (1 - R_w) \tag{2}$$

The Average Latency of Write Requests. We assume the number of nodes in the system is N, and the proportion of the leader data volume of node i to the leader data volume of all nodes is P_i. The average latency of write requests (i.e., L_w) is shown as Eq. (3), where L_w^i is the average write latency of node i.

$$L_w = \sum_{i=1}^{N}(P_i \times L_w^i) \tag{3}$$

When the workload of the system is only writing, the average write latency of node i (i.e., L_w^i) is shown as Eq. (4), where C_w^i is the write concurrency of node i and T_w^i is the write throughput of node i.

$$L_w^i = \frac{C_w^i}{T_w^i} \tag{4}$$

Let the data volume of node i be V_i, and the data volume of the system (excluding redundant replicas) be V_s, then the write concurrency of node i (i.e., C_w^i) is shown in Eq. (5).

$$C_w^i = C_s \times \frac{V_i}{V_s} \tag{5}$$

When the ratio of write requests in the system (i.e., R_w) is greater than 0, the average write latency of node i (i.e., L_w^i) can be calculated as Eq. (6).

$$L_w^i = \frac{C_s \times \frac{V_i}{V_s} \times R_w}{T_w^i \times R_w} = \frac{C_s \times V_i}{T_w^i \times V_s} \tag{6}$$

Combining Eqs. (3) and (6), the average latency of write requests (i.e., L_w) can be obtained, as Eq. (7) shows.

$$L_w = \sum_{i=1}^{N}(P_i \times \frac{C_s \times V_i}{T_w^i \times V_s}) \tag{7}$$

The Average Latency of Read Requests. When the workload of the system is only reading, the read throughput of the system (i.e., T_r) is shown as Eq. (8), where RR is the number of read requests and $Time$ is the processing time.

$$T_r = \frac{RR}{Time} \tag{8}$$

Assuming T_r^i is the read throughput of node i, since each node processes read requests in parallel, the processing time (i.e., $Time$) is shown as Eq. (9).

$$Time = \max(\frac{P_i \times RR}{T_r^i}), \ i \in [1, N] \tag{9}$$

Combining Eqs. (8) and (9), the read throughput of the system (i.e., T_r) is shown in Eq. (10).

$$T_r = \min(\frac{T_r^i}{P_i}), \ i \in [1, N] \tag{10}$$

According to the concurrency of read requests (i.e., C_r), the average latency of read requests (i.e., L_r) can be obtained, as Eq. (11) shows.

$$L_r = \max(\frac{P_i \times C_r}{T_r^i}), \ i \in [1, N] \tag{11}$$

When the ratio of write requests in the system (i.e., R_w) is less than 1, the average latency of read requests (i.e., L_r) can be calculated as Eq. (12).

$$L_r = \max(\frac{P_i \times C_s \times (1 - R_w)}{T_r^i \times (1 - R_w)}) = \max(\frac{P_i \times C_s}{T_r^i}), \ i \in [1, N] \tag{12}$$

The Throughput and Average Latency of the System. According to Eqs. (2), (7) and (12), the average latency of the system (i.e., L_s) is shown as Eq. (13).

$$L_s = \sum_{i=1}^{N} (P_i \times \frac{C_s \times V_i}{T_w^i \times V_s}) \times R_w + \max_{1 \leq i \leq n} (\frac{P_i \times C_s}{T_r^i}) \times (1 - R_w) \tag{13}$$

So the throughput of the system (i.e., T_s) is shown in Eq. (14), where $0 \leq P_i \leq \frac{V_i}{V_s}$ and $\sum_{i=1}^{N} P_i = 1$.

$$T_s = \frac{1}{\sum_{i=1}^{N} (P_i \times \frac{V_i}{T_w^i \times V_s}) \times R_w + \max_{1 \leq i \leq n} \frac{P_i}{T_r^i} \times (1 - R_w)} \tag{14}$$

In Eq. (14), the data volume of node i (i.e., V_i), the data volume of the system (i.e., V_s) and the ratio of write requests in the system (i.e., R_w) can be collected by the system, the write throughput of node i (i.e., T_w^i) and the read throughput of node i (i.e., T_r^i) can be pre-tested.

The problem can be summarized as finding the leader distribution (i.e., P_i) when the throughput of the system (i.e., T_s) is maximum. If the workload of the system is only writing (i.e., $R_w = 1$), in order to maximize the throughput of the system (i.e., T_s), according to Eq. (14), the larger the T_w^i, the larger the P_i. At this time, WALOR also migrates leaders to the node with the best performance (i.e., T_w^i) in Raft groups, same as ALOR.

When the workload of the system is only reading (i.e., $R_w = 0$), in order to maximize the throughput of the system (i.e., T_s), according to Eq. (14), P_i should be proportional to T_r^i. Therefore, for the read-only workload, WALOR's leaders should be distributed according to the proportion of nodes' read performance (i.e., T_r^i).

For read-write mixed workloads (i.e., $0 < R_w < 1$), according to Eq. (14), finding the optimal leader distribution (i.e., P_i) is an NP-hard problem, and an approximate optimal solution can be found through heuristics such as simulated annealing. The approximate optimal solution (i.e., P_i) obtained is the leader distribution of WALOR.

4   Evaluation

We implemented WALOR in TiKV [4].

4.1   Experimental Setup

We compare our proposed WALOR with ALOR [3] and a widely used scheme that evenly distributes (ED) the leaders of all Raft groups in a distributed system. Experiments were conducted on a cluster of 8 nodes; each of them was combined with Linux Centos 7 3.10.0, 2 GB DRAM, and 16GB NVM, where NVM was emulated by DRAM. The disks come in two solid state drives, the 280 GB Intel Optane 900p PCIe SSD (aka high-end SSD) or the 256 GB Intel SATA SSD (aka plain SSD). Among them, 6 nodes serve as TiKV nodes, 1 node serves as PD (the managing component), and 1 node runs the benchmark tool, namely go-YCSB [17].

In the experiments, all the workloads used are listed in Table 2, including an insert-only (*Load*) workload, the read-write mixed workloads consisting of 90%, 70%, 50%, 30%, or 10% of writes (i.e., *W90* ~ *W10*), and a read-only (*C*) workload. Each KV pair contains a 16 B key and a 1 KB value, and each data block has three replicas in TiKV. The requests obey the Zipf distribution.

Table 2. YCSB workloads used in the evaluation.

Workload	Write Type	Category
Load	Insert	Insert Only
W90	Update	90%write 10%read
W70	Update	70%write 30%read
W50	Update	50%write 50%read
W30	Update	30%write 70%read
W10	Update	10%write 90%read
C	/	Read Only

4.2   Overall Results

In this part, for 6 TiKV nodes in the cluster, the data of 1 node is stored on NVM, the data of 2 nodes is stored on high-end SSD, and the data of 3 nodes is stored on the slowest plain SSD. We first load 10 GB data into the cluster, then execute workloads W90, W70, W50, W30, W10, and C, respectively, accessing 10 GB data each.

As Fig. 4 plots, WALOR has higher throughput than both ED and ALOR. For all workloads, WALOR improves the throughput by 72.6% to 101.4% compared to ED, and WALOR also has a greater improvement than ALOR under read-dominant workloads (i.e., W30, W10, and C). On average, WALOR increased the throughput by 82.96% compared with ED, and increased the throughput by 32.42% compared with ALOR. Figure 5 exhibits the average latency of ED, ALOR, and WALOR. For all workloads, WALOR always has lower latency than both ED and ALOR. On average, WALOR reduces the latency by 45.32% compared with ED, and reduces the latency by 19.82% compared with ALOR.

Compared with the ED scheme suitable for homogeneous distributed systems, WALOR appropriately places more leaders on fast nodes according to the heterogeneous capabilities of the nodes. In fact, the actual load balancing of heterogeneous systems is improved in combination with WALOR, resulting in higher throughput. Compared with the ALOR scheme, WALOR has better leader distribution and therefore better performance.

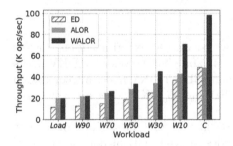

Fig. 4. Overall throughput.   **Fig. 5.** Overall latency.

4.3   Impacts of Different Heterogeneous Configurations

In this section, we evaluate WALOR under different heterogeneous configurations, including two high-end SSDs and four plain SSDs (i.e., 2H4P), one NVM, two high-end SSDs and three plain SSDs (i.e., 1N2H3P), two NVMs, two high-end SSDs and two plain SSDs (i.e., 2N2H2P), and three NVMs, two high-end

SSDs and one plain SSD (i.e., 3N2H1P). We adopt the read/write-balanced workload, i.e., *Workload A (W50)*, to perform the experiments. Specifically, we first load 10 GB data into the cluster, then execute *Workload A* of 10GB data. The throughput and the latencies of performing *Workload A* are exhibited in Figs. 6 and 7, respectively.

In all configurations, WALOR has improved performance compared to ALOR and ED. In 2N2H2P and 3N2H1P configurations, WALOR is more significantly improved than ALOR, because WALOR can take advantage of the performance of most fast nodes, while ALOR can only take advantage of the performance of a small number of fast nodes.

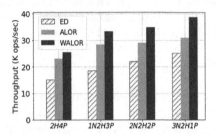

Fig. 6. Throughput for different heterogeneous configurations.

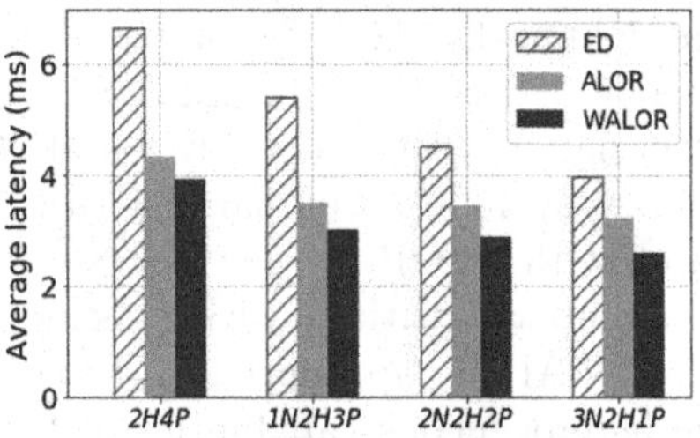

Fig. 7. Latency for different heterogeneous configurations.

4.4 Impacts of System Scale

To evaluate the scalability of WALOR, we conducted experiments on clusters with different numbers of TiKV nodes (i.e. 4, 5 or 6 TiKV nodes). 4 TiKV nodes are configured as 1 high-end SSD and 3 plain SSDs, 5 TiKV nodes are configured as 1 NVM, 1 high-end SSD, and 3 plain SSDs, and 6 TiKV nodes are configured as 1 NVM, 2 high-end SSDs and 3 plain SSDs.

For 6 TiKV nodes, we write 10 GB of data to the cluster; proportionally, we write 8.33 GB of data to 5 TiKV nodes and 6.67 GB of data to 4 TiKV nodes. Then we perform *Workload A* of 10 GB, 8.33 GB, and 6.67 GB on the three clusters, respectively. The throughput and latency results of performing *Workload A* are exhibited in Figs. 8 and 9, respectively. The performance of WALOR, ALOR, and ED increases as the number of cluster nodes increases. Compared with ED and ALOR, WALOR exhibits stable performance advantages at various system scales.

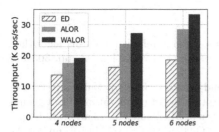

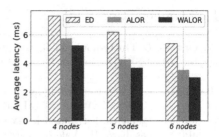

Fig. 8. Throughput for different system scales.

Fig. 9. Latency for different system scales.

5 Related Work

Raft/Paxos. Paxos-based APUS [18] and Mu [19] combine RDMA to reduce network transmission latency. ParallelRaft [20] allows logs to be executed in parallel, breaking Raft's log is a continuous assumption, increasing concurrency, and ensuring consistency through additional restrictions. Some works combine Raft with Software Defined Networking (SDN) [21–23]. In order to solve the consensus problem of the Byzantine scene, BFTRaft [24] is proposed.

Heterogeneous. Dadheech et al. [25] try to increase the performance of Hadoop-based heterogeneous clusters. Zhang et al. considered heterogeneous CPU-GPU and proposed Mega-KV [26], a distributed in-memory key-value storage system on heterogeneous CPU-GPU clusters. Strata [27] and OctopusFS [28] did a heterogeneous situation with multiple devices on one node.

This paper focuses on the performance optimization of Raft-based heterogeneous distributed storage systems.

6 Conclusion

In this section, we summarize the contributions of this paper:

(1) We found that the leader distribution of ALOR [3] is not optimal in heterogeneous clusters.
(2) We propose WALOR, which changes the leader distribution of ALOR to promote the performance further by more fitting the read-write request ratio of the system's workload.
(3) Experiments based on real heterogeneous clusters show that WALOR can increase throughput by 82.96% and 32.42% compared to the even distribution (ED) solution and ALOR, respectively.

Acknowledgement. This work is supported by the National Key Research and Development Program of China (No. 2019YFE0198600), National Natural Science Foundation of China (No. 61972402, 61972275, and 61732014).

References

1. Ongaro, D, Ousterhout, J.: In search of an understandable consensus algorithm. In: 2014 USENIX Annual Technical Conference (USENIXATC 14), pp. 305–319 (2014)
2. Ongaro, D.: Consensus: bridging theory and practice. Stanford University (2014)
3. Wang, Y., Chai, Y., Wang, X.: ALOR: adaptive layout optimization of raft groups for heterogeneous distributed key-Value stores. In: Zhang, F., Zhai, J., Snir, M., Jin, H., Kasahara, H., Valero, M. (eds.) NPC 2018. LNCS, vol. 11276, pp. 13–26. Springer, Cham (2018). https://doi.org/10.1007/978-3-030-05677-3_2
4. TiKV. https://github.com/tikv/tikv (2022)
5. Cooper, B.F., et al.: Benchmarking cloud serving systems with YCSB. In: Proceedings of the 1st ACM symposium on Cloud computing, pp. 143–154. ACM (2010)
6. Lamport, L.: The part-time parliament. ACM Trans. Comput. Syst. (TOCS) **16**(2), 133–169 (1998)
7. Lamport, L.: Paxos made simple. ACM SIGACT News **32**(4), 18–25 (2001)
8. Where can I get Raft? https://raft.github.io/#implementations (2022)
9. Etcd. https://github.com/etcd-io/etcd (2022)
10. Corbett, J.C., Dean, J., Epstein, M., et al.: Spanner: google's globally distributed database. ACM Trans. Comput. Syst. (TOCS) **31**(3), 1–22 (2013)
11. Huang, D., et al.: TiDB: a Raft-based HTAP database. Proc. of the VLDB Endowment **13**(12), 3072–3084 (2020)
12. Cao, W., et al.: POLARDB meets computational storage: efficiently support analytical workloads in cloud-native relational database. In: FAST (2020)
13. Little, J.D.C.: A proof for the queuing formula: L= λW. Oper. Res. **9**(3), 383–387 (1961)
14. Little, J.D.C.: OR FORUM-Little's Law as viewed on its 50th anniversary. Oper. Res. **59**(3), 536–549 (2011)
15. Liu, G., Wang, S., Bao, Y.: SEER: a time prediction model for CNNs from GPU kernel's view. In: 2021 30th International Conference on Parallel Architectures and Compilation Techniques (PACT), pp. 173–185. In: IEEE (2021)
16. Volkov, V.: A microbenchmark to study GPU performance models. ACM SIGPLAN Not. **53**(1), 421–422 (2018)
17. go-ycsb. https://github.com/pingcap/go-ycsb (2022)
18. Wang, C., et al.: Apus: fast and scalable PAXOS on RDMA In: Proceedings of the 2017 Symposium on Cloud Computing, pp. 94–107. ACM (2017)
19. Aguilera, M.K., et al.: Microsecond consensus for microsecond applications. In: Operating Systems Design and Implementation. USENIX ASSOC (2020)
20. Cao, W., Liu, Z., Wang, P., et al.: PolarFS: an ultra-low latency and failure resilient distributed file system for shared storage cloud database. Proc. VLDB Endowment **11**(12), 1849–1862 (2018)
21. Sakic, E., Kellerer, W.: Response time and availability study of RAFT consensus in distributed SDN control plane. IEEE Trans. Netw. Serv. Manag. **15**(1), 304–318 (2017)
22. Zhang, Y., et al.: When raft meets SDN: how to elect a leader and reach consensus in an unruly network. In: Proceedings of the First Asia-Pacific Workshop on Networking, pp. 1–7. ACM (2017)
23. Kim, T., et al.: Load balancing on distributed datastore in opendaylight SDN controller cluster. In: 2017 IEEE Conference on Network Softwarization (NetSoft), pp. 1–3. IEEE (2017)

24. Copeland, C., Zhong, H.: Tangaroa: a byzantine fault tolerant raft (2016)
25. Dadheech, P., et, al.: Performance improvement of heterogeneous cluster of big data using query optimization and mapreduce. In: International Conference on Information Management and Machine Intelligence (ICIMMI 2019) (2020)
26. Yuan, Y., et al.: A distributed in-memory key-value store system on heterogeneous CPU-GPU cluster. VLDB J. **26**(5), 729–750 (2017)
27. Kwon, Y., et al.: Strata: a cross media file system. In: The 26th Symposium (2017)
28. Kakoulli, E., Herodotou, H.: OctopusFS: a distributed file system with tiered storage management. In: The 2017 ACM International Conference. ACM (2017)

Efficient Data Placement for Zoned Namespaces (ZNS) SSDs

Hongtao Wang[1], Yang Liu[1], Peiquan Jin[1(✉)], Mingchen Lu[1],
Xiangyu Zhuang[1], Yuanjing Lin[2], and Kuankuan Guo[2]

[1] University of Science and Technology of China, Hefei, China
`jpq@ustc.edu.cn`
[2] ByteDance Inc., Beijing, China
{`linyuanjin,guokuankuan`}`@bytedance.com`

Abstract. ZNS SSDs (Zone Namespaces SSDs) are a new type of SSDs. It allows the entire SSD space to be divided into multiple zones, and only sequential writes are allowed within each zone. ZNS SSDs effectively improve the read/write throughput of SSDS and reduce write magnification. However, the sequential write and zone partitioning of ZNS SSDs pose challenges to existing storage allocation strategies. In this paper, we propose a new ZNS SSD-aware data placement algorithm. Specifically, the inserted and modified data is placed according to the lifetime of the data, and the variance of the data lifetime in each zone is used for management and garbage collection based on the calculation of the conventional garbage collection strategy. Experiments show that the lifetime-based insertion algorithm has a great improvement in stability compared with the average insertion and polling insertion algorithm, and the time performance is slightly reduced due to the calculation overhead of the lifetime. The lifetime variance-aware garbage collection algorithm is 9% better than the conventional garbage collection algorithm in terms of time performance and is more stable.

Keywords: ZNS SSD · Data placement · Garbage collection · Lifetime

1 Introduction

Recently, ZNS SSD (Zone Namespaces Solid State Drives, ZNS SSD) has gained widespread attention from industry and academia [4,5,7,9,12,13]. ZNS SSD is a new type of SSD. ZNS SSD abstracts the disk into different zones based on spatial distribution, and the zones can only be written sequentially internally. The host manages the disk I/O based on the abstracted interface. This division allows data that fail almost simultaneously to be placed together, reducing the number of write amplifications and improving the performance and longevity of the SSD. Compared with traditional SSD, which uses Flash Translation Layer (FTL) to process storage units and requires operations such as erasing before writing, ZNS SSD reduces the use of DRAM, alleviates the over-provisioning of SSD, and improves the utilization of SSD [11,13].

© IFIP International Federation for Information Processing 2022
Published by Springer Nature Switzerland AG 2022
S. Liu and X. Wei (Eds.): NPC 2022, LNCS 13615, pp. 302–314, 2022.
https://doi.org/10.1007/978-3-031-21395-3_28

While the ZNS SSD has significant advantages, its limitations (e.g., sequential writing and zone partitioning) also challenge existing storage allocation and garbage collection strategies. In terms of storage allocation, ZNS SSD requires that the feature of only sequential writing within the zone must be taken into account when inserting data, namely ZNS-friendliness. Since the zone can not be written randomly, the data within the zone can only be updated offsite, which requires us to perform zone garbage collection operations periodically. The garbage collection operation involves a reset of the whole zone, which introduces a high data migration cost if there is a large amount of valid data in the zone. Therefore, how to reduce the cost of zone garbage collection and avoid the impact of garbage collection on the stability of system performance is another crucial issue that must be considered for data management on ZNS SSDs.

In this paper, we present an efficient ZNS SSD-aware data placement mechanism to address the problems of data storage allocation and garbage collection on ZNS SSDs. Briefly, we make the following contributions in this paper.

- To address the requirement of ZNS friendliness for ZNS SSD data writes, we treat the process from data insertion to garbage collection as its lifetime, and propose a method to calculate the data lifetime based on the access pattern and workload characteristics of the data, and then propose a lifetime-based data insertion algorithm.
- To reduce the cost of zone garbage collection, based on the observation that the lifetime of data differs significantly in different workload environments, we propose a data lifetime variance-aware zone collection algorithm to reduce the cost of data migration during zone collection.
- We conducted an experimental validation using the ZNS SSD simulator null_blk with the libzbd library (since commercial ZNS SSDs are not yet available). The results show that our proposed lifetime-based data insertion algorithm has a more stable insertion performance compared to two baseline methods (average insertion and polled insertion), and the proposed lifetime variance-aware garbage collection algorithm has a 9% improvement in time performance compared with conventional algorithms.

The rest of this paper is organized as follows. Section 2 overviews related work. Section 3 presents the design of the ZNS SSD-aware data placement mechanism. Section 4 presents the experimental results, and finally, Sect. 5 concludes the paper and discusses future work.

2   Relate Work

Traditional SSDs are managed using FTL, and this information is transparent to the host, while ZNS SSDs use the host to manage the SSD, and can then use this information for more intelligent management, such as ZNS SSDs can choose where to place data, and can perform garbage collection and loss balancing [13].

Data placement strategies in traditional SSDs [8], such as the DFTL strategy used by FTL (Flash Translation Layer) for page-based storage or the SAST (Set-Associative Sector Translation) strategy used for log-based storage, are based on segments (2MB or 4MB) rather than zone (0.5GB or 1GB) for data placement and garbage collection, and porting these policies directly to ZNS SSDs would result in longer latency and would not reflect the features of ZNS SSD partition management.

Since only sequential writes are possible within the zone, many applications and systems developed based on the traditional SSD abstraction interface cannot be directly applied to ZNS SSDs. In addition, since ZNS SSD removes the in-device garbage collection, it requires users to design their own garbage collection mechanism, which brings additional complexity. Han et al. took the ZNS interface one step further and proposed the ZNS+ interface [7]. ZNS+ is an LFS-aware ZNS interface that takes a user-defined copy of the valid data generated by garbage collection placed inside the device for this purpose, thus reducing I/O operations and improving the efficiency of file system garbage collection. Choi et al. proposed a new approach for designing the garbage collection required when using ZNS SSDs [6]. They suggested fine-grained garbage collection for ZNS SSDs and storing fine-grained data in different partitions based on data hotness.

Bjørling et al. developed the ZenFS file system based on ZNS SSDs to adapt to the RocksDB file interface, which has been successfully submitted to the RocksDB community [5]. ZenFS is a file system plugin for RocksDB that uses the RocksDB interface to place files into zones on a raw zoned block device. By separating files into zones and utilizing "write lifetime hints" to co-locate data of similar lifetimes, ZenFS can reduce system write amplification as compared to regular file systems on conventional block devices [3].

3   ZNS SSD-Aware Data Placement

Since garbage collection of ZNS SSDs is costly and affects normal read and write operations, the placement of data with different lifetimes affects the garbage collection process. Also, as the workload changes, the data lifetime changes, and timely adjustments need to be made to the data placement. Therefore, we focus on two critical problems, namely the ZNS SSD-aware data insertion problem and the ZNS SSD-aware garbage collection problem, and propose an insertion policy and garbage collection policy based on the data lifetime.

3.1   Lifetime-Based Data Insertion

The ZNS SSD-aware data insertion algorithm needs to use the information about the lifetime of the data to assign the data to be inserted to the best zone, and it needs to optimize the data placement by calling garbage collection according to the changing workload.

When data is inserted into the SSD, the algorithm needs to select the right zone to write it to. This is based on information about the lifetime of the key and the lifetime of the data already in the zone.

Definition 1. *Key Lifetime. For a key record, the lifetime of the corresponding key is the number of updates to other keys since the last write to that key.*

Thus, when an update or deletion is made to a key, the lifetime value of other keys is added by 1, and the corresponding lifetime value of that key becomes 0. A key with a small lifetime value means its value has a short validity period under this workload. The lifetime of data not only effectively characterizes the lifetime of a certain data but also eliminates the need for more memory overhead to keep redundant data history information and allows updating the classification of data lifetime according to changing workloads. To ensure the timeliness of the record's lifetime, we set the maximum lifetime of a key. The lifetime of newly inserted key data is also set to the maximum lifetime since there is no previous record.

After defining the lifetime of the data, we can go on to define the lifetime of the page and the lifetime of the zone on this basis.

Definition 2. *Page Lifetime. The lifetime of a page is defined as the lifetime of the key with the smallest lifetime on that page.*

This is because when the key with the shortest lifetime in the page is changed, the page needs to be read out completely and the block in which the page is located is marked as invalid.

Definition 3. *Zone Lifetime. The lifetime of a zone is defined as the average of the lifetimes of all pages in the zone.*

As shown in Fig. 1, when a page is inserted, the zone with the smallest difference between the lifetime and the lifetime of the page is selected for insertion, which ensures that data with similar lifetimes are stored in the same zone in general and these data will become invalid at a similar time in the future, increasing the proportion of invalid blocks recovered in a single garbage collection and reducing the number of garbage collections per unit of time.

During the initialization process, all zones are reset and restored to the initial state. The zone lifetime record and the garbage collection queue are cleared. Data such as the empty rate and garbage rate of each zone are set to the initial state.

After inserting or modifying a zone, the lifetime update of the key and the zone is required. If a key is modified, add 1 to the lifetime of the other keys in the zone unless it has reached its maximum lifetime. The lifetime of the zone is updated to the average of the lifetime of each page, the lifetime of the block where the inserted page is located is updated to the lifetime of the page, and the lifetime of the zone where it is located is the average of the valid blocks.

When there is data insertion, the lifetime of the inserted page is first taken as the lifetime of the inserted page based on the key with the shortest lifetime among the lifetime of the keys in the inserted page. If the lifetime record of a zone in ZNS SSD is less at this time and there is no valid information to judge the page storage, it is stored equally according to the empty rate of the zone; otherwise, a zone closest to the lifetime of the inserted page is selected for storage

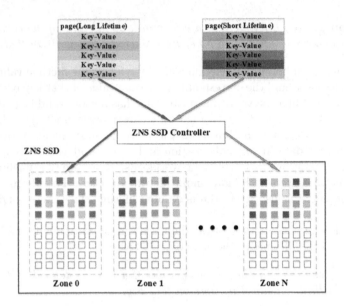

Fig. 1. Illustration of the data insertion based on lifetime

and the block address for storage is returned. After depositing, the lifetime of this zone and the inserted key are updated, and finally, the garbage collection detection algorithm is called. Algorithm 1 shows the process of data insertion.

3.2 Lifetime Variance-Aware Garbage Collection

Another issue with data storage management is garbage collection. Due to the sequential write limitation of the ZNS SSD, the write pointer inside the zone can only move backward, and when data changes, it cannot be updated in place, but only the block that originally held that data is marked as invalid, and then the new data is written. This design makes the garbage rate of the zone grow very fast when the ZNS SSD faces frequent modifications and deletions. So when the empty rate of the zone decreases and the garbage rate increases, a garbage collection operation needs to be called to reclaim the invalid blocks and free up space to store more data. A conventional garbage collection algorithm is called when there is not enough space in the SSD, and the performance improves after adding a garbage collection queue [10].

When the workload changes, the data layout arranged according to the previous workload becomes invalid, which is reflected in the change in the lifetime of the key values, resulting in the lifetime of the pages within the zone becoming more different. This information can be reflected by the variance of the lifetime of the pages within the zone. When the variance is too large, the average value of the intra-zone page lifetime to characterize the lifetime of the zone becomes no longer accurate. Then, it is necessary to garbage collect the zone with a large

---

Algorithm 1: Insert-Page

Data: the *page* to to inserted, the *keySet* of the page, the *OP* that causes an insertion

Result: the block address where the insert page stores

1 pageLifetime ← max(keyLifetime[i in keySet]);
2 **if** *avg(zoneEmptyTable)* <*0.2* **then**
3 | zoneIn ← maxIndex(zoneEmptyTable[i]);
4 **else**
5 | zoneIn ← minIndex(| pageLifetime-zoneLifetime[i] |);
6 **end**
7 blockAddr=writePage(page,zoneIn);
8 OP = ADD;
9 refreshLifetime(page, pageLifetime, blockAddr, zoneIn, OP);
10 GCDetect();
11 **return** blockAddr;

Algorithm 2: Garbage-Collection

---

1 **for** *zone in gcQueue* **do**
2 | **for** *block in zone and block is valid* **do**
3 | | key, value ← readPage(block);
4 | | **if** *data read is large enough to form a page* **then**
5 | | | page ← kv2pages(keyRead, valueRead);
6 | | | InsertPage(page, keyRead);
7 | | **end**
8 | | blockStatus ← empty;
9 | **end**
10 | clear zoneLifetime[zone];
11 **end**
12 clear gcQueue;

---

variance to ensure the effectiveness of the data insertion algorithm. Therefore, the lifetime variance of a zone is added to the conditions for triggering garbage collection, and the lifetime of a key under the current workload is used to redistribute data.

Algorithm 2 gives the process of garbage collection. When garbage collection is triggered, the valid blocks are read and reorganized into new data pages according to the status of the blocks in the recovered zone, and the data insertion algorithm is called to write back to the SSD. When data insertion or modification is performed, the state parameters of the zone are used to determine whether each zone needs to be garbage collected, and the zone that needs to be garbage collected is added to the garbage collection queue *gcQueue*. The zone is detected when its empty rate falls below the threshold *se*, and if the garbage rate of the zone reaches *sg* or when the lifetime variance of the zone is greater than *sl*, the zone is added to the garbage collection queue; and when the zone in the garbage collection queue is greater than

Table 1. Parameters of the GC-Detect algorithm

Parameter	Definition
sl	Lifetime variance threshold for triggering garbage collection
sg	Garbage rate of available zone space
se	Empty rate of the zone for triggering garbage collection
gl	Length of the garbage collection queue

Algorithm 3: GC-Detect

---

1 getZoneEmptyRate(zoneEmptyTable);
2 getZoneGarbageRate(zoneGarbageRateTable);
3 **for** *zone in all zones* **do**
4   **if** *zoneEmptyTable[zone]* $<se$ **then**
5   **if** *zoneGarbageRateTable[zone]* $>sg$ *or LifetimeVarience(zone)* $>sl$ **then**
6   add zone into gcQueue;
7   **end**
8   **end**
9 **end**
10 **if** *len(gcQueue)* $>gl$ **then**
11   GarbageCollection();
12 **end**

---

the upper limit gl of the garbage collection queue, the garbage collection is triggered. These thresholds are shown in Table 1.

At the end of the data insertion process, we need to determine whether we need to perform a garbage collection operation. This process is implemented by the GC-Detect algorithm, which is shown in Algorithm 3.

4 Performance Evaluation

4.1 Setting

Since there is no commercially available ZNS SSD, this paper uses the ZNS SSD emulator null_blk [2] with libzbd [1] library to simulate ZNS SSDs. All experiments were conducted on a server with an Intel(R) Xeon(R) CPU E5-2620 v4 @ 2.10GHz. The operating system is Ubuntu with kernel version 5.4.0 and GCC version 9.3.0. The parameters of the simulated ZNS SSDs are shown in Table 2.

We use a self-made workload to test the ZNS SSD-aware data placement algorithm. The length of keys in the workload is 4 bytes, ranging from 0 to $2^{20} - 1$. There are 4×10^6 write operations in the workload, of which 50% are update operations (including modification and deletion), of which 20% are updates to 5% of the hot data, and the hot data changes randomly after a period of time, for a total of changes 10 times, so as to simulate the workload

Table 2. Parameters of the Simulated ZNS SSD

Parameter	Description
Zone Model	Host-Managed
Capacity	1.047 G
Section Size	512 Bytes
Zone Number	16
Zone Size	64 MB

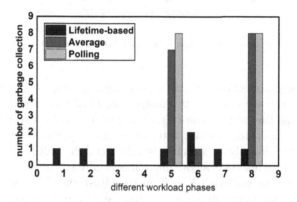

Fig. 2. Number of garbage collections of different insertion algorithms.

changes. The thresholds involved in this experiment are first experimented with to analyze their impact on the performance and stability of this algorithm. Since ZNS SSD-aware data placement is optimized for both data insertion and garbage collection, the comparison experiment is divided into two parts, the first part replaces data insertion with conventional average insertion and polled insertion, and the second part sets the trigger condition of garbage collection to empty rate and garbage rate only, without adding the determination of lifetime variance.

4.2 Results

In this section, we report the experimental results in terms of various metrics, including insertion performance, garbage collection performance, and the impact of the thresholds.

Insertion Performance. In this part, we compare the performance differences between data insertion based on lifetime and polling insertion based on average insert. Garbage collection strategies are all lifetime variance-aware garbage collection strategies, $sg = 0.4$, $se = 0.4$, $sl = 6000$, $gl = 2$.

As shown in Fig. 2, the lifetime-based data insertion algorithm performs 50% less garbage collection compared to average insertion and polled insertion, and

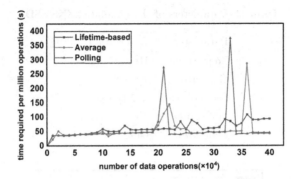

Fig. 3. Performance fluctuations of different insertion algorithms.

50% less garbage collection compared to regular garbage collection. From the figure, we can also see that the two simple algorithms do not classify the data according to the lifetime, so the trigger of garbage collection operation is the low empty rate and high garbage rate, so the garbage collection operation will be triggered continuously at a certain stage to collect multiple zones; while the lifetime-based data insertion algorithm will basically trigger a garbage collection operation when the workload is shifted to adjust the data distribution. The lifetime-based data insertion algorithm basically triggers a garbage collection operation to adjust the data distribution when the workload is shifted, so that the ZNS SSD can be inserted and modified in a stable manner even facing changing workloads.

As shown in Fig. 3, in terms of total runtime, the ZNS SSD-aware data placement algorithm increases the runtime by 11.7% and 8.0% compared to the average placement and polled placement, 2497 s,s, 2234 s,s, and 2311 s,s, respectively, due to the more concentrated garbage collection of these two algorithms, which leads to unstable fluctuations in The lifetime-based insertion algorithm has fewer garbage collections because it can identify the variation of each workload, which makes the operation execution more stable.

Performance of Garbage Collection. As shown in Fig. 4, the lifetime variance-aware garbage collection algorithm is more stable when the zone empty rate decreases. We can see in Fig. 5 that lifetime variance-aware garbage collection is more stable than conventional garbage collection, adjusting the timing of garbage collection according to workload changes, making it more stable to perform data operations when the ZNS SSD empty rate decreases.

On ZNS SSDs with Different Sizes. The parameters of the ZNS SSD simulation device used in the above experiments are shown in Table 2, and since the commercial ZNS SSD is not yet available to predict its specific parameters, we tested the operation of the algorithm for different ZNS SSD sizes with the same total capacity. As shown in Fig. 6, when the number of zones of ZNS SSD is too

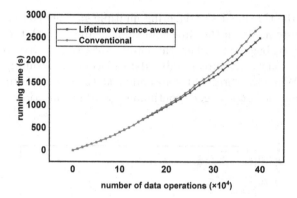

Fig. 4. Performance of different garbage collection algorithms.

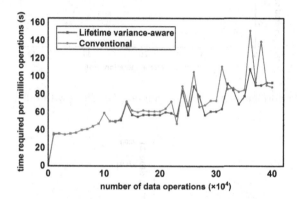

Fig. 5. Performance fluctuations of different garbage collection algorithms.

small, garbage collection is basically triggered by the change of empty rate and garbage rate, which will show relatively large and periodic fluctuations; while when the number of zones is larger than 16, the algorithm classifies the zones more accurately and is more sensitive to the change of lifetime variance, which makes the ZNS SSD run under changing workloads more stable under changing workloads.

Impact of the Thresholds. The thresholds involved in the garbage collection detection algorithm were first tested experimentally, as shown in Fig. 7(a) and Fig. 7(b), where the highest time performance and stability were achieved when the garbage rate se of the non-empty part of the zone triggering garbage collection and the empty rate se of the zone were both controlled at 40%.

As shown in Fig. 7(c), the time performance is better when the threshold sl is below 3000, but due to the low threshold of lifetime variance, when the empty rate of ZNS SSD is low, the valid blocks recovered in one garbage collection operation are inserted into other zone will cause the lifetime variance of this zone to reach the threshold *sl*, triggering multiple garbage collection operations and causing system. When the threshold value is above 5000, the ZNS SSD has a higher total garbage rate when the empty rate is low due to the inability to identify the zone with unreasonable data placement, resulting in poor time performance. While the threshold is around 4000, the time performance becomes better because it does not trigger continuous garbage collections.

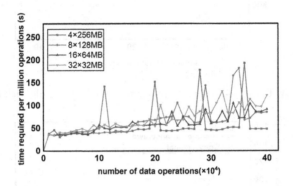

Fig. 6. Performance of our algorithm on ZNS SSDs with different sizes.

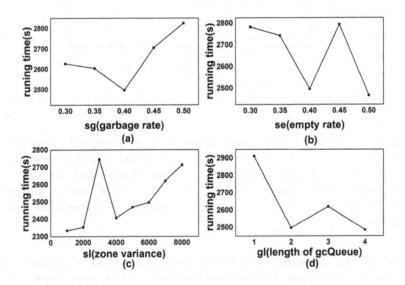

Fig. 7. Impact of the thresholds on the GC-Detect algorithm

Finally, as shown in Fig. 7(d), recycling multiple zones together can significantly improve the time performance. When the garbage collection queue becomes longer, the algorithm timely identifies that the lifetime variance of individual zone has changed, and it will not perform garbage collection operation in time to achieve the goal of optimal data placement, so when the garbage collection queue is set to 2, the system has the best performance and stability.

Memory Cost. In this experiment, we measure the additional memory cost for recording the lifetime of keys, pages, and zones. The total memory consumption is about 8.4 MB, which not a significant cost compared to today's memory space. Note that the size of the recorded data is only affected by the key ranges of the data, meaning that the increase of the ZNS SSD's size will not lead to the increase of memory cost.

5 Conclusion

This paper studied the ZNS SSD-aware data storage management problem and proposed a ZNS SSD-aware data insertion algorithm and garbage collection strategy based on data lifetime. Experiments show that the performance and stability of our proposed algorithm are best when the garbage rate of the non-empty part of the zone triggering garbage collection is 40% compared with the empty rate of the zone. Meanwhile, the lifetime-based insertion algorithm has a significant improvement in stability over the average insertion and polled insertion algorithms, and the lifetime variance-aware garbage collection algorithm outperforms the conventional algorithm.

Acknowledgements. This paper is supported by the National Science Foundation of China (62072419) and ByteDance Inc. Peiquan Jin is the corresponding author of the paper.

References

1. libzbd. https://github.com/westerndigitalcorporation/libzbd (2022)
2. null_blk. https://www.kernel.org/doc/Documentation/block/null_blk.txt (2022)
3. Zoned storage. http://zonedstorage.io (2022)
4. Bae, H., Kim, J., Kwon, M., Jung, M.: What you can't forget: exploiting parallelism for zoned namespaces. In: HotStorage, pp. 79–85 (2022)
5. Bjørling, M., et al.: ZNS: avoiding the block interface tax for flash-based SSDs. In: ATC, pp. 689–703 (2021)
6. Choi, G., Lee, K., Oh, M., Choi, J., Jhin, J., Oh, Y.: A new LSM-style garbage collection scheme for ZNS SSDs. In: HotStorage (2020)
7. Han, K., Gwak, H., Shin, D., Hwang, J.: ZNS+: advanced zoned namespace interface for supporting in-storage zone compaction. In: OSDI, pp. 147–162 (2021)
8. Jin, P., Ou, Y., Härder, T., Li, Z.: AD-LRU: an efficient buffer replacement algorithm for flash-based databases. Data Knowl. Eng. **72**, 83–102 (2012)
9. Jin, P., Zhuang, X., Luo, Y., Lu, M.: Exploring index structures for zoned namespaces SSDs. In: IEEE Big Data, pp. 5919–5922 (2021)
10. Lee, H., Lee, C., Lee, S., Kim, Y.: Compaction-aware zone allocation for LSM based key-value store on ZNS SSDs. In: HotStorage, pp. 93–99 (2022)

11. Maheshwari, U.: From blocks to rocks: a natural extension of zoned namespaces. In: HotStorage (2021)
12. Purandare, D.R., Wilcox, P., Litz, H., Finkelstein, S.: Append is near: log-based data management on ZNS SSDs. In: CIDR (2022)
13. Shin, H., Oh, M., Choi, G., Choi, J.: Exploring performance characteristics of ZNS SSDs: observation and implication. In: NVMSA, pp. 1–5 (2020)

SchedP: I/O-aware Job Scheduling
in Large-Scale Production HPC Systems

Kaiyue Wu, Jianwen Wei[✉], and James Lin

High Performance Computing Center, Shanghai Jiao Tong University,
Shanghai, China
{kaiyuewu,weijianwen,james}@sjtu.edu.cn

Abstract. Job schedulers on High Performance Computing systems can serve more purposes than just maximising computing resource utilisation if they are equipped with more awareness on other aspects of the system. In this work, we focus on making a job scheduler I/O-aware to assist system I/O management. We propose SchedP as the first practical effort on I/O-aware job scheduling that can work in production HPC environment. It trains neural network model to predict each job's I/O pattern, then makes a delay decision if starting a job right away will lead to I/O congestion in the system. We integrate it into Slurm and performed evaluations with real HPC workloads in production environment for about a month. The results show: a) the neural network model of SchedP reached over 99% for both training and test accuracy on predicting jobs' I/O patterns; b) SchedP has obvious effect on alleviating system I/O contention.

Keywords: Job scheduling · I/O pattern prediction · I/O-aware job scheduling · Machine learning

1   Introduction

High Performance Computing (HPC) systems adopt job schedulers to coordinate incoming jobs and manage system resources. As a job comes into the system, it will be assigned a priority and queued in a priority queue, then be allocated the requested resources when it is its turn (based on the priority and scheduling preference), also be monitored throughout its lifetime. All these operations are conducted by a job scheduler. Conventional job schedulers on production HPC systems only concentrate on optimising computing resource utilisation and job throughput as their scheduling goals [2]. However, a lot more issues can be considered at a job scheduler, such as system power usage or I/O performance. It is at the entrance of the system and can act proactively at very early stage to prevent potential problems through coordinating the submitted jobs in a way with more awareness, rather than dealing with ongoing problems as the other parts of the system do at later stages. Thus it is very meaningful to augment a job scheduler to be for example power-aware or I/O-aware to assist system management from those aspects.

© IFIP International Federation for Information Processing 2022
Published by Springer Nature Switzerland AG 2022
S. Liu and X. Wei (Eds.): NPC 2022, LNCS 13615, pp. 315–326, 2022.
https://doi.org/10.1007/978-3-031-21395-3_29

In this work, we target I/O-awareness in a job scheduler. I/O performance is an important part of the overall system performance, and has been studied with various methods [4–6]. In today's production HPC systems, it is still a bottleneck. As the computation capability continues to break the record (Fugaku reaching 442.01 PFLOPS since November 2020), I/O contention has been slowing the system down. Even users can sense the problem (system gets stuck) when the system is overwhelmed by large amounts of I/O. Therefore, we propose to augment job scheduler with I/O-awareness to assist system I/O management, and enable this functionality in real production environment to show its practicality over theoretical research.

This work, which we call SchedP, leverages machine learning method to predict the I/O pattern of each job that enters the system with a submission script, then checks if it will cause I/O contention in the system to start the job right away, and decides whether to delay it based on the check. It is integrated into a real job scheduler in production environment, which is Slurm scheduling system on the *Pi 2.0* HPC cluster at Shanghai Jiao Tong University with 656 CPU computing nodes and 8 GPU computing nodes. This takes a big step further than simulations, as we need to stay practical in our work and consider real-world issues. We developed and set up the necessary software stack on the cluster to enable SchedP, including Timescale database, Slurm components and LDMS monitoring system. The evaluation results show that SchedP's machine learning model reached high accuracy in predicting jobs' I/O patterns, and SchedP is able to alleviate system I/O contention under high I/O pressure.

The main contributions of SchedP are:

- We propose the first per-job I/O pattern prediction mechanism based solely on job scripts. It leverages convolutional neural network to predict the bursty I/O pattern of each job that enters HPC system with a submission script.
- We propose a pre-schedule mechanism which leverages the per-job I/O pattern predictions to enable I/O-aware job scheduling.
- We make the first effort to enable I/O-aware job scheduling in production HPC environment through integrating SchedP into Slurm, proving the practicality of SchedP.

2 Related Work

There are a series of work in which the prediction problem of per-job resource consumption started to be investigated. Different from the common case where the prediction is performed at application level, they focus on discovering the resource consumption of each specific job. McKenna et al. [8] brought in the idea of predicting per-job runtime statistics and I/O counters with historical data. The input to the model was features extracted from job scripts and output was three items, a job's runtime, total bytes read and total bytes written. Later, Wyatt et al. [10] took a big step ahead in which job scripts were transformed into image-like data as a whole instead of being parsed to serve as the only input to the machine learning model. Wyatt et al. [9] followed that, transforming each job script into a 64 × 64 2D character matrix. Leveraging Google's word2vec method, each unique character was converted to a unique 8-dimensional vector, turning the 2D matrix to a 64 × 64 × 8 "image". The prediction output was still a job's runtime and total volume of I/O. Note that we took a big step further in SchedP to predict the I/O pattern of a job over its lifetime, which is the first effort achieving this goal.

I/O-aware job scheduling is a relatively new topic. It coordinates system I/O through scheduling user jobs differently in an I/O-aware manner. Zhou et al. [11] claimed that it is the first work on I/O-aware job scheduling. It works by selecting a subset of jobs to actually perform I/O from the set of jobs which are performing I/O or ready to perform I/O. This is limited by the fact that it only coordinates jobs among the ones that are already started, which depends on operations like suspending running jobs. This would cause much confusion to users, thus is not practical in production environment. The experiments are conducted based on simulations. Herbein et al. [3] explored I/O-aware job scheduling on HPC systems with burst buffer enabled. Burst buffer layer in file system turns jobs' bursty I/O into constant I/O stream. It is restricted by the fact that this layer should exist and be well functional on HPC systems, which is not a common case in current HPC production environment. The experiments are conducted on an emulated system [1] without launching real jobs. Liu et al. [7] developed a tool to discover per-application I/O patterns through server log analysis and give suggestions to batch scheduler on whether a job should be executed now or later. Since no real job scheduler modification is made, they let the jobs run anyway under "later" suggestion and check if a delay suggestion indeed correlates with more congestion. Though they launched real jobs on a production HPC system for evaluations, the applications behind scheduling target jobs (incoming jobs) were completely known, and the tool relies on this information to give suggestions. Real incoming workloads in production HPC environment do not provide direct information on applications behind jobs and modern job scheduling system do not have a mechanism to detect it, which hinders the work from being deployed in a real job scheduler. So far we haven't found any work that is able to provide a practical solution on I/O-aware job scheduling that can work in current production environment.

3 Method Design

SchedP can be divided into two major parts according to whether the part is integrated into job scheduling system or not. One is the per-job I/O pattern prediction mechanism that trains a neural network model with historical data to predict per-job I/O patterns. The model training precess can be performed in parallel with job scheduling procedures and does not need any real-time information from job scheduler, so we maintain it outside of job scheduling system. The other part is the pre-schedule mechanism that leverages the trained neural network model to enable I/O-aware job scheduling. It is integrated into job scheduling system, namely Slurm, to take effect on the job scheduling process. In this section, we will introduce the design of these two parts, while leaving the details of implementation and integration to Sect. 4.

3.1 Per-Job I/O Pattern Prediction Mechanism

We focus on predicting the I/O patterns throughout the lifetime of each job submitted to the cluster with a submission script. The overview of the prediction process is shown in Fig. 1. As introduced in Sect. 2, this mechanism originates from the per-job runtime and I/O prediction method based solely on job scripts. Word2vec method is still leveraged to transform each job script into image-like data as the only input into 2D-CNN deep neural network where there are four convolutional layers followed by four fully-connected layers. The usage of 2D-CNN is due to the demonstrated capability of CNN in image recognition in the past decade. The neural network model configuration and job script processing follow the work described in Sect. 2. Prior to the transformation, we preprocess the job scripts to get rid of contents that are commented out to eliminate the potential interference caused by them.

To realise I/O pattern prediction, we make the output of the neural network a 3360-dimensional I/O pattern vector. The dimension of the vector is decided according to the 7-day runtime limitation configured on the cluster, which will only be extended upon request. We consider the I/O volume introduced by each job within time intervals and take one hour as the minimal time interval, which makes totally 168 time intervals for 7 d. A time interval corresponds to an entry in the I/O pattern vector, so we now have 168 entries in the pattern vector as the first step. Secondly, for each time interval we accumulate read and write volume separately, so we need 2 entries, which then makes 336 entries. The cluster is equipped with Lustre file system, which has Object Storage Servers (OSS) and Object Storage Targets (OST) as data storage backend. Each OSS provides access to a set of OST storage. Since the aim of SchedP is to alleviate system I/O contention and an OSS can be viewed as the smallest unit of storage system, we only reach the level of OSS server. The cluster has totally 10 OSS servers where a job would probably perform I/O differently and have different I/O patterns over time, so each OSS needs to have its own 336 entries for a job. Totally we would have 3360 entries in a job's I/O pattern vector. In more detail, the neural network model would predict 0 I/O for the time intervals beyond a job's runtime when the runtime is less than 7 d, while only predict the I/O within the first 7 d if a job's runtime is longer than 7 d. To clarify, SchedP will predict different I/O patterns for jobs with different submission scripts.

For the neural network model, we adopt multi-label classification. Different from the common multi-class classification where the output vector is one-hot, there could be multiple 1s in the output vector of multi-label classification model. In fact, every entry of the output vector would be somewhere between 0 and 1, independent of each other, which are probabilities of each label being predicted. Probabilities over 0.5 will be determined as 1 meaning that the corresponding labels are predicted, while in multi-class classification the probabilities of all labels sum to 1 and only the label with highest probability is predicted. To clarify, label is a concept in machine learning. Each entry in the output vector corresponds to a label which is a time interval in our case. Here 1 means that there will be an I/O burst in the corresponding time interval. This model is very suitable for SchedP since we want the model to be able to predict all the I/O bursts on each OSS server during a 7-day time period, namely to have multiple 1s in the I/O pattern vector.

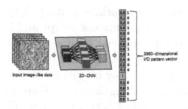

Input image-like data   2D-CNN   3360-dimensional I/O pattern vector

Fig. 1. Overview of the prediction process.

3.2 I/O-aware Pre-schedule Mechanism

The idea is to augment the job scheduler with two abilities: 1) to be able to find out if starting a job right away will cause or increase I/O contention in the system; 2) to be able to delay the job if the answer is yes. Firstly, we need to define a system I/O contention event in order to detect it. I/O contention will happen when there is a big number of jobs all performing I/O simultaneously and the total amount of I/O reaches the system capacity. In our case, this "simultaneously" equals to happening within the same time interval. Therefore, if the total I/O happening within any time interval is above a system threshold, we determine there is an I/O contention event. With this definition, we then need to see if starting a coming job will lead to or exacerbate an I/O contention event. For this purpose, we leverage the trained prediction model to predict the I/O pattern of the current job (the job that just comes and is waiting to be scheduled) and all running jobs, then see if after including the current job, the total number of I/O bursts (which represents the total I/O amount) produced by all running jobs within any time interval would go beyond the threshold. A number beyond the threshold means that the job will cause or increase system I/O contention and should be delayed. The threshold is determined based on the experience operating the cluster. We let Slurm decrease the job's scheduling priority in pending job queue to delay it. The details of the delay operation are described in Sect. 4.3.

The above procedures happen right after jobs are submitted to the system and before the normal Slurm scheduling process happens, so we name it as a "pre-schedule" mechanism. This achieves real I/O-aware job scheduling which happens at job scheduling time, avoiding the situation when we have to manipulate jobs' status after they are started. The latter case is far less graceful and not acceptable in production environment since it may involve many suspend operations on the jobs.

4   Implementations

The major functionalities of `SchedP` are developed in Python, while the integration into Slurm scheduling system is done in C which is Slurm's developing language.

4.1   Training of the Per-Job I/O Pattern Prediction Model

First of all, we need to select appropriate training data set. Historical jobs that are completed normally, have a submission script and have I/O statistic data in the database are selected into training data set. The condition that jobs need to be normally completed is set against failing or cancelled jobs which do not have complete I/O statistics and may originally have wrong submission scripts. For the second condition, job submission scripts are necessary for the training process as the only input to neural network model. The last condition for I/O statistic data is set for the necessity of input data labelling. In general we use supervised machine learning method so that the input data should be correctly labelled, in our case with processed I/O statistics. To clarify, we have monitoring system running on the cluster to collect jobs' I/O statistic data throughout their lifetime and submission scripts. The I/O statistics are then stored into TimescaleDB database.

The next step is training data processing. There are two major parts in this step, one is the processing of model input data and the other is input data labelling, as discussed below.

- *Model input data processing*: We stick with the word2vec plan to transform job scripts into image-like data. Specifically, each job script is converted to a 64×64 2D character matrix where each unique character is further converted to a unique 8-dimensional vector, which makes a $64 \times 64 \times 8$ "image". To clarify, job scripts will be truncated if they are larger than 64×64, or be filled with spaces if they are smaller than 64×64.
- *Data labelling*: What this labelling does is basically generating the 3360-dimensional I/O pattern vectors for every job in training data set. Each of the OSS server has 18 OSTs. Since jobs' I/O statistics are collected per OST, we need to first check that on each OSS server, which OSTs are used by a given job. Then for each OSS server and each time interval, we add up the I/O volume performed by the job on all the used OSTs on this OSS server within this time interval. In more detail, the I/O statistic data is accumulated value of jobs' I/O performed over time, and we need to process it into I/O volume within each time interval. Then we can get a vector whose entries represent the I/O volume performed in corresponding time intervals. Finally, we turn the entries that are above a certain threshold to 1 meaning there's an I/O burst event happening in the time interval, while others to 0 meaning no I/O burst. This threshold is currently set to 100MB according to the experience operating the cluster.

Now we are ready for training. For the neural network model, we have four convolutional layers followed by four fully connected layers and the standard parameter setup for multi-label classification, which is sigmoid activation at the output layer and binary crossentropy loss. Note that the sigmoid activation at the output layer is used instead of softmax activation, since the former makes the output probabilities of each label independent of each other and the latter makes the output probabilities of all labels sum to 1.

4.2   I/O-aware Pre-schedule Mechanism

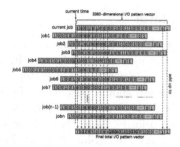

Fig. 2. The add-up process of SchedP's I/O-aware pre-schedule mechanism.

The implementation of the I/O-aware pre-schedule mechanism can be divided into three steps, which are applied sequentially to each job submitted to the system.

- *Step 1*: Get the current job's submission script, feed it into the neural network model after transforming it into image-like data, and get the network output as the job's I/O pattern vector.
- *Step 2*: Traverse all running jobs and get their I/O pattern vectors in the same way as in *Step 1*. Since these jobs have already been in running state for some time, the pattern vectors represent the jobs' I/O patterns from some time point in the past (when the job started running) to some time in the future, instead of from the current time on. Hence, for each running job's pattern vector, we need to find the index of the entry whose time interval corresponds to the current point of time. After that, we add up all the pattern vectors to get a total I/O pattern vector representing the accumulated I/O pattern of all running jobs which should be the current I/O pattern of the system, where each single vector should be added starting from the aforementioned index.
- *Step 3*: Add the I/O pattern vector of the current job to the total I/O pattern vector form *Step 2* to get a final total I/O pattern vector, where they should be both added from the beginning. The add-up process is shown in Fig. 2. Then we check the final total I/O pattern vector to see if there is any entry above

a certain threshold. The threshold is set to 50 according to the experience operating the cluster. If there is such an entry, then we know the current job will generate or increase I/O contention in the system and decide to delay it.

To clarify, the threshold of 50 in *Step 3* means that there are at least 50 I/O burst events happening in the entry's time interval. With over 100 MB per I/O burst, 50 makes over 5 GB read or write volume happening within 1 h on one OSS server. Note that the actual I/O volume could be far beyond 5 GB when any jobs generate I/O burst a lot larger than 100 MB per hour, and SchedP is trying to be more proactive in preventing I/O contention events by setting a moderate threshold.

4.3 Integration into Slurm

We make the integration at Slurm backfill scheduling plugin. In the plugin, we pass the path to the job's submission script (gotten from the job's structure) to our Python function which implements the three steps in Sect. 4.2, then retrieve the decision of whether the job should be delayed from the Python function's return value. If the job is decided to be delayed, we lower its initial priority to half of its default initial priority. Note that all these only change the initial priorities of jobs, which will not affect Slurm's normal backfill scheduling mechanism happening later. With the priority adjusted by SchedP, jobs will still be scheduled under backfill scheme. Normally this priority will not be changed at any later point, unless the system administrator does so intentionally.

Regarding lowering the priority of the job, it is enough to just halve it without having to set multiple levels (probably according to the severity of potential I/O contention) since this is already able to delay the job to some later point and stagger the jobs to avoid the potential I/O contention event currently being considered. And avoiding just this I/O contention event is enough for us since later contention events will be considered at later scheduling cycles. Besides, a job that may cause more severe I/O congestion does not necessarily have to be delayed more, since this severity may well disappear just by staggering the job a little bit and too much staggering may instead invoke other I/O contention events.

5 Evaluations

5.1 Experiment Method

According to SchedP's aim to assist system I/O management, we designed experiments based on system I/O statistics to evaluate performance. Specifically, under real workloads, we monitor the depth of I/O request queues on each OSS server and compare the curve of this parameter before and after deploying SchedP. To clarify, the statistic data of this parameter shows the amount of I/O requests that have ever been queued so far so that it is also accumulated value, meaning that the curve of it will be continuously going up. If there is a sharper increase on the curve than normal, we would know that there are too many I/O requests queued in the system within the corresponding time slot, which shows the emergence of I/O congestion. So if the curve after deploying SchedP looks smoother than before, we would know that it is taking effect. To quantify the results, we also calculate the amount of increase in this depth at each data point compared to the previous data point, which is the amount of I/O requests that have ever been queued within the time slot, showing the effect of SchedP more clearly.

5.2   Results and Analysis

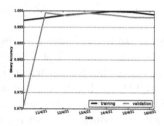

Fig. 3. Training and validation accuracy

Training Results. The 2D-CNN neural network model is implemented with Tensorflow Keras API, where we set binary accuracy as evaluation metric. Binary accuracy in multi-label classification measures the percentage of correctly predicted labels in all labels (totally 3360 in our case). SchedP performs its training in a periodic manner, and the training cycle is set to 7 d. Specifically, we train the model with jobs within a 7-day period (jobs that were started within the time period and have finished), test it and then retrain it with data from the next 7 d. We keep repeating this process throughout our experiment so that the model keeps being updated with new data. In one 7-day period, we randomly pick 1000 jobs that satisfy our training set criteria from each of the 7 d, and train the model with the 7 data batches one by one for 10 epochs each. To clarify, "a job from a day" means that the job started on the day and has finished.

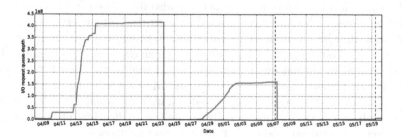

Fig. 4. Curve of I/O request queue depth

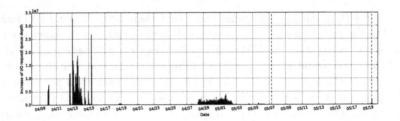

Fig. 5. Increase of I/O request queue depth

`SchedP` separates 100 jobs from each batch (of size 1000) to do validation during training.

Figure 3 shows the results over one 7-day training period from Apr. 10 to Apr. 16, 2021. The accuracy is very high, over 99% across all the training and validation processes. This is due to the sparsity nature of the I/O pattern vectors. An entry of 1 means that an I/O burst happens in the corresponding time interval which should not happen too frequently since only a portion of the user jobs have I/O burst and a job with I/O burst may not have many bursts. Instead an entry of 0 means that no I/O burst happens in the corresponding time interval which should happen very frequently. Hence most of the entries in the predicted I/O pattern vectors should be 0 which are correct predictions. This eases the prediction task since the model can just predict 0 for unsure entries and be correct with high probability.

After this training period, we test the model with statistic data of 1000 jobs from Apr. 17 and got a binary accuracy of 0.9992. We can see that the test results stay in line with training and validation results, which shows that our model is not overfitted and generalises well on workloads that are never seen in training. Benefiting from this nice generalisation property of machine learning method, `SchedP` is confident to work well on future unknown workloads.

Scheduling Results. We want to first emphasis that `SchedP` is not an application-specific approach, but rather works on the basis of each individual job. Though it implicitly considers the application run by each job when the machine learning model studies their submission scripts, this information is only combined with other information which are also discovered from the scripts to make predictions. The model is expected to learn the I/O patterns behind every application that has ever appeared in training data set, and use this information as part of the knowledge that it relies on to make decisions. We monitored the system workloads during our experiment and found application types ranging from biology, physics, math to chemistry and machine learning, which are very diversified. To further avoid being biased towards any application that `SchedP` may work better with, we intentionally ignore the application information when we extract our artificial workloads from past real workloads.

Figure 4 shows a typical curve of the accumulated depth of I/O request queues on OSS servers and Fig. 5 shows the increase at each data point in Fig. 4 compared to its previous data point. The amount of increase in this queue depth shows the level of system I/O congestion at the time, the bigger the amount, the worse the congestion. In Fig. 4, the two drops around Apr. 25 and May 8 are due to cluster maintenance, during which all the servers were down so that the I/O stats were cleaned up. We deployed SchedP on the cluster when it was back up on Apr. 27 and made sure all other aspects of system remain unchanged. We can see in Fig. 4 that before the deployment of SchedP, all the increases on the curve are rather sharp, while the curve turns to go up very smoothly after the deployment. This is shown more clearly in Fig. 5 where the exact amount of increase at each data point is presented. There were some very big increases before deploying SchedP, but such big increases never showed up again after SchedP started to work on the system.

Since it is possible that the I/O just happens to be smoother after Apr. 27, on the morning of May 7 and the afternoon of May 19 we separately launched 100 and 500 I/O-intensive jobs on top of ongoing user workloads. The two workloads were extracted from the workloads on Apr. 13. We monitored the workloads on Apr. 13 and made sure the two extracted workloads made a major contribution to the sharp increases, namely they are able to cause big increments as the ones on Apr. 13. The two black dashed lines mark the time points when these jobs were running. Note that on the afternoon of May 19, we monitored that there were also thousands of other I/O-intensive jobs launched by a user. The workloads were superposed and would only lead to more I/O traffic. We can imagine that without any additional mechanism coordinating this traffic the system would have huge I/O congestion worse than the ones on Apr. 13, however, there is only a very small mild increase at the second dashed line. Since all other aspects of the system stayed the same, we can confirm that it is SchedP taking effect.

6   Conclusions

We propose SchedP as the first practical effort on I/O-aware job scheduling that can work in production HPC environment and made the first effort to enable I/O-aware job scheduling on production HPC clusters. This takes a big step further than simulations, as we need to stay practical in our work and consider real-world issues. The cluster that we work on has hundreds of users and gets thousands of jobs submitted to it every day, which generated high pressure on SchedP. As a research effort, SchedP did well handling it.

Acknowledgements. This work is supported by National Key R&D Programme of China under grant number 2018YFA0404603.

References

1. Ahn, D.H., Garlick, J., Grondona, M., Lipari, D., Springmeyer, B., Schulz, M.: Flux: a next-generation resource management framework for large HPC centers. In: 2014 43rd International Conference on Parallel Processing Workshops, pp. 9–17. IEEE (2014)

2. Fan, Y.: Job scheduling in high performance computing. arXiv preprint arXiv:2109.09269 (2021)
3. Herbein, S., et al.: Scalable I/O-aware job scheduling for burst buffer enabled HPC clusters. In: Proceedings of the 25th ACM International Symposium on High-Performance Parallel and Distributed Computing, pp. 69–80 (2016)
4. Li, D., Dong, M., Tang, Y., Ota, K.: A novel disk I/O scheduling framework of virtualized storage system. Clust. Comput. **22**(1), 2395–2405 (2019)
5. Li, H., Liao, J., Liu, X.: Merging and prioritizing optimization in block I/O scheduling of disk storage. J. Circ. Syst. Comput. **30**(10), 2150186 (2021)
6. Liu, J., Chen, Y., Zhuang, Y.: Hierarchical I/O scheduling for collective I/O. In: 2013 13th IEEE/ACM International Symposium on Cluster, Cloud, and Grid Computing, pp. 211–218 (2013). https://doi.org/10.1109/CCGrid.2013.30
7. Liu, Y., Gunasekaran, R., Ma, X., Vazhkudai, S.S.: Server-side log data analytics for I/O workload characterization and coordination on large shared storage systems. In: SC2016: Proceedings of the International Conference for High Performance Computing, Networking, Storage and Analysis, pp. 819–829. IEEE (2016)
8. McKenna, R., Gamblin, T., Moody, A., de Supinski, B., Taufer, M.: Forecasting storms in parallel file systems
9. Wyatt, M.R., Herbein, S., Gamblin, T., Moody, A., Ahn, D.H., Taufer, M.: PRIONN: predicting runtime and IO using neural networks. In: Proceedings of the 47th International Conference on Parallel Processing, pp. 1–12 (2018)
10. Wyatt II, M.R., Gamblin, T., Moody, A., Taufer, M.: Revealing the power of neural networks to capture accurate job resource usage from unparsed job scripts and application inputs (2017)
11. Zhou, Z., et al.: I/O-aware batch scheduling for petascale computing systems. In: 2015 IEEE International Conference on Cluster Computing, pp. 254–263 (2015). https://doi.org/10.1109/CLUSTER.2015.45

SpacKV: A Pmem-Aware Key-Value Separation Store Based on LSM-Tree

Xuran Ge[1], Mingche Lai[1], Yang Liu[1], Lizhou Wu[1], Zhutao Zhuang[2],
Yang Ou[1(✉)], Zhiguang Chen[2], and Nong Xiao[1]

[1] School of Computer, National University of Defense Technology,Changsha, China
michaelouyang@163.com
[2] School of Computer, Sun Yat-sen University,Guangzhou, China

Abstract. Key-value (KV) stores based on persistent memories such
as Intel Optane Pmem can deliver higher throughput and lower latency,
compared to traditional SSD/HDD. Many KV stores adopt LSM-tree as
the bone index structure. However, LSM-tree suffers from severe write
amplification, which degrades the system's performance and exacerbates
the wearout of persistent memory. In this paper, we propose SpacKV, a
hybrid DRAM-Pmem KV store, which applies a KV separation scheme
and exploits Pmem's device characteristics to achieve high throughput.
We design a dedicated value storage structure to maintain localized order
of values for efficient range queries and a compaction-triggered garbage
collection mechanism to minimize intermediate I/O overhead. Moreover,
we leverage Pmem's key features: byte-addressability, access unit of 256
bytes and specific persistence instructions to further mitigate the write
amplification effect. The experimental results show that SpacKV achieves
1.4–10.8×, 4.7–9.7×, and 6.7–13.5× in terms of write, read, and range
query performance over three state-of-the-art LSM-tree based KV stores:
LevelDB-Pmem, RocksDB-Pmem, and MatrixKV, respectively.

Keywords: Persistent memory · LSM-tree · KV separation · Garbage
collection · Byte-addressability

1 Introduction

KV stores are widely regarded as critical components in modern datacenters
and various data-intensive applications such as cloud storage, e-commerce, social
networks, and search engines. Benefiting from its batch sequential writes, log-
structured merge tree (LSM-tree) is one of the most popular data structures
used in KV stores (e.g., RocksDB [1], LevelDB [2], Cassandra [3], and Bigtable
[4]). Traditional LSM-tree based KV stores [5,6] are deployed on DRAM-SSD
hybrid storage devices to leverage fast speed of DRAM and non-volatility of SSD
for high performance of read and write. However, limited by its coarse access
granularity, high latency, and low endurance, it becomes increasingly difficult to

---

X. Ge and M. Lai—These authors contributed equally to this work.

© IFIP International Federation for Information Processing 2022
Published by Springer Nature Switzerland AG 2022
S. Liu and X. Wei (Eds.): NPC 2022, LNCS 13615, pp. 327–339, 2022.
https://doi.org/10.1007/978-3-031-21395-3_30

boost the performance of KV stores building on SSDs. The advent of persistent memories (PMs) such as Intel Optane Pmem [7] attracts researchers' attention to further improve LSM-tree based KV store by exploiting their byte-addressability, higher throughput, lower latency, and lower power consumption.

Due to the multi-level structure and out-of-place update strategy, LSM-tree suffers from inherent write amplification (WA), which degrades KV stores' read/write throughput and storage devices' endurance [8]. Most of existing works [9–11] only use Pmem as "a higher throughput and lower latency non-volatile storage medium", assisting other optimization methods to mitigate WA and increase system performance. They ignore the following three key characteristics of Pmem: 1) Access unit of 256 bytes [12]; 2) Byte-addressability and higher random write performance in comparison to traditional storage media [7]; 3) Non-temporal store instructions with higher throughput for large writes. Therefore, it is crucial to leverage the above characteristics to design an LSM-tree based persistent KV store with high throughput and low latency.

We present SpacKV, a novel KV store based on a KV separation scheme, which minimizes LSM-tree's write amplification and exploits Pmem's device characteristics to achieve high read and write performance. The KV separation scheme significantly reduces the amount of data in LSM-tree, thereby reducing write amplification. To clean up expired data, we propose compaction-triggered garbage collection by designing a dedicated value storage structure and flexible trigger conditions. It significantly reduces intermediate I/Os generated by cascading compaction operations and realizes localized order for values. In addition, we fully exploit the byte-addressability and fine-grained access unit of Pmem to obtain sufficient Pmem bandwidths. SpacKV has been implemented by redesigning LevelDB; our experimental results suggest that SpacKV outperforms LevelDB-Pmem, RocksDB-Pmem, and MatrixKV by 10.8×, 1.6×, and 1.4× in terms of random write throughput under write-intensive workloads, respectively. It also achieves significant throughput gains in updates, reads and range queries. In summary, the contributions of this work are listed as follows:

- We propose a value manager with a dedicated value storage structure to realize localized order of values for efficient range query performance.
- We design a compaction-triggered garbage collection mechanism to significantly reduce intermediate I/O overhead.
- We present a PM-aware selective KV separation scheme, which leverages the key device characteristics of Pmem to greatly boost access performance.

The rest of the paper is organized as follows. Sections 2 and 3 provide a background and motivations for this work, respectively. Section 4 elaborates the SpacKV design and detailed optimizations. Section 5 shows the experiment and evaluation results. Section 6 introduces related work and Sect. 7 concludes this paper.

2   Background

This section provides a background for LSM-tree based KV store and persistent memory.

2.1 LSM-tree Based KV Store

Log-structured merge tree (LSM-tree) is a write-optimized data structure that takes advantage of efficient sequential writes of SSD/HDD. Next, we use LevelDB [2] as an example to explain in detail a classic block-device-based LSM-tree implementation. As shown in Fig. 1, LevelDB is composed of a memory component and a SSD/HDD component. The memory component mainly consists of two skip-lists (i.e., a MemTable and an immutable MemTable) in DRAM to batch write requests. The SSD/HDD component maintains a multi-level hierarchical structure, from the lowest level to the highest level represented by L_0, L_1, $\cdots$, L_n, respectively. Each level has one or more *sorted string tables* (SSTables). Each level has limited storage capacity, and the storage capacity of L_{i+1} is 10 times larger than that of L_i in LevelDB.

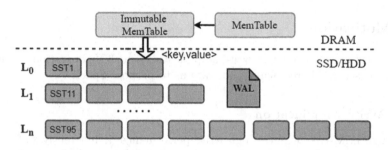

Fig. 1. LevelDB architecture.

For write requests, LevelDB first stores their *key-value* (KV) pairs in a MemTable. When the number of write requests reaches the threshold of MemTable, a MemTable is transformed into an immutable MemTable. Then, the immutable MemTable flushes the data to L_0 on SSD/HDD, generating an SSTable. To ensure crash consistency and tolerate system failures, LSM-tree sets up a *write-ahead log* (WAL) for every MemTable. It performs compaction operations to remove expired KV pairs on SSD/HDD. Specifically, SStables with overlapping ranges at L_i and L_{i+1} are fetched to DRAM for merging sort into new SStables, which are sequentially written back to the next level L_{i+1}. Similarly, the cascading compaction operations can be triggered between adjacent levels of LSM-tree. For read requests, LevelDB first searches in the memory components (i.e., MemTable and immutable MemTable). If not found, it searches SSTables from L_0 to L_n. For each level, it identifies an SSTable and checks its bloom filter to determine if the KV pair exists.

2.2 Intel Optane Persistent Memory

In 2019, Intel released the first commercially available byte-addressable *persistent memory* (PM), which is named as Intel Optane Pmem [7]. It not only features byte-addressability and low latency (only 3–5 times slower than DRAM), but also has non-volatility and large capacity of traditional block devices. Optane

Pmem can work as either far volatile memory with DRAM as cache (memory mode) or persistent memory with DRAM as volatile main memory (app-direct mode). This paper configures it to app-direct mode, where applications can map their physical address space to the user space for direct access.

Next, we elaborate four critical characteristics of Optane Pmem leveraged in this paper. (1) Asymmetric read and write bandwidth, with a maximum read bandwidth of 6.6 GB/s and maximum write bandwidth of 2.3 GB/s for a single Optane Pmem DIMM. (2) Unit write size is 256 bytes; any random write smaller than the unit size requires a read-modify-write operation to generate a 256B write to the storage medium, resulting in the write amplification effect. (3) Random access delivers higher performance than traditional block devices. (4) Leveraging non-temporal store operations to persist data can obtain higher throughput for large writes.

3 Motivation

In this section, we elaborate write amplification and KV separation challenges for PM-based LSM-tree, which motivate us to propose SpacKV.

3.1 Write Amplification

Although LSM-tree achieves high write performance, it inherently suffers from severe write amplification (WA). Specifically, LSM-tree's background threads have to frequently perform compaction operations to remove invalid KV pairs. The SSTables with overlapping key ranges in both L_i and L_{i+1} are read to DRAM and then written back to SSD/HDD multiple times, which exacerbates the wearout of PM and reduces the system's throughput. Figure 2(a) and Fig. 2(b) compare the write amplification and the random write throughput of three state-of-the-art LSM-tree based KV stores: LevelDB-Pmem, MatrixKV and RocksDB-Pmem, when loading random data of 40 GB with different value sizes, respectively. We observed that these three KV stores are afflicted with severe WA effect. In the common case of 4 KB value size, LevelDB-Pmem has

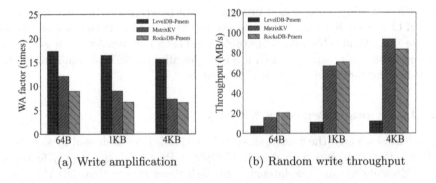

(a) Write amplification   (b) Random write throughput

Fig. 2. Comparison of three typical LSM-tree based KV stores.

a WA factor of 15.5, meaning that the actual data volume written to Pmem is 15.5× the data volume that is supposed to be loaded into the KV store. Although RocksDB-Pmem and MatrixKV reduce WA to some extent, they still write at least 6x extra data. In addition, it can be seen that the larger the WA effect, the lower the system throughput.

3.2 Challenges of KV Separation on Persistent Memory

KV separation [6,13,14] is a well-known optimization scheme to alleviate the write/read amplification effect of LSM-tree. Specifically, it separates the management of keys and values by storing keys and metadata in LSM-tree while storing values in a standalone append-only log. Since the size of keys and metadata is typically much smaller than that of values for KV pairs, KV separation reduces the amount of data involved in compaction operations by only comparing keys instead of bulky KV pairs.

Howerver, the KV separation technique on PM inevitably brings three issues. First, KV separation needs to perform garbage collection to release reserved value space, which introduces additional I/O overhead and impairs system's read and write performance [6]. Second, KV separation makes values corresponding to the keys of consecutive ranges in LSM-tree scattered at different locations, resulting in poor range query performance. Third, the access granularity of Optane Pmem is 256 bytes [12], which leads to write amplification and bandwidth waste for accesses to small values (<256 bytes); thus, the benefit of KV separation on PM for small values is limited when compared to large values.

4   SpacKV Design

In this section, we introduce SpacKV, a hybrid DRAM-Pmem KV store that utilizes the KV separation scheme to reduce WA and exploits Optane Pmem's characteristics to significantly boost read, write, and range query performance.

4.1   System Overview

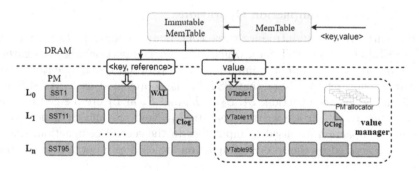

Fig. 3. SpacKV system overview.

As shown in Fig. 3, SpacKV separately stores keys and values when KV pairs are flushed from DRAM to Pmem. Keys and references (the index information of values) are stored in LSM-tree, while values are placed into a reserved storage space named *value manager*.

To manage the reserved storage space in a fine-grained manner, we design a *PM allocator*, which divides the address space of value manager into fixed-size units called *segment*. The default segment size is 256 KB, the maximum value size evaluated in the following experiments. PM allocator is organized as a doubly-linked list, and each linked node stores the metadata $\langle segID, segAddr \rangle$ of a segment.

To maintain *localized order* for efficient range query performance, SpacKV reserves an LSM-tree-like multi-level structure in the value manager, where values are organized as *VTables*. Each VTable corresponds to an SSTable in LSM-tree (e.g., $VTable_1$ contains all values indexed by keys in $SSTable_1$ sequentially). As shown in Fig. 4, a VTable consists of multiple segments, which individually store values without other meta. All segments of a VTable are organized together using implicit links, which means that the last eight bytes of each segment store the address of the next segment. Benefiting from the byte-addressability of Pmem, we can quickly access a single value according to $\langle segAddr, offset \rangle$.

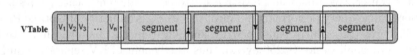

Fig. 4. The structure of VTable.

To be compatible with LevelDB, SpacKV manages the same in-memory component (a MemTable and an immutable MemTable) as conventional LSM-tree KV stores with a persistent write-ahead log (WAL). It also performs cascading compaction operations to remove expired $\langle key, reference \rangle$ pairs. Correspondingly, SpacKV requires a compaction-like operation named as *compaction-triggered garbage collection* to clean up invalid values and realize localized order for values.

4.2   Cascading Compaction Operations

In this part, we mainly introduce three concepts (i.e., input SSTable, intermediate SSTable and live SSTable), which serve the compaction-triggered garbage collection afterward. In update-intensive scenarios, LSM-tree frequently triggers cascading compactions. Note that SSTable is abbreviated as S. As shown in Fig. 5, in the first compaction, S_1, S_2 in L_0 and S_3 in L_1 are merged into new S_4, S_7 and S_8, which are written back to L_1. Next, S_7 and S_8 generated by the first compaction are used as input files in the second compaction; the S_{13} and S_{14} generated by the second compaction are used as input files in the third compaction.

After the above cascading three compaction operations, currently existing SSTables are named as *live SSTables* (e.g., S_4, S_{15}, S_{22} and S_{23}); The SSTables,

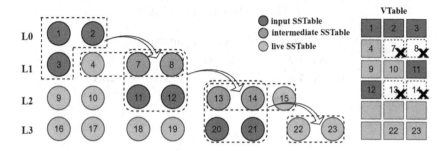

Fig. 5. Cascading compactions process.

which are generated by previous compaction and be used as the input files for the later compaction, are named as *intermediate SSTables* (e.g., S_7, S_8, S_{13} and S_{14}); The input files in each compaction are named as *input SSTables* (e.g., S_1, S_2, S_3, S_{11}, S_{12}, S_{20} and S_{21}).

4.3   Compaction-triggered Garbage Collection

It is inevitable for raw LSM-tree that intermediate SSTables occupy much of the storage and I/O overhead. However, KV separation architecture makes it possible to drop these intermediate data. Therefore, we propose a compaction-triggered garbage collection to release storage space and maintain localized order for values. In SpacKV, garbage collection is performed in the following two steps. (1) Track live SSTables, and relocate their values to new VTables. (2) Pick up input SSTables, and reclaim the corresponding VTables by the PM allocator. The intermediate SSTables are ignored, thus significantly reducing the storage and I/O overhead.

Triggered Conditions. We specify three trigger conditions according to the load of the system: (1) Detect whether the reserved space is running out. (2) Monitor whether the number of invalid keys dismissed by compaction operations reaches the threshold since the last garbage collection in real-time. (3) Statistics whether the number of VTables visited by recent range query operations exceeds the threshold; once it becomes unacceptable, SpacKV necessitates garbage collection to maintain localized order of values for efficient range query performance.

Garbage Collection Strategy. SpacKV sets up a compaction log called *Clog*, which records the sstIDs of input SStables and that of output SStables involved in cascading compaction operations. Table 1. shows the format of Clog.

These three compaction records in Table 1 log the process of cascading compaction operations shown in Fig. 5. According to the Clog, we can drop intermediate SSTables (i.e., S_7, S_8, S_{13} and S_{14}), and identify live SSTables and

Table 1. The format of Clog.

recordID	$Level_i$	input sstID	$Level_{i+1}$	input sstID	output sstID
1	$Level_0$	1,2	$Level_1$	3	4, ~~7, 8~~
2	$Level_1$	~~7,8~~	$Level_2$	11,12	~~13,14~~, 15
3	$Level_2$	~~13,14~~	$Level_3$	20,21	22,23
...	...	...	...	...	...

input SSTables. For a garbage collection operation, first, the background thread locates values according to $\langle key, reference \rangle$ in live SStables, and repositions these values to a new VTable. Second, it packages the new position information $\langle segAddr, offset \rangle$ into a reference, and then updates the $\langle key, reference \rangle$ of LSM-tree. Finally, the PM allocator reclaims all expired VTables corresponding to input SSTables involved in cascading compactions, i.e., VTables in the gray area of Fig. 5. Note that the PM allocator performs fine-grained garbage collection on a segment-by-segment basis to mitigate interference between the garbage collection and the compaction threads.

4.4 PM-aware Optimizations

We further exploit Optane Pmem's characteristics to boost the read and write performance of SpacKV. It mainly involves the following three aspects: (1)Selective KV separation. When MemTable is flushed to L_0, SpacKV stores values smaller than 256 bytes in LSM-tree and separately stores values larger than 256 bytes in the value manager. Optane Pmem has a write unit size of 256B. Selective KV separation avoids write amplification and the waste of Pmem's bandwidth. (2)We use non-temporal stores(ntstores) instead of the common *clwb/clflushopt* instructions to persist data. Because *ntstore* has higher bandwidth for large writes (over 256 bytes), and bypasses the cache to avoid polluting the cache. (3) Benefiting from Pmem's byte-addressability and high random access performance, we directly read values in VTable during query and range query operations. In contrast, the traditional block device reads at least a page of 4 KB.

4.5 Recovery

The recovery of the LSM-tree in SpacKV is similar to the existing work [15]; here, we mainly discuss the two additional recovery overheads introduced by SpacKV: garbage collection operation and VTable metadata. For garbage collection operation, we append the metadata of SSTables and the valid keys to GClog. The recovery performs the following steps: (1) Find the SSTable being inspected according to GClog. (2)Check whether the reference in SSTable is valid. (3) Continue garbage collection starting from the first valid key found. For VTables, When KV pairs are flushed to the value manager, we record the metadata of the current VTables to log and then update keys and references in LSM-tree.

5   Experiments and Evaluation

5.1   Experimental Setup

All experiments are performed on a server with Intel Xeon Gold 6240 CPUs. Each socket is equipped with 256 GB Intel Optane Pmem and 187 GB DRAM. The Optane Pmem DIMMs are configured in App-Direct mode. The kernel version is 64-bit Linux 3.10.0, and the operating system is CentOS 7.6. We implement SpacKV prototype atop LevelDB [2] using the Persistent Memory Development Kit (PMDK) [16] library. Since SpacKV is a persistent key-value store based on hybrid DRAM-Pmem storage devices, we mainly compare SpacKV with LevelDB-Pmem, RocksDB-Pmem and MatrixKV, which correspond to the persistent memory versions of LevelDB, RocksDB, respectively. Note that MatrixKV is a little different from the original version in that it uses only Pmem as persistent storage.

5.2   Overall Performance Evaluation

We compare the overall performance of different KV stores using the microbenchmark db_bench.

Write and Read Performance. For writes, we load 40 GB KV pairs with uniform distribution into KV stores in random or sequential order. For reads, we read 4 GB KV pairs from a 40 GB randomly loaded database to evaluate the random/sequential read performance. Figure 6 shows the random write, sequential write, random read and sequential read performance for different value sizes.

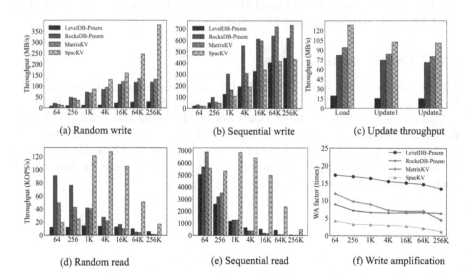

Fig. 6. System performance comparison using the micro-benchmark db_bench with different value sizes.

As shown in Fig. 6(a-b), SpacKV improves random write throughput for all value sizes and has a 10.8x improvement at the common 4 KB value size compared to LevelDB-Pmem. It is also higher than the other three KV stores for large values (>256B). The sequential write throughput of SpacKV is similar to that of LevelDB-Pmem, as sequential writes incur no compaction and garbage collection operations. As shown in Fig. 6(d-e), due to selective KV separation, the improvement of SpacKV's random and sequential read performance is negligible for small values. In the common case of 4 KB value size, the random read throughput of SpacKV is 9.7×, 4.7×, and 5.9× higher than LevelDB-Pmem, RocksDB-Pmem, and MatrixKV, respectively. Morover, the sequential read throughput of SpacKV is significantly higher than the random read.

Load and Update Performance. We first load 40 GB KV pairs(key size is 16B, value size is 4 KB) into each KV store. We then repeatedly update 20 GB of data over the existing 40 GB of KV pairs twice. Figure 6(c) shows the write throughput of each phase. In the load phase, the throughput of SpacKV is 6.7×, 1.6×, and 1.4× over LevelDB-Pmem, RocksDB-Pmem, and MatrixKV. In the update phases, the throughput of SpacKV is 6.8×, 1.4× and 1.3× over LevelDB-Pmem, RocksDB-Pmem and MatrixKV at most, which indicates that SpacKV gains stable performance improvement in update-intensive scenarios.

Write Amplification. We measure the WA of four systems on the same experiment of randomly loading 40 GB KV pairs. Figure 6(f) shows WA factor for different value sizes. Due to the efficient garbage collection method and Pmem-aware optimizations, SpacKV has the smallest WA in all value sizes. In the case of 4 KB value size, the WA of LevelDB-Pmem, RocksDB-Pmem and MatrixKV are 4.3×, 1.2× and 1.5× higher than SpacKV, respectively.

5.3 YCSB Evaluation

We use the real-world workload YCSB [17] macro-benchmarks to generate five types of workloads: workload A(50% read + 50% update), workload B(95% read + 5% update), workload C(100% read), workload D(95% read + 5% insert) and workload E(95% range query + 5% insert), which sets the key size to 16B and the value size to 4 KB. We load and run 10^7 entries for every workload (40 GB data), respectively. Figure 7 shows different KV stores' overall, update, range query performance under different workload types.

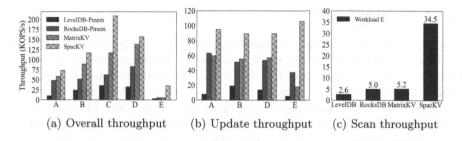

(a) Overall throughput   (b) Update throughput   (c) Scan throughput

Fig. 7. System performance comparison on YCSB

As shown in Fig. 7(a), SpacKV outperforms other KV stores in all types of workloads. Benefiting from byte-addressability and fast random access of Optane Pmem, SpacKV maintains efficient performance over read-dominated workloads, i.e., workloads B to E. Figure 7(b) shows that SpacKV gets the most advantage in updates throughput, which is 1.6–5.9×, 1.5–2.8×, and 4.7–20.9× over LevelDB-Pmem, RocksDB-Pmem, and MatrixKV on the workload A, B, D, and E. Figure 7(c) shows that the range query throughput of SpacKV is 13.49×, 6.9×, and 6.7× higher than LevelDB-Pmem, RocksDB-Pmem, and MatrixKV, respectively, which demonstrates that dynamically monitoring dispersion of VTables can deliver efficient range query performance.

6 Related Work

Many studies exploit persistent memory to optimize the read and write performance of KV stores. SLM-DB [5] is a hybrid Pmem-SSD single-level key-value store, which places MemTable on Pmem and integrates with a persistent B+ tree to provide better query performance. Nevertheless, insertions and updates of B+ tree cause small random write and exacerbate write amplification. NoveLSM [10] is a KV store based on hybrid DRAM-Pmem-SSD storage. It offers two design choices: one is to use Pmem as an alternative to DRAM to increase the capacity of MemTable and immutable MemTable; the other is to enable variable MemTable on Pmem to allow direct updates and avoid logging, but this increases the read path and slow down read performance. MatrixKV [9] places the L_0 on Pmem while the higher levels on SSD. It employs column compaction to achieve fine-grained merge operations in L_0, thus reducing write stalls. Although cross-hint-search is used to compensate for read performance degradation, the read performance of L_0 is sacrificed to some extent. Our SpacKV is a hybrid DRAM-Pmem KV store, which designs compaction-triggered garbage collection under KV separation architecture to reduce inherent write amplification of LSM-tree. Furthermore, we fully use byte-addressability, access unit of 256 B, high random access, and efficient persistence instructions of Optane Pmem to boost the KV store's read and write performance.

7 Conclusion

This paper proposes SpacKV, a persistent LSM-tree based KV store deployed on hybrid DRAM-Pmem storage, which applies a KV separation scheme to improve the system's throughout. SpacKV presents a dedicated value storage structure and compaction-triggered garbage collection mechanism to reduce extra I/O overhead. On this basis, SpacKV optimizes the range query performance by maintaining localized order for values. It also further exploits persistent memory's characteristics to improve large values' access performance. The evaluation results show that SpacKV significantly reduces the write amplification and obtains the best performance in writes, reads, and range queries compared to the other three state-of-the-art KV stores.

Acknowledgments. We thank the reviewers for their insightful feedback to improve this paper. This work was supported by National Key R&D Program of China under Grant NO. 2021YFB0300103, National Natural Science Foundation of China (No. 61872392, 61832020), the Major Program of Guangdong Basic and Applied Research NO.2019B030302002 and the Program for Guangdong Introducing Innovative and Entrepreneurial Teams under Grant NO. 2016ZT06D211.

References

1. Facebook: Rocksdb. http://rocksdb.org
2. Google: Leveldb. https://github.com/google/leveldb
3. Apache: Cassandra. http://cassandra.apache.org
4. Chang, F., et al.: BigTable: a distributed storage system for structured data. ACM Trans. Comput. Syst. **26**(2), 1–26 (2008)
5. Kaiyrakhmet, O., Lee, S., Nam, B., Noh, S.H., Choi, Y.: SLM-DB: single-level key-value store with persistent memory. In: 17th Conference on File and Storage Technologies, FAST 2019, Boston, MA, 25–28 February 2019, pp. 191–205 (2019)
6. Chan, H.H., et al.: Hashkv: enabling efficient updates in KV storage via hashing. In: 2018 USENIX Annual Technical Conference, pp. 1007–1019 (2018)
7. Yang, J., Kim, J., Hoseinzadeh, M., Izraelevitz, J., Swanson, S.: An empirical guide to the behavior and use of scalable persistent memory. In: 18th USENIX Conference on File and Storage Technologies, pp. 169–182 (2020)
8. Luo, C., Carey, M.J.: LSM-based storage techniques: a survey. VLDB J. **29**(1), 393–418 (2020)
9. Yao, T., et al.: MatrixKV: Reducing write stalls and write amplification in LSM-tree based KV stores with matrix container in NVM. In: 2020 USENIX Annual Technical Conference, USENIX ATC 2020, 15–17 July 2020, pp. 17–31 (2020)
10. Kannan, S., Bhat, N., Gavrilovska, A., Arpaci-Dusseau, A.C., Arpaci-Dusseau, R.H.: Redesigning LSMs for nonvolatile memory with NoveLSM. In: 2018 USENIX Annual Technical Conference, USENIX ATC 2018, Boston, MA, USA, 11–13 July 2018, pp. 993–1005 (2018)
11. Zhang, B., Du, D.H.C.: NVLSM: A persistent memory key-value store using log-structured merge tree with accumulative compaction. ACM Trans. Storage. **17**(3), 23:1–23:26 (2021)

12. Zhang, W., Zhao, X., Jiang, S., Jiang, H.: ChameleonDB: a key-value store for Optane persistent memory. In: EuroSys 2021: Sixteenth European Conference on Computer Systems, Online Event, United Kingdom, 26–28 April 2021, pp. 194–209 (2021)
13. Lu, L., Pillai, T.S., Gopalakrishnan, H., Arpaci-Dusseau, A.C., Arpaci-Dusseau, R.H.: WiscKey: separating keys from values in SSD-conscious storage. ACM Trans. Storage (TOS) **13**(1), 1–28 (2017)
14. Li, Y., et al.: Differentiated key-value storage management for balanced i/o performance. In: 2021 USENIX Annual Technical Conference, pp. 673–687 (2021)
15. Raju, P., Kadekodi, R., Chidambaram, V., Abraham, I.: PebblesDB: Building key-value stores using fragmented log-structured merge trees. In: Proceedings of the 26th Symposium on Operating Systems Principles, pp. 497–514 (2017)
16. Intel: Persistent memory development kit. https://github.com/pmem/pmdk
17. Cooper, B.F., Silberstein, A., Tam, E., Ramakrishnan, R., Sears, R.: Benchmarking cloud serving systems with YCSB. In: Proceedings of the 1st ACM Symposium on Cloud Computing, pp. 143–154 (2010)

Consistent and Efficient Batch Operations for NoSQL Databases with Hybrid Timestamp

Qianmian Yu and Jing Zhou[✉]

Shanghai Jiao Tong University, Shanghai, China
`zhoujing2021@sjtu.edu.cn`

Abstract. NoSQL databases, such as HBase or Cassandra employ weak consistency models to provide good scalability and availability. However, they often lack functionality that would help programmers reason about the correctness of their applications. Notably, they do not support consistent batch operations that could be used for important tasks, such as batch updates or maintaining secondary indexes. Some systems add transaction support to NoSQL databases. However, they often bring much overhead to existing single-row operations. This paper proposes an efficient algorithm for supporting batch operations on existing NoSQL databases. It reuses the existing local timestamp and adds a global timestamp to ensure batch operations' consistency. Our implementation based on HBase shows that compared to transactional systems, our algorithm improves the throughput of batch operations by up to 2×. Meanwhile, the latency of single-row operations only increases by around 12%. In comparison, other transactional systems increase their latency by over 3×.

Keywords: Concurrency control · NoSQL Databases · Distributed systems

1   Introduction

Recent demands for storing and querying large amounts of data have led to the emergence of a new kind of non-relational storage system named NoSQL. Examples are HBase [1], BigTable [9], and Cassandra [16]. They have sacrificed rich semantics and consistency guarantees provided by traditional relational database systems to achieve better scalability and availability. However, users are burdened with ensuring the correctness of their applications. Some have tried to provide transaction support to existing NoSQL systems. For example, Google builds Percolator [17] on top of BigTable [9] to satisfy users' complaints about the lack of cross-row consistencies.

NoSQL systems like HBase only support row-level consistency with operations, such as `Get`, `Put`, and `Delete`. Multi-row operations such as `Scan` are supported, but it does not have a consistent view of the data. In other words,

© IFIP International Federation for Information Processing 2022
Published by Springer Nature Switzerland AG 2022
S. Liu and X. Wei (Eds.): NPC 2022, LNCS 13615, pp. 340–351, 2022.
https://doi.org/10.1007/978-3-031-21395-3_31

it does not exhibit snapshot isolation. Other batch operations, such as batch writes, are not supported, partly due to their design that tries to avoid server coordination to achieve better scalability and availability. Users can implement batch writes with multiple Puts, but it is inconsistent.

Some systems are proposed to provide full transaction support for NoSQL databases [12,17]. They often add additional transaction metadata, such as read-write sets or locks. To resolve conflicts, they use two phase commit or centralized transaction server, which brings much overhead. Single-row operations also have to go through the conflict resolution process. We ask if we can provide consistent batch operations for NoSQL databases without the additional overhead of transactional systems.

This paper proposes an efficient algorithm based on hybrid timestamps. NoSQL databases such as HBase are already built on top of versioned storage. However, the version is local and not coordinated across servers. We have observed that we can extend them with a global timestamp shared across servers and only updated by batch operations. Such hybrid design can provide snapshot isolation (SI) for batch operations, while the performance of original single-row operations is not affected much.

We implemented our hybrid timestamp design on top of HBase. It supports simple batch operations such as reading or writing to many rows. More complicated logic, such as maintaining and using secondary indexes, is also supported by our system. Evaluation of our system has shown that while bringing little overhead to existing single-row operations, our system outperforms existing systems that bring transactions to HBase by more than 2x in certain workloads.

2 Background and Motivation

2.1 NoSQL Database and Transactional Support

In recent years, many NoSQL databases have been developed in response to the growing need for storing large amounts of data. They are designed to provide high scalability and availability. In the meantime, they often sacrificed other features such as consistency guarantees and complex query processing. For example, they often lack guarantees for the consistency of cross-row operations. Developers are burdened with ensuring the correctness of their applications.

HBase is among the most popular NoSQL databases, ranked second among wide column databases in DB-Engine Ranking [5]. It is originally inspired by Google BigTable [9]. HBase stores *rows* identified by unique *keys* that are partitioned by keys into many servers. Each row consists of multiple *columns*. The data is multi-versioned at the column level, and multiple versions of the same column may co-exist. It supports single-row operations like Get, Put, Remove, and Scan. Batch operations involving multiple rows like Scan did not provide any consistency guarantees. Because such operations may be executed on multiple servers, ensuring consistency requires coordination between servers.

Many systems tried to provide transactional support to existing NoSQL databases. Tephra [4] and Omid [8,13,20] tried to add transactional support on top of HBase. They utilized the existing multi-versioned storage of HBase and provided transactions with snapshot isolation. Their transactions have a start timestamp and a commit timestamp shared by all servers. However, to support complex transactions, they have to use a centralized transaction server to detect conflicts between concurrent transactions. The centralized transaction server is a bottleneck to the scalability of the system. Even single-row operations like `Get` and `Put` have to go through the centralized transaction server.

2.2 Benefits and Cost of Batch Operations

Batch operations are database operations that may read or write to multiple rows. These rows may belong to different servers. So coordination between servers is required to guarantee consistency. An example of simple batch operations is shown in Fig. 1. Two batch operations try to write the `c1` column of every row in table `t1`. Without any coordination, the result is inconsistent due to different server execution orders.

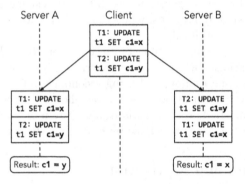

Fig. 1. Batch updates without coordination may result in inconsistency

Batch operations in our definition are more sophisticated than this simple example. Similar to stored procedures in traditional databases, they can execute arbitrary read and write operations, as long as they are for data in one server. That is to say, a batch operation can execute on many servers, but it can not read or write to data on server B when it is executed on server A. Batch operations has many use cases. One common scenario where batch operations become useful is maintaining secondary indexes. Maintaining a consistent secondary index for distributed systems has been a hot topic [11,14,18]. In our system, secondary indexes can be achieved by maintaining a separate table that colocates with the primary table on each server. Updates to the secondary index table are executed in a batch operation.

People often use transactions as a model of consistency for databases. Transactions have richer semantics than batch operations since batch operations are limited to being executed on one server. However, transactions are also more expensive, affecting the performance of single-row operations and limiting the system's scalability.

3 Hybrid Timestamp Design

This paper proposes an efficient algorithm for batch operations based on hybrid timestamps. We now describe the details of the algorithm. Section 3.1 gives an overview of hybrid timestamp design and the architecture of our system. Section 3.2 describes the basic algorithm. Finally, in Sect. 3.3, we introduce an optimistic execution strategy for better scalability of batch operations.

3.1 Timestamp Design and Architecture

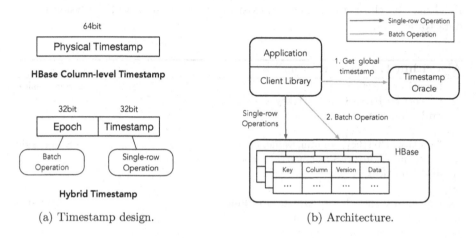

(a) Timestamp design.   (b) Architecture.

Fig. 2. Timestamp design and architecture.

As shown in Fig. 2a, HBase stores a 64-bit timestamp in the version of all data. By default, the physical timestamp is stored. But users can also choose to store the logical timestamp. We modify it to store a combination of a global timestamp and a local timestamp, called hybrid timestamp. For clarity, the global timestamp is called **epoch**, and the local timestamp is called **timestamp**. Each of them takes 32 bits of the original 64-bit timestamp. The hybrid timestamp determines the order of operations, ensuring snapshot isolation of the system. An operation with epoch t can only see data with epochs no more than t. Each batch operation that writes to the database uses a unique epoch. In contrast, read-only batch operations can use an existing epoch. When the local timestamp is used up, a no-op batch operation is triggered to increment the epoch.

Figure 2b shows our architecture. We added a component called *timestamp oracle*, whose sole responsibility is to manage epochs. The timestamp oracle is a single-node server deployed on the same machine as the HBase master. It maintains a monotonically increasing counter. HBase already has a ZooKeeper cluster. So the timestamp oracle will acquire a lease from the ZooKeeper cluster to ensure that no more than one timestamp oracle is running at a time. After the timestamp oracle crashes, recovery is done automatically by reading the latest epoch from every HBase server.

3.2 Basic Algorithm

The basic idea is to add an epoch to the existing column-level timestamp. The epoch is a logical clock to preserve the order of batch operations. Both clients and servers maintain the latest epoch they have seen. The clients' epochs are also carried on every request they send to servers. Batch operations that write data acquire a new epoch from the timestamp oracle and use it as the client's epoch. The server will increment its epoch after executing the write operation. Read-only batch operations use an existing epoch to indicate the version of the data to be read.

Algorithm 1. Basic Algorithm

 1: **function** GET(key, epoch)   ▷ Server-side
 2:     **return** READSNAPSHOT(key, epoch)
 3: **end function**
 4:
 5: **function** PUT(key, column, value, epoch)   ▷ Server-side
 6:     **return** UPDATESNAPSHOT(key, epoch)
 7: **end function**
 8:
 9: **function** CLIENTBATCHOPERATION(func)   ▷ Client-side
10:     **if** func is read-only **then**
11:         epoch ← latestEpoch
12:     **else**
13:         epoch ← NEWEPOCHFROMORACLE()
14:     **end if**
15:     **for** server ∈ all server **do**
16:         server.BATCHUPDATE(func, epoch)
17:     **end for**
18: **end function**
19:
20: **function** SERVERBATCHOPERATION(func, epoch)   ▷ Server-side
21:     **if** func is read-only **then**
22:         EXECUTEONSNAPSHOT(func, epoch)
23:     **else**
24:         BLOCKUNTILEPOCHAVAILABLE(epoch)
25:         EXECUTEONLATEST(func)
26:         server.epoch = epoch
27:     **end if**
28: **end function**

Algorithm 1 shows the basic algorithm for each supported operation. Single-row operations like Get or Put operate on a single row. They will be served by one server and only update the server-local timestamp, which requires no coordination between servers. Therefore, our algorithm adds little overhead to these operations while guaranteeing snapshot isolation. The server will return the latest epoch to the client. The client can update its local epoch to the latest epoch to avoid lagging.

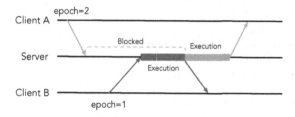

Fig. 3. The Execution of Two batch operation in the basic algorithm.

Batch operations include two steps. First, the client determines the epoch to be used. For read-only operations, the latest epoch seen by the client can be used(line 9). Otherwise, the client should acquire a new epoch from the timestamp oracle(line 11). Second, the client sends the operation along with the epoch to all servers(line 13). They can be executed in epoch order without any coordination between servers. However, a batch operation can not be executed until all operations with lower epochs have been completed, as illustrated in Fig. 3. This could limit the scalability of the system, which we will try to solve in the next section.

3.3   Server-Side Optimistic Execution

In the basic algorithm, batch operations are executed sequentially according to the epoch order. This section describes an optimization to allow parallel execution on the server side. It only applies to read-write operations. Read-only operations use snapshot data and can already be executed in parallel. The basic idea is to execute batch operations optimistically and validate the result in the end. The optimistic execution of every batch operation is composed of four steps:

- **Execution Phase**: Execute each operation and keeps track of its read and write sets.
- **Validation Phase**: After all operations with lower epochs are finished, validate the write sets and retry the operation upon conflict.
- **Commit Phase**: Apply the write sets to the database.
- **Retry Phase**: This is an optional step, only needed for operations that failed the validation phase.

The details are shown in Algorithm 2. We denote O_t as the batch operation with epoch t. S_r is the set of read keys and versions for O_t. S_w is the set of write keys and versions for O_t.

Algorithm 2. Server-side Optimistic Execution

Input:O_t: Batch operation with epoch t

```
 1: function EXECUTEPHASE(O_t)
 2:     for key ∈ O_t do
 3:         value, version ← READSNAPSHOT(key, t)
 4:         if write then
 5:             S_w = S_w∪ (key, version)
 6:         else
 7:             S_r = S_r∪ (key, version)
 8:         end if
 9:     end for
10:     VALIDATEPHASER(O_t, S_r, S_w)
11: end function
12:
13: function VALIDATEPHASE(O_t, S_w, S_r)
14:     BLOCKUNTILEPOCHAVAILABLE(t)
15:     failedKeys ← ∅
16:     for key, epoch ∈ S_r do
17:         latestEpoch ← READLATEST(key)
18:         if epoch ! = latestEpoch then
19:             failedKeys = failedKeys∪ key
20:         end if
21:     end for
22:     if failedKeys ≠ ∅ then
23:         RETRYPHASE(O_t, failedKeys)
24:     else
25:         COMMITPHASE(O_t, S_w)
26:     end if
27: end function
28:
29: function COMMITPHASE(O_t, S_w, S_r)
30:     for key, value ∈ S_w do
31:         WRITE(key, value, t)
32:     end for
33:     MARKASCOMMITTED(O_t)
34: end function
```

Execution Phase. For each key within batch operation O_t, the corresponding value with an epoch less than t is fetched (Line 3). The value and its version are stored in the local read or write set for validation. Arbitrary logic that operates on local data can be executed, including updating secondary indexes or performing other user-defined operations.

Validation Phase. After the execution of O_t finishes, it waits until all batch operations with lower epoch finish. Therefore, O_t can read the latest version of the data for validation. All validation of batch operations is done sequentially due to waiting. It is equivalent to the sequential or lock-based validation phase in other optimistic concurrency control algorithms [22]. For each key, if the latest data version is not the same as the version in the local read set, the operation is aborted and retried.

Commit Phase. If the validation succeeds, the write set is installed to the database with the epoch of t. After O_t finishes, subsequent batch operation with epoch $t + 1$ can starts its validation phase.

Retry Phase. Operations that failed the validation are immediately retried. The retry is guaranteed to succeed because all prior operations are completed. The retry only needs to read keys updated after it is added to the local read set, as shown by the `failedKeys` (line 13). This can further improve the performance of batch operation execution.

4   Evaluation

This section tries to answer the following questions about our algorithm:

- Can our system outperforms existing work?
- How much improvement does server-side optimistic execution bring?
- What overhead do hybrid timestamps add to HBase?

4.1   Exerimantal Setup

Implementation. We implemented our system on top of HBase using its coprocessor mechanism [2]. The timestamp oracle is a new service that the client interacts with RPC. We also implemented a client-side library with similar interfaces to HBase's library. The system is evaluated against the original HBase and Tephra [4]. Tephra is a popular transactional manager used by other systems like Phoenix [3]. It provides general transactions on top of HBase.

Testbed. We used a cluster of six machines. Each machine in our experiment has two 12-core Intel Xeon E5-2650 v4 processors, 128 GiB DDR4 RAM, and a single 1Gbps Ethernet interface connected by the same switch. Five machines run the HBase region server and a zookeeper quorum. The HBase master and the timestamp oracle run on a separate machine.

Workload. YCSB [10] is a benchmark workload for evaluating the performance of NoSQL systems. We modified YCSB to support batch operations. Each row in the table has 10 columns. Each column is 100 bytes long. The table has one million rows that are partitioned into servers in the cluster.

4.2   Operation Latency

Single-row Operation. Figure 4 shows the latencies of single-row operations on different systems. They only increased by about 12% in our system compared to the original HBase. Because of the hybrid timestamp design, single-row operations in our system do not require coordination. However, in Tephra, single-row operations need to be wrapped in a transaction verified at a central server. On average, their latencies increased by 336%.

Batch Operation. We evaluated four scenarios for batch operation: batch read, batch write, secondary index read, and secondary index write. In the simple batch read or write scenario, each operation is composed of a set of keys that the client intends to read or write. These keys may spread across multiple servers. In the secondary index scenario, we implemented a secondary index for a table by colocating an index table with the primary table on every server. It is a popular way to implement secondary indexes for distributed databases [18]. Each server has a shard of the primary table and a shard of the index table for the same set of data. The index is used for reading to writing to multiple rows determined by a condition on the secondary index.

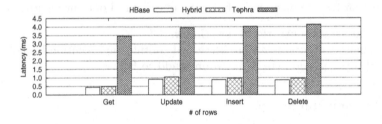

Fig. 4. Single-row operations latency.

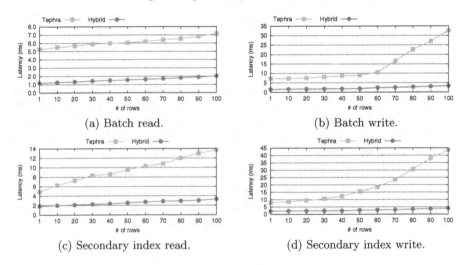

(a) Batch read.

(b) Batch write.

(c) Secondary index read.

(d) Secondary index write.

Fig. 5. Batch operation latency.

Figure 5 shows the latencies of these four scenarios. We tested the latency with varying numbers of rows read or written. In all four scenarios, our system outperforms Tephra. As the number of keys increases, the latency of our system stays relatively stable, while Tephra's latency increases a lot after the number of rows reaches a certain threshold. This is because Tephra needs to verify the read and write set at the central transaction server. As the data volume increases, more computation and network communication are required. With fewer rows, the latency mainly comes from network latency.

4.3   Scalability

This section evaluates the scalability of our system. Both the hybrid timestamp algorithm with (Hybrid-Opt) or without (Hybrid) the server-side optimistic execution optimization in Sect. 3.3 is evaluated.

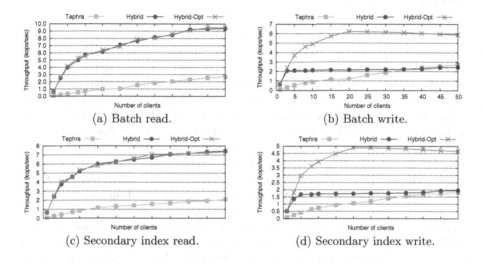

(a) Batch read.   (b) Batch write.

(c) Secondary index read.   (d) Secondary index write.

Fig. 6. Operation scalability.

As shown in Fig. 6, For write operations, without the server-side optimistic execution, the scalability of our system is limited, peaking at three client threads. Tephra can achieve the same throughput with the unoptimized version, though with more clients and higher latencies. The performance of our system with optimistic execution optimization is much better, around 275% better than Tephra. For Tephra, the centralized conflict detection for every transaction limits its scalability. There may also be transaction aborts that will need to be retried for the entire cluster in Tephra. Our system only aborts and retries transactions locally at each server.

5   Related Work

NoSQL Databases. Recent demands for managing big data have led to the emergence of NoSQL databases. Including BigTable [9], Cassandra [16], DynamoDB [21], MongoDB [7], and HBase [1]. Compared to traditional databases, NoSQL databases often have limited consistency models. Some only provide strong consistency over small aggregates of data. For example, IBM Spinnaker [19] and HyperDex [11] enforce serializability over individual data items. Google BigTable [9] and HBase [1] provide serializability over a single row or column of data. Eventual consistency is another weak consistency model that ensures the eventual convergence of system states after receiving asynchronous updates. It is also a popular option for NoSQL databases. Apache Cassandra [16] and early versions of Amazon DynamoDB [21] use syntactic reconciliation based on timestamps. Other novel consistency models are also proposed. For example, SD2DS [15] introduces *component consistency* based on a two-layer data structure.

Transaction Manager for NoSQL Databases. Various efforts have tried to add transaction support to NoSQL databases. Google Percolator [17] is a transactional system built upon BigTable. It uses a centralized server for timestamp allocation and resolves conflict through two phase commit. During transaction execution, clients lock database records to prevent others from accessing them. Additionally, numerous transactional systems are built atop HBase. Hbase-trx [6] is an early attempt to add transaction support with two phase commit. It uses a randomly generated transaction id on each server, and there is no coordination between servers. So transaction's serializability is only ensured on individual servers. Tephra [4] and Omid [8,13,20] are later widely used implementations. They all use an oracle to generate an epoch for each transaction and detect conflicts at a centralized transaction server. Existing single-row operations also need conflict checks. So they become slower than the original HBase. Later versions of Omid [20] propose a fast path for single-row operations. But the centralized conflict detection can still become the bottleneck when the number of servers increases.

6   Conclusion

We proposed an algorithm for implementing batch operations in HBase based on hybrid timestamps. Batch operations provide simpler semantics than transactions but achieve better performance in many cases. This paper proposes a novel algorithm to support batch operations in NoSQL databases based on hybrid timestamps. Compared to existing transactional systems, our algorithm avoids central conflict detection while ensuring the performance of single-row operations. The evaluation shows that compared to transactional systems, our algorithm improves the throughput of batch operations by around 275%. Meanwhile, the latency of single-row operations only increases by around 12%. In comparison, other transactional systems increase their latency by over 3x.

Acknowledgements. We appreciate the anonymous reviewers for their constructive feedback and suggestions.

References

1. Apache HBase. https://hbase.apache.org/. Accessed 30 June 2022
2. Apache HBase: Coprocessor introduction. https://blogs.apache.org/hbase/entry/coprocessor_introduction. Accessed 30 June 2022
3. Apache phoenix. https://phoenix.apache.org/. Accessed 30 June 2022
4. Apache tephra. https://tephra.incubator.apache.org/. Accessed 30 June 2022
5. Db-engines rankings. https://db-engines.com/. Accessed 30 June 2022
6. Hbase-TRX. https://github.com/hbase-trx/hbase-transactional-tableindexed. Accessed 30 June 2022
7. MongoDB. https://www.mongodb.com/. Accessed 30 June 2022
8. Bortnikov, E., et al.: Omid, reloaded: scalable and {Highly-Available} transaction processing. In: FAST 2017, pp. 167–180 (2017)
9. Chang, F., et al.: BigTable: a distributed storage system for structured data. TOCS **26**(2), 1–26 (2008)
10. Cooper, B.F., Silberstein, A., Tam, E., Ramakrishnan, R., Sears, R.: Benchmarking cloud serving systems with YCSB. In: Proceedings of the 1st ACM Symposium on Cloud Computing, pp. 143–154 (2010)
11. Escriva, R., Wong, B., Sirer, E.G.: Hyperdex: a distributed, searchable key-value store. In: ACM SIGCOMM 2012, pp. 25–36 (2012)
12. Ferro, D.G., Junqueira, F., Kelly, I., Reed, B., Yabandeh, M.: Omid: lock-free transactional support for distributed data stores. In: IEEE ICDE, pp. 676–687 (2014)
13. Ferro, D.G., Junqueira, F., Kelly, I., Reed, B., Yabandeh, M.: Omid: lock-free transactional support for distributed data stores. In: ICDE, pp. 676–687. IEEE (2014)
14. Kejriwal, A., Gopalan, A., Gupta, A., Jia, Z., Yang, S., Ousterhout, J.: SLIK: Scalable low-latency indexes for a Key-Value store. In: USENIX ATC 2016, pp. 57–70 (2016)
15. Krechowicz, A., Deniziak, S., Łukawski, G.: Highly scalable distributed architecture for NOSQL datastore supporting strong consistency. IEEE Access (2021)
16. Lakshman, A., Malik, P.: Cassandra: a decentralized structured storage system. ACM SIGOPS Oper. Syst. Rev. **44**(2), 35–40 (2010)
17. Peng, D., Dabek, F.: Large-scale incremental processing using distributed transactions and notifications. In: USENIX OSDI (2010)
18. Qi, H., Chang, X., Liu, X., Zha, L.: The consistency analysis of secondary index on distributed ordered tables. In: 2017 IEEE International Parallel and Distributed Processing Symposium Workshops (IPDPSW), pp. 1058–1067. IEEE (2017)
19. Rao, J., Shekita, E.J., Tata, S.: Using Paxos to build a scalable, consistent, and highly available datastore. VLDB **4**(4), 1–14 (2011)
20. Shacham, O., Gottesman, Y., Bergman, A., Bortnikov, E., Hillel, E., Keidar, I.: Taking Omid to the clouds: fast, scalable transactions for real-time cloud analytics. VLDB **11**(12), 1795–1808 (2018)
21. Sivasubramanian, S.: Amazon DynamoDB: a seamlessly scalable non-relational database service. In: ACM SIGMOD 2012, pp. 729–730 (2012)
22. Tu, S., Zheng, W., Kohler, E., Liskov, B., Madden, S.: Speedy transactions in multicore in-memory databases. In: ACM SOSP 2013, pp. 18–32 (2013)

Author Index

Printed in the United States
by Baker & Taylor Publisher Services